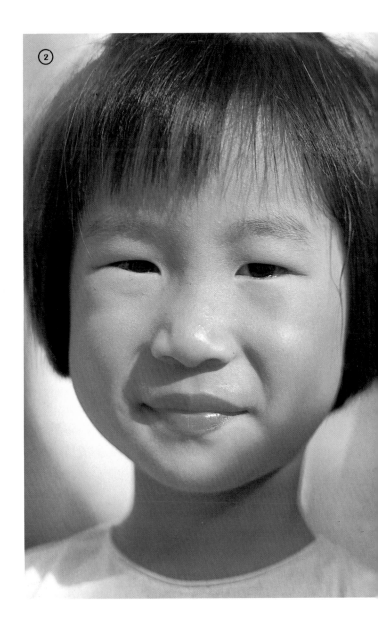

⑦

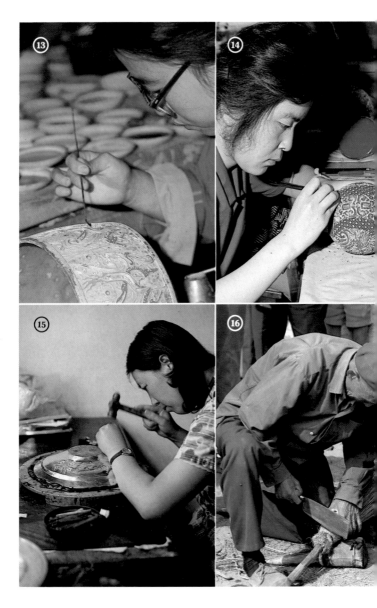

松下问童子
言师采药去
只在此山中
云深不知处

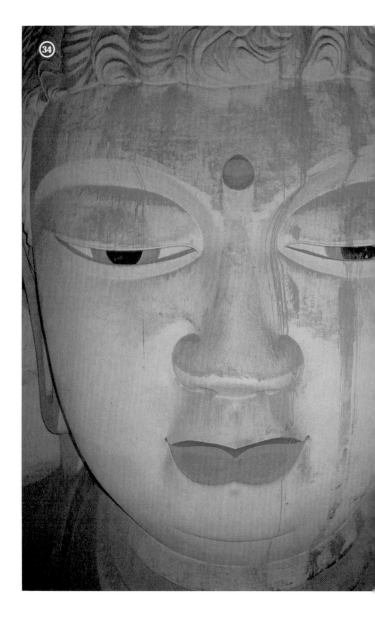

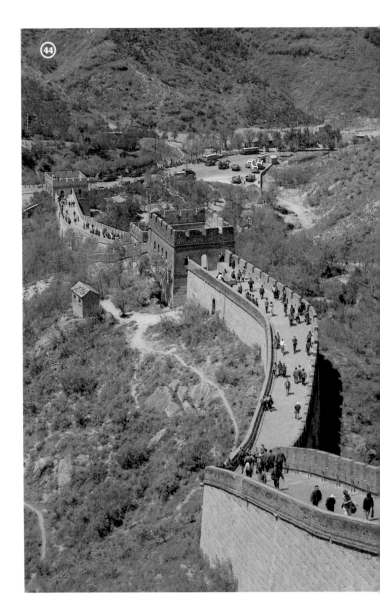

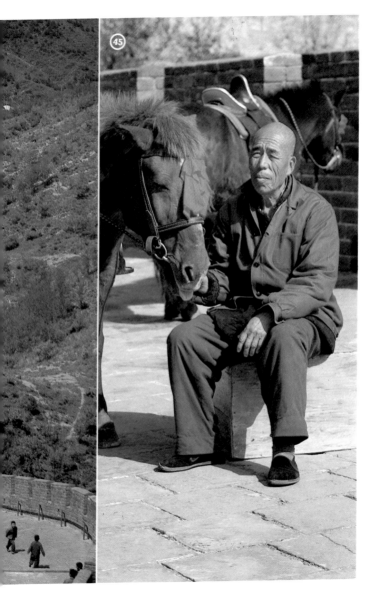

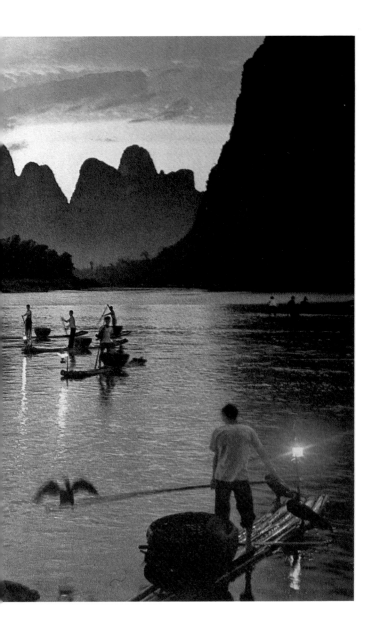

Captions

1. October 1st, 1977 in Changsha, Hunan province. Celebrations take place in the open air to mark the foundation of the People's Republic of China. Young women, dressed in the costumes of rice farmers dance in honour of Hua Guofeng, the former party chairman and Mao Zedong's successor.

2. Efforts are being made in China to bring the country up-to-date and achieve greater prosperity. Hopes for a brighter future are centred on the younger generation. Here, as elsewhere, children are the darlings of their parents.

3. Even in the poorer regions the children wear brightly coloured clothes.

4. Sport, dance and musical subjects are taught even in kindergarten.

5. School is a more serious business than kindergarten. Since classes are large, much emphasis is placed on children acquiring skills of concentration, learning discipline and good social behaviour.

6. For centuries every scholar was expected to be a master of calligraphy – the art of beautiful writing. This schoolboy practises handling brush and ink.

7. A contented Chinese farmer. Farmers are better off today, due to the new agricultural policies.

8. Girl of the Hui nationality.

9. Uighurian girl.

10. Tibetan girl.

11. Tibetan lamas were allowed to return to their monasteries in the post-Mao era.

12. Two Mongolian women in front of their yurts – the traditional felt tents of the Mongolian nomads.

13./14. Arts and crafts have a long tradition in China. These two women are working on cloisonné goods.

15. The arts and crafts industry mainly employs women. For work of this nature, artistic talent, a good eye and a sure hand are needed.

16. Working as a craftsman in China is not perhaps financially rewarding, but it does offer a secure existence. This man is making brooms in the traditional way out of rice straw.

17. During the Cultural Revolution there were only state-owned restaurants and cantines but nowadays privately owned cooking stands are to be seen on the streets again.

18. After a successful day at the market this farmer from Sichuan savours his pipe.

19. Cantonese markets are among the largest and most exotic in China. Nearly every four-legged creature, and others besides (from snakes and frogs to cats and owls), ends up in the cooking pots.

20. The women have rediscovered the hairdresser and done away with the plaits and the boring uniform hairstyles of previous years.

21. The Peking opera is as popular as ever. This actor wears a colourful costume, an intricate headpiece and the typical face mask.

22. This Buddhist monk is printing a sacred book using woodcuts.

23. In most Buddhist monasteries there is a "Hall of the 500 Lohans". Lohans are holy figures whom the Buddhists revere as gods.

24. This Daoist monk displays his religious writing. Daoism knows no gods.

25. The "Hall of Supreme Harmony" in Beijing's Palace Museum (Imperial Palace).

26. The "Hall of Prayer for Good Harvests" in the Heaven Temple.

27. A view of the wood-tiled ceiling which has been constructed without the aid of glue and nails. In the centre is the symbol of a dragon.

28. A detail from one of the four central columns, the "Dragon Spring" columns, which support the inner roof. They represent the four seasons.

29. The edges of the blue-glazed tiles also bear the emperor's symbol: a dragon.

30. The "Pagoda of Glazed Tiles", Liuli Ta, in the western mountains of Beijing.

31. The dragon is the symbol of imperial power. This is a detail from the "Wall of the Nine Dragons" in the Imperial Palace. There are only three such walls in China.

32./33. Heavenly Guards (Tianwang) can be found at every Buddhist temple entrance. Their frightening grimaces and magical weapons are supposed to keep the enemies of Buddhism at bay. Both statues are wearing a five-leaf Bodhisattva crown. A Buddha is depicted in the middle leaf.

34. Buddhism is the most important religion in China. In the famous cave complexes of Dunchuang, Yungang, Longmen and Dazu there are larger than life sized statues of this religion's Indian founder. This head of Buddha is part of the 75 ft statue which stands in the Mongao grottos in Dunhuang.

35. A Buddha from the grottos of Dazu in Sichuan. He is shown seated in the European fashion with a double nimbus. Behind him on the wall, there are several smaller pictures of Buddha.

36. Two figures of Buddha seated in the diamond (lotus) position on the lotus blossom – the Buddhist symbol of purity. Their right hands are raised to their breasts in a gesture of protection.

37. The Potala Palace which the 5th Dalai Lama started building in 1643. It stands on the "Red Mountain" – Marpori, in Lhasa, Tibet.

38. The Fengxian Temple in the Longmen Grottos at Luoyang, which is one of the most important sites of Buddhist religious art. To the right of the central Buddha figure stand a student of Buddha and a Bodhisattva. On the far right, guarding Buddha, are two other gods.

39. The most exciting find in the short history of Chinese archaeology was made in 1974, when the burial site of China's first emperor, Qin Shi Huang Di was found close to Xi'an.

40. Since each head is modelled individually every face looks different. This is a statue of an officer as can be seen by his head gear.

41. Figure of soldier in heavy armour. He wears his hair in a simple knot.

42. Stone figures line the road to the grave (built in 1383) of the first Ming emperor. Among the figures are not only camels, elephants, lions and fabulous animals but also high-ranking officials and generals. They show that the emperor is even now respected and watched over by his subjects.

43. View into Kiziltagh Valley from the Buddhist caves of Beizeklik near Turfan, Xingjian province.

44. The Great Wall at Badaling, north of Beijing. This immense construction – the largest on earth – can even be recognised by astronauts with the naked eye.

45. This man is waiting for customers who want to have their photograph taken on horseback at the Great Wall.

46. Nearly 200 varieties of bamboo grow in China. Bamboo is put to a wide range of uses. It is important building material used e. g. for furniture and scaffolding. The young shoots are edible and taste delicious. Moreover, bamboo is so hard that you can inscribe your name on it – as someone here has done.

47. Lotus fields can be found everywhere in China. Its roots are edible (a tasty vegetable) and the blossoms are used to add flavour and aroma to teas and soups.

48. The lotus blossom, symbol of purity, beauty, the sun and eternal life, is an emblem of Buddhism, as shown by the fact that Buddha's throne is a lotus flower.

49. The most important domestic animal on the Tibetan plateaus is the yak, a relative of the bison able to survive on the sparse vegetation that grows at such high altitudes. Because of its very high fat content, yak butter plays an important part in the Tibetan diet. In extremely cold winters, the Tibetans rub yak butter into their skins to protect themselves from the cold.

50. The water buffalo is the most important domestic animal in southern China, due to its work in the wet, muddy rice fields. It is unlikely that tractors will ever be able to replace the water buffalo on the terraced fields.

51. Mules pull a heavy load over a wide, dried-up river bed.

52. Travelling through the gorges of the Yangzi used to be a dangerous venture in which vessels often had to be towed. Today, the Yangzi is one of China's greatest tourist attractions.

53./54. Junks and sampans are still a common sight on the Yangzi River.

55. The Li River snakes through the fantastic rounded mountains near Guilin. At dusk fishermen go about their work on narrow bamboo rafts. The fish are actually caught by captive cormorants who are prevented from swallowing their catch by a ring placed around their necks.

Trying to reach Heaven

In the middle of the night, we are woken abruptly by ships' sirens. It is 2.30 am., which means that we have only slept a few hours. We are in Yinchang, but have not as yet seen the city since darkness had already fallen when we arrived and the city is still shrouded in darkness now.

Yichang stands on the border between two worlds: to the east lies the flat open country that stretches as far as Shanghai and to the west lie the once feared Yangzi gorges. Behind them is the Four-River-Province of Sichuan. This province used to be virtually inaccessible and was therefore regarded as sinister and alien. Li Taibo, the famous Tang poet (Tang Dynasty, 618–907 A.D.), wrote the following of Sichuan: "Travelling to Sichuan is as difficult as trying to reach heaven."

For centuries sailors tried to storm this heaven with their light junks. No-one can say for sure just how many boats and people were gripped by the rapids and whirlpools in the Yangzi gorges and smashed against the rocks.

If these accidents happened in the summer, when the Yangzi was flooded, then the corpses and wrecks were not discovered until the water level had fallen again (in winter or the following spring). Often they were found caught in the rocks, some 65–100 ft. above the river's surface.

But Sichuan was (and still is) a fertile country and trading with the province a lucrative business. Whoever managed to reach Sichuan and return was a made man. And finally, the most direct route and also the shortest was via the gorges of the Yangzi.

Following their involvement in China in the middle of the 19th century, the Europeans were quick to realize the importance of the Yangzi as regards trade and transport. The British were the first to make a move. In 1898 they laid claim, through their envoy, Sir Claude Mac Donald, in Peking, to the entire Yangzi region and the adjoining provinces.

The British were followed by the Germans whose Kaiser, Wilhelm II, gave them every encouragement to pursue ruthless expansionist policies. A war correspondent, sent by a Berlin newspaper to report on the Boxer Rebellion, wrote in one of his articles, and later in a book, that it was a national duty to "concern ourselves with the Yangzi".

Shortly afterwards, he was himself to attempt to travel through the gorges to Chongqing, in a steamship belonging to a German shipping company. Up until then the lower and middle reaches of the river, as far as Yichang, (the natural barrier before Sichuan) had been filled with European gunboats, whose owners wished to make clear their claims to the region. At the time, a large number of shipping companies sent steamships from Shanghai to Hankou (now known as Wuhan) and a few even sailed as far as Yicheng.

The intrepid correspondent mentioned above set sail for Chongqing from Shanghai in December, 1900. However, despite the ship having been equipped with special paddle-wheels, the narrow gorges still proved difficult to negotiate. The venture, in which large sums of money had been invested, ended in disaster. The hidden reefs of the rapids ripped open the ship's hull and in less than twenty minutes the dream of a German steamship company lay smashed on the bed of the Yangzi.

It goes without saying that we were neither troubled by similar fears and uncertainties about our fate nor stirred by a sense of adventure as we descended the steps to the banks of the river. It was still the middle of the night when we boarded the ship. Our ship was called "The East in Red (Dong feng hong), No. 48". (All Yangzi passenger ships have now been renamed "Tiang yu", "Tiang han", and "Tiang hui", which simply means "river" and designates the ship's home port.)

This morning, though, the east was to remain grey, as our ship set sail on the three-day journey to Chongqing.

Dawn is still breaking an hour later when we reach the Gezhouba-

Lock, which was completed in 1981. It is with the aid of this immense lock that the Chinese have prevented the formation of dangerous rapids beyond Yichang. It prevents the water level from sinking to a depth where rocks emerge from the water and create rapids and whirlpools, thus endangering the ships. In the big floodgate, the ship is raised by something like 20 m (60 ft.), after which we can continue on our journey.

A short while later, the first mountains of the Xiling-Gorge appear. They seem like mighty, natural floodgates, blocking our way. For the pioneers of Yangzi shipping they must have seemed like a warning, a symbol of the danger and the fatal power of this river.

Our boat, however, makes its way steadily, steered by an experienced pilot who directs the helmsman with almost imperceptible movements of his raised thumb. The first of the three Yangzi Gorges is 78 km (48½ miles) long and the scenery is incredible. An old travel guide describes the gorge as follows, "This is indeed a sinister place, in the midst of great danger".

Before our eyes, the towering, almost sheer rocky slopes cast a shadow of perpetual gloom over the gorge. Then cone-shaped mountains loom up – very reminiscent of the Egyptian pyramids. High above us are small mountain settlements or solitary farms. Every accessible piece of land surrounding them has been cultivated. To fetch water or to wash, one has to go down to the banks of the river along steep paths. It is difficult for us to imagine the hardship and loneliness of such a life, cut off from the rest of the world and perpetually subjected to the whims of the river. Sometimes the river appears to be an enormous lake, surrounded by towering mountains, with no visible way out. Then suddenly a way appears, behind a steep rocky wall where the river makes a sharp turn.

Junks pass us swiftly as they sail downriver, laden with grain, animals, or a few passengers. Some of them are towed by motor boats. The junks who, like us, are travelling upriver have a harder time of it. More unfortunate still are the junks who didn't manage to get a tow by boat. They really have to fight every inch of the way and stay close to the embankment to avoid the stronger currents in the middle of the river. These junks are towed by coolies who walk along the banks of the river, pulling from time to time on the ropes which are fastened to the mast and hull of the junk.

Today, you can still make out the towing paths (some of them perhaps thousands of years old) winding their way along the mountain slopes. Sometimes they run along the banks of the river and at other times they are situated on virtually vertical slopes at dizzy heights. At such places, the paths have been hewn out of the rocks. What's more, towing villages have grown up around some especially difficult stretches of the river. The inhabi-

tants earn their living solely from towing ships.

A few years after the unsuccessful attempt by the German steam boat, a young German diplomat, Martin Fischer, left Yichang for Chongqing. He travelled by junk and it took him 25 days under favourable circumstances to make the journey. He vividly describes the physical exertion involved in towing: "The whole river valley echoed with the fiery cries of the overseer, with the monotonous answering cries of the coolies, with the gong beats from the shore and with the drum beats from on board."

Today the river valley echos with the sirens of modern ships. Ours – "The East is Red, No. 48" – has approximately 700 passengers on board. Forty of them are tourists who have relatively comfortable two-berth cabins. The Chinese passengers sleep in 4-berth cabins or communal sleeping quarters. Those who can't afford either sleep in the central corridor above the engine rooms where it is cosy and warm at all times of year – even on cool evenings. During the day, most passengers either remain on deck or in the passenger lounge – a communal room with a broad window at the front. There is no danger of getting bored here, for there is so much to see – the scenery itself and the activity on the river and along its banks.

After an excellent lunch, we reach the second gorge, called Wuxia or the Witches' Gorge. It is some 40 km (25 miles) long and stands out because of its 12 high and very beautiful mountain peaks. We also pass the "Chinese Lorelei". It stands on the peak of a high and spectacular looking mountain. This solitary pointed needle of rock is said to resemble a beautiful girl, provided you use your imagination. This is no Lorelei in the usual sense of the word, however. She does not use her fatal charm to lure sailors into dangerous waters. No, for the Chinese she is the embodiment of the goddess Yao Ji, who Chinese sailors regard as their patron. It was she who calmed the waters and separated them into oceans and rivers together with the mythical Emperor Yu during the creation of the earth. Now she is enthroned high above the Yangzi Gorges, which must have represented her most difficult task.

In the late afternoon we reach the entrance to the Qutang Gorges. Here, the immense mountains have forced the river to make a turn of almost 90°. This last of the three gorges is the shortest, only 5 miles long, but it is also the most threatening, the narrowest of the three, and therefore also the most dangerous. The rocky slopes drop steeply into the water. In some places the river is only 80 m (260 ft.) wide. The water level can vary by as much as 60 m (197 ft.). At high water, the level rises swiftly and the mass of water shoots through this bottle neck with unimaginable speed. Even today, on board a modern boat, the gloominess and oppression are palpable. There is no way out except straight ahead. Beneath us there is the roaring water, whilst above us the smooth, sheer rocks rise up on both sides till their peaks almost meet and only a small patch of sky remains visible.

High above one side of the gorge there is a series of broad, long fissures. Each one is roughly ½ to 1 metre wide (1½ to 3½ feet) and approximately 10 to 15 metres long (33 to 50 feet). Box-like forms can be made out in the fissures – a fact that led earlier travellers to the area to call this spot the Bellows Gorge. More recently, skeletons have been found in the cracks. Some 2,000 years ago, a resident tribe used these crevices to bury their dead in.

Then suddenly the gorge comes to an end as abruptly as it began. (The entrance to these gorges is formed by two, facing, steep mountain sides.) Almost without warning we are in the province of Sichuan. After days of blinkered vision, our view restricted by the steep sides of the gorges, we are once more able to let our eyes roam over distant horizons and wide-open expanses. Sometimes there are even broad, beautiful beaches, which look strangely out of place in this region. Huge bamboo groves line the embankment, the tips of their stems seeming almost to touch the water.

The next morning our ship docks in Wanxian. A strange scene accosts still sleepy eyes. The city lies some 40–50 m (130–160 ft.) above us. From the shore a majestic flight of over 300 steps leads up to the city, which clings to the mountain side on three levels. On the lower steps women are washing their clothes in the muddy waters of the Yangzi.

In China, the most widely used means of transportation is the bicycle. Here, there was not a single one in sight. In this city of steps and serpentine paths a bicycle would only be a hindrance. The busy trade on these steps can be compared to similar activities on Rome's Piazza di Spagna. Cobblers, tailors, and other craftsmen bustle about with artists and clever dealers who are intent on selling modern television sets and stereo units.

Our stay is short and we have to leave this Chinese town with its 300,000 inhabitants. "The East is Red, No. 48" still has to take us to our final destination, the city of Chongqing, which has 6 million inhabitants.

In the past, Chongqing was not only frequented by traders and sailors, who were prepared to risk the dangerous journey on the Yangzi, but also by political refugees. They sought protection in this enclosed hinterland from the might of the central government. The last time this occurred was when the National Government of Tschiang Kai-shek fled from the Japanese in the Thirties and moved the capital here. At low tide, the area in the middle of the Yangzi which was then used as an airfield is still visible.

Chongqing has another, usually irritating, characteristic, one that once saved many lives: for most of

the year it is shrouded in fog. The Japanese had to stop their disastrous bombing attacks because they could not identify the target.

When we arrive, too, the horizon is blurred by a foggy haze. When we leave our ship we have a 3-day journey covering 402 miles on a 3,914-mile river (the longest in China) behind us. We have travelled barely one-tenth of its total length. The Chinese also call the Yangzi "Long River" (Chiangjiang). It has brought catastrophe and death to many people in China's history. The last flood in Sichuan in 1981 cost thousands of people their lives. In Chongqing's harbour at the "Chao Tian Men" (literally, the gate through which one can see heaven), the highwater mark of 1981 can still be seen. On our arrival it is 30 m (98 ft) above the normal water level. There have always been floods, especially in the lower regions where the river flows a great deal slower and deposits thousands of tons of gravel and sand.

But for millions of people, the Yangzi also means life. Over one third of the Chinese population lives in the area around the Yangzi and its many tributaries. It provides farmers with much needed water and it is a major trade and transportation route as well as being China's longest waterway. After the Yellow River (Huanghe) it was the second largest settlement area in the early history of mankind.

It is no wonder that this river has for centuries been a popular subject among artists. The favourite motif has always been the Yangzi Gorges. They have been depicted countless times and brought to paper with brush and ink.

Modern authors have also used them as metaphors, to describe difficulties involved in China's transition from a feudal hierarchy to a modern 20th century state. In the film version of Ba Jin's famous novel, "The Family", the last scene shows the youngest child standing at the prow of a ship as it leaves the Yangzi gorges. Behind him the narrow, threatening mountains recede into the background whilst wide expanses of land open up before him – a symbol of the freedom he has gained.

He had had to struggle long and hard against the constraints of a family hierarchy with Confucian convictions to achieve his freedom. In the end he leaves his family and the provincial narrowness of a Sichuan town behind and makes his way to Shanghai, where he is attracted by the modern and rebellious ideas of the young intellectuals.

Mao Dun, a Chinese author of bestsellers in the Thirties and Forties, sends the heroine through the Yangzi gorges in his novel "Rainbow". This is often considered to be China's first feminist novel. The heroine's reflections on her life are revealed through her description of the gorges:

"So this is what the Yangzi looks like in Sichuan! From a distance it appears as if the river comes to an end here, but once you are in Sichuan itself you realize that the Yangzi does in fact flow further." Later the author comments: "The way in which the Yangzi struggled to force its way through the narrow Wu Gorge seemed to her symbolic for the course her life had taken so far. But she was determined that her life should resemble the course of the river after Kuimen where it flows wide and free." When she finally leaves the oppressive narrowness of the gorges behind her, Mao Dun has her cry out, "Now the twisted and narrow way with its puzzles and dangers has come to an end. Now for the freedom of the big, wide world."

We, however, had come in the other direction – from the big wide world to Sichuan. Today, though, the face of Sichuan is very different. This is where the government's dogmatic reform policies were born. Zhao Ziyang, the present Prime Minister, comes from Sichuan and Deng Xiaoping has been nicknamed "The Good Man from Sichuan" after Brecht's play of the same name.

A typical Tea House

If I were asked which part of China is more Chinese than the rest, the answer would have to be Sichuan. This is the province which lies behind the gorges of the Yangzi at the foot of the Himalayan mountains, a province crossed by four rivers.

Beijing, the capital city, means foreign visitors and affected airs of superiority. In Shanghai, foreign influence began at the start of the present century and still makes itself felt today – not without consequences. In a country where 80% of the population live in villages, many Chinese regard Shanghai as China's only city. As for Canton, it is seen as a suburb of Hong Kong; the young generation has taken over with jeans and stereos.

It would be wrong to say that Sichuan is really behind the times, but new ideas and innovations take longer to get here and are often met with distrust. Old customs die hard here.

For example, you will see more old women with bound feet in Sichuan than anywhere else in China. Here, too, old men still go about dressed in the style of long gown that was popular towards the end of the last dynasty, i. e. around the turn of the century.

Chengdu, the "City of the Hibiscus" on the Jinjiang river, appears much more open, cleaner, and more beautiful than the other cities in Sichuan. It also has more of an official air about it; perhaps because it is the capital of the province.

But my Chinese friend who is acting as guide for our group has offered to steep us in old China. We are going to visit a tea house.

The initial reaction is not exactly one of enthusiasm. Most people in the group are overcome by sinister forebodings where comfort, cleanliness and hygiene etc. are concerned. But in the end we all decide to go.

The Chinese tea house is comparable to our pubs or bars. In China, however, alcohol is only served in the bars of restaurants. The tea house is a place where every class and level of society, with the exception of women, is found. For despite the fact that men and women are officially equal in China, tea houses remain an exclusively male domain. It is here that the problems of day-to-day life are discussed, that opinions about local or central government are bandied about and that the latest sports results are commented on.

The town already lies in darkness as we approach the dimly lit tea house. The folding doors have been pushed back so that the entire tea house front is wide open. This arrangement is very much appreciated in the heat of summer. Indeed no-one can imagine things being done any differently.

A few children dance around in front of the tea house. Inside, their fathers and grandfathers are passing judgment on the politics of the day whilst sipping their tea. We walk across the firm mud floor to the front of the tea house where a table has been reserved for us.

Then we hear an unmistakable sound, which makes some of our stomachs turn. Involuntarily, we glance down at the floor.

And indeed danger lurks for the unwary around the tables in the form of slippery patches.

Whilst in Shanghai a fine of 50 fen or 1 yuan must be paid for spitting on the street, here it is still the done thing, or is at least regarded as socially acceptable.

The smoke-filled air hangs in dark clouds over the bamboo tables. Luckily, the ceiling is porous and so it absorbs some of the smoke. Of course, this has its disadvantages, too. When it rains, the house cannot open.

The table that has been reserved for us is right next to where the musicians sit. There is no stage; they sit at a long table, just like the other guests. A Sichuan opera is being performed. The music is loud, the singing shrill and the combination of the two, pounding on our ears is anything but harmonious. These amateur musicians, who meet here once or twice a week to play together are conducted by the retired director of a local theatre. His baton

is a wooden percussion instrument. There is even a woman among the musicians, but the soprano part is sung by a young man. He forces the high notes out – his face red with exertion. Sometimes he stops and coughs, because he is smoking a cigarette at the same time. And if he's not coughing, he's spitting. There are no sheets of music. The opera usually lasts between two and three hours and the performers usually learn their parts by heart. If the text is lost, or someone forgets

his lines, the others will act as prompters. Payment is in the form of free tea.

In the meantime, we have been served tea. There are no tea cups. Here tea is drunk from traditional tea bowls, which are placed on saucers and covered with a lid.

To drink it, you lift the saucer with one hand and raise the bowl to your lips, lift the lid slightly with the other, and sip the hot, revitalizing drink noisily. You pay a few fen for the tea leaves and these will last you all evening. Expert drinkers swear that the tea tastes best after the second or third infusion because by then the tea's aroma is beginning to develop.

Several waiters spend the entire evening carry kettles of hot water back and forth. The huge stove in the kitchen can heat thirty or forty kettles at the same time.

If you want your "cup" re-filled you simply place the lid on the table next to the bowl. You will then be brought water, without having to say a word. If you leave the table but plan to return, simply put a few tea leaves on the lid's round handle.

Involuntarily, I am reminded of a play written by a Beijing author, Lao She, who was murdered during the Cultural Revolution. He did homage to this Chinese institution by setting every scene of one particular play in a tea house. This was not only a meeting place for bird sellers and fanciers. The author also had marriage brokers and white slave traders meet there to do business. It was there, too, that incredible stories about ghosts and demons started, that politics were discussed and that the best recipes for blending opium were passed around. Tea houses such as that one are just not to be found in the cities anymore.

Here in Chengdu, we sit in a smokefilled room in the midst of spit and shrill sounds. There are no bird dealers to be seen and no marriage brokers. Nonetheless, even today speculations are made here concerning the futures of young men and women who are of marriageable age. It all seems very civilized. You cannot get drunk on tea and there is hardly any time for brawls because the tea houses close early, usually no later than 10 p.m. The people of Chengdu get up early and will have to work long and hard before they can go to the tea house again the next evening.

"Hallo there. How are you?"

"Good morning, ladies and gentlemen. I would like to welcome you to the People's Republic of China. Undeterred by the long and arduous journey here, you have crossed thousands of rivers and mountains in order to visit our beautiful country. China has friends all over the world."

During the first few years of tourism in China it was quite normal for Chinese couriers to give flowery or pompous welcoming addresses like the one above. Their greetings have long since become more matter-of-fact and businesslike. Routine has taken over in China, too.

Nonetheless the Chinese courier remains "persona sine qua non", the most important person on every trip. Without him, it is impossible to get the right bus, to find the right hotel, and to get train or plane tickets. The state-owned Chinese travel agency, Lüxingshe, provides foreign couriers only with general information. This includes notice of the places to be visited, the length of stay in each city, the means of transport, and arrival and departure dates. The rest of the information is contained in the small blue plastic briefcase which nearly every Chinese courier carries around with him. This arrangement often results in bewildering situations arising, where the foreign guide has no option but to trust entirely in the competence and willingness of his Chinese colleagues.

First of all, however, you have to find your guide. In the days when only one group arrived per day this was no problem. Today, though, it is quite a task picking him out from the crowd. Or through determined questioning he will find his way to you, despite the large numbers of tourists. Then you will hear: Are you from England? No, sorry. Sind Sie Deutsche? Ja. How large is your group? No, I'm looking for a group of 13. Which agency are you from? Sorry, wrong again.

On one of my last trips, it took me 20 minutes to find him. My Chinese colleague had actually found my group by the time I found him.

Asked whether they were "delegation 90111" my group had answered that no, unfortunately they were not. Later, it turned out that we were "delegation 90111" after all. We never actually found out where this imposing title had come from. It remained one of those unfathomable mysteries of Chinese tourist bureaucracy. It might have been a relic from the time when every visiting group really was a delegation and they were treated as such – not altogether an unpleasant thing.

Once contact has been established, the two parties start sizing each other up. Can he speak English? Is he friendly and understanding? Will he simply reel off what he's learnt by rote? You will of course encounter experienced couriers but they are not usually very interested or involved in what they are doing. I prefer young couriers who are on their first trip and very enthusiastic. Couriers in China have a certain status. They are respected members of society and their jobs are much sought after. The average Chinese person just can't afford to travel the length and breadth of his own country. For one thing he earns too little.

How do you become a courier in China? This is not an easy question to answer, since Chinese people don't choose a career; they are assigned one. To become a courier you must speak one foreign language fluently. Here, I have to say that I have met people who could say "Good morning", in several languages, but that was all they could say. In Canton an attractive young lady greeted me with the words "Hallo there. How are you?" (She spoke German.) I answered her question with a beaming smile. It is not every day that you are addressed in such a familiar way by a beautiful lady – at least not in a country like China that is known for its prudery. Imagine my confusion when she later spoke to me in English. "Let's go to the bus," she said. I couldn't resist asking, "Which language do you actually speak fluently?" She answered by first giving me another charming smile and then saying, "Ah, yo hablo solo español". After we had boarded the bus, she proceeded to greet every tourist with the words she had used to address me: "Hallo there. How are you?"

Some of my most amusing encounters have been with German-speaking Chinese people who spoke with a strong East German accent. In fact, China used to send people to East Germany to be trained as translators. Then in the early 60's, the ideological conflict with the Soviet Union put a stop to this exchange. Usually these translators speak German better than their younger colleagues whose choice of vocabulary reflects the influence of the Cultural Revolution.

I have met quite a few Chinese people, some of whom were very intelligent, who were exiled to distant provinces during the Cultural Revolution and had to act as couriers because of their excellent command of foreign languages. I hope that these people are now once again in positions in keeping with their intelligence and qualifications.

Up until recently, tourism and other relevant subjects for couriers such as the history of Chinese art and culture simply were not taught. Today, couriers still learn their trade according to the Mao principle that you learn through practice.

During the tourist season, couriers are occasionally lent out to government departments to work as specialist translators. The courier who travelled to Tibet with us was a case in point. He spent hours explaining different aspects of laser technology to me (none of which I understood) and yet he could not put together a simple sentence. I almost had to re-translate everything he said so that the members of my group could understand. In Tibet itself, he came down with altitude sickness and was excused from work. In his defence, I have to say that he was assigned this job very much against his will and was well aware of his own shortcomings.

I have also encountered the perfect courier, however. Such people speak without the trace of an accent, are urbane, charming, highly intelligent and therefore belong to the elite of Chinese couriers. In Wuxi my Chinese guide talked to members of my group about Munich where some of them came from. They discussed streets, squares and museums in Munich, and the beer-gardens, of course. Meanwhile, I was becoming painfully aware of the gaps in my own knowledge when it came to my own country. His information came solely from books and conversations. At other times he would give us a short talk – quite spontaneously – on silk production or the processing of tea.

Luckily, I have seldom come across a courier who is either disinterested or simply lazy. Such people reveal themselves at the latest when the group makes a special request or asks for a change in the schedule. Such couriers detest requests of this nature. They prefer to stick rigidly to their itinerary which means a minimum of initiative on their part. The highlights of the programme for someone like this are the lengthy visits to the "Friendship Stores" where he can take his afternoon nap – "xuixi", a Chinese institution that is almost sacred. Naturally, he will do all he can to fill the programme with such "highlights". It is extremely difficult to motivate people like this. Quotations from Mao's Red Book, like: "You should always strive to give your best", don't seem to help at all. There was a time when such quotations could be used to arouse the masses. And as for offering "material incentives", the authorities only allow these in the form of tips, though officially they are forbidden. For the time being, at least, I wouldn't want things to be any different either. Should you have a disinterested courier, you can always, as a last resort, try praising the person concerned in glowing terms. This does help sometimes because Chinese people cannot bear to receive undeserved praise. The courier would feel that he had to prove himself worthy of your praise. On the whole, however, Chinese couriers are very industrious. Without doubt, they are motivated to some extent by the fact that their profession enjoys such a high status.

I remember on one occasion, however, how a Chinese colleague of mine was trying to give a speech in English. We were travelling by bus at the time and, since the air-conditioning was very noisy, some of the passengers complained that they couldn't hear him properly. He simply picked up his microphone and literally repeated what he had said, word for word, down to the last comma. Even the jokes appeared at the same place as they had done before.

But a Chinese courier is not merely a guide, he is first and foremost a translator. This is by no means an easy task when you consider the things that tourists from the West want to know. The engineer, for example, wants an exact description of how a particular machine works, the doctor is interested in Chinese medicine and the teacher wants information on the principles behind the Chinese education system. Finally, everyone wants to know the translation for various items of food. It will be clear that not every courier has such specialist vocabulary at his fingertips. And where meals are concerned, many things cannot be translated. You have to taste them – and I hope that you will do just that.

Some people even take the courier to be the Chairman of the Communist Party! They imagine that he is responsible for the politics of his country and expect him to go into great detail on the policies etc. This was particularly evident in the early years of tourism in China, but this was partly due to the Chinese. They wanted to show off the new socialist China and prove its superiority. Sometimes such political discussions led to rather embarrassing situations. For example, a Chinese courier set about trying to explain to my group what a good comrade Deng Xiaoping is, a tempered veteran of the Chinese Revolution etc. However, I distinctly remember this very same man trying to convince us, on an earlier trip, that "Mister" Deng Xiaoping was a counter-revolutionary and traitor who wanted to reintroduce capitalism.

But these stories are a thing of the past. Today few couriers are keen to discuss politics; something which not only applies to couriers.

In the early days of tourism the emphasis was placed on touring factories and communes. Today, the Chinese are intent on doing justice to their history, culture and religions, too. This explains why visiting the sites of archaeological excavations, places of cultural interest and monuments feature high on any itinerary. Admiring China's countryside is also an important part of such programmes. Sadly, these are the areas where too many couriers fall short of the mark, especially the ones who qualified during the Cultural Revolution. For these people, Chinese history starts with the founding of the Communist Party. I have no wish to criticise them, however. Many of their lives were marked by very distressing experiences. They suffered directly as a result of the Revolution.

It is at times like this, when the Chinese courier is at a loss for an answer, that the foreign guide must step in and prove his worth. Indeed, my colleagues are usually far better up on Chinese culture and history than their Chinese counterparts. Even for them Buddhism seems almost impenetrable. I have to admit that the pantheon of Buddhist gods and their frightening pandemonium are very confusing. Nevertheless, it remains the guide's duty to help the tourist unravel these facts. It is easier to understand the gaps in knowledge that some couriers have, when you consider that for decades people regarded temples and monasteries as the centres of corruptive feudal superstition. Consequently, every trace of China's religious heritage was wiped out of everyday life.

By the end of your holiday, you will be on friendly terms with your courier, will promise to keep in touch, to send him books .... Perhaps you will invite him to visit your home. Strangely enough, it's at this point (if not before) when the relationship has become more personal, that you realize why it is possible to talk about couriers in general. The Chinese courier is much less an individual than his Western counterpart. Indeed, he is more of an institution – the highest organ of state authority. As such he enjoys a special status, comparable to that of our civil servants. Unlike his colleagues in the West, the Chinese courier does not merely represent some private enterprise or other, he represents his country as far as foreigners are concerned. He is therefore expected to act according to a certain set of rules of behaviour. Many not only do this readily, but are also proud to do so. Patriotism is nothing out of the ordinary for the majority of them. Of course, the courier is also put in a dangerous position because of the constant exposure to corrupting bourgeois influences from abroad: wealth, individualism, anarchy, decadence, and liberalism. The latter is interpreted in the Chinese communist philosophy as representing a shrinking away from bourgeois influences.

The functionaries' fear of detrimental influences intruding from abroad has resulted in the introduction of various rules, regulations and instructions. This means that a barrier has been erected between the Chinese courier and his foreign tourists. During each trip I have been on, I was asked again and again why the couriers did not eat breakfast with us or share any of our meals. Obviously, they might not always want to, preferring to chat to one of their colleagues. What everyone knows, however, is that they are not allowed to. They are simply not encouraged to fraternize with tourists. They won't ever give you their home address, insisting that all letters be sent to the office. Couriers are also instructed not to take groups of tourists into the old, run-down city areas, if this can be at all avoided. In fact, they are not forbidden to take parties of tourists to these poorer areas, but most of them will follow their instructions to the letter and will try to dissuade people from making such trips.

The old styles of architecture found in Luoyang, for example, make its old district particularly fascinating. However, it never features in any sightseeing programme. It requires a great deal of persuasion to get a courier to take you there. The same is true of the old district of Beijing. It is understandable that guides are not keen to show visitors such places. What's more, you can't expect couriers to look on whilst visitors take a grim delight in seeing areas of poverty and destitution. Nevertheless, I believe a case can be made for visitors on educational trips to be shown more than simply attractive façades.

Generally speaking, though, there seems to be a trend for the Chinese tourist authorities to be more open in their dealings with foreign visitors. The Chinese train passengers who spend the night in front of the railway stations are no longer cleared out of the way when foreign tourists arrive. Moreover, tourism has reached such dimensions today that it is impossible to prevent personal contacts being formed between tourists and Chinese people. And what would be the point of preventing such contacts? Visiting foreign countries is, after all, a means of eliminating the fear and ignorance of other people and different cultures and should be treated as such.

Beijing – the City of the Dragon

Visitors to Beijing should spend one morning on Tiananmen Square – "The Square of Heavenly Peace". Parallel to the "Gate of Eternal Peace", the entrance to the Forbidden City, is Chang'an Avenue. This road which is perfectly straight and some 40 km (25 miles) long, runs in an exact east-westerly direction and divides the city into night and day.

Early in the morning, the sun rises red and glowing over the eastern part of Chang'an Avenue. Cyclists pedal past, silently but deliberately; others do their morning exercises. All are bathed in the warming rays of the sun.

In the evening, the sun sets on the western end of Chang'an Avenue, plunging the city into darkness. Night falls in Beijing.

Beijing is a large sprawling city. This means that few people live close to their work; most have a long bicycle journey in front of them every morning. In Beijing the buses are always packed full.

The first joggers run towards the rising sun, while others, who prefer shadow-boxing, have already assembled on the huge Square of Heavenly Peace. Under the direction of several masters of this art, hundreds of people, usually older men and women, start the slow and flowing movements which demand so much concentration, calmness and inner harmony. They all gaze towards the north where the yellow roofs of the Imperial Palace glitter majestically in the morning sun.

Behind them is the final resting place of Mao Zedong – China's last emperor, referred to as such even by the Chinese. This man succeeded in freeing his nation from hunger and misery, but in the last few years of his life he did a great deal of damage to China, too. Moreover, the Chinese have not allowed Mao Zedong to rest. He has remained a powerful figure who plays a significant role in the internal struggles of the party.

The square is empty but for the shadow boxers. The huge grey walls of the concrete palaces which surround the square give it an almost ghostly air.

The picture changes rapidly. The stream of cyclists grows ever larger; the first buses start to move across this unusually wide street. Before long they are moving along in a long convoy, jammed one behind the other, stopping to pick up and set down passengers and full to overflowing. Those who think of the Chinese as a nation of polite and smiling people will quickly realize that this is not always so. You have to jostle and use your elbows in order to board a bus, for example. The rudeness of many passengers seems to be a favourite subject for articles in the evening papers. And so many buses drive along Chang'an Avenue that they are impossible to count.

The city begins to come to life even though there are plenty of tired faces to be seen – not only on buses … some of the cyclists look tired, too. The last vehicles to appear on the streets are the grey Shanghai limousines and the black Japanese cars with their curtained windows – the privileged means of transport for the middle and high ranking Party officials. Members of the party and state administration work from offices in the Great Hall of the People on Tiananmen Square or in Zhongnanhai, to the west of the Imperial Palace. People in government offices and shops usually start work around 9 a.m. A few miles outside the city, the farmers start work at about 6 a.m., or even earlier.

From 9 a.m. onwards, the tourists are flooding into the city centre, kindergartens set out on excursions to Tiananmen Square and grandfathers instruct children in the art of kite-flying.

Then the Imperial Palace opens its gates to the public. For more than 500 years emperors of the Ming and Qing Dynasties resided here, under the symbol of the dragon. Today, Chinese people and tourists alike stroll through the once sacred rooms and courtyards which were formerly filled with courtiers, eunuchs and concubines.

The first emperor in China to select Beijing as his capital city was the great Mongolian emperor, Kublai Khan. Beijing was named Khanbalik by the Mongolians and Dadu, meaning "Big Capital City", by the Chinese. Kublai Khan's palace city occupied the site of the present-day Beihai Park, i. e. it was situated to the west of the Imperial Palace.

After the Mongolians had been defeated and driven out of the country, the first two emperors of the Ming Dynasty made Nanjing their capital city. It was the third Ming emperor, Zhu Di, who moved the capital back to Beijing. Meanwhile, the city had been renamed Beiping (Northern Peace). At the beginning of the 15th century, Zhu Di started building the palace complex as it stands today. Then the city became known as Beijing, which means "Northern Capital". It is only in the West that we refer to it as Peking.

The last emperor of the Qing Dynasty had to abdicate in 1911 and finally left the palace in 1925. This was also the year in which the palace museum was founded.

Five hundred years of imperial residence have also left their mark on the city's architecture. Outside the palace, it was forbidden to build houses that were higher than the palace walls. The use of colours was also forbidden. Most of the colours, yellow, blue and red, were reserved for imperial buildings, nobody being allowed to compete with the magnificent colours of the Imperial Palace.

You will still find only single-storey, dull, grey buildings in the old district of Beijing. But this is nonetheless the real Beijing, and it is here that many Beijingers live. If you have the time then do take a walk through the "Hutongs". No courier will take you

66

there and since the alleys are very narrow, it would be impossible to visit them in a group, anyway. There is just room for one or two people. Perhaps someone will invite you for a cup of tea in one of the beautiful, square courtyards. You enter by a gate and will probably have to walk around the "spirit-wall" (to keep out evil spirits) before you come to the courtyard. The latter is enclosed on three sides by the walls of the single-storey neighbouring houses. Flowers, bicycles, stoves, tables and chairs stand in the courtyard. It is here that water is fetched, food is cooked and on fine days the family eats here, too. Living conditions are cramped with often several families sharing one courtyard. It is not unusual to hear torrents of abuse here, or the curses of bickering women. Living so close together causes aggression here, too.

Every courtyard forms a separate unit. Outsiders are prevented from looking in by a huge grey wall on the side that looks out onto the street. The streets themselves present a dismal picture: grey walls left and right, interrupted only by the courtyard gates. You will come across some strange names, here. Some of the alleys are named according to their shape, e. g. Goat or Pig Tail Alley. Others are given the names of various professions, for example, Paper-Maker Alley or Cloth Alley. Other unusual names are Mutton Alley and Bean Curd Alley.

Here China seems to live on in the style of past decades. There are no traffic wardens, no Japanese cars, no skycrapers, no supermarkets.

In the late afternoon the women return from their shopping. Refrigerators are rare and so shopping daily for fresh meat and vegetables is a must. The alleys are filled with children in the afternoons, and in the evenings chairs are brought out and people sit and chat. During the summer you will find old retired people sitting around in their vests, engrossed in games of chess or involved in a somewhat more heated game of cards.

It is probably these hutongs with their rural character, which are responsible for many Chinese people referring to Beijing as China's largest village. Another factor is no doubt the harsh dialect spoken by the people here. Many Chinese regard it as being somewhat coarse, to put it mildly.

But the city sprawls out way beyond this village. It grows incessantly, like a cancer. Some 7 or 8 years ago, blocks of flats 10 to 15 storeys high were built to the south of Tiananmen Square. It was about this time that the city planners began to argue about redevelopment policies. The fact remains that accommodation is very limited in Beijing. Life in the hutongs may seem idyllic, but for those who have to live there, the hopeless overcrowding has become unbearable. The parts of Beijing which have remained rural will not do so for long. Large ringroads and subways are changing the face of the city and on the outskirts of Beijing huge satellite cities are being built.

Many historical buildings have disappeared in the wake of progress. Before Beijing decided to open its gates to tourists, such buildings were regarded as old and worthless ruins of feudalism. Today, though, people have become wiser. In Xi'an, work is being carried out on the old city walls and gates to restore them to their former splendour. Sadly, it is too late to do such work in Beijing.

However, the citizens of Beijing have taken over the Imperial Gardens. On Sundays and public holidays, you will see them strolling through the gardens – parents, children and grandparents, carrying picnic baskets. These grounds were once reserved exclusively for the imperial family. The favourite excursion destination – next to Beihai Park at the Temple of Heaven – is the Summer Palace.

During the winter, Kunming Lake near the Summer Palace is completely frozen. Skaters gather there to practise their skills, and toboggans fill the surrounding areas. The older men concentrate on the art of kite-flying, practising intricate movements with dedication and unending patience. Quite often competitions are held and then you will see kites of fantastic shapes and colours. During the otherwise grey winter months, these colourful kites against a slate-coloured sky make a beautiful and cheering picture. Building kites is not just the irksome duty performed by some fathers to pacifiy their children. No, it is far more than that – it is almost a craft. There are quite a few famous kite builders in

Beijing. Sometimes you will see them at the Temple of Heaven or at the Tiananmen Square where they try out their latest creations. Some are also keen to sell their work to tourists, but prices are not cheap.

The summer months in the Summer Palace belong to the young generation. They fill the rowing boats that gently skim across Kunming Lake. (It is noticeable that, in the meantime, hi-fi sets are even here regarded as indispensable.) They rest during their walks in the Long Promenade, the covered walk along the shore of the lake, and enjoy the delicate beauty and colours of the lotus flowers.

You can see the Western Mountains from the Summer Palace. They are also a popular destination for excursions.

When the sun reaches the horizon of the Western Mountains, you will know that the city will soon be asleep. Beijing is quite dead in the evenings. It is at such times that its village characteristics become apparent and cannot be denied. Any entertainment in the cultural palaces and theatres usually starts around 7 p.m. and ends no later than 9.30 p.m., the time when all the restaurants close their doors. Then you can start looking for a place to end the evening, but it will be in vain.

This is also the time in the narrow valleys of the old city districts that people are still sitting playing cards. Elsewhere, in hotel bars or on roof gardens people gather to philosophize on China – past and present.

King of the Road

China does have traffic regulations, but I got the impression that the only people who know about them are the police, and they, for reasons of their own, keep them a secret. Indeed they seem to spend most of their time yelling at somebody or other through megaphones and loudspeakers or giving them a ticking off. In Beijing, as in many other cities, the streets are marked clearly. There are policemen at the crossroads and there is a special lane for the literally millions of cyclists. There are rules for overtaking; sometimes there are even pedestrian crossings. No-one who uses one, however, would do so in the belief that the cars are going to stop for him. That would be fatal. Pedestrians are not necessarily harassed, but the drivers do expect some respect for their superior horsepower.

Cyclists are not allowed to carry passengers. It is therefore not unusual to see the passenger jump off the cycle just before the crossroads, run across the street past the policeman and then jump onto the bicycle again when he is at a safe distance from the law.

Usually, tourists get their first shock in a bus, when they notice that the driver has completely ignored a red traffic light. But there is no need for panic. Drivers who are turning right are allowed to do this.

Tourists also have to get used to the fact that in a bus, the driver is king. Because of this they are very self-confident. They wear white gloves as a symbol of their unimpeachable authority and they usually earn more money than their colleagues who work as couriers. They are not allowed to accept tips but small tokens of appreciation certainly do no harm. And once you have shown your respect in this way, it would not be out of place to make a small request.

Drivers have been known to move along so slowly after a shower of rain that they are overtaken by cyclists – and all because they are worried about dirtying their recently washed bus. I would hasten to add that this doesn't happen very often.

You will begin to appreciate the true qualities of your driver once you are outside the city itself. And if your journey takes you through country areas then you will soon realize that a different set of rules applies here. The bus driver has to contend with narrow lanes that are often blocked by convoys of lorries, not to mention the slow moving carts (drawn by people or donkeys). The farmers don't help matters: they put their crops out on the street to dry. And then there are the scores of cyclists. In his Japanese air-conditioned vehicle, your driver truly is the king of the road. If you are of a nervous disposition, I would advise you to sit at the back of the bus and only to look out of the rear and side windows. The driver does not use one particular side of the road – he drives wherever there happens to be space. Overtaking is a risky business which demands courage and a certain assurance that the other person will give way. Anxious couriers will do their best to distract your attention from these dangers either by telling you stories or giving a lecture. They do it for your own good. It may sound ironic, but I must say that in the eight years that I have travelled in China, I have never experienced a serious accident involving tourists.

In fact Chinese chauffeurs are usually very good drivers. After all, they have to work hard for two years before they get their driver's licence. Only a few privileged people are allowed to drive a car in a private capacity. Nearly every driver is a professional, i. e., he either gained his licence in the army or he had to become a car mechanic before being allowed to sit behind the wheel. People wishing to drive tourist buses have to prove their driving skills – often in the form of special tests.

Some high ranking drivers also have permission to direct the traffic. I once met such a "head driver" when I was in Chengdu. He had worked previously for several years on the winding roads of Tibet. Unfortunately, he had never managed to shake off the reckless style of driving he acquired there. This man carried two signal flags about with him – a red and a green one, both with Chinese characters written on them.

And they really worked! We drove through the narrow alleys of several towns, all of them crowded with people – it was market day – in addition to the usual lorries and carts. Miraculously, space was made for our bus with the help of these two flags. No doubt people assumed that we were one of those important delegations who are always given right of way.

Traffic regulations come under the jurisdiction of the provinces or the cities. In Chengdu you will come across a peculiarity which no longer exists elsewhere in China. Children are carried on bicycles, on special rear seats. Here, as elsewhere in China, cyclists are not allowed to take passengers with them, but the law says nothing about carrying passengers on your back. And so parents strap their smaller children onto their backs and the larger ones travel, standing up, on the back seat. It is an ingenious way of bypassing the law and the police are powerless to do anything about it.

In the evenings the streets are in complete darkness. In China, street-lighting is only provided in city centres and cars and buses drive without lights. (Parking lights and side lights are, however, allowed.)

If this all seems totally incomprehensible, you will appreciate why it is done when you see a Chinese lorry with its head-lights on. It is impossible to adjust the lights on these old vehicles and it is easier to spot oncoming cars etc. in the darkness than in bright light. Whenever you're getting around on foot in China, do keep in mind that cyclists can be quite a hazard to pedestrians. It's true that most people in China cycle fairly slowly, but somehow they also seem to come to a halt very slowly, too. Their brakes aren't always in the best working order; sometimes they don't work at all! So being aware of your surroundings and keeping an eye on traffic is as important here as at home.

Guilin – a Landscape Painting

People travel to Rome to see St. Peter's Church and the Vatican museums, to Paris because of the Eiffel Tower and the beautiful women and to Beijing because of its famous palaces (the Imperial Palace and the Summer Palace). Visitors to Guilin, however, go there on account of its unique scenery. There are the bizarre looking hills shaped like a camel's humps, their peaks shrouded in wispy clouds: the water is clear and green and the sky is a marvellous blue. All these elements combine to make a "painting" which is without parallel.

If it were not for its magnificent scenery, this city which, with only 400,000 inhabitants, is small by Chinese standards, and is a mere speck on the map, would have been long forgotten, not least of all by tourists. As it is, poets and artists have, for centuries, been attracted to this region and have used their talents to praise this remarkable achievement of creation.

I am not poet and I just don't have the words to do justice to the beauty of Guilin. In the last few years, I have accompanied many groups to Guilin and have been repeatedly told by people that they never imagined it to be quite like this. All of them had either seen pic-tures of Guilin or had at least heard of it, but it was not until they saw it for themselves that they realized the descriptions had, after all, been accurate.

Countless, talented artists have depicted this scenery, and their work can be seen all over China, from Canton to Beijing, from Shanghai to Urumqi.

When I first visited Guilin, the "Second Liberation" was in progress. This is a term used by the Chinese themselves to describe the fall and condemnation of the "Gang of Four". Caricatures of the "Gang of Four" could be seen in shop windows and on the official notice boards. They were depicted being shot, impaled, boiled in oil etc. No attempt was made to hide the venom behind the attack.

We spent the early hours of evening wandering along Zhongshanlu, Guilin's main shopping street. In the midst of the scenes of horror on display, the only thing that reminded us of Guilin's peaceful and harmonious surrounding landscape was the sweet, heavy perfume of the blossoming cassia trees. The main street is lined with cosy little restaurants, the size of a one-roomed flat. The cooking is unique and you can choose from a wide range of exotic food. The small wire cages in front of the restaurants indicate all too clearly what is on the menu. There can be no mistaking the components of the various dishes: snakes, cats, badgers, armadillos, frogs, etc.

If you find this somewhat off-putting, then you have only yourself to blame; the food here really is excellent, often far superior to what you will be served in hotels. What's more, your stomach can take much more than you think!

The next morning we set off for the Li River (Lijiang). This is our starting-point for a six-hour boat trip to Yangshuo, the final destination on our journey. We plan to return from there by bus.

As it is autumn, the river is high enough for us to be able to board our ship in the town. In the spring you have to travel out of the town, boarding your ship after a two-hour bus ride. This does shorten the boat journey by about three hours, though. At that time, the travel agency in Guilin only had a small boat at its disposal which had to be towed by a motor boat.

Sitting on the upper deck, in well-worn rattan chairs, we enjoy the warm rays of the morning sun. Not long after the boat has left the dock the first hills attract our attention. Though we are still quite close to the city, we can already see the Xiangbi Shan, "Elephant's Trunk Mountain." Nature has done such a wonderful job, here, that you won't need much imagination. On the shore, a cave cuts into the base of the mountain, thus giving it the appearance of an elephant's trunk.

Naturally, the Chinese have a legend about this:

A long time ago, the fertile region of Guilin captured the attention of the Emperor of Heaven. And so he set out with his army to pillage the province. In his retinue was also the aforesaid elephant. Whilst he was on earth the elephant fell ill, but he was nursed back to health by some warm-hearted people. He therefore decided to remain on earth and serve human beings. When the Emperor of Heaven ordered him to return immediately he refused outright. Finally, the emperor had him murdered in cold blood. When the elephant stopped to drink some water at Lijiang river, a sword was driven into his back, right up to the hilt. The hilt of the sword can still be seen today, of course. There is a small pagoda on the hill and with a little imagination you can see it as the hilt of the sword.

On the edge of the city there are also the Pagoda Mountain and the Hole Mountain. The latter derives its name from the story of a legendary general. He is said to have used the mountain as target practice during a session of archery and the hole was made by one of his arrows. The local people also call it the Moon Cave. At dusk the mountain is actually darker than the sky, making the hole seem like a shining moon.

Our boat glides along peacefully and we enjoy the beautiful scenery and the sounds of nature. Small villages line the shore; small, arched bridges span the streams which run into the river; water buffaloes wallow in the water and naked children play in the warm waves.

After travelling for about three hours, we reach the most beautiful part of the landscape. Sights and images start to assault our senses in quick succession. "Nine Oxen Mountain", "Embroidery Mountain", "Apple Mountain" and "Painting Mountain" – an expansive rock face where you can allegedly make out the figures of nine horses. On another mountain slope you can see the profile of two bears, climbing.

Reflected in the clear water, we can see the bizarre looking mountains and the deep green of the phoenix tail bamboo which lines the shore. Our boat seems to glide through these reflected images.

In a poem about Guilin, Han Yu, a poet from the Tang Dynasty (618–907), describes the Lijiang as a blue silk ribbon which winds its way through hair pins made out of green jade. Thus, he compares the scenery to the country's two most important resources.

Occasionally, you will see villagers drying and repairing their nets on the shore. Their fishing boats are made out of 4 or 5 lengths of bamboo which are fastened together to form a raft. Great skill is needed to handle them since they capsize so easily. The boats are steered using a pole or an oar. Suddenly, we spot the first cormorant fishermen.

I am immediately reminded of the philosophical tradition of Taoism. The cormorant fishermen seem to embody perfectly the underlying aim of this religion-cum-philosophy – i. e., the achievement of harmony between man and nature. Squatted one behind the other, fisher and cormorant glide past unhurriedly on their narrow raft. The cormorant is a bird which excels at swimming and diving, skills which the fisherman makes good use of with the aid of some very simple equipment. One of the bird's feet is tied by a piece of string to the boat, thus preventing him from escaping, and a ring is placed around his neck so that he cannot swallow his catch.

One of these small boats drifts towards our ship and the fisherman starts bargaining with our cook. He praises the quality of his catch, using gestures all the while. His catch, strung through the eyes on a string, trails beside his raft in the water. This may seem cruel, but it is the only way of ensuring that the fish remains fresh.

We have been travelling for six hours when we see Yangshuo in front of us. Seven years ago, it was a small village with a dreamy air, our arrival caused a real sensation and half the village gathered on the pier to stare at us.

Today, I have to say that only a complete lack of tourists would cause a sensation. The quiet little village has been transformed into a noisy bazaar. No matter which street you take from the quay, you pass shops.

The hawkers congregate on the landing jetties to sell anything and everything from fruit to souvenirs. They expect people to bargain, and the prices start to fall as the time for the departure of the ships approaches.

Can I still enjoy and appreciate Guilin after the fifth or tenth visit? The answer, without hesitation, has to be "yes!" A trip on the Lijiang is not merely a sightseeing trip; it is a fascinating experience which I can relish over and over again.

Tibet – the Land of Gods and Demons

Shangri-la is the name of a film made in Hollywood in the thirties, which presents the legend of a mythical land on the roof of the world in the form of a modern adventure story. An aeroplane has to make a crash landing in the Himalayas. The survivors are completely cut off from the rest of the world, their chances of contacting anyone, slim. In their search for people and help, they discover a door in the rocks, behind which lies the legendary paradise. In keeping with a modern fairy tale, they find all the things here that man has ever longed for. There is happiness, contentment, harmony and a general love of life. They have already set out, with heavy hearts, for home, when one of them is overcome with the desire to return. He is unable to find the entrance again, however. Finally, it is the snow storms that put an end to his dreams – he dies in sub-zero temperatures.

The myth of a paradise on the roof of the world is now a thing of the past. Today, news does reach the outside world from Tibet. Myths always come about through ignorance and once you have penetrated the veil of mystery surrounding them they are revealed for what they really are. Every paradise loses its attraction once you know it.

I first visited Tibet in 1981. My second visit in 1983 offered me a further opportunity to make observations and comparisons. What changes have taken place since the Tibetans were allowed more freedom under the pragmatic Beijing government? Have the discussions about the return of the Dalai Lama (the chief lama and ruler of Tibet) had any effect?

Nowadays, a trip to Tibet has nothing in common with the adventures of Marco Polo. The journey is no longer a nerve-wracking experience involving hardships, but it will cost you a lot of money. You can travel in comfort, though. The flight from Chengdu, the capital of Sichuan to Lhasa takes about two hours. After driving for two hours, you will see from afar, the golden roofs of the Potala Palace – the seat of the Dalai lamas. Involuntarily, I am reminded of the descriptions of Tibet that feature in old travel reports. Images come to mind of a long forgotten land, where nature has remained unspoilt, a land of religious festivals and mystic ceremonies – images of a society which has remained unchanged for centuries and of a people who have preserved their culture. But what does all of this have to do with today's Tibet?

The nearer you get to Lhasa, the clearer it becomes that progress has entered Tibet. The road is lined with power stations, irrigation plants, oil tanks, military barracks, water towers … Then there are new houses and other buildings – all functional and purpose-built. In fact the tourists live outside the city, to the north, close to the Chinese garrison. Nevertheless, by their mere presence they are messengers from another world which is still unknown to most Tibetans.

The most accurate description of modern Tibet can be gained by visiting the Barkhor in the centre of Lhasa's old district. Here you will meet Tibetans, Chinese, foreigners, beggars, hawkers, monks and innumerable pilgrims. Nowhere else in Tibet does as much news change hands, as here. For over a thousand years, the Barkhor and the Jokhang Temple which surrounds it have represented the focal point of Tibetan Buddhism. It is perhaps easiest to picture the old Tibet by observing the followers of Buddhism as they walk along the 800 metre long (2,625 ft) ritual road. Buddhists walk on this road around the Jokhang Temple in a clockwise direction. It is considered better still to cover the distance by throwing oneself to the ground in a gesture of prayer. The number of pilgrims has risen steadily since the new regime came into power and introduced more liberal policies, including greater religious freedom.

Tibetans from all parts of the country can be seen here: farmers from eastern Tibet who are easily recognizable because of their small stature and Mongolian features, as well as the taller Khampas – a nomad tribe from the north. The latter wear fur-lined coats and carry the usual nomad utensils: a dagger, a "lighter" (a leather pouch with a metal clasp filled with flints), and an amulet bag, which is worn around the neck.

Often, however, Barkhor is more like a bazaar than a place where religious rituals are performed. You will come across far more hawkers than monks engaged in meditation. It is not unusual either to meet Tibetans from India here. Having been granted a visa to visit relatives, many of them earn their fare home by selling souvenirs they have brought with them from India. Even local people, however, find the false god of tourism more attractive than any blessings that their own gods can offer. They sell almost everything, from coins to jewellery and even small statues of Buddha which they carry, well-hidden in their coats or pockets.

Since my last visit, a large number of beggars have settled on the outer edge of the Barkhor – a testimony to the lasting poverty of this country. Followers of Buddhism like to give them something, since this is considered a good deed and will be credited to the positive side of the karma (the sum of all good and bad deeds in life). A good deed automatically cancels out a bad one and will be rewarded by the gods. The wealthier

people usually give 1, 2, or 5 fen coins to the poor or they distribute tsampa – a special Tibetan barley flour. Children, either naked or dressed simply in dirty rags will cling stubbornly to tourists.

A small boy, no more than 5 years old is causing a sensation. He is measuring the length of the Barkhor with his body. With a stone in his hand, he first throws himself onto his knees, then onto his face, so that he is lying stretched out in the dust. He meditates for a while in this position, before standing up again and moving to the spot where he had laid his stone, in order to repeat the procedure again. Hundreds of Tibetans crowd around him. They look at him in awe and give him money as a reward. An elderly man, possibly his father, makes way for him through the crowd. It is possible that the boy is regarded as a reincarnation of one of the Buddhist gods.

Professional prayers, people paid to pray for others, also go about their work. Special clothing is required for this physically demanding work. To protect their hands they wear gloves with a metal "lining". They also wear protective pads on their knees, made either of material or occasionally of metal. Dressed in this way, they spend the whole day throwing themselves onto the ground and imploring Buddha's help.

An old woman with a wrinkled face and unkempt hair sits in one corner of the Barkhor. She is a storyteller and holds a whole group of pilgrims spellbound with her voice and mime. She reads to those who are illiterate, telling them stories and legends; sometimes she will even sing. No doubt, she can also tell them all the latest news.

Jokhang, the holiest temple of Tibetan Buddhism is also being used for prayer once more. Indeed, there seems to be no end to the line of pilgrims: they crowd into the small chapels to fill the lamps with the butter they have brought along. This would all seem to indicate that this religion cannot be stamped out, even using the brutal methods of the Cultural Revolutionaries. And indeed, the temple, which is Lhasa's oldest building, is presently being renovated. When you enter Jokhang, you get the impression that time has stood still.

Although it may sound ironic, Jokhang is also regarded as sacred by the Chinese, though not in a religious sense. As far as they are concerned, Jokhang demonstrates their claim to Tibet as part of the Chinese empire. If you demand historical proof that Tibet belongs to China, the first story you will hear is the one of the Chinese princess, Wen Cheng. In 641 A.D. she married the Tibetan king Strongtsan Gampo, the man regarded as responsible for the unification of Tibet. The wedding present she received from the imperial court was a gem-covered statue of the Buddha Shakyamuni, also known as Jobo. Jokhang, Temple of Jo, was built for this statue. Nevertheless, they often forget to mention

that Stongtsan Gampo had prior to this wedding married a Nepalese princess. So far, Nepal has not used this fact to make any sort of territorial claim on Tibet.

Opposite the entrance to Jokhang, there is a walled mound of earth on which a willow tree grows. It is supposed to have been planted by Princess Wen Cheng as a symbol for the friendship and union between the two countries.

Most of the Chinese living in Tibet are soldiers. The Chinese garrison lies to the north of Lhasa. Chinese and Tibetans rarely speak to one another and if they do, then they converse in Chinese because hardly any of the Chinese who live there have bothered to learn the Tibetan language. In Lhasa itself, Chinese and Tibetans also live apart. This segregation was neither intended nor enforced – it simply happened. No doubt, both sides prefer it that way. The majority of government posts are occupied by Chinese. Very few of the Chinese in Tibet volunteered to come, however. Most of them were ordered to come. Life here at over 4,000 m (13,000 ft) above sea level is both harsh and strange for them and many of them yearn to go home.

The relationship between these two nations suffered badly as a result of the Cultural Revolution. The Red Guards attempted to destroy everything that could be classed as feudal and to drive away the gods by smashing their statues. In doing so, they deprived the people of their religion. Even today, religion incorporates for every Tibetan, both his personal and national identity.

Since then the Tibetans have been granted religious freedom once more, but preaching, or otherwise attempting to spread religious beliefs, is strictly forbidden and is subject to punishment. Where do you draw the boundary between practising a religion and talking about it, though? This distinction seems to have been left to chance.

In Jokhang, a tourist gives a monk a picture of the Dalai Lama. It is impossible to buy such pictures in Tibet, but what you will find in the department stores are pictures of Marx and Engels. You can imagine the monk's pleasure. His face lights up, he is delighted. Full of reverence he gazes at the picture of his god-king. He then places it on his head and murmurs "Yishi Norbu". This means something like "Wish-fulfilling Gem" – an honorific title of the Dalai Lama which is used more often in Tibet than his actual title.

A Chinese courier, having seen what has happened, destroys the monk's happiness by snatching the photograph out of his hand without a word. The monk makes no attempt to voice his protest. His face remains motionless, but it doesn't require much imagination to picture his feelings of hatred and aversion or the desire to gain revenge or how existing feelings of hatred become all the stronger.

Foreigners often bring such photos of the Dalai Lama into Tibet (and these are often to be seen on altars) but the question of the Dalai Lama ever returning in person is one which occupies the thoughts of all Tibetans. His return is wished for by everyone, some even yearn for it. Despite the fact that he has been in exile for over 20 years, he has remained their religious leader. Indeed, he is probably held in greater reverence today than ever before.

This is because, today, all their hopes are centred on him: the desire to be allowed to practise their religion freely, the wish for extensive autonomy, even independence, and a withdrawal of the Chinese, and the hope of leading a freer life. Many people continue to demand total independence from China. It is difficult to judge whether these hopes are shared by all levels of society. Certainly, life under the lamas was no paradise. The aristrocratic families of Tibet (who all lived in Lhasa) may have had an easy time of it, but for the majority of people, life must have been sheer hell. Then, however, even the poorer people had the solace offered by their gods, in difficult times, to whom they could pray and from whom they could expect help. The Chinese, on the other hand, have brought about few improvements, but have succeeded in depriving them of their gods. It is true that there are signs of industrial development everywhere, but even the government in Beijing has had to admit that the standard of living has only improved slightly.

Nowadays, the Dalai Lama's palace, the Potala, is filled with pilgrims again. Back in 1981 a tourist visiting the Potala was almost completely alone. Something else has changed, too, only a minute detail, perhaps, but possibly also a harbinger of an important event. A year ago, visitors were also admitted to the Dalai Lama's private quarters which is situated in the centre of the palace. His bedroom is somewhat humble, containing only a simple bed with a brass frame. At that time, the bed was made and the cover was thrown back at one corner. A sign perhaps that they would like to see the Dalai Lama back in Tibet? That, at least, was how many people interpreted it.

During my last visit in 1983, however, I was told that the Dalai Lama's quarters were locked and that the attendant didn't have a key to the rooms. These rooms are now in the hands of the lamas, who apparently regard it as a blasphemy that nonbelievers, i. e. tourists should set foot in these most holy quarters.

In the autumn of 1982, another Tibetan lama returned after an absence of 18 years: the Panchen Lama. He actually occupies a higher position in the religious hierarchy than the Dalai Lama, being a reincarnation of a Buddha. The Dalai Lama, on the other hand is "merely" revered as an incarnation of a Bodhisattva who are lower in rank than the Buddhas.

In fact the title, Panchen Lama was bestowed by a Dalai Lama. The fifth Dalai Lama chose this method of honouring his old teacher, in

Xigaze, little suspecting the complications it would bring. The present Panchem Lama (the tenth), collaborated with the Chinese in the fifties (whether voluntarily or not is still open to question). He then went to Beijing. During the cultural revolution he was detained and placed under house arrest.

With the exception of some extremists who regard him as a traitor, his countrymen do not resent the fact that he had been absent for so long. (His last visit had been in 1965.) There was talk of him returning for three months to live in his newly renovated summer palace in Xigaze. In 1981, I saw workmen engaged in restoration work on the palace. All of them were convinced that the work was being done for the imminent return of the Panchen Lama, though there had been no official statement to that effect.

When he finally returned after 18 years, in 1983, 50,000 people besieged the summer palace in order to catch a glimpse of him. This is a remarkable turn out when you consider that there are only 60,000 inhabitants in Xigaze, of whom roughly half are Chinese. The whole matter threatened to get out of hand and so the provincial government of Tibet, whose head is Chinese, asked him to cut short his visit after only 25 days.

We stand in front of the palace gate and ask to be let in, so that we can look around, but a Tibetan bars our way and a lengthy discussion ensues. He is dressed in pin-striped trousers, a fashionable cardigan, and wears a pair of tennis shoes with the famous three stripes – altogether very secular in appearance. It turns out, however, that a real-life Buddha in person is standing in front of us. This man is one of the highest dignitaries in the neighbouring monastery of Tashi Lhunpo and one of Panchen Lama's closest advisers. He refuses us permission to enter, pointing out that the palace now belongs to the Panchen Lama again and that no instructions were left for visitors to be admitted. It would seem that the Chinese government is no longer all-powerful; at least in matters such as this they have to defer to the lamas. Meanwhile, the government travel agency has made an official request to the Panchen Lama for permission to conduct sightseeing tours.

It is not difficult to imagine what would happen now if the Dalai Lama were to return. In 1983, restoration work was being carried out on the Norbulingkha, the Dalai Lama's summer palace in Lhasa. A sign that he is going to return, perhaps? On his last visit to Tibet he lived in this palace for the greater part of his stay.

We stand and watch a group of young women dancing, using special rhythmic steps in order to make the mud covering of a roof more firm. As they dance, they sing of Chairman Mao, whose red sun shines over Tibet. Such are the absurdities and contradictions in everyday life here – they don't seem to be in keeping with any of the usually biased conceptions we have of the political situation in Tibet. Reality is far more complex than the theories of politicians and ideologists.

In Lhasa we are allowed to visit a Tibetan family. Naturally they have been specially selected and prepared for our visit. Another sandstorm is presently blasting through the streets of Lhasa and so we run to our host's house, which is built in the traditional style, to take cover in the inner courtyard. Our host offers us yak butter, tea, and tchang which is a Tibetan beer brewed from barley. It is refreshing and tastes delicious but it leaves you with a thick head. The walls are decorated with brightly coloured posters of the kind to be found in any department store. Hanging next to the religious posters, thanka imitations with pictures of Buddhas and Bodhisattvas, there are also examples of the socialist-realist poster art. For outsiders, this mixture of modern Chinese art and traditional Tibetan art is confusing; the two exist here side by side. The socialist poster shows a marshall from the People's Liberation Army, laden with medals. He is depicted riding a horse and smiling broadly, (indeed he exudes energy and authority) against a background of lush green vegetation and bright red flowers.

How do Tibetans cope with the existence of these two art forms? We cannot look inside either their souls or their heads and so the question has to go unanswered. It would also be presumptuous to think that anybody would pour out their hearts to us of all people.

Morning Light

We are on our way to the province of Yunnan. Over twenty different nationalities live in this tropical jungle region which is bordered to the south and west by Vietnam, Laos and Burma.

Our adventure begins at Kunming's airport. We are not travelling alone in the small, Russian twin-engined propeller plane. Apart from several Chinese passengers, we are also accompanied by a fair number of poultry and a great mountain of luggage.

The plane takes off into the clear blue sky, the course set for Simao, a small town in the southern part of Yunnan. Our guide, a Mrs. Wang from Beijing, looks as though she would prefer to get out again – our small plane is quick to react to every turbulence, no matter how slight.

From Simao we travel by minibus to Xishuangbanna, a journey of about 6 hours, taking us through tropical jungle. On the way we see many solitary farms on the hills where land is still cleared by burning. These farmers belong to the smaller ethnic minorities of the province. They were driven away from the valleys centuries ago by the Dai, who are wet-rice cultivators. The dry rice which these farmers cultivate, tastes very good and needs very little water, but the yield is comparatively low. During the trip, we constantly meet people belonging to various ethnic minorities in colourful costumes – worn mainly by the women. Identifying the different minority groups is not easy for us, or our translator. We therefore bombard our local guides from Kunming and Simao with eager questions. Yes, they answer, she is a Dai... No, she belongs to the Hani! No, she is Bai not Yi...

After a while, we are at least able to recognise the Dai by their costumes. This is just as well, since we want to visit some Dai people. Nevertheless, we are only able to tell them apart by their costumes, though many ethnic minorities can be distinguished by their particular build or features. The Bai women tend to be of a fairly hefty build, for example, whereas the Dai are much slimmer. To see the two together you might think they were mother and daughter.

It is late afternoon when we arrive in Xishunagbanna. Before darkness falls we take a look at the unusual animals and plants. We see palms, coconuts, grapefruit but also many beautiful flowers and shrubs that we cannot identify. A parrot is perched on a tree. In the jungle there are said to be elephants, buffalos, peacocks, monkeys and snakes. As darkness descends, colourless, clear lizards, geckos, start gathering on the walls of the guest-house in order to hunt the insects which are attracted to the light from our lamps. We feel distinctly uncomfortable when they start crawling on the ceiling. But we have no need to worry – they keep their distance.

81

Xishuangbanna is a Chinese word given to a name in the Dai language, meaning literally 12,000 fields or 12,000 administrative units. The term stems from the reign of the Dai king, Zhao Yingmeng (15th century), who divided this area into 12 administrative units.

Today, approximately 650,000 people live in Xishuangbanna. A third of them are Han Chinese, a third Dai, and the rest are made up of people from minority groups such as the Wa, Bulong, Hui, Miao, Yi, Nanxi, Hani, Lisu, and Bai.

The town lies only about 100 km (62 miles) from the borders to Laos and Burma, making it strategically important from the point of the central government in Beijing. After all, many members of these ethnic minorities also live beyond the borders of China. Historical proof that these border regions belong to China, forms an important part of the government's policy towards minorities. Our guide tells us that as early as the 2nd century A.D., the Dai king sent his messengers to Luoyang, the capital city of the East Han dynasty, in order to accept various gifts and titles on his behalf. This method of securing such bordering realms for the imperial Chinese court by means of presents and titles, but also through marriage, was widespread, especially during the Han dynasty. The first Han Chinese started settling in Yunnan at the time of the West Han dynasty, i. e., in the first and second centuries A. D. Later people were exiled to Yunnan by their emperors. Eventually, this led to the forced settlement of the town with exiled Han Chinese.

Until the middle of this century, the Dai lived in a feudalistic society, as did many minorities. There were even some vestiges of slavery. All land belonged to the Dai king, and the farmers were his serfs. There was even a special form of compulsory labour. For generations each village was assigned a certain kind of work by the king's court. One village, for example, was responsible for guarding and taking care of the work elephants, another for chopping wood, and another for keeping the royal kitchen supplied. And should a member of court die, there was even a village which had the task of making the necessary preparations for the funeral ceremony. Another village made clothes for the female members of court and the concubines.

The Dai soon developed their own system of writing, but the other smaller minorities (who were often enslaved) resorted to other methods. Up until this century, many of them either carved signs in wood or tied knots in string in order to record facts.

The next morning we visit Mangsha, the Dai village in the district known as Jinghong, or "Morning Light". There is a legend attached to this name, a name which suggests a bright and happy future:

Once upon a time, this area was a huge ocean which dried up and turned into fertile fields. But a devil lived in the forest and he brought misfortune and ruin to the area by setting fire to the bamboo huts. The population was decimated, the birds in the trees stopped singing, and gradually the entire land became desolate. (It is possible that this legend describes a plague.) Then, as befits a story of this nature, a courageous young man appeared on the scene and challenged the devil. The latter fled to the Lancang River (the Mekong) and here the decisive battle took place.

They fought for seven days and in the end, the young man managed to strangle the devil. He then took a giant pearl from the devil's throat and hung it upon a tree. From that time on, the area flourished, again, and was known as Jinghong – Morning Light.

Our arrival causes a tremendous sensation: we are the first foreigners to ever visit the village. We are welcomed in the village square by the chairman of the production brigade and the accountant, both of whom seem very unassuming, almost shy. At this point people start to come forward – they are curious, but for the time being they keep a respectful distance to us. Then the accountant takes out a small notebook and starts to inform us about his village. His report reads like a long list of statistics:

There are 82 households in the village which has 435 inhabitants. Of these, some 205 belong to the work force. They irrigate an area covering 818 mu (approx. 130 acres). Some 230 mu are used for the cultivation of pineapple, 140 mu for rubber, 100 mu for corn…
Last year, the brigade made a total of 120,000 yuan. The average income of each villager amounts to 280 yuan per year and this is paid out in money and food stuffs. There are already 130 bicycles and 165 wrist watches in the village.

When he has finished his speech, he invites us to his house for lunch. The Dai live in bamboo huts, which are erected on poles, to protect them in the case of flooding. The domestic animals are kept in a stall on the ground floor – for a very good reason, as we would later find out. We reach the living quarters via a wooden staircase, and are able to look around. The anteroom, a sort of hallway, has been made ready for the meal. On the side opposite the open stairs there is a terrace where bowls have been placed for us to wash our hands.

The hallway leads into a large living-room which is very simply furnished. In one corner there is a table and chair. On the table lies an abacus, the Chinese calculator, a note book and a pencil, reminding us that our host is the accountant for the brigade. The family of nine all sleep in one large bedroom on mattresses or in hammocks. They have the luxury of electric light. The women of the house are dressed traditionally: in light coloured, close-fitting blouses, long colourful skirts held at the waist by hand-wrought belts of either silver or aluminium. They wear the usual Chinese cloth shoes.

Once we have looked around, we take our places on very low stools, in the hallway. The daughters of the house sit somewhat shyly at our table. The flowers in their hair are made of plastic and come from Shanghai. In the district town there is a store which sells material, dresses and jewellery for the ethnic minorities.

Our meal consists of sticky rice, lots of vegetables and large quantities of incredibly hot, spicy sauces. Chopsticks have been laid out for us, but we eat with our fingers, as the others do. We form the rice into balls with our left hands, examining the dishes in front of us as we do so. Then we work our way through the hot sauces. Any leftovers are dropped onto the floor, but they don't remain there on the bamboo matting – they fall through cracks in the wood and are gulped down greedily by the pigs and hens below.

Conversation isn't easy. First of all our questions have to be translated into Chinese. Unfortunately, the Dai understand very little, if anything of what's said. And our local guides speak the Canton dialect of South China, which is totally incomprehensible for our interpreter from Beijing.

Children are supposed to learn Han Chinese at school, but the bookkeepers' children either can't or won't speak it. Though they are silent, they do smile a great deal, thereby showing off their gold-capped canine teeth. The latter are regarded as a kind of personal decoration as are also the hand wrought silver belts that the girls wear. For centuries now, the Dai have been making belts, arm bracelets, and other jewellery out of this precious metal.

After the meal, we take a walk through the village. We are followed, very hesitatingly and at a great distance by the children. The narrow paths that run through the village are simply mud which has been pressed down to make it firm – work that is undone every time it rains. Cactus-like plants surround the courtyards from which curious eyes follow our movements. An old woman, dressed only in a skirt and chewing betel, is startled when she sees us and decides it is safer to run away. Meanwhile, the children have become both more curious and bold. They send their leaders to us, who converse with our translators in broken Chinese and discuss us, the strange foreigners. After accompanying us for a while, they run back to report all they have heard to their friends, rather proud of their daring.

On the outskirts of the village we see the buildings where the water buffalo are kept. Every family owns one of these animals which are indispensible here. When we later inspect the fields, to round off our tour, the driver has to resort to every trick he knows in order to stop the vehicle getting bogged down in the mud.

As we get ready to leave, half the village gathers to bid us farewell. No doubt, we were a popular topic of conversation for days, or even weeks to come.

The next day is market day in Jinghong. Hundreds of farmers from the surrounding villages come here in the early morning to sell their goods on the main street. Here they are allowed to sell the produce they have grown on their own plots and jewellery and other items they have made at home. You can buy hand wrought silver belts here. It has been drizzling the whole morning, but nobody seems to mind in this warm tropical air.

We conclude our visit to Jinghong with a boat trip on the Lancang River, which is known further south in Indo-China as the Mekong. We pass by the summer residence of the last Dai king, Zhao Benling. The building is dilapidated now. Zhao Benling is still alive today, we are told, as are also several of his cabinet ministers. Indeed one of his former ministers is chairman of the revolutionary committee for the district of Xishuangbanna. The daughter of the last king is acting chairwomen to the local women's association and the king's uncle is vice-chairman of the political consultant committee in Beijing. The committee is under the direction of the Communist Party and is made up of members of the various political parties as well as other leading figures. Integration is part of China's policy towards the minority groupings and is reminiscent of the "embrace" policy which was practised under the Han dynasty. Now, as then, it helps to defuse the border situation.

When we arrive back in Simao we are told that there will be no flight from Kunming today. Flights only operate to such remote places, wea-

ther permitting, and cancellations and delays have to be reckoned with. Thus our stay in Simao is extended by two full days. So we set about organising impromptu visits, which turn out to be real experiences because people are not as well prepared for our arrival. We cause chaos in the primary school in Simao by announcing ourselves and then appearing in person just one hour later. This is the first time that foreigners have visited the school and the children are beyond themselves with excitement. Classes continue during our visit, but despite this the reception building where we are welcomed by the headmistress is soon thronging with scores of curious children. The teachers look on, helpless. Later an unrehearsed song and dance demonstration is put on for us in the school playground. Understandably, the school children find us more interesting than the performance that their classmates are giving. Each individual performance is followed by a heated discusion as to what should come next. Finally, someone suggests that we sing something. Our performance was not particularly good, but the children seemed to enjoy it. The headmistress is obviously relieved when we start to leave. She had never known such chaos as this in her school, not even in the turbulent days of the cultural revolution.

A girl from the dance group whose burning ambition it is to become an actress when she grows up, gives me her school badge. The red characters on a white background read: Simao Hongqi Xiao

Xue – Simao's Red Flag Primary School.

In our two extra days in Simao we are served some delicious meals, as our host attempts to console us for the fact that we are having to leave later than planned. In actual fact we weren't all that upset, but we tasted some wonderful local delicacies in that time. The most exotic dish we had was deep-fried bees which were twice as big as any I have ever seen.

Zhongguo – the Middle Kingdom

For many of us China is still some-what of a mystery – a mosaic from which several pieces are missing – so that the complete picture continues to elude us. China's rulers pursued a policy of isolation for not just hundreds, but thousands of years and the country has always assimilated foreign culture and influences whilst exporting very little of its own culture. This explains why China has attracted so much curiosity over the centuries.

However, China has since opened her doors to the West, anxious to gain access to western technology. In doing so, she has raised the hopes of many industrial giants that there are profits to be made in China. Nevertheless, China is intent on preventing western influence from gaining too great a hold.

China as the central kingdom – a concept which is thousands of years old, but which is still alive today in the word Chinese people use to refer to their country: Zhong-guo means literally middle-kingdom. The official designation is Zhonghua Renmin Gongheguo – The People's Republic of China.

If you visit the Heavenly Temple in Beijing, then you will be able to see for yourself the centre point of this kingdom, which according to the Chinese formed the centre of the cosmos. A round stone on the upper level of the Heavenly Altar marks the centre of the earth. The idea is not so unusual when we consider that for the Romans the Forum was the centre of the earth.

And in fact the Heavenly Altar was built as a representation of the Chinese view of the world. Thus the altar is surrounded by a circular wall which is symbolic of the limits of the heavens. Outside the circular wall is a square-shaped wall to represent the boundaries of an earth which they thought was flat. The arched heavens only cover the middle section of the earth – the Central Empire, and the dark corners are populated by the barbarian peoples. For the Chinese, anyone who was not Chinese was barbarian. The Chinese emperor and Son of Heaven had to place his sacrifices under the arch of heaven.

According to history, China's centre lay further to the west, in the fertile loess plains of the Yellow River. It was here that the first communities, principalities and kingdoms originated. From here, too, the King of Qin succeeded in conquering six other kingdoms. Then in 221 B.C. he founded the first Chinese empire, at roughly the same time as the Romans started to build up their empire in faraway Europe. The King of Qin gave himself the title: Qin Shi Huang Di, First Sovereign Emperor. He wanted his empire to last for a thousand years with the emperors who succeeded him also bearing his name. This was not to be, however. The second emperor was followed by another dynasty. It is very likely that the name we use in the West – i.e., China, originates from the time of the Qin dynasty, since the name Qin is often transcribed as "Ch'in". In old historical documents in the Indo-Germanic language area, the name appears as: Ts'in, Tshin, Tschina, Tzinistan etc. In India the name Mahatchina is used and translated as "Great China".

The first mention of China can be found in the works of the Greek, Ptolemy – the father of geography. He mentions two cities for the first time: Issedon skythica and Issedon serica, probably identical with the cities of Kashgar and Khotan in the provinces of Xinjiang. They were once important trading centres – caravansaries along the Silk Road. In fact, it was the news of this delicate and valuable material which first aroused the curiosity of the European nations, especially the traders. Alexander the Great, Herodotus, Isaiah and others mention the land of Sera or the race of Serer, which means simply "the silk bringers".

This was the only information people had about this unknown race in the country of the rising sun.

Moreover, it is very likely that the race concerned was actually the Issedones, who lived in the Tarim Basin. They received their silk from the Chinese and monopolised trade with the West. Thus they effectively prevented direct contact between Western civilization and the Chinese for several centuries. Another name for China can be found in the Russian language, namely "Khitai". The name originates from the warrior nomadic race of Khitan. They founded their own dynasty in the northern border regions of the Chinese empire from the 10th to the 12th century. Hong Kong's airline company uses the name today: Cathay Airways.

A busy shipping trade began to develop between the Arabs and the southern Chinese at about the same time. And so another name made its way to the West, possible by way of the Malaysian language: Sinai.

Today you no longer have to face arduous adventures, endless expeditions across mountain ranges or deserts, or undertake dangerous sailing trips in order to reach China. You can travel by plane to Beijing from Los Angeles in less than 20 hours; or in 30 hours if you are flying from London. Even today, though, we are still accompanied by a certain amount of curiosity, and silk, which was the first message from China to the West, is still a much coveted article.

An Audience with China's First Emperor

For more than 2,100 years, his body lay hidden beneath the yellow, loess earth of the Shaanxi Province, not far from its capital, Xi'an. As a historical figure he is still alive, however. Indeed, more recently, his name was used during the cultural revolution by various fractions of the Communist Party. The man in question is the Emperor Qin Shi Huang Di, the founder of the united Chinese empire.

In the spring of 1974, farmers from the village of Xiyang in the district of Lintong, disturbed his peace of over 2,000 years. They had only wanted to dig a well and made the find of a lifetime, comparable to the large excavations of Roman and Egyptian civilizations.

Archaeologists (in common with other scientists) did not have a particularly easy time of it during the chaotic and turbulent days of the Cultural Revolution. The fact that it was farmers and workers who had chanced upon the grave site meant that leading figures of the revolution could underline the important role played by the worker in the sciences. Luckily, archaeologists were soon able to take over the grave site. I shudder to think what damage might have been done otherwise through ideological stubbornness and general ignorance. Perhaps it is significant that Mao Zedong, who is said to have been very interested

and well read in both history and classical literature, had a weak spot for this emperor.

The grave site of the Emperor Qin Shi Huang Di has become a standard feature on the sightseeing programme of visitors to Xi'an. Xi'an is China's oldest city and is also of the greatest historical significance. The excavations made in the early stone-age village of Banpo near Xi'an prove that there were settlements in the fertile valley of the Wei River as long as 6,000 years ago. One thousand years before our western history begins, the Western Zhou dynasty already had its capital here. The founder of the empire, Qin Shi Huang Di, lived in the town of Xianyang some 40 km (25 miles) east of the present-day Xi'an. Little remains of Xianyang today, which according to historical documents, was once a large and beautiful city. The grave site of Qin Shi Huang Di on Li Mountain is the only thing that has remained intact.

Xi'an also served as capital city for subsequent dynasties, when it was known as Chang'an. Over one million people lived here during the Tang Dynasty (618–907 A.D.), making it very probably the largest city in the world at that time. Chang'an was also known to European and Middle Eastern civilizations since it was situated at the end of the Silk Road and was therefore of strategic importance for trade with other countries. Archaeological finds, historical documents, paintings and drawings all attest to the encounter with western civilizations.

Today, Emperor Qin Shi Huang Di receives visitors with all military honours. First of all you enter an immense hall which was built to protect the grave site. Constructed of steel tubing, the building is supposed to withstand earthquakes. From a gallery, you look down onto the formation of an infantry division. The main excavation site covers an area of 12,600 sq. metres (136,625 sq. ft). It is 210 m (689 ft) long and 60 m (197 ft) wide. Here, there are more than 6,000 terra-cotta figures. So far only about one tenth of the site has been excavated by archaeologists. Some 500 soldiers, 25 horses and 6 war chariots are now standing again and restoration work has been carried out on them. It is in this section of the site that more than 7,000 weapons have been found, made largely of bronze, together with ornaments of gold, bronze or stone, and also parts of the building. Among the finds was also a sword which was still so sharp, despite being more than 2,000 years old, that it can cut a piece of paper clean in two as archaeologists were able to demonstrate.

The first thing the visitor sees is a formation of men in three columns, made up of marksmen, archers and crossbowmen. Directly behind them stand six war chariots. Each chariot is drawn by four horses and manned by a charioteer and two soldiers.

Behind these war chariots there are eleven corridors. In nine of them the infantry soldiers stand four abreast. In the two outer corridors, the soldiers posted on the flanks stand lookout, thus protecting the troops. Officers can be distinguished from the soldiers by their clothing and equipment. What is really impressive is that no two faces are exactly alike. Archaeologists think that the figures were probably modelled on the emperor's guard of honour. All the figures are life-sized, measuring between 1.75 and 1.86 metres (5' 7" and 6' 1"). They were originally painted and carried real weapons. There are reconstructions of soldiers and chariots in their original colours in the exhibition hall.

The hard grey clay that the figures are made of comes from the area surrounding the Li Mountain. This hard material made it possible to form such large figures, which were then fired at high temperatures. The figures were put together out of individual sections, though the lower part of the torso had to be made of solid clay because of the weight it had to support. The upper parts are all hollow. Arms, head and hands were formed separately and then attached to the figures. There appears to have been one standard mould for the body, whilst the head, hairstyle and any other details had to be fashioned individually and then fitted to each body.

Apart from the main excavation site there are two further sites which have not yet been excavated. However sample excavations have been carried out and archaeologists now know what the sites contain. The second site contains a cavalry consisting of more than 1,400 warriors and horses. In addition to the archers, spearmen, and armoured cavalrymen, 64 war chariots lie buried here. Two commanders were also found here. The third grave most

Statue from the grave site of Emperor Qin Shi Huang Di near Xi'an.

probably contains the command post of the commander in chief. Here, too, excavations are not yet complete, but so far it is mainly officers who have been found – their height of over 1.90 m (6' 2") distinguishing them from the ordinary foot soldiers. Although there have been speculations about the commander in chief, his figure has so far not been found. Indeed it is even thought that this officer's corpse might be buried here. Possibly he was one of the emperor's ministers, perhaps even his defence minister. This is just one of the many puzzles that the archaeologists still have to solve.

The soldiers of the Emperor Qin Shi Huang Di have already made a trip around the world. In Europe they have been on display in Zurich, Berlin and Cologne, for example. The emperor himself remains majestically reticent. Although archaeologists know that his mausoleum is situated in a grave mound at the foot of the Li Mountain, roughly a mile to the west of the terracotta army, they have not yet penetrated inside it.

Originally, the hill was to be planted with fir trees and cypresses, but today there are orchards here, which together with the cultivated fields surrounding the hill, form the livelihood of the farmers here. The foreigner who visits the site usually finds that there is something both fascinating and awe-inspiring about climbing this hill. The farmers, however, go about their daily lives, obviously little impressed by the history in their midst. Perhaps they are more worried about their orchard which will no doubt end up in the hands of the archaeologists in the not too distant future.

We know something about the contents of the grave from the records of the historian, Sima Qian (145 until 90 B. C.). He writes: "On the first emperor becoming king of Qin (in 246 B. C.) work was begun on the grave at Li Mountain. After the empire had been united under him (221 B. C.), more than 700,000 people were conscripted to work there from all parts of the country. They dug through the courses of three streams and cast the molten copper for the outer coffin. They also fitted out the tomb with models of palaces, pavilions and public buildings as well as exquisite objects used in everyday life, precious stones and various rare objects. The workers were ordered to set up the crossbows in such a manner that anyone attempting to break in would be shot. Furthermore, the country's main rivers, the Yangzi and the Yellow River, were reproduced in quicksilver and were even made to flow by some mechanical means. The heavenly constellations were portrayed above and the earth was depicted below."

What makes the archaeologists' work so difficult is the fact that the grave was first discovered just a few years after the emperor's death. This means that they have only ruins to work on today and everything must be laboriously classified and restored. The grave's first "discoverers" did not come here to carry out research work; their intentions were much less noble. They came to seek retribution for the wrongs they had suffered under the tyrannical reign of Qin Shi Huang Di. Having plundered and destroyed the site, they set it on fire.

In southern Europe, Hellenism was at its height, the Celts dominated central and northern Europe and the Carthaginians were losing Sicily to the Romans in the first Punic War ... And in distant China, the thirteen year old Lord Zheng was crowned king of Qin, in the province of the same name (roughly corresponding to today's Shaanxi Province in the North-West of China). The year was 246 B. C. Lord Zheng was helped by a rich businessman, who secured him the succession to the throne through his money and connections.

He had to contend with intrigues against him at an early age. His own mother was even involved in one of them. In fact he escaped several assassination attempts, mainly due to luck and chance. Between 230 and 221 B. C. he annexed the remaining six large kingdoms and divided the country into thirty-six provinces each headed by a governor. He thus united his empire and founded a new dynasty, the Qin Dynasty. He gave himself the name, "First Sovereign Emperor of Qin" – Qin Shi Huang Di. It was his wish that all his successors should be named after him, i. e., "Second Sovereign Emperor of Qin" – Qin Er Huang Di, and so on.

In the first seven years of his reign soldiers were sent on numerous military expeditions and campaigns taking them as far as Canton in the south, Fujian on the south-east coast and even to Vietnam and Mongolia. In effect, therefore, he controlled an area which corresponds to the territory of modern China excluding the larger regions of Tibet, Xinjiang, Qinghai and the north-eastern province of Heilongjiang.

He rightly recognised the aristocracy as representing the greatest threat to the unity of his empire, aware that they feared for their privileges should they be made subordinate to the state. The emperor therefore issued an edict abolishing serfdom and introduced a system under which land was owned by the farmers themselves. The farmers were subject to taxes, were forced to do unpaid building work and could be conscripted for military service.

In order to nip resistance in the bud, the emperor ordered that 120,000 aristrocratic families be resettled in the capital, Xianyang. This meant that they were moved away from the influences of home and were under the direct control of the court. The empire was divided into administrative districts which were governed by officials appointed by the central government. (Each administrative district was sub-divided into smaller units.) This system of administration has survived almost unchanged up until the present day.

Further reforms were carried out to strengthen both the unity of the empire and the central system of administration. A single, nationwide system of law was established, weights and measures were standardized and unified coinage was introduced. The coins were round with square holes, so that they could be threaded onto a string and remained in this form until the last century. He also insisted that all carriages be built with a uniform wheel gauge. The emperor had roads built to reach far-flung provinces. According to history books, a road was built to Yunnan (not then part of the empire) consisting of wooden balconies, to make the steep, rocky slopes passable. Such roads had posts at various points which were manned by soldiers. The farmers who lived along these roads were responsible for keeping the road in good repair and were expected to provide board and lodging for travelling officials.

The only external threat to the empire was posed by the Xionghu (possibly ancestors of the Huns) who would come down from the Mongolian steppe and invade the northern border regions.

The Great Wall was built by slave labour, with hundreds of thousands of farmers and convicts being press-ganged into working for the emperor.

This enormous construction stretches from present-day Gansu Province in the south to Inner Mongolia in the north. It extends eastwards, skirting the north of Beijing, ending in what is now Liaoning Province. Thousands upon thousands of people died during the construction of this wall.

We can read of the misery of the workers and their feelings of resentment towards the emperor in a legend written during the Tang period (618–907). Meng Jiangnu, the beautiful wife of a scholar who was forced to work on the Great Wall makes the arduous journey there in search of her husband. When she arrives, she is told that he is dead. Her sorrow and tears so move the gods that they make part of the wall crack, thus releasing his corpse. The woman insists that the emperor (who was on a tour of inspection of the wall at the time) give her husband a state funeral. However, she must promise to become his concubine and follow him to the palace as he has taken a liking to her. Following the funeral service on the coast of the eastern ocean, she throws herself from the cliffs into the ocean, to be united with him in death.

There are still several memorials in Shanhaiguan at the eastern end of the wall to remind us of this legend.

The emperor was influenced by Taoism and surrounded himself with counsellors who belonged to the philosphical school of Legalism which is also anti-Confucian. The scholars, who were nearly all Confucianists, greatly resented his abolishment of the feudal system. In addition, he ordered the scholars in the capital to bring him the elixir of immortality. Since the scholars could not find the elixir and also continued to undermine his divine authority as emperor, he had all Confucian writings destroyed. All privately owned books with the exception of those in the imperial library were duly collected and burnt. To make his intentions quite clear he had 460 Confucian scholars living in Xianyang buried alive (as a further deterrent!). But it was not only the scholars who suffered under this emperor. He also introduced a series of restrictive measures and regulations which applied to businessmen. Perhaps he was afraid they would form a lobby against him which would pose a further threat to his power.

He freed the farmers from feudal serfdom, but they did not benefit as a result. On the contrary, the emperor's measures brought widespread misery and poverty to the rural areas: high taxes and forced labour on huge construction sites. In 210 B.C., a year after his death, the farmers joined forces and formed a rebel army which toppled the emperor's son from the throne. The latter – Qin Er Huang Di – had acted according to his father's wishes and adopted the dynastic title. Then in 206 B.C., the rebel leader Xiangyu and his 400,000 soldiers reached the capital city of Xianyang. An awful massacre followed. They beheaded every single member of the emperor's family and set palaces and other buildings on fire. Qin Shi Huang Di's grave was robbed and then destroyed. And the imperial library which was stocked with the entire works of every writer of that period, was burnt to the ground. Thus the fifteen year reign of the Qin Dynasty ended in a terrible massacre. Nevertheless, the empire he unified and the administration system he founded have remained intact up until the present; his reforms have proved enduring, too.

In 1973, i. e., before his discovery by the archaeologists, mention of Qin Shi Huang Di had already been made in articles written by counter-revolutionaries. In the anti-Confucius campaign of 1973, he was praised as a progressive emperor. This campaign was in all prabobility directed against those advocates of a pragmatic line in politics – followers of Zhou Enlai. Accordingly, the burning of the emperor's books, the persecution of the scholars and other tyrannical measures had been necessary in order to strengthen the new system, to unify thought, and to prevent the restoration of the old feudal order. These articles proceed to explain in a fairly blunt manner that such actions form part of the duties of the dictatorship of the proletariat.

And so, during the cultural revolution history repeated itself: books were burnt, there was widespread persecution, intellectuals were murdered and a uniform system of thought was achieved by means of the Little Red Book (The Thoughts of Chairman Mao). It has been repeatedly pointed out that Chairman Mao always thought highly of the Qin emperor. He is said to have first expressed his admiration for the emperor during the eighth Party Congress in 1958. "What significance can the first emperor of Qin have anyway? He was satisfied with having 460 Confucian scholars buried alive; we have buried 460,000!" This was not the only measure of the first Qin emperor that was followed during the Cultural Revolution. Farmers were press-ganged into doing construction work and intellectuals and students were sent to the country to work.

The farmers who live at the foot of Li Mountain have survived both reigns of terror. They are not interested in hearing anything else about the Cultural Revolution. Very probably, they were never told about the tyranny of the emperor buried beneath their land. Today, their gain is two-fold. Not only does the old tyrant at whose hands their ancestors suffered misery and poverty attract tourists and foreign exchange. The present government also allows them to make a personal profit.

Before you reach the grave mound you will pass through whole hordes of hawkers. The women from the surrounding villages sell their handicrafts – dresses with imaginative embroidery in glowing colours. Bargaining about the price is expected here. It is something the women have experience in and they drive a hard bargain. With this secondary source of income they can easily double or treble their revenue from farming. They need fear neither the tax collector of the Qin emperor nor the ideologists and red guards of the Cultural Revolution.

China's History

You are on your first visit to China and your guide is talking about the Tang, the Ming, or the Qing Dynasty. It is at this point that most people realise just how little they know of Asian or Chinese history. Our western-oriented history lessons may have taught us something about the Greeks, the Romans, even the Egyptians, but the Chinese civilization was probably hardly ever mentioned. And yet the Chinese played at least as important a role in the development of Asia as the Greeks did in the development of Europe.

A trip to China is therefore also a voyage of discovery into history. After all, the Chinese civilization was at times far more advanced than our western culture. Two thousand years ago, the Chinese had already established trading and cultural links with countries in the Near East and Europe. For a short time their empire covered the largest territorial area known to history.

The strong influence that Chinese culture had on Asia can still be seen today. For centuries, however, the Chinese preferred to isolate themselves completely from all the "barbarian" nations. It was this behaviour that really provoked the curiosity of the rest of the world.

Chinese historians present their country's history, up to the foundation of the first republic in 1911, as a long succession of dynasties. This is where the difficulties begin for us. For most of us in the western world, on the other hand, history is a series of events with dates attached to them.

And then there are mnemonics to help us remember just what happened when. "In 1675, hardly a soul was left alive" – a memory aid to help pupils remember the date of the Great Plague. Chinese tour guides often have difficulty remembering historical dates, but they will certainly know which dynasty succeeded which. They remember which dynasty an event happened in rather than the year itself. In older history books, events are rarely associated with years, at least not in the western sense. What you will see written is: "In the tenth year of Qianlong's reign ...".

Generally speaking, the emperors of the Ming and Qing Dynasties, i.e. from the 14th century onwards were referred to by their particular dynasty, an imperial title and their own name. Thus emperor Qianlong (mentioned earlier) who reigned from 1736 to 1795 as the seventh emperor of the Qing Dynasty had the imperial title of Gaozong, but his own name was Aisin Gioro Hong Li.

In the following account, we have concentrated on the most significant periods of China's four thousand year history. However, it is important to bear in mind that the Chinese civilization also had its ups and downs, and that periods of prosperity were often followed by wars or disasters.

Myths

Myths and legends occupy a special place in China's history; they account for the periods of history for which history provides no explanation.

The creator of the world according to the Chinese is called **Pangu.** Before the world came into being, all that existed were an egg-shaped primal mass and **the cosmic principle of Yin and Yang.** Yin and Yang are two poles which interact and complement each other. They are the origin as well as the essence of all things. Pangu was created from Yin and Yang. Every day he underwent nine changes as a result of which the clear and pure elements condensed to form the heaven, the stars and the sun, whilst the earth was created from the dark and dirty elements. These changes are supposed to have taken place over a period of 18,000 years. During this time, both heaven and earth and Pangu himself grew larger. Finally, a thousand years later, Pangu died. His body then disintegrated into wind and clouds, mountains and rivers, fields and forests. The parasites in his body became the human race.

Today, Pangu is just as popular as the other figures who took part in the creation of the world, or in the taming of nature. **Nüwa,** for example, is a truly legendary figure who courageously intervened when the arch of heaven broke apart. She cut off the legs of the **giant turtle** and used them as columns to support the arch. **Houyi** is another popular mythical figure, who is said to have freed humanity of ten burn-ing suns which were causing drought and famine. Being an excellent archer he shot the suns down using magic arrows.

Another heroic figure who must be mentioned is **Yu the Great.** He tamed water according to the following legend. Once upon a time, the heaven in the West fell down. The earth sank and large floods covered the land. Then Yu the Great arrived and averted the disaster. He forced the water to retreat to oceans and rivers. It is said that in return for his services, his son Qi was made first emperor of the first Chinese dynasty, the Xia.

Peking Man

In 1927, a Swedish scientist made a discovery which constituted the first proof of man's early existence in China. In **Zhoukoudian,** about 50 km (30 miles) from Beijing, he found fossil human teeth which were 500,000 years old. The discovery of Peking man (Sinanthropus pekinensis), named after the place where he was found, caused a great sensation. At the time, there had only been two previous finds of this nature – the Java man and the Homo erectus heidelbergensis.

Further discoveries have been made at this site, more recently, including skulls and tools. These finds have given us a better insight into Peking man's existence.

He knew how to handle fire and used it as a means of providing warmth as well as for cooking the game he had hunted. The tools he used were made out of either stone or animal bones.

The Yangshao and Longshan Civilizations

The cradle of Chinese civilization lies in northern China, in the fertile valleys of the Huanghe (the Yellow River) and its tributaries. This is where the first settlements grew up, a development which has parallels in Europe and the Near East. Here, too, the first communities and states were established close to rivers: in the area between the Euphrates and Tigris and along the banks of the river Nile.

The two **neolithic civilizations in northern China** were (like Peking man) named after the places where they were discovered. One of them is referred to as **Yangshao,** after a village in Henan province and the other is called **Longshan** which is an area in today's Shandong province.

The most important site of the Yangshao civilization is **Banpo,** formerly a small village and now the eastern suburb of Xi'an. A large number of discoveries were made in an area covering 50,000 sq. km (19,305 sq. miles). These finds have provided scientists with precise information about working and living conditions at this time. Banpo stood on a river bank and was home to a number of family groups. These early settlers dug a deep trench on the other side of the village, as protection against fire and wild animals. Some six or seven thousand years ago, the villagers built rectangular community halls and round living quarters out of mud and a wooden framework. Some houses were literally souterrain, with only the roof being above the ground.

The people of the **Yangshao civilization** were gatherers and hunters, but they had also mastered the art of cultivation. They used stones and bones to make tools and weapons. These implements included fishing hooks, needles and knives of bone and axes hewn out of stone. They knew how to spin, to weave and make pottery. Communal storehouses were built for provisions, but large clay vessels were also used for storage by individual families.

Such clay vessels were decorated with pictures of fish or birds, the designs generally being conventional ones. An alternative form of decoration was the imprint left by wickerwork or woven cloth. A reddish brown or black was usually used for this. Some of the drawings found on clay vessels are regarded as being Chinese characters in their earliest form.

A special piece of land was set aside for the burial of the dead. For children a separate burial site was used, their remains being kept in clay urns.

The nature of the burial rites, but other factors, too, would indicate that this was a matriarchal society. The Yangshao civilization extended along the river Wei from South Gansu, and encompassed the area from Shaanxi to Shanxi and northwestern Henan.

The **Longshan civilization** dates back to the same period as the Yangshao. It had its centre in Shandong but also extended westwards into Henan province. It was here that the two civilizations, which were so similar, met. And it is in Henan province that archaeologists have discovered evidence of both civilizations. It has been proved that the Longshans used potter's wheels, whereas the Yangshaos did not. Above all, fine, black pottery was produced. The two civilizations had practically identical tools. Both built walls of mud in order to protect their villages.

Xia Dynasty
(c. 2100–1600 B. C.)

Traditionally, the Xia Dynasty is referred to as the first Chinese imperial dynasty, making it also the first political system. However, this has not, as yet been adequately substantiated. Early historical documents do contain information about this period but it should be relegated to the realm of myths. Sometimes, Yu the Great is mentioned as the first emperor of the Xia Dynasty – the heroic figure who tamed the destructive powers of water. Other sources name his son Qi as the first emperor.

According to the legends, there are other heroes who were called either "majesty" or emperor. One of them is **Huang Di,** the Yellow Emperor or the Sovereign Emperor. He is said to have vanquished and conquered other tribes with weapons made out of jade. His wife, **Lei Zu,** is credited with the discovery of silkworm cultivation. **Shen Nung,** who taught people about agriculture, and **Yu the Great,** who tamed water, are also referred to as emperors. Yu was the feudal lord of **Xia** and gave this name to the first dynasty. Scholars, who write in the classical style, still use this name as a synonym for China.

Shang Dynasty
(c. 1600–1100 B. C.)

Xia was followed by Shang. According to Chinese legends, the reasons for one dynasty being succeeded by another were always the same: corruption, excesses, and neglecting official duties. Records have been found from the Shang Dynasty – also known as the **Yin Dynasty.** (The name is derived from the capital city.) This first written evidence was found inscribed on bronzes, animal bones, or tortoise shells. These discoveries were made in the district of Anyang in Henan Province and in the vicinity of the city Zhengzhou, these being two major centres of the Shang Dynasty.

The beginning of the Shang Dynasty coincides with the beginning of the **Bronze Age** in China. The reign of the Shang emperors (there were supposed to be as many as 30 of them) was based on the awarding of fiefs. They took prisoners from neighbouring tribes as their slaves. The art of cultivation was as highly developed as writing. The records contain prophecies regarding harvests and rain, and they even mention silk. There is evidence to suggest that the emperor and his lords wore clothes of silk. As in the earlier Yangshao civilization, the domestic animals included horses, pigs and dogs, but occasionally they also kept sheep and cattle. It also seems more than likely that elephants once lived in the area of the Huanghe and were used as war animals. The bronzes from the Shang period feature among the most important dis-

Bronze, sacrificial wine vessels of the "jia" (left) and "ding" (right) types from the early Shang Dynasty.

coveries made by Chinese archaeologists. Finds include wine goblets, arrow-heads, spoons, the first tripod vessels and other containers. The Shang bronzes can be seen in many Chinese museums.

The Shang Dynasty ruled over a territory that stretched from Shaanxi in the west to Shandong in the east; from Hebei in the North to the Yangzi River (also called Changjiang) in the South.

The Shang Dynasty ended because their brutal reign, their excesses, and their incompetence incurred the wrath of the lords. The lord of Zhou gathered an army and defeated the last ruler of the Shang Dynasty.

Zhou Dynasty
(c. 1100–221 B. C.)

Zhou was a vassal state under the Shang Dynasty and lay in the valley of the Wei River, to the west of the Shang capital cities. The first ruler of the Zhou Dynasty was called **Qi**. He was known as the "Divine Farmer" because he is supposed to have cultivated a new kind of millet and raised cultivation in general to a new level.

King Wen led the insurrection against Shang and conquered several states. His son, **King Wu,** succeeded in putting an end to the insurrection against the Shang and established the Zhou Dynasty. He founded his capital in **Haojing,** close to the present day city of Xi'an.

Chinese historians also call the period from **1100 until 771 B. C. Western Zhou,** because the capital at that time lay in the western part of the Zhou kingdom. The territory of the Zhou kingdom extended along the lower course of the Huanghe River. In order to administer this empire, fiefs were given to the aristocracy. A fief generally consisted of a walled city plus the surrounding agricultural land. Conquered vassal states had to pay tribute to the ruler of Zhou.

The Western Zhou strengthened the system of patriarchal hierarchy. The oldest son inherited the title and property from his father. The allotment of fiefs by the emperor strengthened the position of the landed gentry. Their power was based on the ownership of both land and people. The people were serfs, but they owned their tools and had private plots, which they cultivated for their own subsistence.

In the **8th century,** the emperor's authority began to wane and the power of the lords and princes grew as they took advantage of the weak court. **King Ping** felt threatened by the alien nations from the North and therefore moved his capital to **Luoyi,** today's Luoyang. That is why the **period from 771 to 221 B. C.** is also called the **Eastern Zhou.**

They discovered and worked iron in the **6th century B. C.** The use of iron tools meant that methods of cultivation could be improved and greater success in war was guaranteed by the employment of weapons made of iron. Cities developed and soon it was nothing unusual to have cities of 10,000 households. The landed gentry became an independent group and refused to give the emperor their allegiance. There had been a ruling which stipulated that land could not be sold to the aristocracy. When this was changed and land could be bought it resulted in the growth of a new class of landowners who leased land to the farmers in return for rent. Thus the emperor was left with only his title. He no longer had the followers to support his authority and at the same time the system of administration broke down.

The gap left by the aristocrats was filled by learned people and scholars – a group in society which grew up out of the former military class. This was the beginning of a centralized, bureaucratic system of administration by scholars. Protected by the lords, this class of scholars enjoyed both material advantages and a high social prestige. Many worked as counsellors at court; others founded schools, as did for example, **Confucius.** The school he founded was in the state of Lu, which lies in today's Shandong Province.

According to a chronicle on the State of Lu, the first period of Eastern Zhou was also called the **Spring and Autumn Period (771–476 B. C.).** The succeeding period is named after a historical chronicle: **Era of the Warring Kingdoms (476–221 B. C.).**

A struggle for power took place within the Eastern Zhou, as various leaders waged war against each other in an attempt to fill the vacuum of power left by a weak emperor. The growth of new social classes, such as farmers, craftsmen and businessmen, brought a boost to trade and cultural exchange. It became clear that the benefit to both would be even greater if the empire were united. The scholars gave their support by providing philosophical teachings and systems. It was during this period that Confucianism and Taoism developed. They were to influence people's thoughts for thousands of years to come.

Qin Dynasty
(221–206 B. C.)

The kingdom of Qin was established in the valley of the Wei River, and it competed for the hegemony of China in wars with six other states – Han, Zhao, Wei, Chu, Yan, and Qi.

In **246 B.C.,** at the age of thirteen, **Lord Zheng** became the **King of Qin,** and by age 25 had conquered and subjugated all the other states. His superiority was based on a highly developed art of warfare, which combined the superbly equipped infantry troops with the mobility of cavalry. The kingdom of Qin extended as far as Gansu in the west, where there were constant confrontations with the nomad tribes from the steppes. It was from them that the king of Qin adopted techniques of warfare on horse back.

In **221 B.C.** he founded the first centralized, autocratic, Chinese feudal state. To the west it extended as far as Gansu, to the east it reached Korea, to the southwest Vietnam, and to the south Fujian. He gave his

Qin Shi Huang Di, the first emperor of China.

dynasty the name **Qin,** and he called himself **Qin Shi Huang Di,** which means the "First Sovereign Emperor of Qin". He wanted his dynasty to last a thousand years and it was his wish that every emperor who succeeded him should also be called Qin. Later his son called himself **Qin Er Huang Di,** Second Sovereign Emperor of Qin.

During his short reign, Qin Shi Huang Di introduced a series of reforms to strengthen imperial power and to maintain the unity of the empire. These reforms survived for centuries and also formed the basis of the reigns of later dynasties.

First of all, he destroyed the power of the landed gentry, whom he held responsible for separatist trends. The aristocratic families were forced to resettle in his capital **Xianyang,** near today's Xi'an, where they would be under the court's direct control. Others were exiled to border regions or press-ganged into working on the Great Wall.

He created a new administrative system. The country was divided into 36 administrative districts, each with a governor and an inspector from the imperial central government.

He standardized measurements and weights, even the gauges of carriages, created a calendar, and unified the various forms of writing. All these reforms, especially the introduction of a unified monetary system, encouraged trade and undermined the power of the old landed gentry.

As the founder of the Chinese empire, Qin Shi Huang Di is worthy of praise and yet, in history books, he is described as a tyrant. His immense plans could only be realized by means of a reign of terror and the brutal exploitation of people.

In order to protect the empire from the warlike, nomadic tribes in the North, he used the remaining walls from former kingdoms and decreed that they be joined together to form the **Great Wall.** Nearly 300,000 people are supposed to have been engaged in its construction. Most of them were either exiles

or were press-ganged into working here. A further 700,000 construction workers, craftsmen and artists worked for decades on palaces and on his mausoleum. Moreover, hundreds of thousands of people were forced to build huge roads from the centre of the country to the remote border regions. The land was given over to the ordinary people but the farmers who owned it were often forced to sell because of the high taxes. Such measures brought extreme poverty leading to the growth of strong opposition among the people. This was to manifest itself in violence and brutality.

Qin Shi Huang Di has also made Confucian scholars his enemies. His counsellors belonged to the Legalist school. In contrast to Confucius, they believed that human beings were basically evil. They based their theory of statehood on this concept: a strong, central power of government supported by military power and a rigid system of punishment.

In **213 B.C.,** Qin Shi Huang Di ordered the **mass burning of books,** the first of its kind in history. All Confucian writings were burnt. Because he feared the Confucianists due to their different view of the state and their support of the old landed gentry, he ordered 460 of them to be buried alive as a deterrent. In fact, this action merely united the various social classes within in the empire against him. Opposition centred around the aristocratic family of Han. In **211 B.C.,** Qin Shi Huang Di died during an inspection trip. He placed the power into the hands of his son. The second Emperor of Qin was a weak emperor and his reign was short. In **206 B. C.** he was defeated and hanged by rebels who were led by **Liu Bang.** The rebels caused a terrible massacre in the capital city. Palaces, libraries, and the mausoleum of the First Emperor were set on fire and his entire family was murdered. The empire that was to last a thousand years came to an end exactly 5 years after Qin Shi Huang Di's death.

Han Dynasty (206 B. C.–220 A. D.)

Liu Bang, a former minor official who was made a lord by the Han nobles, defeated the mighty Qin and nominated himself **Emperor Gao Di** of the Han Dynasty. His capital city, contemporary Xían, bore the name **Changan** (Eternal Peace).

Although the Han essentially retained and formed the basis of their power on the reforms introduced by the Qin, they still had to ameliorate the situation of the peasants. Their decrees were directed primarily at the merchants, who were manipulating the prices on the market through speculation and thereby creating a shortage in supplies.

These in turn reacted by forming an alliance against the central authority with separatist forces. Hence the first half of the **2nd century B. C.** was plagued by constant power struggles and conflicts that went on until Emperor Jing Di was able to put an end to them. Under the reign of his successor **Wu Di**

(140–87 B. C.), the Han Dynasty reached the height of its power. During his reign, Confucianism became the official doctrine of the state and all other schools of thought were prohibited. The imperial examinations for scholars were first instituted in **124 B. C.**

A rapid improvement in the economy and trade occurred during the first decades of the reign of the Han Dynasty. The growth in the production of iron was especially beneficial to the situation of the artisans. The merchants were able to take advantage of the system of roads and canals that had already been built under Emperor Qin Shi Huang Di. The flourishing trade also helped to further integrate each one of the regions. Emperor Wu Di had established new prefectures in Fujian and Guangdong and his successors extended the empire northwestward.

This region, today's Xinjiang, was under the control of the **Xiongnu** (Huns), a warlike people who posed a permanent threat to the northern borders of the empire. Wu Di had paved the way for the development of this region. In **138 B. C.** he had sent **Zhang Qian** out on an expedition to the west. In an alliance with other nations, the Xiongnu were defeated and the western trade route along the Silk Road was opened. During the reign of the Han Dynasty, silk was already taken to India, Persia, and all the way to the larger trading centres of the Roman Empire, which was known to the Chinese as **Da Qin** (Great Qin Empire).

Under the reign of Wu Di's successors, the empire steadily disintegrated. The increasing involvement of the consort families in the instigation of intrigues, the concentration of landed property, and the burdens of high taxation for the peasants finally augmented social conflicts to the point that peasant uprisings ensued.

In **30 B. C.,** when natural disasters made the situation much more drastic, **Emperor Wang Mang** was forced to introduce clear-cut reforms. From then on, all lands were to belong solely to the emperor and private ownership as well as the sale of land was prohibited. Imperial officials were to control prices and protect the peasants from excessive taxation. The salt and iron production was nationalized and a currency reform carried through. However, his intercession came too late. Under the leadership of a gang calling itself "Red Eyebrows", peasant armies conquered the capital, deposed Wang Mang, and thus put an end to the **Era of the Western Han Dynasty. Liu Xiu,** a landed aristocrat from the house of Han, managed to put down the peasant revolt and re-establish the Han Dynasty.

As **Emperor Guang Wu Di,** he had the capital moved further east to Luoyang. For this reason historians name the period **Eastern Han Dynasty.**

He redistributed the land among the peasants and set those free, who had desperately sold themselves in order to survive. The ruined irrigation systems were set in order and agriculture began to recover. With **Cai Lun's invention of paper in 105 A. D.** and the **introduction of porcelain manufactories,** new skilled trades began to develop. Guangzhou (Canton) and Xuwen in Guangdong Province developed as seaports and trading centres. The Xiongnu, who had posed a permanent threat to the western trade routes, were finally subdued and new expeditions sent on their way to the west. Imperial official **Ben Chao** managed to establish tributary relationships between various western and northern ethnic peoples and the imperial court. Another emissary, **Gan Ying,** was able to advance all the way to the Persian Gulf and establish contact with the Roman Empire.

The successful expansion towards the west was only accomplished at the cost of internal security. Tribes under tribute to Emperor Guang Wu Di in the region of Gansu rebelled against the domination of the Chinese. They blocked the Silk Road and forced the Han into a **war that lasted forty years.**

As usual, the burdens of war were placed on the shoulders of the peasants. Now, however, even the young scholars and students began to show opposition to court nepotism and the dominant position of the eunuchs. A **national uprising** occurred in **184 A. D.** under the leadership of the **Yellow Turbans,** a secret society from Sichuan.

The Disunited Empire (220–589)

The rebellion of the Yellow Turbans terminated the Han rule. The emperor managed to stay on for a few decades, but then had to abdicate in **220 A.D.** The whole country was in disarray and the population decimated. Peasants who had lost their lands roamed the country in bands and feuding families fought each other for control of the empire. Each one of the war lords who managed to survive this struggle established his own empire. The period between **220 and 265** is therefore referred to as the **Era of Three Empires** in Chinese history. **Cao Cao** founded the **Kingdom of Wei** in the Huanghe (Yellow River) Valley and founded his capital in **Luoyang. Liu Bei** reigned over the **Kingdom of Shu** from **Chengdu,** which corresponds approximately to the area of today's Sichuan. From **Nanjing, Sun Quan** ruled over the **Kingdom of Wu,** which included the regions at the estuary of the Yangzi.

The demand for a reunited empire was emblazoned on the banners of the noble family of **Sima.** After first having subdued Shu and Wei, they proclaimed a new dynasty, that of the **Jin (265–316).** In **280,** they were also able to conquer the Kingdom of Wu and it appeared as if the **unity of the empire** had been established once again. However, the reign of the Jin was based on a weak foundation. Continuous encroachments by the northern ethnic minorities and internal rivalries undermined the authority of the Jin rulers. Several tribes conquered the northern regions during the **4th century** and established their own states there. The **Xiongnu** conquered **Luoyang** in **311** and the old capital of **Chang'an** in **316.** Together with many of the feudal land-lords, nobles, and state officials, the Jin rulers fled southward to establish their capital at **Nanjing.** As the **Eastern Jin Dynasty,** they ruled over southern China until the year **420.**

The period between **304** and **439** is known as the **Era of the Sixteen Kingdoms.** Numerous conflicts and wars occurred among the nomadic people who had annexed northern China. A total of sixteen kingdoms were established, all of which did not last very long. Among others, the Tibetans gained control over almost the entire north for the first time. The western trade routes were reopened during the time in which a nomadic people ruled in northern China and **Buddhism** slowly began to penetrate into the area, coming from India by way of Turkestan. The great Buddhist worshipping centres at the grottoes of Dunhuang, Longmen (close to Luoyang), and Yungang (near Datong) were established during the **4th and 5th century.** Although Confucianism was displaced, many of the northern rulers gathered Chinese officials around them and some even adopted Chinese names, dress, and customs.

The **Toba** were able to conquer the disunited north in **386** and founded the **Northern Wei**

Dynasty. As nomad warriors, they could depend primarily on their highly mobile and effective cavalry. Their capital was called **Pingcheng;** today's Datong. The Wei emperors themselves fostered the adoption of Chinese ways. They surrounded themselves with Chinese officials, took on Chinese names, forced their women to marry Chinese nobles, and even made the use of their own language subject to punishment.

Between **386 and 589,** a total of **nine dynasties** ruled over China at the same time. Four were part of the southern dynasties and five were established in northern China.

The Sui Dynasty (581–618)
Yang Jiang, the Han Chinese who had served the Toba as chancellor of the Northern Zhou Dynasty, was able to assume power in **581** and bring the southern dynasties back into the empire. He reigned in Chang'an under the title of **Emperor Wen Di.** He relieved the plight of the peasants by reducing forced labour and lowering the taxes. As a result of this, the situation in agriculture began to improve and, for the first time in centuries, the population started to grow again. In order to stimulate trade, he had to implement the reforms that had been introduced 800 years earlier by Qin Shi Huang Di, namely the establishment of a standard monetary system and a uniform system of measure and weight. His successor **Yang Di** anounced a great restoration programme. Two million labourers had to rebuild the devastated city of Luoyang. Since the fear of the

northern "barbarians" was still very acute, another million were sent to repair and enlarge the Great Wall. Furthermore, the emperor ordered the construction of the Grand Canal, which was to connect Hangzhou in the south with the city of Beijing (then called Zhoujun).

He sent military expeditions to the west, where Turkic peoples were threatening the border, and to Korea, where the rulers were refusing to pay tribute. Soon the first peasants began to rebell because of the new burdens placed on them. Yang Di reacted by confiscating all arms and prohibiting their possession. Nevertheless, the revolt could no longer be stopped. The Sui Dynasty lasted for only 27 years. Their historical importance, however, was equal to that of the Qin Dynasty. After nearly 400 years of turmoil and disaccord, the Sui did manage to reunite the empire and **centralize authority.** Thus they paved the way for the **Tang Dynasty,** under which Chinese culture was to experience an unprecedented upswing.

Tang Dynasty (618–907)
Li Yuan, a provincial governor under the last Sui emperor, placed himself at the head of the rebellion and then ascended the throne. As **Emperor Gao Zu,** he founded the Tang Dynasty in **618.** Yet it was his son, **Li Shimin,** who unified the empire in military campaigns. He succeeded his father as **Tai Zong** (627–649) and became one of the most powerful of the Tang emperors. During his reign, economic sta-

bility brought peace to the country. The redistribution of lands among the peasants, as well as improvements in the system of irrigation, resulted in the increase of agricultural productivity. The state established many manufactures e. g. for the production of brocaded silk, rugs, dyes and the working of metal. Courier services and stage-coaches promoted trade and the Grand Canal was completed. Large cities developed into trading, religious, and artistic centres. **Chang'an** became the **largest city of the world** with over 1.5 million inhabitants. Merchants from Europe, the Near East, and central Asia met in this city located at the beginning of the Silk Road. Foreign religions such as Nestorianism, Islam, Judaism, and Manichaeism found their way into China and established communities there.

The Tang emperors subjugated Turkestan (contemporary Xinjiang) once again and garrisoned the trading centres and caravanseries along the Silk Road such as Kuqu, Hotan, and Kashi (former Kashgar) located at the foot of the Pamirs. The **trade in silk** thus **flourished** as never before; sometimes there were four to five thousand merchants living in Chang'an.

At the same time, however, the first powerful policy began to develop on the **Tibet/Qinghai Plateau** under the **Tibetan King Strongstan Gampo,** who also sought to extend his kingdom eastward. The Tang Dynasty countered this new challenge with a clever diplomatic ruse that had already been applied successfully by the Han Dynasty to pacify the northern tribes. They offered to give the Tibetan king one of the princesses for a wife. **Princess Weng Cheng** soon departed for Lhasa with a large entourage and many presents. There are people in China today who continue to put forward this marriage as proof of Tibet's belonging to China.

Chinese culture spread northeastward all the way to Korea and Japan. Countless Japanese monks came to study in Chang'an. Once they were back in Japan, they also made sure that the city of Kyoto was patterned exactly after Chang'an.

First traces of deterioration already began to appear under the successor of Tai Zong. Once again, the intrigues of the concubines ultimately undermined the authority of the imperial family. Following the death of **Emperor Gao Zong,** the concubine **Wu Zhao** managed to override his family and seize the title of empress. Under the name of **Wu Zetian,** the **only empress in the history of China** she reigned for almost two decades over an empire that had been dominated by the strict patriarchal teachings of the great philosopher Confucius for more than a thousand years. Since she could not count on the imperial family or the nobility for support, she made use of Buddhism and the scholarly caste to consolidate her powers. Buddhist monks spread the notion that she was the incarnation of Buddha Maitreya, the ruler of the coming Buddha-world. A 56-foot statue of Buddha was set up in the Longmen Grottoes, which is said to bear Wu Zetian's facial features. The imperial examinations were upgraded to insure that only the most loyal officials would find a place in the state apparatus. Finally, however, she had to comply with the pressure exerted by numerous ministers and relinquish the throne to her son. He, in turn, allowed himself to be dominated by another concubine. Thus it wasn't until **Xuan Zong** came to power in **712** that an emperor reigned with the necessary authority and power. He brought back the flourishing times of **Emperor Tai Zong.**

In the first place, he put an end to the extravagances of court and curtailed the influence of the consort families. His consolidation of state finances and regimentation of the administration system spurred the economy again. But Xuang Zong made a name for himself above all as patron of the arts. Himself an active poet and composer, he called numerous artists, poets, singers, and scholars to his court. His love of the arts finally led him to neglect the affairs of the state. As usual, a concubine, **Yang Guifei,** seems to have played a major part in this turn of events. Her beauty was celebrated in many songs and her name continues to be a synonym for extraordinary looks. The Tang poet Bai Yuji once wrote: "When she turns to show her smile of a hundred charms, all of the beauties of the six palacial courtyards simply fade away". She, however, well knew how to make use of her beauty in order to have totally inefficient and incompetent relatives placed in high positions, as in the case of her nephew **Yang Guozhong,** who advanced to the position of chancellor as her favourite.

This prompted a rival to instigate a rebellion, during the course of which Yang Guifei ended up on the gallows.

An Lushan, a commander from Youzhou, took advantage of the instability at the palace and marched into Chang'an. Emperor Xuan Zong fled to Sichuan. Although he was able to put down the rebellion with the help of the **Uighur,** Xuang Zong ultimately had to abdicate.

An Lushan's rebellion had deeply upset the nation both economically and politically. Commerce and trade in those cities struck by the rebellion stagnated, while the provincial governors and the military leaders took advantage of the political vacuum to expand their own powers. They refused to pay the court taxes, using the money to finance their own armies instead. Some of them even broke away from the imperial court altogether. In the meantime, the palace fell under the control of the eunuchs. They appointed the officials, had control over the military, and had enough power to enthrone eight of the nine successors of Xuan Zong.

The nation was now constantly being ravaged by **peasant revolts.** Buddhism was made the scapegoat for this development. After having provided vital impulses in politics and the arts during the heyday of the Tang Dynasty, it was now being slowly displaced again by Taoism and Confucianism. In **845**, Emperor Wu Zong passed an edict making the Buddhists responsible for the decline of the empire. He accused them of being exploiters, extravagant, lazy, and immoral. His edict unleashed the **worst wave of persecutions against the Buddhists in the history of China.** Temples and monasteries were burned down and the monks enslaved or forced to pay taxes again. Tens of thousands of them fled to Sichuan.

Five Dynasties and Ten States (907–960)

In **907, Zhu Wen** overthrew the Tang Dynasty and founded the **Later Liang Dynasty (907/923).** Four other dynasties followed in rapid succession: the **Later Tang (923–937),** the **Later Qin (937–946),** the **Later Han (947–950),** and the **Later Zhou (951–960).** By adopting the names of former dynasties, the rulers showed that they still sought to re-establish a united empire. But these five dynasties only really had control over the regions along the Huanghe.

In the same period, **10 other states emerged in the south,** all under the control of military governors. Only the last of these dynasties, the Zhou, actually managed to reunite nearly all of northern China and to reconquer a few other regions in Sichuan and along the Yangzi.

In the northwest, where the contemporary provinces of Liaoning and Jilin along the Liao River are situated, the **Mongolian Khitan** had established a powerful empire that would last for more than two hundred years. They conquered the prefectures at Shanxi and northern Hebei and then made **Yanjing** (today's Beijing) their capital. They called their **dynasty the Liao.**

As a result of the wars that had been going on for decades since the fall of the Tang Dynasty, all of northern China was in turmoil. The inhabitants of Chang'an are said to have fled to the mountains and the fields to have been abandoned. Chang'an, like many other cities, was a ruin. Only a few of the palaces and buildings had survived the inferno. Just a few hundred families are said to have remained in this old imperial city.

The rulers of the short-lived dynasties and the regional states tried to maintain internal and external power by keeping large military forces. This could only be financed by the further exploitation of the peasants in the form of higher taxation and increased forced labour.

Since less warfare occurred in the south, southern and central Chinese cities emerged as metropoli during this period. These included Chengdu, Nanjing, Fuzhou, Hangzhou, Guangzhou, and Changsha. Commerce and cultural life concentrated in these cities – all at the cost of neglect in the rural areas.

Song Dynasty (960–1279)

For the first time in Chinese history, a general was elected emperor by his own troops in **960**. **Zhao Kuangyin,** a general of the Later Zhou, managed to wrest the power from this house and thus establish the **Song Dynasty.** From his capital **Kaifeng,** he began to plan the **unification of the empire.** He subdued the ten southern states one after the other and, at the same time, developed a policy of peaceful coexistence on the borders. The Khitan **Liao Dynasty** was still in power in the northeast. To the west of them, along the lower course of the Huanghe, was the Turkic and Tibetan state of **Xixia.** Zhao Kuangyin sought to pacify these neighbours with enormous tributes, usually paid in gold and silver.

With great patience he was able to put an end to the rivalries between the nobility and thus concentrate on the establishment of internal order. The powerful military leaders, whose separatist ambitions had been one of the main causes for the downfall of the Tang Dynasty, were slowly displaced and military affairs turned over to civilians. A **secret council** was established at court and the administration of finances was shifted from the regional rulers to the central government.

In the sector of agriculture, the irrigation systems were renewed and the migrating peasants were aided in the cultivation of new lands. But the decentralization of the lands owned by the nobles, officials, feudal landlords, and merchants was not accomplished. These were usually able to find some way in which to evade the recently instituted land taxes.

Industry, however, made great progress. Gold, silver, copper, iron, and tin mines were in operation and there was widespread use of coal as fuel, e. g. in the process of smelting iron.

Shipbuilding techniques were making rapid advances: the compass was in use for navigation, and gunpowder was invented. The printing of books, already developed during the Tang Dynasty, became more practical with the invention of movable type, nearly 400 years before Gutenberg started printing in Europe.

Paper money was first used to a greater extent during the reign of **Zhen Zhong (998–1022).** Even bills of exchange were being used as currency.

On the other hand, the situation of the peasants was becoming progressively worse. This was due primarily to the higher tributes demanded by the Khitan and western **Xia.** Whole regions were facing famine. Thus, in addition to the external threats, the Song rulers now were confronted with new internal problems. The sixth Song emperor, **Shen Zhong,** finally had to institute the extensive reform programme suggested to him by his first advisor Wang Anshi. It included a renewed survey and distribution of land, low interest state loans for the peasants, laws and administrative measures designed to control prices, and taxation of the landowners.

The primary intention behind this reform programme was the protection of the peasants from excessive exploitation so that internal stability and order could be restored. As a measure to strengthen the military and its defence capacity, the army was reorganized and issued new weapons. Horses were bred for the cavalry on a state operated farm. Thirty-six garrisons were built north of the Yellow River to provide more adequate defence against the Khitan and Xia.

In the long run, however, all these measures proved to be futile. The Chinese were not able to withstand the steady onslaught of the nomadic minority groups from the north.

The Khitan were the first to seriously threaten the Song empire. The Song rulers had to pay dearly for the peace on their borders. Following the **Peace Treaty of 1004,** they were committed to a yearly tribute of 100,000 ounces of silver and 200,000 bales of silk.

The Khitan were displaced by the **Nüzhen** (Jurchen). They came from the valleys of **Heilongjiang,** where they had established the **Kingdom of Jin** in **1115.** Only a few years later, in **1126,** they conquered the capital of the Song empire, **Kaifeng,** after first having subdued the Khitan Liao Dynasty. Thus the nation was once again split into two large empires. The Jin Dynasty of the Nüzhen reigned over the north and the Song rulers withdrew to the south. Therefore, the following period in the history of the Chinese dynasties is called the **Southern Song Dynasty (1127–1279).**

This era was also dominated by constant warfare with the northern Jin Dynasty of the Nüzhen. Whereas the Song regime was willing to comply with the demands of the Nüzhen in order to safeguard the peace on the northern borders, the belligerent patriots began to form themselves under the leadership of General **Yue Fei.** He led campaigns against the Jin Dynasty and was determined to resist them militarily.

He was betrayed by his own followers, who accused him of treason and then had him executed. Today, the people still pay homage to him and continue to visit his grave in Hangzhou. He has become a symbol of Chinese patriotism. Hangzhou, then called **Linan,** was the capital of the Song rulers. During this period, the cities situated near the estuary of the Yangzi and a few of the cities in southern China were developing into important trading centres. New markets flourished along with the maritime trade in the cities on the southern coast.

Porcelain vase of the Yuan Dynasty.

Yuan Dynasty (1271–1368)

A new threat emerged in the north towards the **end of the 12th century,** which was not only to afflict the Chinese, but the entire Asian continent and Europe as well.

A Mongolian Khan was able to gain the support of many Mongolian and Turkic minority groups for the first time and thus establish a Mongolian empire. **Genghis Khan** was their supreme leader and he **initiated what is probably the greatest expansionist movement in the history of mankind.**

The mounted hordes of the **Mongolians,** feared for their mobility and cruelty, conquered all of central Asia, Russia, and a number of eastern European nations between **1218** and **1253.** The Mongolian empire ultimately spread from Manchuria to Poland and Hungary, as well as from Siberia to southern China and the Persian Gulf. They overthrew the northern Chinese Jin Dynasty in **1234.**

For 46 years they posed a threat to the Southern Song Dynasty. In **1276** they finally took the capital, Linan (Hangzhou). Prior to their capture of the city they had encircled the entire country from the west. First of all they thrust forward into Tibet across Qinghai, moving on through Yunnan and Sichuan. They were led by one of Genghis Khan's grandsons – **Kublai Khan.** He later became the **first emperor of the Yuan Dynasty** and called himself **Shi Zu.** Kublai Khan adopted **Beijing** as his imperial capital and it was given the name **Khanbalik** ("City of the Khan"). The Chinese referred to Beijing as **Dadu** ("Large Capital"). With the taking of the province of Guandong **in 1279 the Mongolian conquest of China was complete.**

For the Chinese, the period under Mongolian rule was truly one of extreme social oppression. The social hierarchy was restructured along ethnic lines. The Mongolians made up the ruling and privileged class. All land and property belonging to the state were confiscated and then redistributed among the Mongolian nobles. Next in rank were the other racial groups from central

Asia. After them came the Han Chinese, who had already had contact with the Mongolians for a longer period of time. The southern Chinese found themselves at the bottom of the social hierarchy, probably because they had resisted the Mongolians till then. At first, all Chinese were excluded from high political and military office. At the very best, they were allowed to hold local positions under the supervision of Mongolians. It was generally prohibited for them to either carry or own weapons.

The mounted armies of the Mongolians consumed vast resources, which had to be provided by the Chinese peasants. It is said that in the brief duration of the Mongolian rule 700,000 houses were confiscated as well as innumerable boats and carts. The expropriation of the land and its redistribution among the Mongolian nobles and Lamaist monasteries led to the rapid impoverishment of the peasants, who also had to pay horrendously high taxes.

Although they did promote Tibetan Buddhism (Lamaism), the religious policy of the Mongolians was quite tolerant and liberal. Islam, Nestorianism, and other religions developed freely while Confucianism and Taoism where pushed into the background.

It did not take long for the Mongolians to realize that the knowledge they had acquired, gained largely in military conquests, was of little use to them in the administration of such a huge empire. It is said that a Chinese monk serving the Khan as advisor formulated the following in a memorandum: One may conquer a great empire on a horse, but one cannot rule it from the back of a horse.

Thus the Mongolians soon took advantage of the administrative experience of the Chinese officials and scholars. Within their own ranks, however, first signs of deterioration began to appear after the death of Kublai Khan. In the brief period between **1307 and 1333,** there were **eight Yuan emperors.** Violent conflicts between the court princes and attempted uprisings were soon the rule rather than the exception.

During the reign of Kublai Khan, handicrafts and foreign trade prospered once again. Whereas agriculture soon began to decline, the artisans and craftsmen were kept busy producing the luxury items and other consumer goods required by the Mongolian ruling class. The sections of industry that most flourished were the nationalized and private manufactories in which gold, silver, iron, jade, gems, and porcelain were worked into luxury items. The armaments industry was also operating on a large scale.

Foreign trade thrived in an unprecedented manner. Since the Mongolians had been able to subjugate all of the nations along the Silk Road, trade between Europe and Asia by way of these routes that were more than 1,000 years old could develop unhindered.

The Venetian merchant **Marco Polo** came along this route to Khanbalik in the company of his father and uncle. He was so fascinated and inspired by both the strangeness and the advanced cultural development of this empire, that he remained for seventeen years serving the Khan and undertaking several voyages throughout the land. Back home, his accounts were first taken to be a product of the imagination or plain insanity. He had to dictate all of his travel experiences while serving a sentence in jail.

Mediated by the trade, there was also a cultural exchange between east and west. Silk, porcelain, paper currency, and gunpowder were introduced in the Near East and Europe. The Mongolians, on the other hand, were interested in astronomy and mathematics, both of which had reached a high stage of development in the Arabian regions.

The Chinese rebellion against the foreign Mongolian rule was long and violent. Social distress, oppression, and discrimination all added impetus to the rebellion. The rapid rate of impoverishment among the peasants led to the formation of bands of robbers all over the land, who often gained control of entire regions. One of the best Chinese adventure novels, "The Bandits of Liangshan Moor", describes this period. Rebellious members of the class of feudal landlords and scholars joined together in secret associations. The focal point of the rebellion was the densely populated province of Anhui. Here the monk **Zhu Yuanzhang,** who was the son of a peasant, managed to unite the rebels under his command. Together with the troops of the **secret association** called **Red Scarves,** he was able to conquer section after section of central China. Khanbalik and with it the Yuan Dynasty fell in **1368.** That same year, Zhu Yuanzhang proclaimed the **Ming Dynasty,** and announced himself first emperor. He was the first and only "peasant emperor" of China.

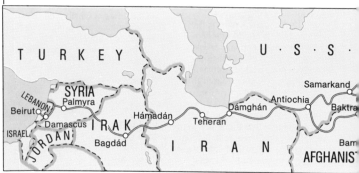

Ming Dynasty (1368–1644)

To Zhu Yuangzhang, the south seemed to be safe enough for the time being. He removed his capital to Nanjing and made preparations there for the **final expulsion of the Mongolians.** After having disposed of his rivals and executed some of the generals accused of treason, he managed to assume total power and consequently establish the first absolutist regime in China. The administration of military and political affairs was kept strictly separate. There were six ministries, directly and solely answerable to him. He abolished the chancellor's office, which had existed unchanged since its institution during the Han era, in order to have more personal control over political matters and the military. Since he mistrusted scholars and officials, he came to depend more and more on the services of the eunuchs (mere court domestics originally) in the affairs of state. Under the succeeding emperors of the Ming Dynasty, they became the secret rulers of the court. They increased their influence in politics by means of secret dosiers, intrigues, and conspiracies. They did not even shy away from committing murder.

The third Ming emperor **Cheng Zu,** also referred to as Yong Le, who had disposed of the legitimate successor to the throne, was the first of the Chinese emperors to remove the capital of the Chinese empire to **Beijing.** Only the northern tribes – the last to do so being the Mongolians – had used Beijing as a capital so far. Consequently, the old imperial cities of Xi'an and Luoyang lost their former importance. From Beijing, **Emperor Yong Le** hoped to establish better control over the Mongolians. The Great Wall was expanded as a defence measure against their attacks. The construction of the Imperial Palace, erected on top of the ruins of Khanbalik, was begun in **1407.**

The Ming empire reached the height of its power during the reign of Emperor Yong Le. A Chinese fleet made its first appearance on

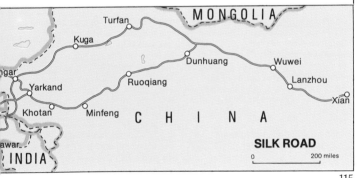

SILK ROAD

0   200 miles

the world's seas. Commanded by the eunuch **Zheng He,** the fleet sailed on several expeditions to the South Seas and the Pacific Ocean, establishing trade and the first Chinese foreign settlements. The fleet even reached the eastern coast of Africa. This maritime traffic was later discontinued, most likely as a result of dwindling funds. The Mongolian incursions continued up until the 15th century. The sixth Ming emperor **Zhengtong,** who had personally gone to the front lines, was captured and held prisoner by the Mongolians for eight years.

Agriculture profited from the supportive measures instituted by the first Ming emperor. The cultivation of lands was subsidized, irrigation systems were improved, and cotton was first planted in the outlying regions. Taxes were lowered – in some cases lands were even exempted from taxation by public order – and the trade in seeds allowed to go on unrestricted. Nevertheless, the situation in the rural regions again worsened drastically towards the end of the dynasty. The concentration of land among a few landlords, the increasing of tributes, and the introduction of pecuniary taxation to replace payments in the form of natural goods finally resulted in widespread indebtedness among the peasants. As it had occurred so often in the history of China, the peasant revolts portended the fall of a dynasty.

The handicrafts witnessed a new upswing. Inhibiting restrictions were removed and private enterprise became possible. Furthermore, the western techniques introduced during the period of Mongolian rule improved the means of production. Movable type made of lead or wood was already being put to use in the printing presses of Bilin and Suzhou. Guangdong and Fujian developed into centres for shipbuilding. The textile factories in Suzhou and Hangzhou became famous throughout the land and the large porcelain factories of Jingdezhen in the province of Jiangsu were producing the blue on white porcelain that was to become renowned later as Ming porcelain.

The merchants founded their own organizations such as guildlike associations or inns offering lodging for travelling merchants from specific regions. First capitalistic relations also developed between the merchants and the spinners and weavers. The merchants provided the spinners and weavers with the necessary appliances and paid them in cash for their products.

The beginning of the **16th century** saw the commencement of maritime trade with European nations. The first Portuguese ships arrived in Guangzhou (Canton) in **1516** to establish a permanent sea route between China and Europe. They were followed by the Spaniards, Dutch, and English. The missionaries came after the merchants. In the earlier centuries they still had to make their way to China along the Silk Road. Now they could get directly to the east coast of China by sea and reach the interior from there. The Italian Matteo Ricci is often cited as being the founder of the first Catholic missions. Well versed in the modern sciences, he became the first Jesuit advisor of the imperial court. He was followed by the first German to reach the country, the Jesuit **Adam Schall von Bell.** Although the missionaries failed in their main objective, the diffusion of Christian teachings, the Chinese still welcomed their scientific knowledge. Chinese scientists began to get involved with disciplines hitherto little developed in China such as mathematics, astronomy, the calendar, mechanics, and psychology.

The Confucians met these western missionaries with suspicion. The latter rejected the Chinese practice of ancestor worship as idolatry and spread the notion of one true God. The Chinese rulers saw in this doctrine a grave danger for the state.

But among the ruling class itself, it was the court eunuchs who undermined imperial authority with their intrigues. Taxes had to be increased drastically once more at the beginning of the **17th century** because a new great power was forming itself in the north: that of the Manzhu (Manchu). Great peasant uprisings recurred in **1628,** shaking the Ming empire from within.

Qing Dynasty (1644–1911)
The **Manchu** (Manzhu) were a tribe of the Nüzhen, who had established the great Jin Dynasty in northern China 500 years earlier. They lived in northeast China, in the area of the contemporary province of Heilongjiang, where the Songhua and the Mudan flow together. They continued to raise stock as in earlier times, but by then they had also adopted agriculture. Their feudal lord **Nurhaci** had been able to subjugate the other tribes by **1580.** In **1616** he founded the state of Jin, in deference to the ancient dynasty of the Nüzhen, and brought the North of China under his control. In the years that followed, he conquered the cities of Liaoyang and Shenyang as well as Mongolia and other regions and cities in the northeast.

With the help of a general in the Ming army, the Manchu also succeeded in surmounting the Great Wall at Shanghaiguan Pass, where the Great Wall connects up with the sea. The Manchu prince **Fu Lin** was then able to conquer Beijing, have himself enthroned as the first emperor of the **Qing Dynasty,** and erect his capital there.

The inner decay of the Ming Dynasty was also manifest in the general attitude towards the new rulers. Quite a number of high officials, scholars, and army officers openly collaborated with the Manchu. This was especially true for the northern Chinese, for whom the Manchu were no strangers. But others retreated farther and farther south, where they resisted the Qing troops with bitter determination for several decades. The attempt to establish a southern Ming Dynasty failed, however, because of internal quarrels.

It took until **1683** for the Qing to conquer all of China, including the island of Taiwan. They reached the zenith of their power in the middle of the **18th century.** At that time they had control over a territory of more than 4 million square miles. The empire had never been as large before and never would be again. For the first time as well, the population grew to a total of more than 400 million inhabitants.

During the reign of **Emperor Qianlong,** the Qing subjugated the Dsungarei and the Uighurs, consolidating their entire territory into one province named Xingjiang (New Territories).

Suzereinty over Tibet was re-established by imperial decree and commissioners, so-called Ambanes, were sent to administer the country. The subjugation of Tibet was preceded by a campaign of pro-Lamaism. The 6th Dalai Lama had already been received with great pomp in Beijing as early as **1652** and then accompanied on his way back to Tibet by Qing troops. Eight years later, **Emperor Yong-Zheng** had his palace in northeastern Beijing rebuilt as a Lamaist monastery. It can still be seen today. In the northeast, the Qing extended their territory beyond the Heilong River (Amur) all the way to the Sea of Okhotsk. Neighbouring states to the south, in Nepal, Burma, Vietnam, and elsewhere had to recognize the dominance of China as the most powerful nation in Asia.

The last years of the 60-year reign of Qianlong were beset with mis-

management and corruption. When his successor ascended the throne, the nation was in turmoil once again.

Wang Lun, a peasant leader from Shandong, had started the first uprising in **1774.** The Hui, a Moslem minority, followed suit shortly afterwards in Gansu and then the Miao tribes in Hunan and Guizhou also rebelled. The secret associations were growing in number and providing the leadership for several peasant revolts. Their sphere of influence increased in Hebei, Sichuan, and Shaanxi. These uprisings occurred incessantly and finally led to the great **Taiping Rebellion** in the middle of the **19th century.**

The period of the Qing Dynasty was one of imposed foreign rule for the Han Chinese. Like the Mongolians before them, the Qing emperors also created a strict hierarchy on the basis of nationality. Certain influential positions were reserved for the Manchu. The Han Chinese were allowed to hold other administrative offices, but only under Manchurian supervision. The landed property of the Ming emperors and the consort families, as well as that of the Han Chinese nobles, was confiscated and redistributed among the families of the Qing rulers. The Chinese were restricted to a certain area in the capital situated to the south of the Imperial Palace. Only the Manchu were allowed to settle in the vicinity of the palace itself. The Qing rulers also made it illegal for Chinese and Manchurians to intermarry and forced the Chinese men to wear queues (pigtails) as a sign of submission. This discrimination and the overbearing manner of the Manchurians in their dealings with the Chinese stirred up national sentiment against the foreign rulers.

The whole nation was placed **under the strict control of banners,** military organizations with a rigid hierarchical structure. The inner banners were only open to the Manchu and the Jurchen (Nüzhen), whereas the collaborating Chinese troops were placed in the outer banners.

As far as the administration of state affairs was concerned, the Qing emperors maintained the absolutism of the Ming. The main administrative body was the **Grand Council.** It made all of the political and military decisions under the supervision of the emperor. The ministers were reduced to strictly executive personages.

The Qing rulers also established Confucianism as the doctrine of the state. The imperial examinations were upgraded and the so-called **Holy Oaths** promulgated, short proverbs on the proper conduct of each citizen towards family, ancestors, state, and emperor. These rules were continuously being made public throughout the nation. The original Confucian ethics, which put forward loyalty and obedience as great human virtues, were thus reduced to the level of cheap legitimations for absolutist rule and a morality of unconditional submission.

The Qing rulers themselves adopted the practices of the eunuchs during the Ming period; the employment of spies and the writing of dossiers. The officials of the state were kept under close surveillance by anonymous informers. Fear of persecution eventually prevented any initiative whatsoever on their part.

During the reign of the Qing Dynasty, there was a period of economic and cultural prosperity under **Emperor Qianlong.** Though agriculture still occupied an important position in the Chinese empire, handicrafts, industry, and trade in particular made unexpected progress at this time. Unprecedented quantities of gold, silver, copper, tin, lead, and coal were being mined. According to one source, more than 10 mines employed over 100,000 people in the province of Guangxi alone. There were 45 mines in Yunnan, operated both by the state and privately.

Sichuan was the centre for salt mining. In the porcelain manufactories at Jiangxi, which had already been producing at an astonishing rate during the Ming era, a high level of division of labour was practised. In Guangdong there were tea-processing industries employing more than 500 labourers. Additionally, some 50,000 people were receiving wages as spinners and as weavers. The greatest economic power was in the hands of the salt traders and the newly established financial institutions of the Shanxi. These had already assumed some of the functions of modern banking, such as the handling of investments, the transaction with bills of exchange, the granting of credit, and the collecting of taxes on behalf of the state.

One of the most remarkable developments of this period was the expansion in trading, especially in the foreign and maritime sector.

However, it was this particular development that would ultimately bring about the fall of the Qing Dynasty and initiate one of the darkest chapters in Chinese history: the humiliating subjugation under various foreign powers. The trade relations begun in the Ming era with the Portuguese, Dutch, and English now reached new levels in the extent of trading as well as in the aggressive way in which the European powers were trying to penetrate the Chinese market.

The English established a trading post at Guangzhou in **1685** and began to expand their commercial activities under the **East India Company.** In **1793,** the English made their first demands at the imperial court for access to further northern ports such as Zhoushan, Ningbo, and Tianjin – practically at the very gates of Beijing. But the Qing rulers, fearing for their own feudal powers, implemented a **policy of Isolationism** and only handed out trading licenses for the port of Guangzhou (Canton) for the time being.

The English in particular were dissatisfied with this situation as they hoped to open up the huge Chinese market for their inexpensive Manchester cloth in exchange for valuable tea and even more precious silk to bring back to Europe. Since they were not willing to pay for these commodities in hard cash, they involved themselves in the **opium trade.** There were more than enough consumers in the disrupted nation for this drug, so that the English were soon only accepting silver dollars in payment for it. The illegal outflow of this silver currency brought the imperial finances to the brink of ruin, so that the government was forced to take action. Some of the members of the government were prepared to comply with the demands of the English, but there was still a patriotic faction at this time that favoured resistance. In **1839,** 1,000 tons of confiscated opium were set on fire in the vicinity of Guangzhou.

The English countered with armed aggression. They quickly occupied the seaports along the southeastern coast and then pushed their way to the interior from there. The imperial family only offered brief resistance. On **August 29, 1842,** under the **Treaty of Nanjing,** China ceded Hong Kong to the British and had to open the seaports of Guanzhou, Xiamen, Fuzhou, Ningbo, and Shanghai. The Qing government pledged to pay 21 million silver dollars as indemnity. Furthermore, Chinese autonomy in matters of customs was breached for the first time. Tariff rates now had to be approved by the British. In a supplementary treaty, the British secured **most-**

favoured-nation status. This, guaranteed that all concessions made to other governments would also automatically apply to the British.

As a direct result of these agreements, other powers like France, Belgium, Norway, Sweden, the United States and, somewhat later, Germany also compelled the Chinese to sign equally one-sided treaties.

The foreign powers did not limit their incursions to the cities along the coast. They soon demanded special traffic rights for the Yangzi River, using their canon boats as a means of blackmail. The trade in opium went on unimpeded and the cheap mass-produced products coming from the European factories crippled the rural Chinese handicrafts, thereby also destroying the basis of existance for millions of peasants.

Britain used an incident as an excuse to start the **Second Opium War (1856–1860),** which ended with more one-sided treaties. Additional sea- and riverports were opened up for the free market, foreign administrators ran the Chinese customs bureau, foreign warships obtained permission to dock at Chinese harbours, and even the trade in opium was legalized. In **1860,** French and English troops advanced all the way to Beijing, where they laid the Summer Palace and other buildings to waste. The emperor fled to Jehol (Chengde).

China, once the greatest power in all of Asia, was reduced to the status of a poverty stricken semi-colonized nation after the two Opium Wars. The foreign powers were not at all interested in overthrowing the Qing regime as it was increasingly willing to comply with their demands. Foreign troops even supported its efforts to subdue the uprisings in its own country.

The **Taiping rebels** almost brought about the collapse of the empire. Burdened by higher taxes levied in order to make indemnity payments to the foreign powers, the artisans and merchants, as well as the peasants, joined **secret associations.** The general turmoil finally culminated in the **Taiping Rebellion,** which spread throughout the nation. Its leader **Hong Xiuguan** was a village teacher of humble origins, from the province of Guangdong. Next to the doctrines of the different secret associations, he was especially impressed by the Christian sermons of the missionaries. In the name of Jesus Christ, he demanded social rights and equality for all of the people. In a few years his armed troops swelled in numbers from 10,000 to more than one million men. Within three years they conquered half of southern China and advanced from the province of Guangxi all the way to Nanjing, where they established their own government. The fact that they did not take Beijing as well, was probably a fatal mistake. This gave the imperial court time enough to mobilize its troops and put down the rebellion with the aid of foreign troops. The Taiping Rebellion was followed by innumerable revolts, most of which were initiated by the national minorities.

During the **Sino-Japanese War (1894–95),** the Chinese suffered even heavier losses of land. Under the **Treaty of Shimonoseki,** Liaodong Peninsula, the Penghu Islands, and Taiwan were ceded to the Japanese, who also obtained the right to establish their own industry in the Chinese seaports.

In keeping with the stipulations of the most-favoured-nation status clause, this right also fell to most of the other foreign powers. There began a renewed race for spheres of influence. Japan claimed Taiwan and the province of Fujian, but they had also set their sights on the entire northeast. Czarist Russia demanded all of the regions north of the Great Wall for itself, the British focused on the regions around the Yangzi, Germany (under Kaiser Wilhelm II) obtained Shandong, and the French fought the British over the southern provinces of Yunnan, Guangxi, and Guangdong.

All the same, modern ideas and sciences reached China as well as the canon boats and machines of the foreign powers. Under the leadership of **Kang Youwei,** the first middle-class reform movement in China emerged and even gained the attention of the youthful **Emperor Guangxu.** Kang Youwei, who had a following of more than 1,000 scholars, combined the Asian notions of equality and justice inherent in Buddhism and Confucianism with occidental Christian ideas as well as new perceptions and concepts of the natural sciences into a new system of social thought. All social and class barriers were to be removed and prosperity, peace, and joy were to accrue to all members of the society.

The actual period of reform only lasted for 103 days, which is why it is referred to in history as the **Hundred Days Reform.** Although Emperor Guangxu did incorporate several of the reformers' demands into laws, such as the introduction of western school systems, the establishment of academic associations, freedom of the press, and the establishment of banks and railroad companies, these reforms were never actually realized. The real political and military power was in the hands of **Empress Dowager Ci Xi,** who stubbornly maintained feudal notions and structures while at the same time willingly complying with the demands of the foreign powers. She had the young emperor Guangxu placed under house arrest in the Summer Palace for several years. On **September 21st, 1898,** she assumed the throne.

The failure or unwillingness of the Qing ruling family to implement the extensive reforms needed to solve the growing social and political problems, made the abrupt end of dynastic rule in China inevitable. The people's annoyance with Empress Dowager Ci Xi's yielding stance towards the foreigners turned into more and more hatred for the foreigners and culminated in the **Yi He Tuan Movement.** It was called the **Boxer Rebellion** by the

Europeans because its followers practised Chinese martial arts. The rebellion started up in the province of Shandong and rapidly spread to Tianjin and Beijing. The killing of a German envoy and a secretary of the Japanese embassy prompted a military intervention by foreign troops that brought about the brutal suppression of the rebellion. A **protocol of peace** forced upon the government in **1901** requiring the Chinese to pay another indemnity of 450 million silver dollars certainly did not promote peaceful relations. On the contrary, it only deepened the growing anti-imperialist sentiment and quickened the fall of the Qing Dynasty. After the death of Emperor Guanxu, the empress dowager installed three-year-old **Pu Yi** on the throne, shortly before her own death. Only two years after his ascension to the throne in **1909,** he was forced to abdicate. And so the republican revolution had been victorious.

The Republic and the Period of Revolutionary Civil War (1911–1949)

At first, the republican idea only found support among the western oriented intelligentsia. They had their centre in Tokyo, where many young Chinese were studying. One of them was **Sun Yatsen (1866– 1925).** A young doctor of medicine, born in Macao, he had studied in Hong Kong. lived and practised there as well as in Honolulu, until he had decided to join the revolutionary movement and moved to Tokyo. There he was soon elected leader of the **Revolutionary League of**

China, which oriented itself in part on the ideals of the French Revolution. It had as its goals: the overthrowal of the Manchu Dynasty, the founding of a democratic republic and the equal redistribution of the land. Sun Yatsen himself formulated the **Three People's Principles: nationalism, democracy, and prosperity.**

Between **1906** and **1911,** he instigated several rebellions in Guangdong, all of which were unsuccessful. Nevertheless, the republican movement soon gained

Dr. Sun Yatsen (1866–1925) first President of the Republic.

the support of the labourers, peasants, and intellectuals, as well as the Qing soldiers. Far-sighted politicians of the imperial government were already acting with careful restraint and remaining passively observant of the likely new rulers.

The **downfall of the dynasty** was brought about by the Qing regime itself. Annoyance with the sale of Chinese resources was already pronounced enough. It reached the boiling point when the imperial government announced plans to nationalize the railroads with foreign loans. Since these companies provided the provinces with much needed income, the latter concertedly refused to comply. Within a short period, 15 provinces disclaimed any loyalty to the emperor and established revolutionary provincial governments. Their delegates met in Nanjing to elect **Dr. Sun Yatsen as the first President of the Republic of China.**

However, the young republic lacked both the instruments of power and military forces. **Yuan Shikai,** commander of the northern armies, had become the most powerful person in the nation some time back and now gained control over the imperial family. Yuan forced the emperor to abdicate and then accepted Sun Yatsen's offer of the presidency of the republic. **A monarchy that had lasted for more than two thousand years was overthrown**, and, in the true sense of the word, pigtails began to fall. All over the country, Chinese

people cut off their prescribed pigtails in a demonstration of liberation from foreign rule.

But the republik proved not to be viable enough, as the changes had occurred too abruptly. Two milleniums of culture and tradition simply could not be revolutionized in just a few years.

The president of the republic, Yuan Shikai, decided to re-establish the monarchy and assume the title of emperor.

Only his early death in **1916** prevented this plan. Rival military leaders took over in the north and led the nation into a civil war that lasted for many years. Sun Yatsen, who had since then fled to Japan, then founded his own republic in southern China. He went into opposition against the feudal military leaders and united the forces of resistance under the National People's Party, the **Guomindang.**

With the exception of a brief period during World War I, the influence of the foreign powers remained unbroken. The **Treaty of Versailles,** which required Germany to give up its territory in Shandong to the Japanese, produced a wave of anti-imperialist protest among the Chinese students, who gained the sympathy of the whole nation. They demanded that this territory be returned to China. This revolution, known in China as the May 4th Movement, brought out a new and radical orientation among younger intellectuals, who drew their ideo-logial concepts from the successful October Revolution in Russia.

The first **Marxist associations** were founded at the University of Beijing, where **Mao Zedong** was also studying. In **1921,** thirteen dele-gates representing a mere fifty members met in Shanghai for the **Founding Congress of the Chinese Communist Party.** Inspired by the proletarian revolts in Europe and basing their hopes on the grow-ing Chinese working class, they decided to concentrate their activi-ties in the cities for the time being. However, all of the uprisings they instigated failed and involved great sacrifices. A pragmatic reorientation taking into consideration the realities of China had already occurred in 1923. They decided to cooperate with the Guomindang under Sun Yatsen and his brother-in-law **Tshiang Kai-shek** to defeat the military leaders of the north. Com-munists and Nationalists founded a joint military academy to provide training for the officers. **Zhou Enlai** became one of its representative directors. Many Communists were also members of the Guomindang.

The new supreme commander of the National People's Army, Tshiang Kai-shek, was at last able to defeat the rebellious northern armies and to unite the empire under his leader-ship. **Nanjing** became the seat of the newly instituted republican regime. Since Tibet, under the influ-ence of the British, and Mongolia, urged by the Russians, had broken

*Mao Zedong
(1893–1976),
founder of the
People's Republic of China.*

away from the empire in **1911,** the territory of the new republic was much smaller than it had been under the Qing Dynasty.

After his victory, Tshiang Kai-shek turned against the Communists. **Terrible massacres** took place in the cities, especially in Shanghai, where Communists, labourers, and intellectuals were beheaded in public.

Despite intensive resistance and continuous warfare, Tshiang managed to establish a system of administration with a set of laws based on European models, and to

125

stimulate the economy. The internal rupture of the republic was portended by his close association with high finance – exemplified in his marriage to the daughter of an important banker – and his request for foreign aid to combat the Communists. The failure to implement land reforms in particular, strengthened the influence of the Communists among the rural population, which still made up over 80% of the total population.

In order to escape the continuing persecutions and extermination campaigns of the Guomindang, the Communists began their legendary **Long March. The Red Army covered over 7,500 miles through 11 provinces.** The loss of lives and possessions was great, but the prestige and influence of the Communists grew from day to day. **Revolutionary bases** were established throughout the country under Communist administration, which in fact were like small states within the state.

As a result of the Long March, Mao Zedong was able to assert himself against the dogma of working class revolts. **For Mao Zedong the peasant was the most important force behind the Chinese revolution and guerrilla warfare the best form of military resistance.** The march ended at **Yan'an** and here they set up a revolutionary base to which more and more supporters flocked, especially urban intellectuals.

The **Japanese** had steadily increased their influence in China during the civil war and annexed more and more territory. They had conquered **Mukden** (Shenyang) by **1931,** as well as other regions throughout the northeast. A year later, the Japanese founded the puppet state of **Manzuguo** (Manchuria) and nominated **Pu Yi** as emperor and head of state. They moved into Shanghai in **1932** and conquered other regions in the north. An incident at the Marco Polo Bridge near Beijing that was instigated by the Japanese in **1937** started the Sino-Japanese war.

A year earlier, two generals belonging to the left wing of the Guomindang had arrested their party leader Tshiang Kai-shek and forced him to negotiate with the Communists. The latter had long favoured a united national front against the Japanese. After negotiating with Tshiang, they placed a large part of the Red Army under a joint command and temporarily abandoned their revolutionary programme.

The country was torn apart by the civil war and the Japanese invasion. The rival groups were situated in four capital cities. The last of the Qing emperors, Pu Yi, reigned in Mukden (Shenyang) over the state of Manchuria, a dependency of the Japanese. A Guomindang leader established another puppet state in Nanjing that was under the direct control of the Japanese. Tshiang Kai-shek was forced by the Japanese to retreat to Chongqing, while Mao Zedong established himself in Yan'an.

There was no decisive turn of events until the Japanese got involved in the great naval battles of the Pacific. In spite of continuing internal struggles, the combined Chinese armies finally managed to oust the Japanese from their country.

With the **capitulation** of the Japanese at the end of **World War II,** the alliance between the Chinese parties was terminated and the third major **civil war** erupted. The Communists had already borne the brunt of the anti-Japanese war, even though most of the foreign aid, especially armaments, had gone to the Guomindang. Nevertheless, they were able to march southward from Manchuria to the Yangzi River relatively unhindered, where they won a decisive battle against the Guomindang.

Together with the rest of his army and about 2 million Chinese, **Tshiang Kai-shek had to flee to the island of Taiwan.** Under the protection of the **U. S. A.,** he proclaimed the **Republic of China** on **March 1st, 1950.** Six months before, on **October 1st, 1949,** Mao Zedong had proclaimed the **Foundation of the People's Republic of China** from the Gate of Heavenly Peace.

The primary reason for the victory of the Red Army was that it was **the only party offering a programme of land reforms** promising the abolishment of the feudal system and distribution of lands to each peasant. In contrast to the Guomin-

dang soldiers, the Red Army had also gained the confidence of the general population with its **strict discipline, unselfishness, helpfulness, and idealism.** In this respect, **the Red Army truly distinguished itself from all other armies** spreading war throughout China for the greater part of the first half of the 20th century.

The People's Republic of China (1949–1984)

One of the first tasks undertaken by the young People's Republic was land reform; after all it now had to feed about **half a billion people.** Then there were the damages left behind by decades of warfare and catastrophies that needed to be taken care of. All landed property was immediately expropriated and nationalized. Hundreds of thousands, perhaps even more, of the landowners were brought before **national tribunals** during the campaign of expropriation and most of them were sentenced to death.

Expropriated land was redistributed among the peasants, whereby private initiative was still condoned for the time being. The Communist functionaries were well versed in matters pertaining to agriculture. For years, they had had to deal with these matters as well as with problems of economic and political organization in the former revolutionary bases. The situation in industry was much more problematic. Here they first tried out a policy of so-called **New Democracy,** formulated by Mao Zedong. It was a **class-alli-**

ance between labourers, peasants, and those national capitalists who had not collaborated with the foreign imperialists. The latter were allowed to retain and manage their factories. Due to the employment of this policy, the initial years of the People's Republic were weathered fairly well with considerable economic progress. The first five-year plan came into operation in **1954** heralding the **adoption of Soviet-Stalinist economic policy.** The major goal behind this policy was to focus on the advancement of heavy industry, a result of the Socialist utopia, which measured progress in tons of steel at the cost of the peasants. At times their standard of living stagnated and even deteriorated.

The first manifestations of discontent among the peasants were countered with an acceleration of the collectivization initiative. The peasants had been encouraged as early as **1953** to join in mutual-aid teams, but the question of private property had not been touched upon. Soon after, however, a programme of collectivization was set in motion. Agricultural co-operatives were established and then in **1958,** after a positive vote by Mao Zedong, the first **people's communes** began to appear throughout the nation. At that time, the Chinese believed that the communes were the ultimate stage of collectivism and a necessary step towards a Communist society.

The economic results, however, were more disastrous than inspiring.

The bureaucracy developing at the communes prevented any initiative on the part of the peasants.

The **Great Leap Forward,** one of the first mass movements to stimulate the initiative of the general population, was launched in **1957.** Hundreds of thousands were employed in labour projects while an unprecedented **wave of propaganda** flooded the country.

The nationalization of private industrial enterprises was completed by **1957.** In many cases, the former owners were kept as managers and compensated with an annual pension.

During the mid 50's, the Communist party had its first conflict with intellectuals. Quite a few of them voiced criticism about the policies of the party in the **Let One Hundred Flowers Blossom** campaign initiated by Mao Zedong. When some of them even began to challenge the leadership role of the party and to demand a **democratic parliamentary system,** the party simply turned the tables on them. What had apparently started off as a first step towards founding a democratic and liberal system ended up in brutal repression. Many of those who were convicted and persecuted back then, were not rehabilitated until the end of the 70's.

The ultimate failure of this mass movement, as well as the catastrophic results of the "great leap forward" and the people's communes, unsettled Mao Zedong's leadership position within the party. Mao, who had been elected as the first president of the state in 1954, right after the adoption of the first constitution of the People's Republic, had to relinquish this position to **Liu Shaoqi** in **1959.** He was a major adversary of Mao's and considered to be an advocate of a more pragmatic course. The technocrats and bureaucrats of the party had already tried to remove the rebellious Mao from the political process in **1956.**

The People's Republic of China was able to register successes with its early foreign policies. **Tibet, Xinjiang, and Inner Mongolia,** which had only kept loose ties with the empire and republic since the fall of the Qing Dynasty, were won back again and integrated into the People's Republic as **autonomous regions. Manchuria,** which had been occupied by Russia just before the war ended, was returned. The Red Army also marched into **Yunnan,** at that time still under the influence of the French. Furthermore, China gained in influence over the Third World.

Another major conflict began to develop at the close of the 50's, which was to dominate Chinese foreign policy for the next two decades: the **break with the Soviet Union.** On **April 22nd, 1960,** the Chinese published a polemic treatise commemorating Lenin's 90th birthday, which made the conflict obvious to the world. The ideological controversy carried on in the years that followed was in reality a hard political confrontation over the position of leadership within the international Communist movement. Each one accused the other of having betrayed Lenin's teachings, as well as the goals of the proletarian revolution. The **Soviet Union** had earlier denied the Chinese access to the atom bomb and now it also withdrew its experts and **terminated all economic aid.**

The **Great Proletarian Cultural Revolution** that broke out in the mid 60's was the result of both the ideological conflict with the Soviet Union and internal disputes which led to splits within the party.

The pragmatists Liu Shaoqi and Deng Xiaoping were increasing their influence in the party over Mao Zedong, who accused them of being revisionists, i. e. of wanting to bring capitalism back to China. This set off a **massive movement of the Red Guards** against the supposed "buourgeois headquarters".

The revolution quickly got out of hand and armed conflicts broke out all over the country. Countless politicians and intellectuals were banished to prisons or exiled to isolated regions of China. Some were even murdered. The party finally called on the army to intervene. **Lin Biao,** its commander, gained so much in prestige that he virtually functioned as **Mao's designated successor** after the **9th party congress in 1969.** The conflicts within the party

The Emperors of the Ming Dynasty

Imperial Title	Name of Emperor	Period	From – To
Taizu	Zhu Yuanzhang	Hongwu	1368–1398
Huidi	Zhu Yunwen	Jianwen	1399–1402
Chengzu	Zhu Di	Yongle	1403–1424
Renzong	Zhu Gaochi	Hongxi	1425
Xuanzong	Zhu Zhanji	Xuande	1426–1435
Yingzong	Zhu Qizhen	Zhengtong	1436–1449
Daizong	Zhu Qiyu	Jiangtai	1450–1456
Yingzong	Zhu Qizhen	Tianshun	1457–1464
Xianzong	Zhu Jianshen	Chenghua	1465–1487
Xiaozong	Zhu Youtang	Hongzhi	1488–1505
Wuzong	Zhu Houzhao	Zhengde	1506–1521
Shizong	Zhu Houcong	Jiajing	1522–1566
Muzong	Zhu Zaihou	Longqing	1567–1572
Shenzong	Zhu Yijun	Wanli	1573–1620
Guangzong	Zhu Changluo	Taichang	1620
Xizong	Zhu Youxiao	Tianqi	1621–1627
Sizong	Zhu Youjian	Chongzhen	1628–1644

grew more and more involved. Finally, Lin Biao disappeared, supposedly killed in a plane crash over the People's Republic of Mongolia while he was trying to flee to the Soviet Union. With him, or rather after him, many other political and military leaders also fell. Den Xiaoping returned to politics in **1973** to become **Zhou Enlai's** closest ally. A new group was forming itself at the same time in Shanghai, later known and condemned as the **Gang of Four.**

The **annoyance of the populace** with the political leadership **manifested itself** for the first time at the **death of Zhou Enlai** on January, **1976,** and then again on the commemorative day of his death in the following April. For the first time since **1949,** spontaneous and unorganized **mass demonstrations** took place in the capital city of Beijing, in which several hundred thousand people participated. Critical speeches and poems were directed primarily at **Mao's wife Jiang Qing** and the Gang of Four. But even Mao was not spared criticism. The radicals were able to gain the upper hand at first. They made **Deng Xiaoping** responsible for the demonstrations and he had to give up his official positions for the second time. This time, however, it was only for the period of a few months. **Mao Zedong died on September 9th, 1976,** and immediately a power struggle broke out among the leading factions of the party. The radical leaders Jiang Qing, Yao Wenyuan, Zhang Chun-

The Emperors of the Qing Dynasty

Imperial Title	Name of Emperor	Period	From – To
Shizu	Aisin-Gioro Fu Lin	Shunzhi	1644–1661
Shengzu	Aisin-Gioro Xuan Ye	Kangxi	1662–1722
Shizong	Aisin-Gioro Yin Zhen	Yongzheng	1723–1735
Gaozong	Aisin-Gioro Hong Li	Qianlong	1736–1795
Renzong	Aisin-Gioro Yong Yan	Jiaqing	1796–1820
Xuanzong	Aisin-Gioro Min Ning	Daoguang	1821–1850
Wenzong	Aisin-Gioro Yi Zhu	Xianfeng	1851–1861
Muzong	Aisin-Gioro Zai Chun	Tongzhi	1862–1874
Dezong	Aisin-Gioro Zhi Tian	Guangxu	1875–1908
(no title)	Aisin-Gioro Pu Yi	Xuantong	1909–1911

qiao, and Wang Hongwen were arrested on the 7th of October. The compromise candidate after the death of Mao, **Hua Guofeng,** had joined sides with the moderates.

Once the radicals were ousted, a truly new policy began to evolve in many sectors. A new **policy** in the **sector of agriculture** stood at the centre of the **political reforms.** The **people's communes** were abolished in many regions of the country and the peasants encouraged to work on a pivate basis once again, under contract by the state. This, together with the increasing prices paid by the state for agricultural products and the re-establishment of open markets, raised the income of the peasants rapidly. There was also a marked improvement in the supplies situation. Investments – especially in heavy industry – were reduced.

Today, it is hoped that the economy will be stimulated by higher incomes and the consequent rise in demand.

Supportive measures in the sector of light industry are aimed at improving the supply of durable products. **Private property** is limited rather than being prohibited altogether and **private enterprise** in commercial and service industries is also permitted.

The Chinese Dynasties

Xia	2100–1600 B.C.	North and	
Shang	1600–1100	South Dynasties	420– 589
Western Zhou	1100– 770	Sui	581– 618
Eastern Zhou or		Tang	618– 907
Spring and		The Five	
Autumn Period	770– 476	Dynasties	907– 960
Era of the Warring		Song (North	
Kingdoms	476– 221	and South)	960–1279
Qin	221– 207	Liao (Khitan)	916–1125
Western Han	206– 24 A.D.	Western Xia	1038–1227
Eastern Han	25– 220	Jin	1115–1234
Three Kingdoms		Yuan	
(Wei, Shu and		(Mongolen)	1271–1368
Wu)	220– 265	Ming	1368–1644
Western Jin	265– 316	Qing	
Eastern Jin	317– 420	(Mandschu)	1644–1911

There has also been a process of **liberalization** in religious policy, especially in the case of the national minorities living in the border regions, and in cultural policy. As far as the latter is concerned, however, it is still very much subject to change. Periods of liberalization alternate with periods of reinforced criticism and repression.

On various occasions, the party has made it clear where it draws the line. **The fundamental arguments of Marxism-Leninism and above all the absolute authority of the party are not to be questioned.**

This new political course has been combined with an **open policy towards the west** in **foreign relations.** The conflict with the Soviet Union, as well as the self-imposed isolation during the Cultural Revolution, had hampered the flexibility of Chinese foreign relations a great deal. First contacts were established with the **U.S.A.** at the beginning of the 70's. **Diplomatic relations** with several western countries soon followed, together with the first major **commercial exchanges.**

After the initial euphoric exaggeration on both sides, trade relations with the west have become more stable. From this new position, the attempt is also being made to normalize relations with the Soviet Union and eastern European countries.

The goal of this new Chinese policy is to carry out the **Four Modernization Programmes: the modernization of agriculture, industry, science and technology, and national defence.** Today, the Chinese are prepared and even consider it necessary to achieve this end with foreign help.

The People's Republic of China

On October 1st, 1949, the Chairman of the Chinese Communist Party, Mao Zedong, proclaimed the People's Republic of China. This important proclamation was made from the rostrum of Tiananmen – the Gate of Heavenly Peace which is located in front of the Imperial Palace.

It took a few more years until the new rulers were able to bring the border regions of China under their control so that it was 1954 before the first constitution was introduced. Since then it has been amended several times. The present constitution was adopted at the 5th national people's congress on December 4, 1982.

The **national flag** is red with five stars in the top left-hand corner. The large star in the middle represents the leading role of the Communist party, and the four smaller ones surrounding it stand for the revolutionary classes that were involved in the revolution.

The **national coat of arms** depicts the Gate of Heavenly Peace, Tiananmen, on a red background. Above it there are five stars and it is surrounded by a wreath made from bunches of grain. Below the wreath is a cogwheel.

Beijing has been the **capital** of the People's Republic of China since the latter's foundation.

The constitution defines the People's Republic as a socialist state under the democratic dictatorship of the people. The labourers, together with the peasantry, form China's **leading class.**

For administrative purposes, the country is divided into 22 provinces, which include Taiwan, 5 autonomous regions (Inner Mongolia, Xinjiang, Tibet, Ningxia, and Guangxi), and three administrative cities (Beijing, Shanghai, and Tianjin). The provinces and autonomous regions are further subdivided into autonomous counties, and cities. The counties are in turn subdivided into municipal districts and administrative villages.

The **autonomous regions** are areas primarily inhabited by national minority peoples with autonomous rights in specific areas.

The cities are also subdivided into districts and precincts.

The constitution of 1982 contains the first provisions for the establishment of **special administrative areas,** a few of which already exist in the vicinity of Guangzhou and the province of Fujian. These special areas are designated for foreign investors, whose commercial enterprises are subject to special laws. It is also intended that Hong Kong become a special area once the leasing contract expires in 1997. A similar arrangement is being contemplated by the Chinese should the province of Taiwan ever be reintegrated into the People's Republic.

The **highest organ of state authority** is the National People's Congress (NPC), together with the local people's congresses found at various levels of administration, all of which are established by vote. The people's congresses at the basic level either vote for, or nominate, the candidates for the people's congresses at the next level higher up. A democratic voting system in which all citizens participate is thus only in practice during the election of the people's congresses at the county levels.

The National People's Congress is elected for a term of five years and its membership includes delegates from the provinces, autonomous regions, administrative cities, and those representing the armed forces. Since the ethnic minorities have special rights, even the smallest group (with only about 600 members) is still represented by one delegate. The National People's Congress is elected for a period of five years – a provision which has not always been complied with in the past. In the years of the Cultural Revolution, from 1964–1975, for example, the National People's Congress did not convene at all. What is more, under the new constitution, the NPC may, in special circumstances, remain in office for longer, providing that two-thirds of the electorate vote in favour of an extension.

The NPC convenes annually. Its functions are:
– the amendment, the ratification and the supervision of the constitution;
– the election of the Chairman (formerly the President) of the People's Republic of China and his representatives;
– the nomination of the Prime Minister and the State Council;

– the election of the Chairman of the Central Military Commission, the President of the Supreme Court of the People and the Procurator General;
– discussion and approval of plans for the national economy and the state budget;
– decision-making on matters of war and peace, among other things. The standing committee of the NPC exercises these functions during the interval between the annual sessions. The **executive organ** is the State council, headed by the Prime Minister. Aside from the Prime Minister its membership includes four vice-premiers, state commissioners, ministers, chairmen of commissions, a President of the Supreme Auditing Office, and a Secretary General. Like the National People's Congress, it is also elected for five years. New regulations prohibit the same persons from occupying the above posts for more than two terms.

The State Council assumes all legislative and administrative functions and is accountable for them before the National People's Congress.

The Central Military Commission, which is appointed by the NPC as well, commands the armed forces of the nation.

The constitution also enumerates the duties and rights of China's citizens in 24 articles. These include freedom of speech, press, assembly, association, religion, correspondence, the inviolability of domicile, the freedom to criticize organs of the state, and the equal status of men and women in society. The constitution further qualifies some of these rights, however. Freedom of correspondence, for example, may be suspended if the organs of state security find it necessary to impose censorship for the purpose of investigation. Other regulations are supplemented by laws and executive orders. For instance, freedom of speech and press have been repeatedly curtailed in the past under the clause prohibiting "counter-revolutionary attacks on the socialist system".

The preamble of the constitution outlines the future task of socialist modernization and the leading role of the Communist party. Almost all of the leading functionaries of the state machinery also hold high positions within the party. These interrelationships are visible right down to the lowest levels of the political system.

The Communist party was founded in Shanghai on July 1st, 1921, by just 13 delegates representing a mere 50 members. It was able to assume power within only 28 years, since its policies conformed to the expectations of the peasants and labourers, but also because of its extraordinary discipline which formed a contrast to the corrupt practices of the Guomindang regime and gained the confidence of the populace. When the coalition with the Nationalist Party collapsed following the defeat of the Japanese in World War II, the Communists were the first to take advantage of the vacuum this left. And indeed, its plans to reconstruct the nation, and especially the land reform programmes, were widely supported by the people.

Today, it is not unusual for leading members of the Party to admit that drastic mistakes were made in the past – i. e. the policies of the Great Leap Forward at the end of the fifties or the Cultural Revolution of the sixties and seventies – and that these did much damage to the Party's political standing and credibility.

The numerous factional conflicts that had a crippling effect on the Party from the middle of the sixties onwards, and which remained largely incomprehensible to the people, undoubtedly did nothing to improve its poor image. Some important changes also took place within the organization of the party machinery during the **post-maoist era.** It was decided to replace the near religious personality cult associated with Mao, with a more collective form of leadership. The omnipotence of the Party Chairman and the standing committee was curtailed by the creation of a secretariat within the Central Committee.

The National Party Congress, which convenes every five years, is technically the **highest organ of the party.** It elects the members and candidates of the Central Committee, the Central Disciplinary Commission, and the Central Advisory Commission. The latter has been established provisionally in order to make the notion of retiring from politics more appealing to the old party functionaries and thus make room for the appointment of younger men among the leading cadres. The Central Disciplinary Commission is responsible for ensuring that the Party carries out its work conscientiously and in keeping with Party guidelines.

The higher committees still retain some control over the decisions of the National Party Congress, however, because they determine the number of delegates, the electoral procedure for the delegates, and set the date of convocation. This precedence is legitimized by a party statute making "democratic centralism" the mandatory principle in the organization of the party. It requires the subordination of all members and committees to the highest organs of party leadership.

The Politburo, its standing committee, the secretariat of the Central Committee, the Secretary General of the Party, and the members of the Military Commission within the Central Committee (the leading organ of the armed forces) are nominated at the annual plenary sessions of the Central Committee. The **most powerful organ** is the standing committee of the Politburo, which makes all the major decisions concerning the daily activities of the party. At present, it has six members:

Hu Yaobang, also Secretary General of the Party;
Chen Yun, also Chairman of the Central Disciplinary Commission;
Deng Xiaoping, Chairman of the Central Military Commission and the Central Advisory Committee;
Li Xiannian, Chairman of the People's Republic (President of State);
Ye Jianying, Chairman of the National People's Congress;
Zhao Ziyang, also Prime Minister.

The Central Committee's secretariat – currently headed by the Secretary General, Hu Yaobang, is, however, responsible for dealing with all routine matters and is in charge of the Party administrative machinery. The secretariat supervises the Central Bureau and its several departments and research offices, as well as the Party school.

The patterns of organization described above are also found in the lower echelons of the party hierarchy, at the provincial and district levels.

Apart from the Communist Party, there are also a few so-called "democratic parties", such as the leftist branch of the National People's Party (Guomindang) or the Democratic League, which take part in the Political Consultative Conference. Leading personalities in public life also attend, as well as Chinese from Hong Kong. This institution does not exercise any power, though. It convenes at the same time as the National People's Congress and its primary function is to unite all national forces under the leadership of the Communist Party.

The different mass organizations such as the unions, women's associations, or youth associations, are also supervised by the Communist Party. The **organisational structure** for each person's daily activities is the unit, or **danwei.** This could be a factory, a hospital, a university, an office, or part of a city. **Every Chinese belongs to one of these units; it is a part of his identity.** In certain situations, a person's unit is even inquired about before his name is asked. **The unit is an**

organization which determines the nature of the individual's work and life. Aside from assigning people their place of work, it also provides housing, distributes the ration cards for food, sanctions marriages, and is responsible for the physical and social welfare of its members, e. g. children and old people. It also approves holidays and bonuses, and either metes out praise or punishment, with minor offences often being dealt with by the unit rather than being referred to the police or the courts. At present, it even decides which family can have a child and when. The unit is responsible for carrying out the new population growth policy, the **one-child family.** And if someone would like to take advantage of certain privileges, such as travelling, shopping at a Friendship Store, purchasing a bicycle, or simply obtaining furniture without having to wait until it is allocated to them, then it helps if he or she has a letter of recommendation from the unit.

The **managing committee** of such a unit is headed by a Party secretary. There is no doubt that this is a powerful person, whose author-ity, influence, and good will affect the well-being of the entire unit.

To us this system may appear to be too patronizing and an unwarranted interference in the private life of the individual, but this is not how the unit is viewed by the majority of the Chinese. For them, the unit is a kind of comfortable nest, as well as a replacement for the disappearing extended family, or clan, which once had fairly similar functions to the unit.

However, this **organizational network** is also being undermined by the new pragmatic policies of the party. Above all, it is the young people and the intellectuals who feel that they are too restricted by the unit. Although the process of indoctrination through political schooling has been abandoned to a great extent, the unit will continue to function as a social network for the time being. The units are even losing their function as a collective organization in the rural areas. The new agricultural policy allows the peasants to work on their own allotted lands, which in turn promotes personal initiative and self-reliance.

Geography

China covers the eastern and south-eastern part of the Asian continent and has a **total area** of 9,560,900 square kilometres (3,691,463 square miles). It is the **third largest country in the world,** after the U. S. S. R. and Canada, and is approximately the same size as Europe. China extends from the **Heilong River** in the far north of former Manchuria to the **Nansha Islands** in the South China Sea and from the **Wusuli River** (Ussuri) close to the eastern border of Siberia, as far as the **Pamir Mountains** in the regions bordering on Afghanistan. From north to south it extends over 5,500 kilometres (3,418 miles) spanning across 49 degrees of latitude, and from east to west it covers roughly 5,200 kilometres (3,231 miles) and over 60 degrees of longitude.

If one were to transpose the Chinese borders to Europe, they would cover an area from Portugal to the Urals and from the North Sea all the way to the Sahel zone in Africa.

China borders on 12 countries: **Korea, the Soviet Union, Mongolia, Afghanistan, Pakistan, India, Nepal, Sikkim, Bhutan, Burma, Laos, and Vietnam.** Its borders cover a total length of about 28,000 kilometres (17,399 miles).

China has nearly 18,000 km (11,185 miles) of coastline in the east and north. These 18,000 kilometres consist of the Bay of Bohai to the west of Beijing, the Yellow Sea coast, along the provinces of Shandong and Jiangsu, the East China Sea coast, which takes in Zhejiang and Fujian, Taiwan, and, the South China Sea coast in the vicinity of Guandong. And finally, there is Hainan Island and thousands of other smaller islands.

China declared a 12 mile zone along its coastlines as its own territorial waters as early as 1958.

If one considers the vast expanse of this country, it is not surprising that the landscape should be so varied. In China, you will encounter artic-like temperatures as well as tropical climes, deserts and rich loess plains, deep basins and the loftiest mountains in the world.

Geographically, China can be divided into five major regions:

The Northeast

The Chinese call this region northeast of **Beijing** "Dongbei". It incorporates the provinces of **Heilongjiang, Jilin,** and **Liaoning,** as well as the area we still refer to as **Manchuria,** a name that originates from the Japanese invasion of the thirties.

At the centre of this region lies the **North China Plain,** one of China's major grain producing areas. This plain is enclosed by mountain ranges on three sides, the only break coming in the side on which the Bay of Bohai is located. The northeast is the region of China most subject to snow and ice. The winters here can be as cold and harsh as those experienced in Siberia. The mountain regions are predominantly inhabited by **Mongolian and Tungusic tribes,** whereas the lowlands are mostly settled by **Han Chinese,** who practised agriculture much earlier than the northern tribes.

The Desert Regions

China's north and northwest, or the provinces of **Inner Mongolia, Ningxia, Gansu,** and **Xinjian,** are steppe and desert regions for the greater part.

For centuries, the **nomadic Mongolian peoples** made use of the steppe regions of the **Gobi** as grazing lands. Due to the sparse vegetation, however, only sheep or goats could ever be raised in this area. As there is no form of natural protective barrier to the north, the cold Siberian winds sweep across the Gobi during the winter. In the winter months, these winds carry sand from the desert all the way to Beijing, where the roofs virtually turn loess yellow. Inner Mongolia is thinly populated. There are approximately 16 inhabitants per square kilometre (40 per square mile), 80% of which are **Han Chinese** who settled there in the last few decades. The only fertile areas are located along the **Yellow River** (Huanghe), which makes a wide arch through the western part of Inner Mongolia and then turns southward towards the provinces of **Shaanxi** and **Shanxi.** More recently, attempts have been made to make the steppe regions suitable for arable farming. By planting several million acres of **timber,** the Chinese hope they will be able to put an end to soil erosion.

The desert and steppe regions extend westward across the provinces of Ningxia and Gansu, all the way to Xinjiang, formerly called **Turkistan.**

The **Junggar Basin,** better know to some as **Dzungaria,** lies in the northern part of Xinjiang Province. This somewhat more humid steppe region is separated from the **Mongolian People's Republic** by the **Altai Mountains** in the northeast, while the northwestern **Tarbagatai Mountains** form a natural barrier to the Soviet Union. Several glacial rivers coming from the **Tianshan Mountains** in the south flow into the Junggar Basin, which lies at an altitude of approximately 270 metres (886 feet).

The loftiest peaks of the Tianshan range (Tianshan means Mountain of Heaven), rise above 6,000 metres (19,685 feet). Running in an east to west direction to the south of this mountain range, lie the great Tarim

Basin and the **Taklimakan Desert.** It is one of the largest sand deserts on earth, covering over 300,000 square kilometres (115,830 square miles). Towards the southern border of Xinjian Province, the **Kunlun Mountains** merge into the **Tibetan plateau.**

In spite of these desolate and barren conditions, the **Tarim Basin** has been a sort of junction between the cultures of the Near East, Europe, and China since the first centuries B. C. The few rivers flowing to the edges of the Tarim Basin from the Tianshan and Kunlun ranges, gave rise to early **oasis cultures** which developed into caravansaries and trading centres. It was from this area that **Chinese silk** was transported to the Near East and to Europe. Two routes existed: one led along the north of the Tarim Basin, following the southern periphery of the Tianshan, and the other was south of the Tarim Basin, moving along the northern edge of the Kunlun Mountains. Both circumvented the desert to meet again in Kashgar, and continued across the **Pamir Mountains** towards the west.

The great religions like Buddhism, Islam, Christianity, and the Nestorian sect especially, also made their way into China through this region. The **Turfan Depression** is situated to the southeast of the provincial capital of **Urumqui.** At 154 metres (505 feet) below sea level, it is the lowest spot in China. There is a difference of more than 9,000 metres (29,528 feet) between this depression and the highest mountain in Tibet, the **Qomolongma** (Mt. Everest).

The Tibet/Qinghai Plateau

Covering an area larger than 2 million square kilometres (772,200 square miles) and situated at altitudes between 4,000 and 5,000 metres (13,124 and 16,405 feet), the plateau is the largest highland region in the world. Two-thirds of China's surface area is made up of highlands and mountain ranges. To the north, the plateau is enclosed by the **Kunlun Mountains** and the **Qilin Shan.** To the south rise the mighty **Himalayas,** the highest peaks on earth. The west is cut off by the **Karakoram** and **Pamir** mountain ranges. To the east, the **Tanggula Shan** and the **Daxue Shan** separate the plateau from the **Red Basin** in **Sichuan.**

The largest rivers in China and Indochina are in the Tibet/Qinghai Plateau. The **Yarlung Zangbo** has its source in western Tibet, from where it flows for almost 1,500 kilomtres (1,000 miles) along the Himalayas in an easterly direction, before turning southward at the eastern edge of the Himalayas to empty into the **Gulf of Bengali** under the name **Brahmaputra.** The **Lancang River** flows through the province of Tibet in a southerly direction and then, under the name of **Mekong,** it forms the border between Thailand and Laos, before emptying into the **South China Sea** due south of **Ho-Tschi-Minh City,** formerly **Saigon.** The **Changjiang** (Yangtsekiang) also emerges on this plateau under the name **Jinsha,** which can be translated as Gold Dust River. The source of the **Yellow River** is also in Qinghai. Lake Qinghai, better known to some

as Koko Nor, is the largest lake in the whole of China, having a surface area of 4,200 square kilometres (1,622 square miles).

On top of the world's roof, in Tibet and Qinghai, there are only 5,8 million inhabitants, which averages out to less than 3 people per square kilometre (9 people per square mile). The Tibetan settlements are concentrated in the alluvial valleys of the Yarlang Zangbo and in **Chamdo,** the eastern portion of Tibet, where large rivers flowing in a southerly direction and heavier rains irrigate the land enough to allow farming. For the same reasons, the settlements in Qinghai are concentrated in the eastern part of the province, where the Yellow River has its source.

Central China

Central China is made up of several regions: **the northern Chinese lowlands, the central Chinese loess regions, the Red Basin in Sichuan, and the lowlands of the Chengjiang** (Yangtsekiang). They have been dealt with together here because their climatic conditions and types of soil are similarly advantageous, which led to the development of the first advanced civilizations in this region thousands of years ago.

Basically, the central Chinese loess regions include the provinces of **Shaanxi** and **Shanxi.** The **Yellow River** flows between the two provinces and the **Wei River** runs through Shaanxi. The latter has come to be regarded as the cradle of Chinese culture. Thousands of years ago, the soft and rich loess soil blown in from the Gobi by strong winds provided men with the means of growing their own food. The **first agricultural societies** emerged here. Since loess is highly subject to erosion, men had to work in teams in order to construct terraces, walls and irrigation systems. It was out of this need for co-operation and concerted action that the first Chinese communities and states emerged.

The remains of former cities are found in the vicinity of **Xi'an.** This region was the cultural centre of China for nearly three thousand years. Plentiful rains that fall mainly in the summer months, and the Yellow River provide the much needed water for agriculture. At the same time, these have also brought about natural disasters.

The northern Chinese lowlands include the provinces of **Hebei, Shandong, Henan, Anhui, and Jiangsu,** which are all located to the south of Beijing. For the greater part, the northern Chinese lowlands are the work of the **Huanghe.** It got its name from the great quantities of loess and sand it gathers on its way through Mongolia and the central Chinese loess regions and which it has been depositing in the northern Chinese lowlands for thousands of years. Its course and estuary have shifted position many times, thus enlarging the lowlands of the **Shandong Peninsula.** Nevertheless, fertile soil has not been the only result of this process. The Huanghe also deposits some of the sediments it carries on its own bed, with the result that the water level rises constantly and the river overflows its banks from time to time. Within the present century, disastrous floods have taken the lives of hundreds of thousands. One-third of the Chinese population, more than 300 million people, live in this region. It has a density of approximately 420 inhabitants per square kilometre.

The 3,915 mile long **Changjiang** (Long River) is the longest river in China and, after the Amazon and the Nile, the third-longest in the world. Emerging in **Sichuan,** it forces its way through the **Yangzi gorges.** The lowlands begin where it exits from these again, near **Yichang.** They extend along the course of the river all the way to **Shanghai,** forming two central regions on the extensive lake plateau to the southwest of **Wuhan** and the area surrounding the **Poyang Hu** near **Nanchang.** The numerous lakes play an important role in regulating the tremendous masses of water carried by this river, 20 times as much as the Huanghe. This is China's main rice growing region, wheat being cultivated in the northern regions.

The **Yangzi** region is also vital for the Chinese in the sector of transportation. Nearly 400 million people live along the course of the Yangzi and its tributaries. Countless large cities have emerged here as a result of the numerous waterways. Ocean-going vessels can journey as far as Wuhan and smaller craft pass through the Yangzi gorges today to sail far into Sichuan. The Yangzi also divides the country into a northern and a southern half. This division is even evident in local administrative measures: the buildings north of the Yangzi are provided with heating systems, those to the south of it are not. This division also applies to cities that are intersected by the Yangzi, such as Wuhan.

The last of the great central Chinese granaries to be mentioned here is the **Red Basin** in Sichuan. In prehistoric times, a huge lake existed here, and it was from the red deposits it left behind that the basin got its name. Entirely surrounded by mountain ranges, the Red Basin forms the central region of **Sichuan.** With more than 100 million inhabitants, it is China's most densely populated province. The basin is put to intensive agricultural use. The advantageous climate of this basin, located at an altitude between 300 and 700 metres (985 and 2,297 feet), permits up to three harvests annually. Crops are even successfully grown in terraced fields on the hill-sides. On the **Chengdu Plain,** one can visit China's oldest and largest irrigation system, **Dujiangyan,** which is still in use today. As long as 2,000 years ago, the natural features of the plain were being skillfully taken advantage of, to irrigate the entire basin.

Southern China

To the south, the Red Basin borders on the **Yunnan-Guizhou Plateau.** These highlands are situated at an altitude of about 2,000 metres (6,560 feet). The eastern section of **Yunnan** Province and the capital city of **Kunming** are both protected from the cold northern winds by mountain ranges and thus enjoy a mild climate. Towards the west, and especially in the province of **Guizhou,** one encounters the **great karst regions.** These are the remains of large lakes. Wind erosion then formed the rounded karst configurations, scenery which will be familiar to those who have visited **Guilin.** Conditions here are not favourable for agriculture, so that only 10% of the total area is actually put to use. Both provinces are inhabited by numerous non-Chinese minorities. The provinces of **Guangdong, Fujian,** and **Taiwan** form part of the Southeast. This region is densely populated. Due to the subtropical climate, conditions for agriculture are perfect in the valleys and estuaries. Up to three harvests can be brought in annually.

Climate

Considering the size of China – the southernmost regions, such as the islands in the South China Sea, are near the equator and the northernmost regions in the province of Heilongjiang are actually a part of the Siberian sector of the Asian continent – it is not surprising that the climate is extremely varied. Tropical

plants grow in the southern regions at the same time that cold storm winds sweep over the land in northeastern China, where the ground is covered with frost for months. While winter conditions exist practically the whole year round in the northern part of the Tibetan highlands, the Turfan Depression some

1,000 km (620 miles) farther north is one of the warmest regions in China.

Three basic factors are responsible for these differences in climate:

Latitudinal Range. There are 49 degrees of latitude between the northern and southern shores of the South China Sea and another 35 degrees of latitude from the Heilong River to Hainan Island in the Gulf of Tonkin.

Longitudinal Range. The surface of China resembles a staircase with several steps leading down towards the sea in a west to east direction. To the southwest and west are the highland regions of Tibet/Qinghai and Yunnan/Guizhou. Central China is made up of mountain and hill country, interspersed with plains along the river valleys. The lowland regions are concentrated in the coastal areas.

Location. China is located between the immense land mass of the Asian continent and the equally large Pacific Ocean. These regions have different heat storage capacities which in turn gives rise to the monsoon winds, the permanent air-currents that move from high-pressure to low-pressure zones and are crucial for the type of climate that exists in China.

High-pressure zones develop over Siberia and the People's Republic of Mongolia during the winter. Cold air masses flow southward from the eastern edges of these zones towards central and eastern China. Temperatures and precipitation are determined by the location of these northern high-pressure zones. If the high-pressure zones are located more to the west, then the dry-cold air masses will cause low temperatures with little rainfall. Should the high-pressure zones move to the east, then the escaping currents of air will flow along the coast, warm up, and transport humid air masses to southern China. This constellation results in warmer winters and more abundant rainfall along the southern and southeastern coastal regions. Under such conditions, the temperatures in Guangzhou vary between 50°F (10°C) and 60°F (15°C). If, however, the cold air masses move in across land, the greater part of China will be cold and dry during the winter. This makes China exceptional among all other countries in these latitudes.

Summers in China are dominated by a maritime climate. The continental landmasses warm the air very quickly. High-pressure zones develop over the Pacific and the Indian oceans and send humid air-currents to China. These summer monsoons coming from the southeast and southwest bring the much needed rains. The southeastern monsoon affects the eastern half of China, the lowlands along the coast, and the southwestern monsoon coming from the Indian Ocean affects the south and the southwest. Therefore, in almost all regions of China, the rain usually falls during the summer months. The first rainfall occurs on the southern slopes of the mountain

Month / Town	1	2	3	4	5	6	7	8	9	10	11	12
Average Monthly Temperatures (°C)												
Harbin	−19.7	−15.4	− 5.1	6.1	14.3	20.0	22.7	21.4	14.3	5.9	− 5.8	−15.5
Hohhot	−13.5	− 9.3	− 0.4	7.7	15.2	20.0	21.8	19.9	13.8	6.5	− 3.0	−11.4
Beijing	− 4.7	− 2.3	4.4	13.2	20.2	24.2	26.0	24.6	19.5	12.5	4.0	− 2.8
Taiyuan	− 7.0	− 3.3	3.6	11.2	17.5	21.7	23.7	21.9	16.1	9.8	1.8	− 5.1
Jinan	− 1.7	0.9	7.3	15.1	21.9	26.3	27.6	26.3	21.7	15.8	7.8	0.8
Qingdao	− 2.6	− 0.5	4.6	10.9	16.7	20.9	24.7	25.4	20.5	14.3	7.4	0.5
Nanjing	1.9	3.8	8.4	14.7	20.0	24.5	28.2	27.9	22.9	16.9	10.7	4.5
Shanghai	3.3	4.6	8.3	13.8	18.8	23.2	27.9	27.8	23.8	17.9	12.5	6.2
Hangzhou	3.6	5.0	9.2	15.1	20.3	24.3	28.7	28.2	23.5	17.4	12.1	6.1
Fuzhou	10.4	10.6	13.4	18.1	22.2	25.3	28.7	28.2	26.0	21.6	17.8	13.1
Nanchang	4.9	6.3	10.9	17.0	22.0	25.7	29.7	29.4	25.1	18.9	13.1	7.3
Wuhan	2.8	5.0	10.0	16.0	21.3	25.8	29.0	28.5	23.6	17.5	11.2	5.3
Changsha	4.6	6.2	10.9	16.7	21.7	26.0	29.5	28.9	24.5	18.2	12.5	7.0
Guangzhou	13.4	14.2	17.7	21.8	25.7	27.2	28.3	28.2	27.0	23.8	19.7	15.2
Guilin	8.0	9.0	13.1	18.4	23.1	26.2	28.3	27.8	25.8	20.7	15.2	10.1
Nanning	12.9	13.9	17.3	21.9	26.0	27.4	28.3	27.9	26.7	23.3	18.9	14.8
Chongqing	7.5	9.4	14.0	18.8	22.2	25.2	28.6	28.4	24.0	18.4	13.9	9.4
Chengdu	9.1	11.4	16.6	22.0	25.3	28.1	29.7	30.1	24.9	20.8	15.4	11.1
Kunming	7.8	9.8	13.2	16.7	19.3	19.5	19.9	19.2	17.6	15.0	11.5	8.3
Lhasa	− 2.3	0.8	4.3	8.3	12.6	15.5	14.9	14.1	12.8	8.1	1.9	− 1.9
Xi'an	− 1.3	2.1	8.0	14.0	19.2	25.3	26.7	25.4	19.4	13.9	6.5	0.6
Lanzhou	− 7.3	− 2.5	5.3	11.7	16.7	20.5	22.4	21.0	15.9	9.4	1.6	− 5.7
Turpan	− 9.5	− 2.0	9.6	18.9	25.9	31.2	33.0	30.7	23.6	12.6	1.5	− 7.2
Urumqi	−15.2	−12.2	0.7	10.8	18.9	23.4	25.7	23.8	17.4	8.2	− 2.6	−12.0

Average Monthly Rainfall (mm)													

Month Town	1	2	3	4	5	6	7	8	9	10	11	12	Total
Harbin	4.3	3.9	12.5	25.3	33.8	77.7	176.5	107.0	72.7	26.6	7.5	5.9	553.7
Hohhot	2.4	6.1	10.1	19.9	28.4	46.2	104.4	136.9	40.4	24.1	5.9	1.4	426.2
Beijing	2.6	7.7	9.1	22.4	36.1	70.4	196.6	243.5	63.9	21.1	7.9	1.6	682.9
Taiyuan	2.9	5.3	9.9	25.7	37.0	46.5	124.6	99.3	65.8	32.4	14.8	2.3	466.5
Jinan	6.2	10.4	16.1	36.1	36.8	73.7	214.0	147.9	60.9	33.0	28.9	8.2	672.2
Qingdao	7.8	11.4	12.5	33.3	48.7	92.2	209.7	155.2	108.2	45.5	34.8	9.7	768.8
Nanjing	31.8	52.9	78.6	98.3	97.3	140.2	181.7	121.7	101.2	44.1	53.1	30.2	1031.1
Shanghai	44.3	63.0	80.5	111.1	129.3	156.6	142.4	116.0	145.9	46.8	54.3	39.2	1129.4
Hangzhou	64.3	84.4	116.7	130.4	185.8	191.6	131.6	135.5	183.0	67.0	61.2	49.1	1400.6
Fuzhou	52.6	79.9	121.4	136.2	210.0	223.5	118.5	142.2	155.3	31.0	28.8	28.7	1328.1
Nanchang	59.1	93.8	170.2	221.1	306.5	277.3	127.0	93.8	85.1	57.2	62.2	44.9	1598.2
Wuhan	35.5	60.5	104.5	144.4	161.2	218.0	119.0	133.4	80.6	53.2	56.6	33.5	1200.4
Changsha	53.1	87.2	152.3	199.2	244.5	184.5	123.2	106.3	69.3	84.8	69.9	48.1	1422.5
Guangzhou	39.1	62.5	91.5	158.5	267.2	299.0	219.6	225.3	204.4	52.0	41.9	19.6	1680.6
Guilin	55.6	76.0	133.8	279.7	318.7	316.2	224.0	167.2	65.7	97.3	83.1	58.4	1875.7
Nanning	40.0	41.6	62.8	84.0	183.1	241.3	180.0	203.5	109.6	66.6	43.5	24.9	1280.9
Chongqing	18.8	20.9	43.2	72.3	155.4	165.4	156.7	141.0	132.3	99.2	51.2	24.7	1081.1
Chengdu	5.0	11.4	21.8	51.2	88.3	119.4	228.9	265.8	113.5	47.9	16.5	6.4	976.0
Kunming	10.0	9.8	13.6	19.6	78.0	181.7	216.4	195.2	122.9	94.9	33.7	15.9	991.7
Lhasa	0.2	0.1	1.5	4.4	20.6	73.1	141.7	149.1	57.3	4.8	0.8	0.3	453.9
Xi'an	7.6	10.3	24.7	53.0	62.3	57.6	105.9	80.1	100.2	61.5	34.0	7.1	604.3
Lanzhou	1.4	1.8	7.4	19.0	40.0	33.0	59.3	85.6	51.0	26.9	4.9	1.5	331.8
Turfan	1.0	0.1	1.7	0.4	0.6	3.6	2.5	3.7	0.9	0.5	0.5	1.1	16.6
Urumqi	5.6	4.0	18.8	22.6	25.1	29.1	16.4	18.9	14.2	17.2	15.2	7.4	194.6

Seasons in China

Season	Spring			Summer			Autumn			Winter		
Town	Start	End	Days	Start	End	Days	Start	End	Days	Start	End	Days
Harbin	26.4	25.6	61	26.6	15.8	51	16.8	10.10	56	11.10	25.4	197
Hohhot	26.4	15.7	81	16.7	25.7	10	26.7	30.9	67	1.10	25.4	207
Taiyuan	21.4	10.6	51	11.6	20.8	71	21.8	20.10	61	21.10	20.4	182
Beijing	1.4	25.5	55	26.5	5.9	103	6.9	25.10	50	26.10	31.3	157
Qingdao	11.4	5.7	86	6.7	15.9	72	16.9	15.11	61	16.11	10.4	146
Jinan	26.3	15.5	51	16.5	20.9	128	21.9	15.11	56	16.11	25.3	130
Nanjing	21.3	25.5	66	26.5	20.9	118	21.9	20.11	61	21.11	20.3	120
Shanghai	26.3	5.6	72	6.6	25.9	112	26.9	25.11	61	26.11	25.3	120
Hangzhou	21.3	25.5	66	26.5	30.9	126	1.10	30.11	61	1.12	20.3	110
Wuhan	16.3	15.5	61	16.5	30.9	138	1.10	30.11	61	1.12	15.3	105
Changsha	6.3	10.5	66	11.5	30.9	143	1.10	30.11	61	1.12	5.3	95
Chongqing	21.2	5.5	74	6.5	30.9	148	1.10	5.12	66	6.12	20.2	77
Chengdu	26.2	10.5	74	11.5	15.9	128	16.9	30.11	76	1.12	25.2	87
Kunming	1.2	10.12	313							11.12	31.1	52
Guangzhou				21.4	5.11	199	6.11	20.4	166			
Guilin	21.2	30.4	69	1.5	20.10	173	21.10	5.1	77	6.1	20.2	46
Nanning				16.4	10.11	209	11.11	15.4	156			
Xi'an	21.3	25.5	66	26.5	5.9	103	6.9	10.11	66	11.11	20.3	130
Urumqi	16.4	5.7	81	6.7	20.7	15	21.7	5.10	77	6.10	15.4	192

Average emperatures were used to divide the year into Spring,
Summer, Autumn and Winter:

Spring and Autumn: 10° to 22°C
Winter: below 10°C
Summer: above 22°C

ranges. Humid air-currents then meet up with dry air coming from the northern part of central China, causing heavy precipitation. However, the summer monsoon is not always predictable. If strong winds should carry the humid air towards central and northern China too quickly, then the central regions of the Yangzi remain without rain while the northern regions are virtually flooded. When northern air-currents keep the summer monsoon from advancing further, it rains in central China and the northern provinces face the prospect of drought. This climatic instability is one of the reasons why the Chinese mastered the difficult task of irrigation as well as the construction of large irrigation systems, so early.

Since the summer monsoons virtually affect the entire country, differences in temperature are less felt in the summer than in winter. In the south, the average temperatures in July are 84°F (29°C) in Guangzhou, 82°F (28°C) in Shanghai, and 79°F (26°C) in Beijing. Even in the northernmost province of Heilongjiang, the average temperature still remains around 68°F (20°C).

However, significant differences in temperature are revealed when several regions of greatly varying altitudes are compared. The average temperature drops 5 to 6 degrees for every 1,000 metres (3,280 feet) of altitude. Thus the average temperature in the northern part of the Tibet Plateau will even remain below 50°F (10°C) at the height of the summer.

The division of China into geographical regions in the previous section is also used in the description of the country's climate.

The northeast has brief and warm summers. The growing season lasts 4 to 5 months and there is little rain. Correspondingly, the winters are long and very cold.

The desert regions of Xinjiang and Inner Mongolia have hot and dry summers with occasional strong winds. The winters are cold and dry.

Due to the altitude (4,000 to 5,000 metres/13,125 to 16,405 feet) the brief summers of the **Tibet/Qinghai Plateau** are temperate. The winters are very cold and there is little rainfall throughout the year. However, temperatures vary extremely between day and night.

Central China largely has hot and humid summers and abundant rainfall during the late summer months. The winters in the lowland regions of the Yangzi are somewhat milder than those in the northern Chinese lowlands or the central Chinese loess regions. The winters in Sichuan are also mild and humid because of its location among mountain ranges. The growing season here lasts up to 11 months, in contrast to other central Chinese regions, where it only lasts 8 to 9 months.

The **Yunnan-Guizhou Plateau** enjoys a truly mild climate with warm summers and cool winters. This is why Kunming, the capital of the province of Yunnan, bears the name of "City of Spring". There is little rainfall and, in spite of the high altitude (1,000 to 2,000 metres/ 3,280 to 6,560 feet) seldom ever any frost.

Southern China experiences no winters. Here autumn follows spring and the growing season lasts all year. Rainfall is spread fairly evenly throughout the year. It is very hot in the summer and humidity is high. Winters are mild, almost warm, with somewhat less precipitation than in the summer.

Soil, Resources, and Agriculture

Anyone who travels through China will inevitably notice the various **colourations of soil,** especially in central China. In the vicinity of **Xi'an,** for instance, you come across yellow loess soil. In the **provinces along the Yangzi,** such as **Hunan,** you will immediately be struck by the red soil. The Chinese have been categorizing their soil according to colour, ever since the 14th century.

Northeast China has **black earth,** while the **soil of the desert and steppe regions in north and northwest China** is referred to as **white.** The soil in **central China is yellow** and that of the region south of the Yangzi is **red** (podsol and laterite soil). The **marsh soils of the southwest** are either called **blue** or **green.**

This categorization of the soils indicates that the more fertile agricultural regions are located in southern and eastern China, whereas the north and the west are covered with grazing land. Here lies the source of centuries of armed conflict between the Chinese farmers and the nomadic stock raisers of the north and northwest.

Only about **40% of China's total surface is suitable for farming** or growing timber. The remaining **60%** consists of **wastelands.** The **timber regions make up 10%** and are mainly located in the far northeast, in western Sichuan, at the lower end of the Tibetan highlands, and at the western border of Yunnan. The **grazing areas,** which **make up 18%,** are located in Mongolia and the steppe regions of Xinjiang and Tibet. Only 11% of the total surface area can be used for agriculture. This is a very low percentage especially when you consider that India can use 50% of its lands for farming. In order to be able to feed 1 billion people, the Chinese have to use their farming areas intensively. The most important farming products are grains. Wheat is primarily grown in the north. The lowlands along the Yangzi River alternately produce wheat and rice. Irrigated rice fields are common in the south. Some of the major products grown in the north are millet (gaoliang), cotton, maize, soya beans, and tobacco. Apart from rice, the south also produces rape, tea, and sugar cane.

Nevertheless, the northern and northwestern wastelands are of great importance for China's future. Here lie the **energy** and **mineral resources** that are essential to the modernization of China. China is thought to have the **richest coal deposits in the world.** Coal deposits occur throughout the whole country (with the exception of Qinghai and Tibet). The largest deposits are located in the central Chinese loess regions, in the provinces of Shaanxi and Shanxi, as well as in the province of Sichuan. Efforts have also been made recently to find **oil and natural gas deposits.** Some of these projects involved foreign help. According to the Chinese, rich deposits have been found off the coast of Guangdong Province. **Large oil fields** have also been found underneath the Tarim Basin, in Guizhou, off the coast of Beijing and Tianjin, in the northeastern region between Harbin and Shenyang, and all along the east coast.

These fossil fuels and the **tremendous potential in hydraulic power** could supply the Chinese with enough energy for the coming decades.

Further prospecting for mineral resources is still going on and attempts have been made in recent years to exploit the minerals which occur in Tibet and Xinjiang. China has deposits of iron, lead, zinc, copper, mercury, antimony, bauxite, tungsten, silver, gold, uranium, and platinum – enough mineral resources to support the modernization of China's industry without resort to outside help.

The **main problem** here, however, is the **proper means to exploit** these mineral resources. Most of them, especially the oil and natural gas deposits, are usually found in the thinly populated and remote regions of the country, so that they must first be transported to the industrial centres of central China.

Flora and Fauna

In China there are more than **30,000 higher forms of plantlife.** These also include those that are common throughout the northern hemisphere. China's climate is influenced by both the continental landmasses in the north and northwest and the monsoon winds coming in from the south and southwest. The vegetation zones therefore run along this southeast to northwest axis. In accordance with the actual range of the monsoon winds, **wet woodland zones** are found in the far south, the southeast, and along the coast towards the north. Adjoining these forests there are the **temperate grasslands,** followed by the **steppe and desert regions** of the north and northwest. The **cold coniferous zone** is found in the woodland regions in the far north of China, along the Hinggan Mountains. Larch, spruce, and pine grow in this region and the winters are extremely cold. The wood from these trees is used to manufacture boats, carts, musical instruments, and paper. This area forms one of China's major timber reserves.

The remaining areas of northern China belong to the **temperate deciduous forest zone.** Here one finds deciduous forests that are similar to those in Europe and North America, with elm, maple, birch, ash, and oak. Extensive oak forests and mixed oak and pine forests exist in the Liaodong and Shandong peninsulas. The leaves of the oak are used as nourishment for the silkworms that produce the so-called raw silk. This region is also well suited for

growing other temperate zone products such as apples, peaches, dates, persimmons, walnuts, chestnuts, and grapes. Furthermore, the plains of this region are major areas for the cultivation of cotton, wheat and other grain crops.

The **subtropical forest regions** extend northward along the east coast from Shanghai to Fujian and westward down the Yangzi River to the province of Sichuan and northern Yunnan. It is the largest region of subtropical forests to be found in these latitudes. Along the same latitudes, America, Africa, and south-west Asia generally have dry climate and deserts. More than 10,000 types of plants grow alone in the fertile

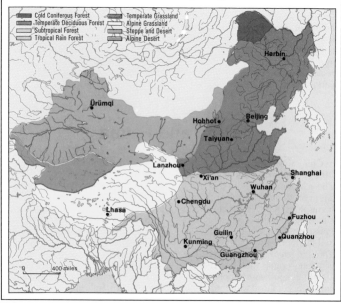

Cold Coniferous Forest
Temperate Deciduous Forest
Subtropical Forest
Tropical Rain Forest
Temperate Grassland
Alpine Grassland
Steppe and Desert
Alpine Desert

Herbin
Ürümqi
Hohhot • Beijing
Taiyuan •
Lanzhou •
• Xi'an
Wuhan
Shanghai
• Chengdu
Lhasa
Fuzhou
Guilin
Kunming
Quanzhou
Guangzhou

0   400 miles

province of Sichuan. Here one can even find forms of plant life which existed in different parts of the world several million years ago, during the Tertiary period, e. g. the **ginkgo tree.** Some of these trees are over 1,000 years old. The wood of the ginkgo is used in building, for carvings, and to make printing blocks. The seeds are edible and are used as a remedy for bronchial illnesses. The **metasequoia tree,** found on the border between Sichuan and Hubei, is also a relic from the flora of the Tertiary period.

Bamboo grows all over the mountains and there are **tea plantations** in the red earth regions of Sichuan and Hebei. Olives are important products of this region, especially the **tung tree** and **lacquer tree,** the wood of which is used for manufacturing various articles of daily use and handicrafts. The **tallow tree** is valued for the oil which is extracted from its seeds. **Oranges** and **tangerines** are also grown here in large plantations, while **Chinese conifers** provide the farming industry with valuable wood. Huge **forests of bamboo** grow in the province of Sichuan at altitudes of between 2,000 and 3,000 metres (6,560 and 9,840 feet). The leaves and sprouts of the bamboo serve the **giant panda** as nourishment. The **mountain country** of the southwest might be likened to a large natural garden being an area where **azaleas, primroses, and camellias** flourish.

Tropical rain forests are to be found in the southern part of Guangdong Province, Fujian, Taiwan, Yunnan, and Guangxi. Various types of trees grow in this hot and humid climate, some of which reach a height of 40 metres (130 feet) or more. Many of the thick trunks are supported by mighty roots that also grow several yards high. **Epiphytic farns** and **orchids** adorn the trees.

Mangroves form huge **aquatic forests.** These trees are supported and protected from wind and weather by a network of roots growing above the surface. The tips of the roots, which project out of the water, supply the trees with fresh oxygen. Obviously numerous tropical fruits also thrive here, such as **bananas, lychees,** and **mangoes.** The brigades and communes cultivate **betel nuts, rubber, coconuts, coffee, cocoa, black pepper, oil palms, pineapples, sugar cane,** and **hemp.** Taiwan and Guangdong are among the major producers of **sugar cane** and **camphor,** a distillate of camphor wood which is used in both medicinal and technical fields.

The northeastern plains and the eastern part of Inner Mongolia form an extensive steppe region with a temperate and dry climate. The ground here is predominantly covered with various kinds of grasses. Despite continued efforts to increase arable farming, the raising of livestock such as **sheep, goats, cattle,** and **horses** still predominates in this area. Summers are brief here, but when the flowers of the steppe come into bloom, the area is transformed into a mass of brilliant colours.

Some of the major products of this region are **soya beans, sorghum, and sugar-beet.** Due to the

Lotus Blossom

rich soil and conditions which are favourable to irrigation, the northern Chinese loess lands which form part of the pasture region have been widely cultivated.

The **alpine steppe regions** are located in the eastern and southern part of the Tibet/Qinghai Plateau. Here, at an average altitude of 4,000 metres (13,120 feet), there is hardly any summer at all. And yet the season is long enough for the melting glaciers to bring about the formation of rivers, brooks and lakes. Thus sufficient water is provided for a single, albeit meagre harvest. **Yaks,** goats, and sheep can survive on the short and hard grasses that grow on the slopes of the mountains. **Winter grain crops** such as **barley** but also **peas,** are

cultivated along the valleys of this region.

Xinjiang, Gansu, and the Quaidam Basin are **desert regions.** Very sparse vegetation, if any at all, can grow in these sand and gravel deserts.

Vermouth and **tamarisk** are among the few plants that still thrive in this extreme climate. A remedy for intestinal ailments was once extracted from the bark and fruits of the latter. **Zygophytes, chenopudirceae and ephedra** also grow in the gravel deserts. The adrenalinlike alkaloid known as ephedrin is extracted from the ephedra (a kind of tree or bush), and it is put to various uses in medical science. Most of these sparse grasses serve as nourishment for camels. Some of the plants have very long roots reaching far into the ground in order to obtain water. In places where the ground water is closer to the surface, one can find the **Euphrates poplar,** a special species bearing two kinds of leaves. One sort looks just like regular poplar leaves, while the other resembles those of the willow. Extremely sweet **grapes** and **watermelons** also grow in oasis areas together with the **hami melon,** which is so popular all over Xinjiang.

An **alpine desert** is found in the northwestern regions at an altitude of 5,000 metres (16,400 feet). Only low **bushes** or **creepers** can survive here. Along the sides of the glacial lakes one also comes across the **tamareerceae,** a plant that is resistant to the cold and dry climate and that bears green leaves and red blossoms in the brief summer season.

The Panda

The panda bear – sometimes also called bamboo bear – has come to be regarded as something of a (Chinese) national mascot. It has even figured in the diplomatic scene.

In 1972, the Chinese sent their best table tennis players to the U. S. A. as a sign of their desire to establish diplomatic relations. In a similar gesture, former prime minister Hua Guofeng brought along a number of panda bears as diplomatic gifts on his tour of Europe in 1979. In the past, bears have, for example, also been presented to Britain and America.

These popular bears with their soft black and white fur are truly appealing – one is very tempted to cuddle them as one would a teddy bear. In the meantime, even the **World Wildlife Fund** (WWF) has made use of the panda's general popularity. They have adopted the panda bear as the emblem of their organization. Today, pandas are no longer given away as gifts because they are threatened by extinction in China. Additionally, these sensitive animals are difficult to keep in captivity and they usually will not mate under such conditions. The first time that a panda gave birth to a cub in captivity was at the Beijing zoo in 1963. At birth, the panda cub is no larger than a full-grown white mouse and only weighs 100 grammes. It is covered with thin white hair and is quite unable to crawl for the first three months. During this time, it is always carried by the female.

It is no longer dependent on its mother after 6 months and is sexually mature in 6 to 7 years.

A full-grown panda weighs somewhere between 100 and 130 kilos (220 to 285 pounds). It dislikes either extreme heat or cold, preferring temperatures between 50°F (10°C) and 77°F (25°C).

Zoologists assume that the panda was common throughout southern China during the Pleistocene, 500,000 to 600,000 years ago. Later on, vast regions with bamboo groves were cleared for cultivation by an ever spreading civilization. The panda was progressively displaced until its natural habitat was reduced to a small area located at higher elevations. Today, it only appears in Sichuan and the regions along the borders of Shaanxi and Gansu. In the meantime, it has also lost most of its predatory functions as its teeth have degenerated. Although it will occasionally prey on smaller animals, its major source of nourishment is bamboo. It feeds on the leaves and young shoots, as well as on the bark of the Chinese fir. The **Chinacane bamboo** preferred by the panda characteristically blossoms every 50 to 60 years and then withers away. This means that the panda is regularly threatened by starvation. A full-grown panda can consume up to 20 kilos (45 pounds) of bamboo leaves daily.

At present, efforts to preserve this species are being made by both Chinese and international organizations. It is strictly forbidden to hunt them and, furthermore, whoever happens to find and feed one that is starving, will receive a bounty from the government. Nearly all areas forming the natural habitat of the panda have officially been declared wild-life preserves.

China's varied climatic and vegetation zones also have many forms of **animal life.** Over 1,000 species of birds have been categorized, together with more than 400 different mammals, many of which are endemic.

The animals found in northeastern China are adapted to the cold climate. The **rodents** include **squirrels** and **chipmunks.** Among the larger herbivores there are **moose, sika, wapiti,** and **roe deer.** These in turn provide ample nourishment for the predaceous animals, the most prominent of which are **the North Chinese tiger, the leopard,** and various species of **weasels,** such as the **sable.**

The most common species of birds are the **hazelhen, pheasant, and partridge.** In northern China, along the valleys of the Huanghe and Huaihe and the loess plains, there are numerous pests, such as **field-voles, moles,** and **rabbits.**

The forests in this region were cleared at random over the generations with little thought for the future, so that only few large forest animals are left, with the exception of **deer** and **wild boars.** Only small predaceous animals still exist, such as the **badgers** and **weasels.** There are also some species of birds that only occurr in this region, like

the **reeves' pheasant** and the **rock partridge.**

Inner Mongolia, Xinjiang, and parts of Gansu and Ningxia have a dry climate and are composed of **steppe and desert regions.** The most common animals found here are rodents, like **desert rats,** and various species of hoofed animals. Large herds of **Mongolian gazelles** and **goitred gazelles** wander over the vast steppe. The **saiga** (a kind of antelope) found in the regions along the western border of Xinjiang Province is valued for its horns, which are used for medicinal purposes. The **Asian wild ass, Przevolski's horse,** and the **wild baktrian camel** only occur in this region. The most common predators are the **grey wolf** and the **corsac.**

Notable species of birds include the **Houbara bustard, sand partridge, desert lark,** a species of the jackdaw, **cranes,** and **pheasants.**

The **Mongolian beaver,** which has a very valuable pelt, only lives in the Mongolian Altai Mountains which extend all the way to the province of Xinjiang.

The sparse vegetation of the cold and desolate Tibet/Qinghai regions offer little means of sustenance for

Pandas enjoy their meals in a relaxed position.

animal life. The **yak** and the **Tibetan antilope** are able to live off the sparse grasses. The rodents include a **species of rabbit** with long and thick fur and the **Himalayan marmot,** which also has a valuable pelt. The **snow leopard** and the **Tibetan sand fox** are very rare predators.

Some of the species of birds worth mentioning are **vulture, snow cock, sand partridge,** and **snow finch.**

The mountain country in southwestern China, the provinces of Sichuan and Yunnan, and eastern Tibet are the natural habitat of the **giant panda.** It lives at altitudes of between 2,500 and 3,500 metres (8,200 and 11,500 feet). It belongs in the category of herbivores among the predators, because it feeds on **Chinacane bamboo.** This type of bamboo blossoms every 50 to 60 years and then withers. This is currently happening in many regions, so that the few pandas still living in a wild state are threatened by starvation. With the help of international organizations, the Chinese government is doing all it can to preserve this rare species. Other animals of this region include the **lesser panda,** a feline species, and the **snub-nosed langur. Marmots, musk deer,** and **hazelhens** live in the higher mountain regions. The **Great Indian Zibet** and more than ten species of **pheasants** live in the lower regions.

Central China encloses the middle and lower Yangzi regions, as well as all of its tributaries. Among the remarkable species in this area are the **stump-tailed macaque,** the **zibet** (a member of the civet family), the **Chinese pangolin** (or scaly anteater), the **great white eagret,** and the **woodpecker.** Another rare species is the blue-feathered **magpie.**

Other noteworthy animals of this region are **Chinese water deer, whitefin dolphin, Chinese bamboo partridge,** and the **golden pheasant.** The greatest number of animal species can be found in the south, in the southern part of Guangdong and Fujian and the southern Chinese islands. The **tree shrew, bats, plumploris** (a species of lemur), and the **gibbon** live among the trees of the jungles. The predators worth mentioning include the **South Chinese tiger,** the **zibet** and the **leopard. Indian elephants** live in the southern regions of Yunnan. Among the birds are such rare species as **parakeets, hornbills,** and **sunbirds.** The **green peafowl** and the **red jungle fowl** (the ancestor of the Chinese domesticated hen) are also found in southern Yunnan. The southern Chinese islands are the natural habitat of the **gannets,** whose excrement makes an excellent fertilizer.

Population

How many Chinese people are there? Has their number already exceeded one billion? These questions preoccupied both scholars and politicians during the 70's. Not that they were of vital importance, but they did arouse curiosity.

Since July, 1982, we know for certain that there are more than 1 billion Chinese. At exactly midnight on July 1st, 1982, there were 1,031,882,511 Chinese. This number included the inhabitants of Taiwan, Hong Kong, and the islands located between the provinces of Fujian and Taiwan. The number of people living on the mainland amounted to 1,008,175,288. (End of 1983: 1,024 billion). **Thus a quarter of the world's population lives in China, on 6.4% of the earth's surface.**

Enormous efforts were needed to conduct this census. The preparations for this project, which was also supported by international organizations like the U. N., went on for three years. The data was processed by 29 large computers. The census was carried out by several million officials whose task it was to ask people questions about their personal background, pertaining to such things as religion, profession and education.

One of the things to emerge from the census was that there still were **23.5% illiterates** or semi-literates among the population (as compared with 38.1% in 1964). Approximately 6 million people were attending institutions of higher learning or were in possession of a university qualification or its equivalent, 66 million passed school leaving certificate, 178 million merely fulfilled the minimum requirements for leaving school, and about 355 million only received an elementary education.

There is a **surplus of males** in China. The men make up 51.5% of the population and the women 48.5%.

The Han Chinese make up 93.3% of the total population and the rest is comprised of national minorities. One fifth of the Chinese live in cities, which means that 80% still live in the country. If one compares the 1964 estimates, the urban population has grown by 62.5%.

The **largest cities** are **Shanghai,** with 11.8 million inhabitants, **Beijing,** with 9.2 million, and **Tianjin,** with 7.7 million. If one compares these figures with those of other countries, however, one must take into consideration that Chinese cities are drawn up as very large administrative sectors. This means that the inhabitants of surrounding districts are counted as well as those living in the cities themselves. In Beijing, for instance, only some 6 million people actually live within the city. The remaining 3 million are spread throughout the districts administratively affiliated with the city.

A **large administrative sector** was just recently established in the province of Sichuan that takes in some 13 million people. As one consequence of this bureaucratic measure, Dazu now belongs to the administrative sector of Chongqing, even though it is 180 kilometres (112 miles) away.

The average **density of population** in China is calculated at approximately **108 inhabitants per square kilometre** (280 per square mile). This, however, is a misleading figure, because there are few countries in the world with such an **uneven distribution of population** as China. Whereas **in Shanghai there are 2,000 inhabitants per square kilometre** (5,000 per square mile), the figure for the whole of **Tibet is only 1.5** per square kilometre (3.8 per square mile). The most densely populated regions are those of the **North Chinese Lowlands,** including the provinces of **Shandong, Jiangsu,** and **Henan,** as well as those of the province of **Sichuan** in China's interior. The regions around the estuary of the Yangzi River are also heavily populated. This means that about 80% of the Chinese population lives in the eastern and southeastern regions of the country, on only one fifth of China's territory.

The **North Chinese Lowlands** and the **loess regions along the Yellow River** are the **cradles of Chinese civilization.** This is where historians and archaeologists discovered the earliest settlements. The very first dynasties emerged in the valley of the Wei River, a tributary of the Huanghe (Yellow River). The first historically documented census in China was taken **in the year 2 A.D.** At this time, the imperial territory of the Han Dynasty had a population of **57.6 million.** Several other counts were made by various dynasties. Quite unlike Europe, with its small feudal states, in China a centralized form of government played an important role quite early.

The major reason for repeated census taking was the enlistment of subjects for compulsory labour or military service. Later, it was instituted for taxation purposes.

The development of the Chinese population was continually affected by the warlike nomadic tribes living along the northern borders of the empire. Their unrelenting wars of conquest pushed the Chinese farther and farther south in the course of the centuries. Only in this region were the peasants able to find suitable conditions for agriculture. The Chinese in turn either displaced the inhabitants of these areas or eventually assimilated them. During the **period of the Mongolian invasions,** when Genghis Khan and his successors led campaigns to conquer China, there was a **drastic reduction of the population.** The population did not start to grow again noticeably until the 17th and 18th centuries.

China experienced its first great increase in population, **a veritable explosion,** during **modern times.** The **1953** census, the first one taken after the founding of the People's Republic of China, registered **583 million inhabitants on the mainland.** When we compare this to the 1982 census, it becomes obvious that **the Chinese population has nearly doubled since the People's Republic was first established in 1949.** This could very well be an even greater problem for the economic development of China than her lack of modern technology. The population explosion came about because of improvements in social and medical facilities, which reduced infant mortality rates and raised the average life expectancy substantially. Famines and natural disasters could now also be averted – factors that had previously decimated the population by millions in a most brutal manner.

The problem was not taken seriously enough in the first decades of the People's Republic. Although warnings were uttered, Mao Zedong's notion that a large population constituted China's greatest wealth carried the day.

Today efforts are being made to rectify the mistakes of the past by implementing a **strict policy of population control. Chinese families are required to have one child only,** in the hopes that this measure will eventually bring about a marked reduction in the growth of the population. Chinese demographers expect this plan to stabilize the population at 1.2 billion and slowly bring it back again to 1 billion in the coming decades. The programme for the one-child-family has been accepted by the urban population, but the peasants still cling to traditional concepts. For many of them a lot of children still stand for happiness, prosperity and, above all, a secure old age. By offering material benefits to those who comply with this directive and penalising the families who do not, it is hoped that the programme will eventually succeed in lowering and stabilizing the growth of population.

National Minorities

All citizens of the People's Republic of China are called **Zhong uoren** which literally means people from the Middle Kingdom. When talking in ethnic terms, however, Han is used to designate the largest group of the population – i. e the Chinese people themselves. The term Han was borrowed from the 2,000-year-old Han Dynasty. The **Han Chinese** presently make up **93.3%** of the entire population.

The remaining 6.7%, or approximately 68 million people, belong to a total of **56 ethnic minorities.**

The 56 nationalities are officially recognized as minorities and are granted **special rights.** The ethnic minorities have cultural, social, linguistic, and psychological characteristics that clearly set them apart from the society they live in. In previous centuries they had often set up their own kingdoms. At times they had even managed to subjugate the Middle Kingdom, i. e. the Mongols, Manchurians, or Tibetans.

Emperors of various dynasties were dependent upon the goodwill of the ethnic peoples living along the borders. Sometimes they accomplished this with military force, but the practice of making gifts was also common, as was the offer of a princess's hand in marriage.

Reference is still made today to the fact that Tibetan King Srongstan Gampo married a Chinese princess, Wen Cheng, in 641 and some people still insist that this is proof of Tibet belonging to China.

After the founding of the People's Republic of China in 1949, the minorities were granted **autonomous regions.** These are territories with the same status as provinces, districts, or municipalities. The rights of autonomy include the independent regulation of economic, financial, and cultural matters and the prerogative of sending a representative to the National People's Congress. The languages of the individual minority groups are also maintained. They are **officially recognized as secondary languages** and are taught as part of the school curriculum. Newspapers in the languages of the minorities are published as well. Large minorities like the Tibetans, Mongols, Manzhu, or Uighurs are able to look back on their own great cultures, histories, and traditions. Many of the smaller minorities in the south on the other hand, (especially those from the province of Yunnan) only have between ten and one hundred thousand members who have been living in relatively primitive social conditions up until this century. Many of these minority groups did not even have a system of writing.

Minority institutes were established in several towns for the purpose of conducting research on the history of these ehtnic peoples and to promote their welfare. Efforts have also been made to develop native orthographies. Members of these minorities are being trained as cadres, teachers, and civil servants at these institutes.

National Minorities in China

Name	Numbers	Settlement Areas	Language Religion
Mongols (Mongolians)	2.7 mil.	Inner Mongolia, Liaoning, Xinjiang, Jilin, Heilongjiang, Qinghai, Hebei, Gansu	Mongolian Lamaism
Hui	6.5 mil.	primarily in Ningxia, Gansu, and Shaanxi, but also in many other provinces	Chinese Islam (religious minority group)
Tibetans	3.5 mil.	Tibet, Sichuan, Qinghai, Gansu, Yunnan	Tibetan, Lamaism
Uighurs	5.5 mil.	Xinjiang	Uighur, Islam
Miao	4.0 mil.	Guizhou, Yunnan, Guangxi	Miao, some are Christian
Yi	4.9 mil.	Yunnan, Sichuan, Guizhou	Yi, none
Zhuang	12.1 mil.	Guangxi	Zhuang and Chinese, none
Bouyei	1.7 mil.	Guizhou	Bouyei and Chinese, none
Koreans	1.7 mil.	Jilin, Heilongjiang, Liaoning, Inner Mongolia	Korean, some Buddhists
Manzhu (Manchus)	2.7 mil.	Liaoning, Heilongjiang, Jilin, Hebei, Beijing, Inner Mongolia	Chinese, none
Dong	1.2 mil.	Guizhou, Hunan, Guangxi	Dong and Chinese
Yao	1.3 mil.	Guangxi, Hunan, Yunnan, Guizhou, Guangdong	Yao and Chinese
Bai	1.1 mil.	Yunnan	Bai and Chinese

It is very much in the interests of the central government in Beijing to maintain good relations with the minority groups. **Even though they only make up 6.7% of the population, they nevertheless inhabit approximately half of China's territory and almost all of the border regions.** Kinship ties among the ethnic peoples extend beyond the borders of China. In the north, the autonomous regions of the Mongols and the Uighurs border on the Soviet Union. In the south and the southwest, the province of Yunnan which borders on Burma, Laos, and Vietnam, is inhabited by Tibetans and many other minorities.

However, one should not over-look the fact that the central government has also had troubles with these minorities. During the border conflicts with the Soviet Union towards the end of the sixties, several thousand people moved from the autonomous region of Xinjiang to the Soviet Union. During the Cultural Revolution, demands were made for the process of assimilation among the ethnic minorities to be speeded up. Consequently, nearly half of Inner Mongolia's territory was added to the northern provinces of Heilongjiang, Jilin, and Liaoning, and to the western autonomous region of Ningxia during the middle of the sixties. This policy has only recently been reversed again.

Even the Chinese admit to having made grave mistakes as far as Tibet is concerned. What promoted separatist actions in Tibet more than anything else, was the suppression of religion and the lowering of living standards. The Dalai Lama, currently living in exile in India, is still regarded as the supreme leader by the Tibetan population and tensions

are bound to exist as long as no settlement is reached between him and the Chinese government.

The post-Maoist leaders have drawn consequences out of these problems and errors. Rights of autonomy were either reinstated or expanded. The granting of religious freedom once again is primarily a concession to the minorities, many of whom are Buddhists.

The one exception among the minorities are the Hui. Ethnically they belong to the Han Chinese, but they are considered a minority because of their Islamic beliefs. Most of them live in the provinces of Gansu, Ningxia, and Shaanxi. They have a large community with several mosques in the capital city of Xi'an.

The above table lists the 13 largest minorities with more than 1 million members. The smallest minorities are the Hezhen from the province of Heilongjiang, with just 800 members, and the Russian community in Xinjiang which has a mere 600 members.

Writing and Language

Writing is one of the most ancient cultural achievements of this country, but it is also one of the things that causes Westerners consternation making us aware of the vast differences between China and the West. Without the help of our accustomed Latin letters, most of what we (as tourists) see and experience in China will appear like an impenetrable labyrinth to us. What is one to do if the names of streets are

undecipherable or if one is confronted by signs covered with inextricable Chinese characters while searching for a toilet?

We also ask ourselves just how the Chinese can cope with such a vast number of characters. It is not easy for them either, because day to day life alone requires a knowledge of about 3,000 characters. Some 800 to 1,000 symbols will suffice to understand simple newspaper texts, however. **The Chinese system of writing has produced a total of 50,000 characters in the course of its development.** Although Chinese children learn to speak the language as quickly as say English or French children learn to speak their own language, it still requires much time and practice for them to learn how to use the characters.

Undoubtedly this system of writing, which is partially based on pictographs, also has its advantages. It is probably true to say that the Chinese do not have too many problems reading and understanding ancient Chinese, even though it has undergone many changes. (The interpretation given to certain characters has changed, too.) It is not uncommon, however, for Chinese guides to have difficulties interpreting ancient inscriptions on tombs and temples. They may still be able to read them, but not necessarily be able to understand them.

Chinese people speaking different dialects can still communicate with each other by using the written characters. Occasionally, one may observe how someone conducting a conversation with a person unfamiliar with his own dialect will outline characters on the palm of his hand with his forefinger. This suffices to establish some kind of understanding. Even the Japanese understand sufficient Chinese characters to enable them to grasp the basic meaning of a written text.

Although children have to do a lot of "cramming" in order to learn how to use and pronounce the numerous characters, they have little difficulty with grammar, as there are

no inflections in Chinese. One merely needs to pay attention to the sentence structure. Tenses are formed by using auxiliary words, or syllables.

The word chi, for example, means eat. "Chi le ma?" is a common form of greeting meaning: "Have you eaten?" The word, or syllable, chi remains unchanged. In order to use the past tense, the auxiliary syllable "le" is added and the "ma" indicates that the interrogatory form is being used.

Consequently, it is much easier for foreigners to learn how to speak the language than to write it.

An additional difficulty, however, is the matter of **intonation.** The use of 4 different tones of voice in pronunciation increases the phonetic store of syllables from 400 to about 1,600.

The first tone sounds somewhat high pitched, but is evenly spoken. It is represented by a straight dash in Latin transcription, as in the word Chī. The second tone rises, Chí; the third falls and then rises, Chǐ; and the fourth falls abruptly, Chì. **Proper intonation is absolutely necessary for the understanding of single words, because each tone of voice gives them a different meaning.** It is often easier to sense the meaning out of the context of longer sentences.

It is not uncommon for the same syllables pronounced in the same way to still have different meanings. If we continue with the example Chi:

Chī (first tone) could mean:
  spirits, owl, eat, stupid
Chí (second tone) could mean:
  pond, arrest, running, slow
Chǐ (third tone) could mean:
  undress, wasteful, shame, tooth
Chì (fourth tone) could mean:
  burning, wing, red, command.
Of course, the written character for each one of these is also different.

The people who complain the most about the disadvantages of this pictographic system of writing patterned after the environment are the scientists. Indeed, there are a series of problems. New knowledge and inventions are continually being brought forth by the sciences and these in turn require new terminology. How is one to describe complicated acids or other chemical compounds in Chinese? It is either necessary to create new characters or make up a series of words composed of several syllables, each one having its own meaning. **Unlike our own alphabet, Chinese characters cannot simply be interchanged in order to make new words.**

Furthermore, how is one to deal with thousands of characters in the new age of computerized information? Chinese scientists have actually experimented in this sector and it appears that it is indeed possible to use characters in computers. Nevertheless, this would require much more expensive storage facilities.

There have been efforts to reform the system of writing since the beginning of this century. These have been renewed recently, but the solution is still not in sight. The more radical reforms attempted to introduce the Latin alphabet as quickly as possible. **Today, students are required to learn Latin transcription, Hanyu pinyin, as well as the old characters.** Now one can see transcription used more frequently in the cities for street-signs, billboards, and information boards. It has been in use for some time among the minorities (who often speak a completely different language) in order to make it easier for them to learn Chinese. But the use of the Latin alphabet has continuously been hampered by the passive resistance of the population. This does not come as too much of a surprise in a country in which the majority of the inhabitants were illiterate until fairly recently.

Nevertheless, the characters have been simplified by several reforms. Symbols that were once composed of 15 to 20 brush strokes, only need 5, 6, or maybe 7 of them today.

Chinese writing is more than 4,000 years old. The earliest records (in the form of symbols or marks) are those found on the neolithic pottery of the Yangshao and Longshan cultures. Then there are the oracles carved on bones or tortoiseshells that date back to the Shang Dynasty (1600–1100 B. C.).

Emperor Qin Shi Huang Di (221–206) passed the first reform of the writing system, making it more unified. His chancellor Li Si compiled a register of seals containing about 3,000 characters.

Meng Tiang, a Qin general, is credited with introducing the writing brush and the process of making paper was discovered in 105 A.D. by the eunuch Cai Lun. However, with the development of the political system and the progressive polarization of the social classes, written language became the exclusive art of scholars. The simple people remained illiterate and had to make do with the spoken language only.

The classical form of written language, in which every syllable represents a word and whose meaning is generally only apparent to people skilled in the interpretation of these syllables, has remained a mystery to most of the common people. Literary publications in the vernacular were not considered to be acceptable until the Yuan Era, during the reign of the Mongols. People continued to disdain this particular genre up until the present century.

The vernacular was not really socially acceptable until the cultural and literary revolutions of the 4th of May Movement took place in 1919. Above all it was the students and younger intellectuals who wanted to make the written language more accessible to the general population.

Modern Chinese has little in common with the classical written form. One obvious change is that contemporary Chinese people write from left to right (horizontally). But the old style of writing from top right to bottom left is still being practiced by calligraphers and lyricists.

A reform in the system of writing is also complicated by the fact that so many dialects are spoken. The dialects of the northern Chinese and Cantonese people for instance, are so different from each other that the only way to communicate is through a common system of writing.

The Shanghai, or Wu, dialect is spoken in the regions along the estuary of the Yangzi and the Hokkien dialect is common for Fujian. There are eight major dialects and more than 100 local variations in all. The government has been trying to establish a standard language since the days of the Republic. **Mandarin (putong hua), the northern Chinese dialect, is recognized as being the standard language.**

Although the national minorities only make up approximately 6% of the population, they in fact represent a number of major linguistic families. The languages spoken by the minorities of the southwest and Tibet belong to the Tibeto-Chinese family.

Altaic languages are spoken by the minorities in Xinjiang, among them the Uighurs, Kazakhs, Usbeks, Kirghiz, Mongols, and Manchus. The Tajiks and the few Russians living in China belong to a branch of the Indo-European linguistic family.

The number of different transcriptions of the Chinese language available often cause some confusion among foreigners. Does one write Peking or Beijing; Mao Zedong or Mao Tsetung; Guanzhou, Guangchou, or Canton? Matteo Ricci, the Jesuit priest who lived in China from 1583 to 1610, was the first to make a Latin transcription. In the centuries that followed, a whole series of new and different transcriptions were developed.

Every single European nation likes to use a transcription that is adapted to its own language.

The system of transcription used throughout this guide is the Hanyu-Pinyin transcription which was introduced by the Chinese government on January 1st, 1979. The reason for this is that it is currently being used in all Chinese publications and it is the most widely used form in China itself.

No transcription can possibly give an exact rendition of the correct Chinese pronunciation. Therefore, we are including a brief guide to pronunciation here, which tries to render the proper pronunciation of Chinese as **accurately** as possible.

In the following table, sounds of the Chinese phonetic alphabet have been allocated equivalent or similar sounds which occur in the English language. (Where no equivalent exists in English examples have been taken from German and French.)

1. Consonants

Chinese	Equivalent
b (o)	**b**ar
p (o)	**p**artner
m (o)	**m**ile
f (o)	**f**arm
d (e)	**d**art
t (e)	**t**ap
n (e)	**n**arrow
l (e)	**l**augh
g (e)	**R**eagan
k (e)	**k**id
h (e)	**h**at
j (i)	**j**eep
q (i)	**ch**eer
x (i)	like the German i**ch**
zh (i)	**j**uniper
ch (i)	i**tch**
sh (i)	**sh**ort
r (i)	a sound between r and j, similar to French rou**ge**, (tongue curved upwards without touching palate)
z (i)	ban**ds**
c (i)	le**ts**
s (i)	li**st** (voiceless)
y (i)	p**ie**ce
w (u)	**w**hisky

2. Vowels

Chinese	English
a	**a**rt
o	**o**pen
e	broth**er**
i (after z, c, s, zh, ch, sh, r)	i not voiced, the initial consonant is drawn out, nearly hummed
i	m**e**
u	m**oo**t
ü	f**ew**
er	**are**
ai	l**ie**
ei	**ate**
ao	t**ow**n
ou	**o** short, **u** long
an	c**an**
en	Rub**en**
ang	s**ang**
eng	nasal sound
ong	l**ung**
ia	**ya**cht
ie	**ye**t
iao	m**eow**
iu	**you**
ian	**yen**
in	**in**
iang	**Yang**zi River
ing	s**ing** (voiceless g)
ion	(voiceless g)

ua	**va**t
uo	**vo**te
uai	**vi**tal
ui	**ve**t
uan	**va**n
un	like German **wun**derbar, or **fun** with v instead of f
uang	**vang**uard
üe	short **ü**, then **e** as in y**et**
üan	short **ü**, then an
ün	as in French **une**, fort**une**

The general rule for all vowels beginning with u is that the u is barely indicated and is then followed by the next sound, which is voiced briefly.

The last three vowels beginning with ü are not mutated in the Hanyu-Pinyin transcription. But if a u directly follows the consonants j, q, x, or y, it is mutated: thus the word **yun** (cloud) is actually pronounced **yün** (yuen).

Philosophies and Religions

Confucianism

In contrast to many other cultures, Chinese thought has never manifested itself in just one religion. China has never had a religious system or an ecclesiastical organization comparable to Christianity, Buddhism, or Islam – unless it was introduced from the outside, by another culture.

Confucianism is a realistic and worldly oriented moral philosophy. Like many other religions, it has influenced Chinese life and thought for two thousand years, but only as a series of **guidelines designed to perfect life and human nature.** It should not be understood as any kind of promise for a life after death. **Kong Fuzi** – the name can be loosely translated as "Great Master Kong", whereas Confucius is just a commonly used transcription – was born 551 B.C. in Qufu, in the state of Lu. Being the son of wealthy parents he was able to obtain a comprehensive education. Like most other scholars of his

times, he first wandered around the country seeking employment with one of the nobles. The great Zhou Dynasty was on the verge of collapse at that time and numerous small and independent feudal states had begun to emerge. At a later date he began to instruct the students who had gathered around him. Nothing written by Confucius himself has been preserved. Everything that has remained was taken down by his students. **Four canonical volumes – the Yijing** (I Ching), a book of oracles, **the Shijing** (Book of Poetry), **the Liji** (Book of Rites), and **the Shujing** (Book of History) – are attributed to him, as well as **the Chunqiu** (Spring and Autumn Annals), a chronicle of the state Lu. Historical proof for this, however, is not readily available. For centuries, all Chinese scholars had to study and master these writings in order to take the imperial examinations. One of the most authentic works is the **Lunyu**, which contains conversations with

An Imperial state official. The European word "Mandarin" comes from the Sanscrit and means "advisor".

Confucius recorded by his students. Central to the Confucian philosophy is the basic assumption that man is naturally good and able to perfect his human nature by conducting himself according to certain principles. By behaving in a humane way towards others and observing the five cardinal virtues of love, honesty, wisdom, sincerity, and morality, he may become a noble person. **Such a noble person can be recognized by his comportment, rather than his social status.** To be able to attain human perfection, however, it is absolutely necessary to follow specific rules. Confucius had the social relationships between people in mind when he formulated these ethic rules. According to Confucian belief women have to subordinate themselves to men, sons must obey their fathers, younger brothers must do as their older brothers tell them, and so forth. The relationships that are supposed to create harmony within the family, the microcosm of the state, are also applied to the state as a whole. Consequently, Confucianism demands the strict loyalty of all subjects to their rulers. On the other hand, the latter should base their power on trust instead of tyranny.

This particular aspect of his philosophy has often led modern historians to see Confucius as a reactionary, who contributed to the maintenance of slavery during the Zhou Dynasty. This view, which was most vehemently postulated by the leftist historians during the Cultural Revolution, is no longer strictly adhered to. Today, one is also willing to point out the aspects of humaneness and equality inherent in his teachings.

Confucianism became the state cult during the Han Dynasty. Nevertheless, it had to compete continuously with other teachings or religions, such as Taoism, Moism, and above all Buddhism. Confucianism experienced a renaissance after the persecution of Buddhists during the Tang Dynasty. The scholar **Zhu Xi** (1130–1200) is said to be the founder of **Neo-Confucianism.** He formulated the concept of the **Great Ultimate,** the highest of all principles. It becomes manifest in things and human beings through a certain force. Depending on the distribution of this force, mankind can either be good or evil. But moral and ethical behaviour can help him achieve the Great Ultimate and become a noble person.

The idealistic philosophy of Confucianism can no longer withstand **the challenges posed by the natural sciences.** Still, its ethic and moral codes regulating social behaviour have persevered in modern times. The lowly status of the women in the rural areas, the wish for a first-born son among the peasants, and the partial subservience towards superiors would indicate that more Confucian traditions have persisted up until today than one might suppose.

Moism

Mozi (or Mo Ti) lived in the state of Song about one hundred years after Confucius' death. His philosophy is more radical than Confucius'. This is probably why it didn't gain much support from the educated circles which were composed primarily of noble families at that time. **The central issue in his philosophy is the condemnation of war and he was, in all likelihood, the first** **author of pacifist essays in the history of philosophy.** Confucius had also condemned war occasionally, but never in such detail and in such a decided manner. The important difference between them was that Confucius condemned war as a vice whereas Mozi rejected offensive warfare on the basis of rational considerations. He simply felt that it was harmful for the people. Virtue itself was not so much an issue for Mozi, but rather the notion that **all activity, especially that of the rulers, had to be based on the simple principle of whether or not it served the good of the people.** According to him, offensive wars are reprehensible because they are detrimental to the people, who have to bear all of the consequences. In this sense, he accused the rulers of having double standards, for they openly condemned the theft of a peach out of a neighbour's garden yet at the same time rejoiced at the occupation of another country. **His notions of morality are also more radical than those of Confucius.** His argument was that since all men were created equal by nature, the same standard of virtue and morality applied to everyone. His philosophy left no room for hierarchical structures in social relationships. He even condemned the extravagances and expenditures incurred by rulers during rituals. One of his essays is aptly titled "Simplicity at Burials". **According to Mozi, the guiding principle for all actions should be the will of Heaven.** The latter demands **justice, humaneness, and prosperity for all.** Heaven will punish wrong deeds by actively interfering in earthly affairs. By rejecting their belief in fate, people should be instilled with courage to **actively participate in the process of life,** rather than accepting all things as given. The Moists were critical of Confucianists' conservative bearing, which was due to their belief in irrefutable social hierarchies.

Legalism

The Legalists posed the first major threat to Confucianists. The fore-runners of Legalism were **Guanzi** (7th century B. C.), who first developed the idea of a constitutional state, and **Shang Yang** (390–338 B. C.), who developed a system of laws based on punishments and rewards. The foremost scholar of the Legalist school was **Han Feizi** (280–233 B. C.). He combined all of the ideas of his predecessors and reshaped them into a uniform theory of government, which he helped to put into practice in the state of Qin.

The Legalists had little faith in the goodness of man, considering him to be naturally evil. They did nod even believe that trust was any basis for the authority and power of a ruler. If the laws are weak, they argued, then the system of government will also be weak. **Whoever places trust in others, will himself be ruled.** According to Legalist doctrines, sovereigns should rule on the basis of strict laws that prescribe exactly the function of each individual. Any violations of these laws were to be punished most severely.

Because they regarded the landed nobility as being responsible for the disruption of the empire, they turned instead to the state officials, peasants, and soldiers for support.

Only the ruler is above the law and, with the aid of his state officials, he should have a firm hold on the government. **Power is to be solely concentrated in the hands of the ruler.** In Emperor Qin Shi Huang Di the Legalists found a sovereign who was eager to adopt their ideas. The tyrannical notions of government were combined with a **disdain for culture and literature.** In 213 B. C. they carried out the first book-burnings in history. All of the Confucian writings were fed to the flames. But the Legalists did not stop here. Since the law demanded the severe punishment of all violators of the law, they had 400 Confucianists publicly executed at the capital city of Xianyang.

The confrontation between Confucianists and Legalists flared up again during the Cultural Revolution. By criticizing Confucius, the radicals actually intended to strike a blow against the moderates around Zhou Enlai. The Legalist notions of a rigid and centralized state machinery went well in hand with the demand for an omnipotent proletarian dictatorship under the Gang of Four. This probably explains why they chose the Legalists for propaganda purposes rather than Mozi, whose philosophy was much more closely related to the ideals of Communism.

Popular Beliefs

The various philosophical schools obviously found supporters primarily from among the educated classes; their teachings remained inaccessible to the common people. **The desire in China to find explanations for natural and social phenomena also manifested itself in archaic cults and beliefs,** such as animism, shamanism, and ancestor worship.

Ancestor worship is one of the more basic forms of popular beliefs, going back to the mythical beginnings of Chinese history. Since it was a private matter for each family to pay homage to its ancestors, there was no reason for a priesthood to develop. **The highest official ceremonies in honour of the ancestors were conducted by the emperors themselves.** The peasants' wish for a first-born son – still common in the rural areas today – stems from the belief that **only the eldest son may continue the practice of ancestor worship.** Every household has its own ancestral altar. The wealthier families of the feudal lords always began the day with a ceremony in honour of the ancestors. These ceremonies were considered to be absolutely necessary, as there was a common belief in the existence of spirits that could determine the fate of humans.

The souls of humans leave the body after death to become either benevolent or evil spirits. The souls of those ancestors who had misbehaved or met with an accident would turn into evil spirits. They had to be appeased with daily ceremonies, in the hope that they would eventually find peace again and become benevolent spirits. The benevolent spirits were asked to intercede with the gods.

It is impossible to assess how many deities there were. River and mountain gods were commonly worshipped as well as deities of the sun, wind, thunder, and rain. **Local cults** developed in every region. In some places, the people worshipped deities that were exclusively known to their villages. Shamans cured the sick, prayed for rain, ended misfortunes among families, and guaranteed a good harvest.

One of the most popular deities was the **Kitchen God.** He was said to live above every hearth, from where he would observe what the families were doing. Once every year he would climb up to heaven and deliver a report. On this specific day, various ceremonies would take place in order to encourage the Kitchen God to make a positive report.

Many of the old houses still have **spirit walls.** These are supposed to prevent evil spirits from entering because the latter are quite unable to turn corners. The high thresholds in older palaces e. g. the Imperial Palace, and simple residences fulfill the same purpose.

The people also paid homage to **mythical figures** or alternatively to **actual persons,** who had achieved something great, elevating both to the level of gods. One of them was the **War God Guandi.** Guandi was a general in the Han Dynasty, whose glorious deeds were recorded in a novel entitled "History of the Three Kingdoms". He is still quite often depicted dressed in a fine brocaded robe and having a bright red face, which is symbolic for loyalty, sincerity, and bravery.

Taoism

Taoism emerged at about the same time as Confucianism. Whereas much is known about Confucius, there is very little evidence of the existence of **Laozi,** the supposed founder of Taosim. Laozi simply means "Old Master". He is still portrayed as an ancient old man with a bald head and a large, round forehead. In his left hand he holds the Peach of Immortality. Some consider it possible that the Taoists teachings do not stem from one scholar alone, but from several different individuals. **It would be very much in keeping with Taoist beliefs if its founder and foremost teacher had actually renounced any claim to notoriety and fame.**

This mystery has stimulated the fabrication of legends surrounding his life. The most famous of these is about the origin of the **Tao-te Ching** (Book of the Way and Virtue). It recounts that Laozi was emigrating to western China on a black ox, when a customs official asked him to leave something set down in writing behind. Thereupon Laozi wrote down the 5,000-word Tao-te Ching.

Tin Hai, the heavenly mother of the West, is also often seen.

Tao is usually translated as **"way"**, although some consider that **"reason"** or **"mind"** would be a more appropriate rendering. **Te** is commonly translated as **"virtue"**, but it can also mean **"nature"** or **"being"**.

Tao is an eternal cosmic principle inherent in all things. **Nature itself stands at the centre of the Taoist teachings,** and not mankind, as is the case with Confucianism. All of man's actions should be aimed at living in total harmony with nature. Man can live in spontaneous harmony with nature through frugality and meditation, without having to act rationally. In order to understand nature, or Tao, one must first refrain from earthly endeavours and desires. **The Taoist chooses meditation and solitude.** According to the Taoist theory of government, taking no action at all is the best maxim for rulers. It says in the Tao-te Ching that the best kind of government is one that the people are not even aware of. **Rather than the centralized form of civil government sought by the Confucianists, the ideal of the Taoists** would be **a number of smaller and peacefully coexisting communities.** Numerous references are made in Taoist legends to scholars stubbornly refusing to assume any political obligations.

Here there are **certain similarities to Buddhism,** which also teaches that one must turn away from human desires and passions in order to reach salvation. Even though Tao is not the same as the Buddhist Nirvana, both philosophies are in agreement that earthly endeavours only lead to disharmony, harm, and misfortune. **Chan Buddhism** ultimately emerged out of the meeting between these two teachings and rapidly spread in Japan under the name of **Zen Buddhism.**

One of the Taoist schools also involved itself with **magical practices.** Taoist alchemists tried early on to find potions for immortality. The taking of such remedies or drugs was supposed to preserve the vitality of the body and to strengthen the organs. Others tried to attain the same goal through strict meditation, asceticism, breathing exercises, or sexual practices.

The popularization of Taoism also led to the development of a pantheon. The most important deities include **Pangu,** the creator of the world, the **Jade Emperor,** and **Laozi** himself. The Taoist temples are much more modest than the Buddhist ones. Nevertheless, the Taoist places of worship are often the scenes of colourful ceremonies, quite in contrast to Confucian temples, where only wise and benevolent rulers are paid homage.

Taoism has never played a major role in politics. The reason for it being badly received in this sphere is probably due to its central concept of taking no action, which obviously would not seem to be a practical ideology for most sovereigns.

Buddhism

For the Chinese, Buddhism is an alien religion. This doctrine of salvation developed by **Siddharta Gautama** came to China from India. As **Mahayana Buddhism,** it was passed on to the Chinese by the inhabitants of central Asia. In **Hinayana Buddhism,** the teachings of the "Lesser Vehicle", homage is only paid to the founder of Buddhism, Siddharta. Mental and spiritual efforts must be made by an individual wanting to reach **Nirvana,** which is to be understood as the permanent release from all earthly grief and not as some sort of paradise. Hinayana Buddhism also rejects the corporeal depiction of Buddha in religious art. In other words, **only symbols** are ever used, e. g. the **Teaching Wheel** or the **Bhodi Tree** of perception. Mahayana Buddhism can be said to be a popularized form of this teaching. Here a number of **Bodhisattvas** also play an important role after Buddha. Bodhisattvas have already reached the highest stages of perception, but they refrain from releasing themselves into Nirvana in order to bring salvation to the rest of mankind.

Buddhism divides the history of the world into various stages, each one being presided over by a Buddha. One will commonly see a **Buddha trinity** at monasteries and temples throughout China and Tibet. Apart from **Buddha Sakyamuni**, the trinity includes **Kasyapa,** the Buddha of the Past, and **Maitreya,** the Buddha of the Future. Some sects have established 5 or 7 such stages and the corresponding number of Buddhas. According to Mahayana teachings, every earthly Buddha has a counterpart in heaven. In the case of Buddha Sakyamuni it is **Buddha Atimabha,** the Buddha of Eternal Light. Presiding over all of the Buddhas is **Adibuddha,** the prime principle.

The Buddhas and Bodhisattvas on the altars are often flanked by Buddha Sakyamuni's pupils, of whom **Ananda,** Buddha's favorite pupil, is the most common.

Also to be seen in practically all of the temples are the **Lohans,** who

Head of a Bodhisattva (Tang Dynasty approx. 760).

are called **Arhats** in Sanskrit. Lohans are saints or sages, who have attained the highest stage of enlightenment. Only 18 of them were originally represented, but their number increased to 500 in the Chinese monasteries. The Lohans are often of strange appearance; some have extremely long arms, others have three eyes, and a few make very grim or very amused faces. Chinese Buddhism ascribes a legend to each Lohan, usually a very amusing but nevertheless instructive account of their lives.

The first reference to Buddhism in historical writings goes back to 65 B. C. We are told that Emperor Meng Di of the Eastern Han Dynasty once had a vision that was identified by his dream-readers as the image of Buddha. He then sent two emissaries to the west in order to get information on this god. Presumably they journeyed all the way to Baktrien which is located to the west of the Pamir Mountains. Here they came across two Indian monks, whom they bade to come with them to Luoyang. According to the legend, the monks arrived on two white horses and were carrying the Buddhist writings with them. The **Monastery of the White Horse, Baimasi,** which is located in the vicinity of Luoyang, is said to have been erected in commemoration of this historical event. It is supposed to be the **oldest monastery in China.** A relatively lively exchange took place between India and China in the centuries that followed. **Kamarajiva,** an Indian monk, came to China at the beginning of the 5th century. **Xuanzong, a Chinese monk** who had undertaken a lengthy journey to study in India, also did much for the diffusion of Buddhism. Upon his return to Xi'an, he left an important body of translation work as his legacy.

The new religion first gained support among the nomadic peoples living along China's northern borders. Thus all three of the great Buddhist places of worship are in northern China. The earliest of these were the **Mogao Grottoes,** erected near Dunhuang during the second half of the 4th century. Then came the **Yungang Grottoes** near Datong, followed by the **Longmen Grottoes** in the vicinity of Luoyang. **Buddhism had its heyday in the 7th and 8th centuries, under the rule of the first Tang emperors.** However, its popularity was dealt a severe blow by the Confucianists in 843, who blamed the Buddhists for the deterioration of the empire. In fact, they accused the Buddhists of extravagance, sloth, and subversive activities. In 843, Emperor Wuzong passed an edict as a result of which

40,000 monasteries were destroyed and more than 250,000 monks were relegated to the status of laity and made subject to taxation.

Tens of thousands then fled to Sichuan, where they still had supporters, and established a new and **huge place of worship** there, the **Dazu Grottoes** near Chongqing.

Buddhism owes its rapid diffusion to its inherent tolerance. It makes no pretentions of absolutism or exclusiveness and it is willing to accept other deities or religions. On the other hand, the ability of the Chinese culture to adopt and assimilate foreign elements also aided this process.

A number of peculiarities characterize the Chinese version of Mahayana Buddhism. Although goddesses were originally unknown to Buddhism one of the most adored deities is **Guanyin,** the **Goddess of Mercy.** She is an emanation of **Bodhisattva Avalokiteshvara.** The latter is commonly shown with eleven heads and one thousand arms, whose presence is merely indicated. A small Buddha statue rests on top of the highest head. According to the legend, Avalokiteshvara was so grieved because his efforts to attain salvation remained fruitless, that his head and body burst. When this happened, Buddha picked him up and put him back together again, thereby endowing him with one thousand arms and eleven heads so that he would be able to pursue his duties more effectively from then on. In China, this Bodhisattva was transformed into the goddess Guanyin. It is usually the women who pray to her; they ask her to bring happiness to their homes or to bless them with a large family.

Another typical figure in Chinese Buddhism is **Mi Le.** This seated figure with its large belly and a smile playing on its lips can be seen in the second hall of every temple, just behind the heavenly temple guards. He is the Buddha of the coming Buddha world. Legend has it that he failed the test which he was subjected to by Buddha Sakyamuni, the ruler of the current Buddha World. It appears that his powers of concentration and his ability to meditate were not sufficiently developed for the children were able to move him to laughter. Now he has to wait for the next Buddha world.

In the popular form of Buddhism, Nirvana also has a different meaning. The release into nothingness is a difficult notion for most believers to grasp. Consequently, many people prefer to believe in the rebirth at the Paradise of the Western Heaven, which is presided over by Amitabha Buddha. A concept of hell also exists, but the unfortunate ones are not lost forever because the ruler over hell, **Bodhisattva Ksitigarbha,** takes care of them and ultimately leads them to the **Western Paradise** after they have been purified. This concept came from the **Pure Land Sect,** which emerged in the 5th century. According to its doctrine, even the ignorant can be saved. All they have to do is to make as many appeals to Buddha Amithaba as they possibly can.

Although many monasteries and temples still exist in China, Buddhism has not been able to attract many young people since the right to religious freedom has been reinstated. Some are still attracted by the more exotic offshoots of this religion, such as **Kungfu Boxing** which was developed by the monks of the **Shaolin Monastery.**

Lamaism

The common term Lamaism is inaccurate and misleading. In Tibet, the **Lama** is a fully ordained monk. The most appropriate term for the religious school existing in Tibet is **Vajrayana** which translated means **Diamond Vehicle. Vajrayana Buddhism is in Mongolia, Nepal, Sikkim, and Bhutan, as well as in Tibet. It can be described as a mixture between Mahayana Buddhism, Hinduistic Shiva Cult, Tibetan natural religion (Bonpo), and Tantric practices.** Tantric monks perform a number of magical practices during meditation, which are supposed to release them into the form of a certain deity. These include the **Mandalas** (sacred circles), **Dharanis** (sacred formulas), and **Mantras** (sacred syllables).

The most important symbol of this teaching is the **Vajra,** the Thunderbolt. The principal deity is **Bodhisattva Avalokiteshvara,** the tutelar god of the Tibetans. The Dalai Lama is worshipped as his incarnation. Apart from the **Dalai Lama,** the spiritual head and ruler of the Tibetan Buddhists, there is also the **Panchen Lama.** The latter is believed to be an **incarnation of Buddha Amitabha.** He actually occupies a higher position than the Dalai Lama in the religious hierarchy, but he has always played a lesser role historically.

Vajrayana Buddhism knows a number of deities other than the Buddhas and Bodhisattvas, some of which are adaptations of deities of the **Tibetan Bon religion.** These include the **Dakinis** (witches), the **Dharmapalas** (ferocious looking tutelar gods), the **Yidams** (personal tutelar gods), and the sacred Lamas. Tutelar deities are usually represented in the Yab-Yum position, in sexual union with their female counterparts. This has less to do with notions of sexuality than it does with the concept of a Great Harmony, which is symbolized by the fusion of opposites.

Vajrayana Buddhism emerged in northern India during the 5th century and then slowly diffused to Tibet. The foremost teacher of this school was **Padmasambhava,** an **Indian monk** who came to Tibet in the 8th century and did very effective missionary work. He simply converted the deities of the Tibetan Bon religion and integrated them into the Buddhist pantheon as tutelar gods. Furthermore, homage is paid to **Atisha** (958–1054), another Indian teacher, and to **Tsongkhapa,** who is thought to be the founder of the **Gelupga Sect** (Yellow Cap Sect). Through Tantric practices, a Lama is

The Thunderbolt (Vajra), Lamaism's most important symbol.

able to find a direct path to salvation. Accounts of Lamas who had themselves walled in for decades in order to meditate are quite common. The lay people, however, can only hope not to fall further in the eternal cycle of reincarnations, but to be born again at the highest possible level. This will depend entirely upon their **Karma,** the sum total of all their good and bad deeds.

Other Religions

Next to Buddhism, the most common religion is **Islam.** This is especially true in the northwest. Islam reached China by way of the Silk Road during the Tang Dynasty, between the 7th and the 10th centuries. The Islamic faith is primarily represented by the national minorities in Xinjiang and the Hui, Chinese officially classified as a minority because of their religious beliefs. The autonomous region of the Hui is Ningxia.

The Christian religion has never been able to gain a foothold in China. The **Nestorians** first established Christian communities. They rejected the cult of Mary and had repeatedly broken away from other Christians in the 4th, the 6th, and the 7th centuries. They no longer play a role in contemporary China.

The first Christian missionaries arrived after young Marco Polo had completed his voyages. Most of them were **Jesuits.** One can still find churches and sometimes even smaller parishes in Chinese cities as a reminder of these missionaries' activities, but **a true diffusion of Christian beliefs never did occur.** The Confucians resisted it most vehemently and it also found very little support among the general population because of its condemnation of ancestor worship as idolatry. This meant that it required its perspective followers to distance themselves from their own cultural circles. Nevertheless, the Jesuits at least managed to capture the interest of the imperial court, thanks to their knowledge of the sciences. The emperors were very willing to enlist their services as advisors. For this reason, the Jesuits were the first to be able to transmit reliable information about the Middle Kingdom to Europe.

Art and Culture

Literature
Chinese literature is not very well known to us, although sinologists have been busy for some time translating works. The sinologists are primarily preoccupied with classical literature, but modern Chinese literature is now also being translated and disseminated by younger sinologists, who were able to study in China after it opened its doors to visitors in the seventies. In the meantime, the major publications in modern Chinese literature have been translated into English.

The following survey of Chinese literary production is far from being complete and is simply intended to provide the reader with an insight into the subject. It tries to focus on those writers and works that are better known to us and are generally easier to obtain.

The four canonical works ranking as Confucian classics are among the earliest literary products of China:
− the **Shijing** is a collection of songs from the Zhou Dynasty;
− the **Yijing** (I Ching) is a book of divination with oracular passages dating back to the Shang era;
− the **Shujing** contains historical documents as well as speeches by sovereigns from the Zhou era;

– the **Liji** describes the classical rites and the

– **Chungiu** is the first historical chronicle. This volume, which is better known under the title "Springs and Autumns", outlines the history of the state of Lu during the Zhou Dynasty. An era in history has been named after it: the Spring and Autumn Period (770–476 B.C.).

Also to be mentioned here is the **Lunyu,** recordings of remarks made by Confucius. One of the earliest known poets is **Qu Yuan** (330–295 B.C.), a civil servant who had given up his position because of intrigues against him as well as out of personal disappointment and had then turned to writing. His own melancholy, sorrow, and disillusionment over the decline of the nation set the tone of his writings. Not even writing could help him get over his depressions, so he finally committed suicide. At the Dragon Boat Festival, held every fifth day of the fifth moon month, the Chinese still honour this poet.

Sima Qian is China's first major historiographer. He lived during the Western Han Dynasty, from 145 to 86 B.C., and finally completed the task his father had set out to do, the compiling of a comprehensive history of China.

Literary productivity reached a climax during the Tang Dynasty, a period when quite a few emperors dedicated themselves to the arts or patronized them. **Li Bai** (or Li Taibo) had only been working at the imperial court for a few years, when he was overcome by the great urge to travel. After nature, he is supposed to have loved wine above all other things, something he openly admits to in his poetry. It is said that he fell overboard completely drunk one moonlit night because he was trying to embrace the moon's reflection on the surface of the water.

He was a very close friend of **Du Fu,** who spent a long time at Chengdu and wrote most of his works there. His poetry is highly critical of society, dealing with the life and problems of the common people. One of the greatest poets of the succeeding Song Dynasty was **Su Dongpo.** His work was to have a lasting influence on the poetry of later writers.

The first great works of fiction appeared during the Ming Dynasty. **The writers of prose also made use of the vernacular for the first time, this making literature accessible to those who had not enjoyed a Confucian education.**

Water Margin (or All Men Are Brothers) is a famous novel. The story takes place during the Northern Song era (10th to 12th century). It tells about some daring bandits who, much like Robin Hood, have kept their sense of justice and come to the aid of the poor. The novel is still very popular in China today and supposedly it was one of Mao Zedong's favourite books.

Also to appear during the Ming era was the great **Journey to the West,** which is a clever combination of the legends of the monkey king Sun Wukong with the historical journey of the monk Xuangzong. Sun Wukong is still very much alive today. His image has even appeared in more recent advertisements for modern products. Within the context of Confucian ethics, the monkey king represents the urge for individuality, rebellion, and anarchy. Sun Wukong is a monkey endowed with magical powers. He has absolutely no respect for gods or emperors and his rebellious nature brings heaven into turmoil.

The **first of the erotic novels** began to appear early in the 17th century. In the meantime, these have come to be among the best known Chinese works abroad. **Jin Ping Mei** is one of the most famous works of this particular genre. Concealed behind the flowery but very blunt descriptions of the sexual escapades of the privileged classes is a sharp critique on the lifestyles of the rulers and the wealthy, for whom intrigue, corruption, passion, and selfish lust are common daily experiences.

Dream of the Red Chamber, which was brought out in the 18th century, also deals with a wealthy feudal family. It is basically a sentimental love story, developed against the background of the decline of a family. Since its publication, it has been one of the favourite books of the younger generations.

The period of modern Chinese literature was initiated by the Literary Revolution of the 4th of May, 1919. The younger intellectuals began to criticize Confucian rigidity and conservativeness, making them responsible for the decline of the nation. They wanted to communicate with the population in general by means of a genre of literature dealing with the country's political problems in an intelligible language. **Literary circles** sprang up in the cities and newspapers began to appear with one common word in their title names: New.

One of the major writers of the modern period is **Lu Xun.** He wanted to study medicine at first, but then turned to writing instead. In his essays and stories he takes up the cause of the poor and criticizes the corrupt rule of feudal emperors and their families. He vehemently denounced superstition and fatalism on the one hand, and condemned the ignorance and arrogance among many of the intellectuals on the other. Although he supported the politics of the Communists and Mao Zedong, he never joined the party. He was able to maintain his independence as an intellectual and writer by openly expressing criticism of the Communists. He died from a severe malady at the age of 55. His works have undoubtedly found their place in world literature.

Mao Dun (or Tun) and **Ba Jin** (or Chin) have produced great novels about the decline of feudal China and the emergence of modern ideas and concepts.

Mao Dun's most famous novel is **Midnight,** an account of the rise and fall of a family that also reflects social developments. The characters are personifications of intellectual decadence and social deterioration, but they also represent the budding of new expectations.

Ba Tin also writes about a family in his trilogy of novels **Families, Spring,** and **Autumn. Families** is a story about a young man trying to break away from the fetters of Confucian traditions. His works have inspired several generations of young readers.

Equally renowned is **Lao She,** a writer who does not shy away from using the rough Beijing dialect for his naturalistic stories. Many of them deal with the desperate situation of outcasts. One of his more famous works is **Rickshaw Boy,** the account of a person with a blind

faith in justice who tries very hard to find his place in society and is continuously reduced to misery.

Architecture

One place where the basics of Chinese architecture can be seen is the **Imperial Palace in Beijing.** It contains all of the elements inherent in Chinese architecture, executed to their utmost perfection. Pala or residences of wealthy families are always entered through a folding-door in the wall surrounding them.

A **spirit wall** just behind the entrance gate obstructs the view towards the courtyard and the main building. Spirits apparently can't turn corners and thus the wall prevents them from intruding.

Greater constructions, such as the three large halls of the Imperial Palace, are built upon terraces. The terrace is also the foundation of the building. It fulfills a practical function by protecting the building from moisture, but it also has a symbolic meaning: it represents the earth and the roof stands for heaven.

The Chinese showed an early preference for **wood** as a building material. Other materials were less readily available and more difficult to transport and work with. In time, highly complicated and skilfully constructed **frameworks** began to appear.

The roof is entirely supported by wooden columns. On top of the columns are cross-beams and ingen-

iously sectionalized bracketing systems which carry the roof-beams. Most of the halls within the palace buildings of Beijing were made without the use of nails or cement. Occasionally the interior part of the ceiling has been left open, enabling one to get a good view of the bracketing system, but usually it has been covered with painted coffers.

The roof is covered by glazed tiles. Those of the Imperial Palace are yellow, the colour of the emperor, and those of the Temple of Heaven are blue, the colour of heaven. The eaves are turned up at the corners, making the heavy construction seem much lighter and giving it a wavelike appearance. Figures of animals that are supposed to keep misfortune from the buildings have been carved at the ends of the turned up eaves. The circular construction of the Temple of Heaven shows another style of roof. It is built in three stages, a type of construction also commonly used for square roofs.

Since the walls have no supporting function, they can be used for purely decorative purposes. Typical are wooden partitions with cut out patterns. Following the Taoist principle of harmony between man and nature, the external environment is incorporated into the interior of the building. This is often observed in the construction of **pavilions** as well as in horticulture, where wooden structures are used to form part of an artistic landscape.

In the construction of palaces, stone and other hard materials have usually only been used for the outside walls and the balustrades enclosing the terraces. In the Imperial Palace these are made of white marble.

Most of the religious buildings also have wooden frameworks. Different principles apply to the construction of monasteries than to palaces, but a similar style was still used for both.

Different styles of pagodas. From left to right:
Burial Pagoda, Storeyed Pagoda, Ring Pagoda, Gallery Pagoda,
Glazed Pagoda.

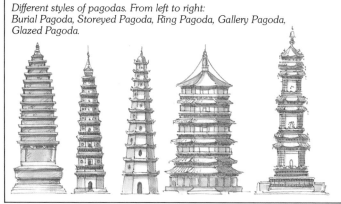

What will immediately catch the eye of every visitor are the **pagodas,** one of China's most typical architectural features. The pagoda has its roots in India, where feudal lords or kings were buried in domed structures placed on a square foundation. The dome was topped by the **chatra,** a prominent mast with finial disks or parasols. In terms of historical development, the Tibetan urn pagodas still bear the closest resemblance to the Indian original.

The Chinese pagoda is a large-scale extension of this prominent mast. The finial disks were transformed into storeys. The farther removed the style of a pagoda is from the original structure, the less it is related to religious or cult matters.

In Xi'an it is possible to see the typical styles of early pagodas. Ranking among the most important in China are the **Great Gander and the Small Gander pagodas,** multi-storeyed brick structures erected during the Tang era. Later pagodas also had wooden frameworks. In order to give more stability to high pagodas, the wooden exterior was often constructed around a solid brick core. This kind of pseudo-pagoda will often give the external appearance of having more stories than it actually has internally.

Decorative gates, called **pailu** in Chinese, are a common feature at temples, palaces, and parks. They will usually have a wooden frame-work and one, three, or five arch-ways.

Horticulture has to be consid-ered as one of the more interesting Chinese architectural achievements. It is an integral aspect of every palace site and has become one of the major attractions for tourists in Suzhou and Wuxi. Centuries ago, Suzhou had already become a kind of paradise for retired civil servants, rich merchants, and established artists. They set up horticultural landscapes in even the smallest available space. Here nature and architecture are joined in perfect harmony. The small areas have been extended optically by the con-struction of pavilions, halls, ponds, bridges, archways, and walkways. Every minor shift in position will open up new perspectives. It appears as if the landscape were permanently changing. Numerous resting places are also available, inviting one to remain for some time, observing and relaxing. The wooden pavilions with their open walls seem to be elements created by nature itself. They do not seem to close a person in, but rather to place him in his natural environment.

Painting

Many styles have emerged in the 2,000-year old development of Chi-nese painting. **Contemporary painters have also begun to experiment with European forms and techniques.**

Nevertheless, traditional Chinese painting differs from European painting in both form and technique, as well as choice of motifs and expression.

A style of **portrait painting** with pedagogical functions was developed under Confucian influence during the Han Dynasty. Important personalities were painted as representations of ideals, as were legendary or historical events, especially when these communicated patriotism or loyalty to the state.

A form of **religious figural painting** emerged under the influence of Buddhism, which can still be seen at various ancient Buddhist places of worship, such as the Magao Grottoes of Dunhuang. This style of painting was perfected during the Tang Dynasty, when it was used primarily for murals at burial sites.

Taoism, however, with its tendency to place more emphasis on nature than on humans, was to have a more lasting influence on Chinese painting. The favourite motifs in this style of painting are **landscapes, plants,** and **animals.** Man merely appears as a subordinate subject to nature in these paintings and he is usually depicted as being at great peace of mind and in solitude.

The brushstroke itself is the essential part of this technique and is supposed to convey the feelings of the artists. A Chinese artist might spend years observing his subject, be it mountains, landscapes, plants, or animals. **He will, however, never paint a naturalistic image.** Once he is ready to begin, he will retire to his studio and paint his subject by memory only. **This will insure that he paints his perception of the subject and not the subject itself.** One of the central aspects of

this style is to express the inner "force", or "breath" in Taoist terms, of all things. **These paintings were usually executed with a brush and Indian ink on rice paper.** The artist is able to give expression to his emotions with his brush. He can make the strokes vigorous or delicate, gentle or hard, dynamic or calm. Perspective is created by applying various shadings of Indian ink.

Traditional artists may finish a painting in a matter of minutes, applying just a few lines, smears, or dabs. However, years of study and a lot of practice are required to master this technique.

Another important aspect of this kind of painting is **emptiness,** also a central concept in Chinese philosophy. The space in the painting referred to as "uninhabited" is an integral and dynamic component of the entire composition. Empty white space in a landscape may represent fog, clouds, a river, or something else. This technique also gives the painting a sense of depth.

Landscaping is called "drawing mountains and water" in Chinese. Both elements signify much more than just two poles of nature to the Chinese. They are also symbolic for the two human polarities of emotion and comprehension, the heart and the mind.

Individual artists often have surnames based on their favourie motifs like Painter of Horses, Painter of Donkeys, and so on. A Chinese artist does not content himself with just one rendition of a particular motif. Since his painting is the expression of a momentary feeling or emotion and not a naturalistic image, he may paint the same motif over and over again and still create a new piece each time. One of the most famous artists of this century is the deceased **Qi Baishi.** Next to landscapes, plants, and animals, he had a strong penchant to paint crabs. His pupil **Li Keran** is sometimes referred to as Painter of Buffaloes. A contemporary of Qi Baishi's, the equally famous **Xu Beihong,** is known for his paintings of horses.

There is a close association in technique between traditional Indian ink drawings and **calligraphy,** the art of drawing Chinese characters that had to be learned by every scholar. A calligrapher must master every style of writing. The real art in calligraphy, however, is the ability to develop a personal and unique style of writing **that meets all aesthetic demands on the one hand and gives expression to individual character and feelings on the other.**

The art of calligraphy has been preserved and cherished up to the present. Even Mao Zedong, whose classical education is often overlooked, wrote calligraphic poems patterned after classical models.

The more popular styles of writing are **seal-writing,** which dates back to the Shang Dynasty, and **cursive** or **grass-writing.** The former is used by most artists for their own

seals, which are stamped in red on every painting. Cursive-writing, or **Xingshu,** is called "running hand" in Chinese. Full cursive-writing, **Caoshu,** commonly known as grass-writing, is the most popular. In this style of writing the artist can condense the numerous brush-strokes making up the characters into one quick flourish. This style is more open to the artist's own creative notions.

Poetry, painting, and calligraphy are virtually inseparable elements of the Chinese arts. All three flow together in **lyrical painting,** an art form that emerged during the Tang Dynasty. It soon became the foremost movement in Chinese painting and it continues to be so up to the present. The three elements above are integrated into one piece. The inspiration is usually brought about by a poem, which is then transferred to the painting. The poem takes up a particular place in the composition. By making use of calligraphy, the artist can further express his feeling for the poem.

One of the great masters of **lyrical painting** is **Su Dongpo** (1035–1101), an artist of the Song era.

Although socialist realism was adopted from the Soviet Union and often promoted by the government after the foundation of the People's Republic, it could not displace the traditional styles of painting. In the wake of the liberalization process following the death of Mao Zedong and the ousting of the Gang of Four, the traditional art forms have regained their former status of importance.

Ceramics

Ceramics is a major art form in the history of China, which has also gained international recognition.

The **earliest pottery** that has been preserved dates back to the **Neolithic Period.** The early Stone Age potters of the Yangshao Culture which grew up along the valleys of the Huanghe produced hand-made pots that were decorated with geometric designs or representations of animals. The Longshan Culture, which emerged at about the same time in the area of contemporary Shandong, already knew the potter's wheel. They had a preference for earthenware with a blackish body and burnished surface.

This early earthenware was soft and porous, but by the late Neolithic age it had become common to fire kaolin, or **China clay** at 1,832 °F (1,000 °C). At this time pottery was definitely being employed for various items of domestic use e. g. food and storage vessels, or burial urns for infants.

It is quite likely that the process of **glazing** was also discovered in China by coincidence, perhaps when alkaline ash had caused a few lustrous spots to appear on the surface of the fired material. Glazing smoothed out the surface of the material and made it denser, thus **leaving more room for creativity.**

The **celadon** produced 3,000 years ago during the Shang Dynasty are basically identical to the porcelain of later times. Bronze casting also emerged during the Shang era and displaced ceramics to a certain extent.

During the Qin and Han era ceramics were primarily used as **burial objects.** At last the rulers had given up the practice of taking human sacrifices, household goods, and animals with them to the grave. Now they contented themselves with ceramics.

Life-sized figures of humans and animals were made for the first Qin emperor, but with the advent of the Han Dynasty this practice was reduced to the production of mere **statuettes.** The figures were first pressed into a mould, then fired, and finally decorated with **mineral colours** after cooling off.

The firing process was constantly being improved up to the 6th century so that the surface of the earthenware became progressively smoother. Celadon developed at about this time, usually a pale green glaze applied in various shades of green, sometimes also in blue or gray. These colours were made by applying a coating of watered down clay with a high iron content just prior to glazing.

The famous **tricolour glaze** (brown, green, red) made by the addition of copper, iron, and cobalt was developed during the Tang Dynasty. The colours were usually applied close enough to each other so that they would mingle while being fired.

The museums of central China have excellent samples of Tang ceramics. The horse was one of the more popular motifs. Tang horses are cherished and have been copied all over the world. They are symbolic for the flourishing trade in silk at that time, when the horse figured as the prominent pack animal. Furthermore, the Tang nobles were then entertaining themselves with a kind of mounted game imported from Persia, namely polo.

The **art of ceramics** reached its peak during the succeeding Song Dynasty. There was a marked preference at this time for **monochrome glazing.** The greenish **celadon** was brought to perfection and was even exported to other Asian countries.

At this point we should also mention **Ding ceramics,** which were being produced in Dingzhou in the province of Hebei. They show a definite preference for cream-coloured glazes and moderate decor.

Ming porcelain with its blue decor on a white background has also achieved worldwide fame.

Jingdezhen in the province of Jiangxi became best known for the production of Chinese porcelain. Blue and white porcelain was primarily produced here, though occasionally it was produced in red. Jingdezhen was destroyed during the Taiping Rebellion, but is currently being restored as a centre for Chinese ceramics.

A porcelain Ming vase with its typical blue on white decor.

Famille rose porcelain was produced at Jingdezhen during the Qing era. The **rose colour** that is dominant in this kind of enameled porcelain was extracted from gold chloride.

Bronzes

Bronze casting is about 4,000 years old in China. It flourished from the time of the Shang, Zhou, and Han dynasties, that is to say the 16th century B.C., until the beginning of modern time reckoning.

During the **Shang Dynasty,** bronze was worked into **sacrificial or cult vessels, weapons,** and **tools. Bronze mirrors** were common products of the **Han Dynasty.**

The centres for the bronze art of the Shang Dynasty were located near Zhengzhou and Anyang, in the province of Henan, where the Shang rulers had established their capital. The **ritual vessels** of the Shang Dynasty are usually very sturdy and **richly decorated.** Animals were the preferred motif. The most common example is the **taotie,** the so-called **devil's mask.** It depicts two symmetrically opposed demonic figures. Other common motifs are **figures of animals, dragons, tigers, and turtles.** Later during the Shang era, the vessels were actually cast in the form of animals. Shang bronzes have inscriptions on the inside – later they were also applied to the exterior – giving information about who made the bronze, for which client, and for what purpose. These inscriptions have provided scholars with valuable information for their research. **Ding vessels** (heavy round pots standing on three legs) are characteristic of the Shang era.

Large chimes were cast in bronze during the **Zhou Dynasty.**

A 2,300-year old princely tomb was discovered near Wuhan in 1978 containing a large and well preserved bronze chime. It has a total of 65 large and small bells attached to a wooden frame. The largest bell weighs more than 200 kg (440 lbs). Wooden clappers were used to strike the bells, wooden poles were used for the larger ones. The **production of bronze mirrors** grew in importance during the **Han Dynasty.** They found use as household objects, jewellery, or burial objects. The reflecting side was made of polished bronze, but the often richly ornamented rear sides are usually more interesting.

Peking Opera

Few things are more difficult to comprehend for a foreigner than a Chinese opera. The reactions of the Chinese public is even more inscrutable. They start to clap just as soon as an actor appears on the stage, long before he has had the chance to say anything. They remain impassive during the presentation of acrobatic feats, just when the foreigners will burst into applause. An old man runs around the stage in circles constantly wagging his head in quick motions and the Chinese public will virtually go into ecstasy.

The Chinese, especially the older men, know their operas very well, including the songs, dialogues, and the subjects themselves. Just a regular performance will hardly exite them. They go to the opera when they want to see a certain actor or a particular cast. They can recognize the finer points, the special talents, and the notable accomplishments of an actor.

The **Peking Opera,** which is only one of approximately one hundred types of Chinese opera, is fairly accessible to foreigners with little knowledge of the language and the singing. They would obviously have great problems understanding the content, but in this case pantomime and acrobatics play an important role along with recitation and singing. The pantomime elements can be understood if one is willing to pay attention and use a little fantasy. It also helps to have some previous knowledge of their place and function in the opera. The stage setting has very few props or decorations. Things and actions are described through pantomime. **Each motion with the hand, stroking the beard, rolling up a sleeve, lifting a foot, all of these follow exact rules and ancient patterns that are immediately recognized by the Chinese spectator.**

The lifting of a whip, for example, means that the actor is riding; a paddle or just a paddling motion denotes a boat ride; if an actor runs around in a circle once, he has just covered a very long distance; stroking the beard slowly implies thinking; two flags depicting wheels stand for a carriage; four generals and four soldiers represent an army of thousands; and so forth. All of this happens on a stage that is almost bare. One table and a few chairs would therefore be considered a lot of props.

A special visual treat for the spectators are the luxurious and colourful costumes. The colours of the costumes also provide information on the social status of their wearers. Yellow is solely the colour of the emperor, red is worn by the nobles, and black is the bandits' colour.

There are **four types of roles** in the Peking Opera: **Dan,** the female roles which were only played by men in the past; **Sheng,** the male roles; **Chou,** a kind of comedian or clown whose task it is to make the audience laugh; and the **Jing,**

*Character actor
in the Peking Opera.*

colourful masks which, depending on their colour, will either represent good or bad characters. A mask that is nearly all red will stand for a brave and loyal man. A black one symbolizes a man who is rough and strict, but also honest. Blue will be a cruel person, yellow a false one, and white will denote craftiness. Spirits may also appear occasionally, in which case they will be wearing gold or silver masks.

Due to the marked symbolic content of the opera, it is hardly necessary to understand the language. As both the songs and the dialogues are presented in Peking dialect, even the southern Chinese will have some difficulty understanding them. When the actors begin to sing in their high-pitched voices, the words of the song are projected onto the side-walls of the stage.

It is advisable to wear casual clothes to the opera. Exclusive evening apparel may mean that the members of the audience pay more attention to you than they do to the actors up on stage.

Chinese Medicine

Chinese medicine has attracted international attention primarily because of **acupuncture,** a form of treating illnesses by applying needles to specific spots on the body. Presently, 780 such spots are known, which are all joined to each other by 14 meridians (body lines).

Every spot to which a needle can be applied is defined exactly, both in terms of position and effect. The needles are inserted to various depths and then left in the body anywhere from a few minutes to half an hour. Additional stimulation is achieved by turning the needles or sending electric impulses through them.

Acupuncture, which is a form of treatment based on experience, has probably been known in China for nearly 5,000 years. Early historical records credit the legendary Emperor Huang Di with having developed acupuncture. The Neijing, a medical handbook attributed to Emperor Huang Di, was available during the Han Dynasty. It shows the correct spots for the application of the needles, describes the meridians, lists the therapeutic effects of the needles, and provides prescriptions for their proper use.

Archaeological finds show that stone needles were used as early as the Stone Age for blood-letting, pus removal, and other purposes. These were then replaced by needles made of bamboo or bone, which in turn made way for copper or iron needles at a later period. Today, needles are either made of gold, silver, or steel.

Acupuncture is strictly empiric and does not rely on any scientific theory, which is probably why it is often rejected in orthodox medical practice. Scientists continue to disagree about the function of this kind of treatment. The most controversial question is whether or not acupuncture reduces pain. Allergies and functional disorders can supposedly also be treated in this way.

Chinese medicine is based on holistic thinking, which is derived from the ancient principles of Chinese philosophy. It was scholars of the Han Dynasty who took up the task of placing acupuncture within a theoretical context.

The **polarity of Ying and Yang,** that cosmic principle of Chinese philosophy that accounts for all harmony, was also applied to the practice of medicine. All organs and parts of the body were accordingly categorized as being either Ying or Yang. Human ailments are then understood as a disturbance in this balanced system and the therapy is consequently aimed at re-establishing the harmony.

In traditional medicine, the doctor makes a diagnosis after having completed a checkup. As well as asking questions and taking his patient's pulse, the senses of seeing, hearing and smell are involved in the checkup. After the doctor has been able to diagnose which organ is malfunctioning, the therapy is begun by finding the correct spots that will stimulate the organ when the needles are inserted.

Depending on just how the needle is inserted – deep or not deep – and the type of stimulation which is applied, either plain puncture or turning the needle, the doctor can either soothe or activate the organ in question.

Acupuncture usually requires a longer period of treatment for it to be effective.

Acupuncture is painless; one merely feels slight warmth at the points where the needles are inserted.

Acupuncture is still widely practised in the rural areas because it is

Panax ginseng

relatively simple, has no side effects, and requires very few technical appliances.

Very controversial in China as well, is the question of acupuncture applied for anaesthetic purposes. As one of the traditional forms of Chinese medicine, acupuncture became very popular during the Cultural Revolution, at a time when western medicine was rejected. The photographs showing sensational operations of patients who had been anaesthetized with acupuncture and could consciously observe what was going on while holding a copy of the Red Book in their hands all date back to this period. Doctors have since discovered, however, that these events were staged for propaganda purposes. Anaesthesia with acupuncture seems plausible, but as yet no concrete data is available on how it affects individual patients.

Of much greater importance is **herbal medicine.** It is also an empirical form of medicine that became based on the philosophy of Ying and Yang in the course of its development. Herbs were the only source of medicine available in the past for the poorer inhabitants of the rural areas. Herbal medicine still plays a major role today, if only because it is much cheaper than western medicine.

Moxibustion is a form of acupuncture performed with herbs. The specific spots on the body are stimulated by warmth rather than by the insertion of needles. This is accomplished by burning balls of pressed herbs over the indicated spots.

Chinese Martial Arts

All over Chinese cities, in squares, parks, or courtyards, people gather in the early morning hours and prepare themselves for the working day by doing **gymnastics.** Although a few of the young people have also found a liking for jogging in the meantime, traditional **shadow-boxing** is still the most popular form of exercise. The harbour promenade in Shanghai is transformed into a huge sports arena in the early morning, where one can observe practically every style of Chinese martial arts. The elderly prefer the calm and flowing motions of shadow-boxing while the young like the hard and aggressive style of **kung fu,** which also entails the use of arms.

The martial arts are called **Wushu** in China. What is being practised today as a form of exercise, started many centuries ago as a serious matter of warfare.

Wushu, as well as **archery and riding,** were already being practised during the Western Zhou Dynasty (1100–771 B. C.). **Xiangpu,** a style of wrestling, was developed during the Han Dynasty. **Shaolin boxing** was probably developed in the 5th century by the monks of the Shaolin Monastery near Luoyang. They served as bodyguards to the first Tang emperor after they had actively helped to eliminate a rival and thus made it possible for him to ascend the throne.

The martial arts lost much of their importance with the advent of firearms. Wushu survived as a form of exercise and has since then developed many variations and styles.

Two major schools can be recognized. The "external" martial arts are aggressive and seek to defeat an opponent. Speed, quick reactions, agility, toughness, and strength are consequently of importance for these styles of martial arts. The best known of these is Shaolin boxing, which was popularized internationally by the Hong Kong film industry under the name Kung fu.

The moves in Shaolin boxing imitate the motions of animals, such as the lightning strike of a tiger, the suppleness of a snake, the springing agility of the leopard, and so forth. The fingers, hands, and feet are used for fighting. Quick movements, turns, jumps, and lightning blows are characteristic of this style of boxing which requires a lot of hard training. In the early days, training was begun by striking the trunk of a tree repeatedly with spread fingers every single day, for a continuation of years or even decades. One of the masters of Shaolin boxing, who was the abbot of the monastery some decades ago, could still stand on two fingers in spite of his advanced age. Legends mention ancient masters with supernatural powers: merely pointing a finger at an opponent was sufficient to kill him.

Shaolin boxing spread to Japan during the Ming Dynasty, where it merged with other endemic styles of martial arts to become what is now well known as **judo.**

The older people tend to prefer those martial arts which are rather - less active; not just because these are slower and much more gentle, but because they also require a great deal of mental discipline and concentration. The most important style of the "internal" school is **Taiji-guan,** or shadow-boxing. **Taiji** is based on Taoist conceptions and its object is to **unify all human forces,** the physical, the mental, and the spiritual. The movements are slow and gentle but require balance, peace of mind, and a lot of concentration. The flowing movements have to be in unison with the respiration. For this reason there are closing exercises, during which one must inhale, and opening exercises, during which one exhales. The highest stage in Taiji are the partner exercises. The motions in these very difficult exercises not only flow together, they also flow from one person to another. The opening moves made by one of the partners are taken up by the other and then neutralized with a circular motion.

This style of shadow-boxing best exemplifies the unison with Chinese philosophy, which revolves around the opposites of Ying and Yang, the two polarities of life reflected in all things.

Other than these two major styles there are still a number of additional ones, a few of which ought to be mentioned at this point.

"Long boxing" is popular amongst the young because it requires coordination, elasticity, and speed.

The same applies to **Nanguan,** or **southern boxing.** The latter is easily recognized because the fighters issue loud cries when they make their attacking moves. Much more legwork is done in this style than in the others.

There are a few peculiar styles that somewhat resemble Shaolin boxing, such as **Ziuguan,** or **drunken boxing.** Making believe that one is drunk, is supposed to fool the opponent. At an unexpected moment, the fighter will quickly change his reeling motions into a direct assault.

Monkey boxing imitates the motions of a monkey. Another rather peculiar style is **crane boxing.** Aside from these pugilistic forms of the martial arts there are also a number of styles which use both "short" and "long" weapons.

Short weapons include daggers, short swords, and hooks. Long weapons are canes, spears, and broadswords. There are also several jointed types of weapons, such as the hammer chain, made up of three connected canes, and a whip with nine links. Obviously, only wooden imitations of these are still in use today.

The martial arts have recently gained in popularity. Wushu sports festivals are being held all over the country and are usually covered by television.

Chinese Cooking

The Chinese cuisine is undoubtedly ranked among the best and most noted of the world. Chinese restaurants can be found in nearly all parts of the globe. However, what you might have come to know of Chinese restaurants in your own country may not necessarily have much in common with true Chinese cooking. Clients will ultimately force their tastes on restaurants and as a result, meals come to be prepared in a specific way. Furthermore, it would be highly unusual to make do with just one or two dishes at a Chinese banquet.

Chinese food often has a lasting impression on visitors to China. For some people it remains their most vivid impression, whether this be favourable or unfavourable. Open-mindedness, healthy curiosity, and an inclination for the pleasures of taste are all that is required to be able to enjoy Chinese food.

Forget your prejudices and all that nonsense about dogs, cats, snakes, and rotten eggs. Dogs and cats are only seldom eaten, snakes can taste very good, and even the "rotten eggs" in no way deserve to be referred to as rotten. **It just might reassure you somewhat to know that the Chinese have similar doubts about our food.** They consider cheese to be little more than sour milk and that eating steak is a relic from the age of barbarism.

In China one will usually dine with eight people at a round table. Several courses are served, or at least as many as there are people sitting at the table. A regular meal includes small appetizers, assorted meat dishes, various vegetables, soup, and desert.

Rice is usually served last. The host expects his guests to eat their fill of the finer dishes of a good meal, without having to resort to the rice. In China the soup is not served as an entreé, but either during or at the end of a meal.

Very complicated rules prescribe the proper succession of the individual dishes, which are not always adhered to in simpler meals. Nevertheless, only a meal in which the proper and well balanced succession of dishes is observed will reveal the true delicacy of Chinese cooking. Thus "solid" dishes are alternated with "soft" ones, spicy with mild, sweet with sour. Poultry has to be succeeded by fish or meat; duck will never be served after chicken, and so forth.

Ingredients and preparation will vary according to the soil, rainfall etc. of a particular region. The principal grains are rice, millet, and wheat. Since rice is more widely cultivated in the south, it also features prominently in the cuisine of the area whereas noodles are more popular in the north.

195

The arable soil is so limited, making up a mere 11% of the total surface area, that it would be uneconomical to raise stock on it. Consequently beef hardly features at all in Chinese cooking. It is replaced by pork and poultry, animals that can easily be kept in the courtyard at a small cost. Dairy products are also scarce for the same reason.

The Chinese use a lot of natural plant food, such as roots, tubers, seaweed and other marine plants, water chestnuts, bamboo, and even some flowers.

Since the available soil has always been used intensively, materials to use as fuel have also been limited. It is therefore important that a minimum amount of energy is used during cooking. Therefore, meat is cut into small cubes or strips and then quickly fried in the **wok,** the Chinese frying-pan. The same is done with vegetables. Even poultry is cooked quickly and then left to simmer in sauce. One will often observe food being steamed in an energy saving fashion at the eating places along the roadsides. Several bamboo steamers, or round baskets, are piled up one on top of the other and then placed over the fire.

Preserving the ingredients was also a major problem. Even today, very few households will have a refrigerator. The housewives and cooks have to get the ingredients fresh from the markets. Poultry will be butchered just before it is cooked. This may seem somewhat troublesome to us, but there is really

nothing wrong with having fresh ingredients in the kitchen; quite the opposite in fact.

Whatever needs to be preserved is usually air-dried. This is done primarily with vegetables, but it is not unusual to preserve meat and poultry in this way, too. Curing is another common form of preserving food.

Obviously the art of Chinese cooking was refined by the upper classes. The common people often had to be content with just a handful of rice. The regular diet today still consists of either rice or noodles with vegetables for the greater part. Meat is certainly not eaten every day.

The rich upper classes, however, wanted quality and variation in their food. The palace cooks were constantly called upon to create new dishes, even if the ingredients available were always limited. For this reason, spices with which to enrich or change the flavour of foods is an absolute must in the Chinese cuisine.

The Chinese like to invite relatives and friends for a large dinner on all major festive occasions. Then several members of the family will be out shopping the whole day in order to obtain all of the necessary fresh ingredients. Guests usually come earlier than they are expected. It is considered polite to offer the host help with the preparations. Indeed, there is a great deal to be done. Everything has to be washed, cleaned, and chopped up before it can be cooked.

It is considered impolite if a guest does not try each and every course. Thus it is usual to limit oneself to just a few morsels of each. There will be a number of pauses during every meal, when people often smoke.

Foreigners inevitably have problems using chopsticks to eat with. Depending on the restaurant, you may be offered a knife and fork anyway, but you really should not give up right away. The food will always be cut up into morsels that are easy to handle with chopsticks.

It is important to learn the right way of holding them from the very start.

Pick up the first chopstick at the middle, place it on the crook of your thumb and let the lower end rest on the tip of the ring finger. The first chopstick has to be held firmly because it is not moved when in use.

The second chopstick is held between the thumb, index, and middle finger. You can easily bring the tip of the upper chopstick to push down on the lower one by applying a little pressure with your index finger. Food can thus be held between the lower ends of the chopsticks. Do not apply too much pressure or the morsel will slip off again.

This may take a little practice, but by the time you finish your round trip you will undoubtedly have mastered the art.

Chinese cooking is not the same throughout the country, **it varies according to the region.** Cantonese cooking is better known in the west because most of the Chinese living abroad come from the southern province of Guangdong or from Hong Kong.

Cantonese cooking is mild; very little salt and not many spices are used. A strong chicken broth is fairly common. Roasted duck, smoked pork, pork meat balls, and various types of pasta filled with either meat or condiments are some of dishes served in Cantonese cooking.

The most common form of preparing food in Canton is steaming. The area is rich in seafood, which appears quite often on the menus. Lobsters, oysters, mussels, abalone, and sea cucumbers are a few of the specialties. The Cantonese even have reputation in China for eating absolutely everything that can possibly be consumed. At the markets one can buy frogs, toads, salamanders, snakes, cats, owls, as well as all kinds of fish or seafood.

Peking cooking is also mild, but somewhat richer. Staple foods are noodles and dumplings. Most foods are fried. Since the grasslands of the north are not far away, beef or even lamb are available more often. Onions, garlic, green onions, and leeks are used quite frequently.

The presence of the imperial court for 600 years obviously had an influence on Peking cooking. There is not enough space here to list nearly all of the specialties. The most famous one is Peking duck (see separate section).

Peking Duck

The tourist who travels to Beijing will certainly want to try some of the world famous Peking duck. Since this is true for practically every tourist, it is almost impossible to get a table anywhere unless you reserve one beforehand. Those people who have already been to Beijing will know that the best place to go is **Quanjude Peking Duck Restaurant,** at Qianmen Gate. The restaurant has also been operating a second establishment for some years now, located on Hepingmen Road and accommodating **3,000** guests. Unfortunately, the new restaurant's large seating capacity has been gained at a cost to its atmosphere.

Peking ducks have to be fattened in Beijing itself. The restaurant gets its ducks from some of the farms located on the outskirts of the city. The ducks are just perfect for the grill when they are about 65 days old and weigh some 2 kg (4.5 lbs). In the last 20 days they are given special feed and their movement is restricted as much as possible. This will make the meat tender and keep the skin thin.

The ducks are drawn, scalded, and then basted with sugared water so that the skin will turn deep red and be crisp and sweet when barbecued. Just before they are barbecued, the ducks are filled with boiling water and then sown up. After that they are barbecued over an open fire for about 30 to 40 minutes. Only the wood from date-palms, peach trees, or pear trees may be used for the fire.

When the duck is ready it is cut into thin slices, which are rolled up in flat wheat cakes along with sauce and some leeks and then eaten.

A complete duck dinner will include several entreés of duck parts, such as entrails, tongue, head, wings, and webbed feet. There are about 100 variations in the way these can be prepared.

Customarily, one will accompany the meal with Maotai, a Chinese dinner brandy. It is 60% proof or more and will ensure that you have no digestion problems.

Shanghai cooking is very tasty. Many of the dishes are sweet or are served with sweet sauces. Shanghai's hinterland is one of the most fertile regions in the country and the sea is also rich in fish, prawns, crabs, and seaplants. Sharkfin or prawns in ginger are typical specialties of Shanghai.

Sichuan cooking is noted for its very spicy dishes. Some may be a little too hot for our taste, but most of them are quite savory. Mountain pepper, better known to us as Sichuan pepper, is used a lot for seasoning. Sichuan duck is as popular specialty. Another typical dish is a hot but very tasty noodle soup.

Obviously this huge country has many other local cuisines (Fujian,

Hunan, etc.) and famous specialties to offer.

The restaurants in Beijing will often serve Mongolian firepot or Xinjiang lamb on the spit.

There are many kinds of tropical fruit in Yunnan and fried pears is one of the specialties there.

Tea is the Chinese **national beverage.** A day is started off with tea, tea is drunk during breaks and mealtimes, it is served when guests are received, and in the evenings people will often visit their local tea house.

Tea once had to be imported to China. It was first brought over to China from Assam around the 4th century. Now tea is being cultivated primarily in southern China. It needs warm temperatures and high humidity and thus grows best in tropical or subtropical regions.

The quality of tea not only depends on climatic conditions, but also on the type of soil, the time of the harvest, the way it is treated, and the kind of water used in its preparation.

The Chinese prefer **green tea.** In order to make green tea, the young leaves are picked and then dried briefly in the sun before being dried again indoors either by hand or machinery. The first harvest, which is usually in April, will make the best tea.

As mentioned above, the early leaves are first dried in the sun and then later dried again by hand in small pans. The hand dried variety apparently makes the finest quality of tea.

One of the better known brands is **Longjing,** or Dragon Well Tea, from Hangzhou.

You drop a few leaves into a cup and then pour hot water over them. The leaves give off their fragrance and then sink to the bottom of the cup. The Chinese traditionally drink their tea in bowls placed on saucers and covered with lids. In order to take a drink, you simply lift the lid a little and sip the tea. The lid will also keep back the leaves.

For **black tea,** which is not as popular in China, the leaves are picked when they are older and have begun to dry. Then they are fermented before they are left to dry.

Another variety is **Wulong tea,** a semi-fermented kind of tea. The leaves are only partially dried and the process of fermentation is interrupted. Wulong has a golden, or amber-like color.

Blossom teas are also very popular in China, especially **jasmine tea.** The dried blossoms are simply added on to the tea leaves.

Thermos flasks full of hot water to make tea with can be found every where in China, in apartments, offices, trains and people's homes. Occasionally one may have to do without certain things, but thermos flasks will always be available.

Pidan

The legendary "hundred-year old" or "thousand-year old eggs" – either called **Pidan** or **Choudan** (stink eggs) – are made from duck eggs. In order to transform a normal egg into a Pidan it has to go through a special process: the egg is placed in a mixture of wet clay, unslaked lime, and chaff. The moisture slakes the lime and the heat developed in the process turns the egg-white into a dark green to black gelatinous substance. The egg-yolk turns green. Pidan eggs can't always be bought at the market. Normally, one takes fresh eggs to a special dealer at the market and he will place them in the clay mixture right then and there. The exact mixture of ingredients is the dealer's secret. At home the eggs are left in jars that are permanently kept moist. The eggs will be ready in two to three weeks. If they are kept longer than that they become inedible.

Pidan eggs neither smell rotten nor bad and the mildly sweet taste is quite delicious.

The choice of wine in China is not very great, especially away from the major centres. China is not particularly a wine country. The wines from the province of Xinjiang are usually very sweet. Many of them actually taste more like a liqueur. Dry wines tend to be difficult to come by.

Wine is called **jiu** in Chinese, but the word is usually applied to any of the several **grain spirits** available there, all of which are very strong.

Spirits are distilled from wheat, millet, rice, sorghum, and other grains. One of the better known brands is **Wuliangyie,** which is distilled from five kinds of grain. Another one is **Daqu.** Both are made in the province of Sichuan. **Maotai** is considered to be the best brandy in China. It is called "dinner brandy" because it is always served at festive meals. This brandy is very expensive (about 15 Yuan) and few Chinese are able to afford it. Maotai is distilled in a region with the same name, located in the province of Guizhou.

The ingredients include wheat, sorghum, and the excellent water of this region.

Shaoxing Jiu is the best rice brandy. It is named after a small town, Shaoxing, in the province of Jiangsu. It is made with sticky rice mixed together with water from Lake Jianhu. It can be drunk either cold or warm, much like Japanese sake.

In the meantime **beer** has become a popular beverage, even though not all of the Chinese are able to afford it. Chinese beer is rather spicy and quite refreshing. The most popular brand is **Qingdao Pijiu.** The Qingdao brewery was originally constructed by German colonists and then taken over by the Chinese after the former had left the country.

Beer is almost always served along with meals for tourists. One may also order soft drinks, however, most of which are very sweet, or **mineral water.** The most common brand of the latter is **Laoshan,** named after a mountain in the vicinity of Qingdao.

Regular western drinks have also become available recently, but these can only be purchased with either foreign currency or certificates. Hotel bars have been offering international spirits and mixed drinks for some time now.

China's Economy

In 1949, the new government of the People's Republic took control of a desolate country that had suffered tremendously under the Japanese invasion and the ensuing four years of civil war. Millions of peasants had also perished in natural disasters or famines.

The new regime first turned its attention to the agricultural sector: 80% of the population in China lives in rural areas. The distribution of wealth in these areas was highly disproportionate: 10% of the rural population, that is the landowners and rich peasants, owned 70–80% of the land while the remaining 90% had to make an existence as tenant farmers or simple farm hands. At times the taxes were so high that two thirds of the harvest had to be turned over to the landlord. It was not even unusual for tax monies to be collected for years in advance. The exorbitant interest rates demanded by the usurers had also left the peasants hopelessly in debt.

Industry had been developed somewhat in the coastal cities, but it was almost entirely under the control of foreigners.

The government initiated a **land reform** policy in 1950. The landowners were expropriated without any compensation and the lands were distributed among the peasants. At first, there was no attempt to collectivize the peasants.

The government also refrained from nationalizing industry all at once, trying instead to get the capitalists involved in the process of revitalizing the nation.

As far as foreign affairs were concerned, the good relations that had developed with the U. S. A. during World War II began to deteriorate rapidly as a result of the Korean War and anti-Communist agitation in the U. S.

Consequently, the U. S. S. R. evolved as the only partner of the young republic. The first Five-Year Plan was developed with the assistance of Soviet advisors. It was during this period that the process of nationalization was stepped up, **collectivization** initiated, and the machinery of central administration was perfected.

The conflict with the Soviet Union over the leadership role in the international Communist movement began to crystallize as early as the latter part of the 50's. China hoped to make a "great leap" in the direction of becoming a Communist society. Backyard furnaces began to crop up all over the countryside, which were supposed to be the first step towards the total industrialization of the nation. **People's communes** were introduced in the sector of agriculture. Not only the means of production were made public property, but also cooking utensils and other personal belongings in some cases.

By 1961, the chaos in the economy had grown out of hand. In many regions the peasants simply didn't have enough to eat. **Mao Zedong** assumed all responsibility for this situation and relinquished his position as president of the state.

He was succeeded by **Liu Shaoqi,** a pragmatist who set about reversing the process of overcollectivization and stimulating the diligence of the population with material benefits.

Retaliation followed in just a few years. The radical forces behind Mao Zedong accused the pragmatists gathered around Liu Shaoqi, which already included **Deng Xiaoping,** of wanting to reinstate capitalism. As a preventive measure they unleashed the **Great Proletarian Cultural Revolution.**

The revolution continued until 1976, when the **Gang of Four** was arrested. This factionalist conflict within the party, which had lasted for ten years, left the country on the verge of ruin once again.

The dissatisfaction among the peasants was quite obvious, cities could no longer be supplied properly, and the intellectuals needed to bring the economy to order again had withdrawn in fear and resignation.

After the deposition of the Gang of Four and the death of Mao Zedong, the new leaders made their goal of socialist modernization public. In recent years, a number of reforms have been carried out in the economic and administrative sectors which represent a radical departure from a centrally planned economy.

Collectivization in agriculture ceased and the people's communes have been terminated. A **system of private responsibilities** prevails today. The land was distributed among peasant families who in turn signed contracts with **brigades,** pledging to turn over a certain amount of their products at prices fixed by the state. The peasants themselves decide what they want to grow. The peasant families are allowed to keep all surplus products. They can either turn these over to the state at higher prices or sell them at one of the free markets.

The establishment of markets has greatly improved the supply of goods to the rural areas and created a marked increase in the peasants' incomes. The monopolistic system of state distribution was broken.

Private ownership is allowed once again, e. g. of utilities, sections of land, domestic animals, houses, and cars.

The government promotes a spirit of enterprise among the peasants.

Those peasants who can't or don't want to work their section of land can either lease it or hire others to work on it.

Some drastic changes have also occurred in industry.

In the first place, political administrators of business enterprises were replaced by competent managers. Responsibility was turned over once again to the professionals, who were awarded higher salaries Material benefits, such as bonuses or piece-wages, were incorporated into the wage system in order to encourage workers to be more industrious. If an enterprise had been operating at a loss and it seemed highly unlikely that it could be made viable again, it was simply shut down.

It is hoped that with the adoption of modern management and the introduction of company accounting systems, in which profit is the standard, efficiency in the industrial sector will increase. Individual enterprises are now responsible once again for decision-making, something which used to be the province of higher administrative offices. Plans to establish a limited market for industry have also been formulated recently. Whatever industries produce in surplus of the planned quota, may be sold directly to consumers.

The rule by which all profits had to be turned over to the state was eliminated in order to stimulate the growth of business enterprises. Most enterprises are now subject to a system of taxation: the enterprises retain their profits and can draw up their own investment policies, but they must pay the state a tax on the profit.

The decision to turn away from the policy of self-sufficiency has been of vital importance for the moderni-zation of the nation's economy. By adhering to an open door policy towards the west, the government hopes to be able to speed up the process of modernizing the econo-my with the aid of western tech-nology. By 1978 the Chinese had started to deal and make contracts with foreign partners in a very credulous manner. Their initial euphoria and conviction that the import of advanced technology was sufficient to modernize industry quickly changed into disillusionment. The construction of huge industrial complexes only led to imbalances in the country's economy. Additionally, there was a dire lack of foreign currency.

Therefore, the original plans have recently been revised. Light industry was given priority over heavy industry in order to be able to meet the demand resulting from the increased spending power of the general population i. e. to supply them with sufficient goods. Another reason for the change of policy was to increase the rate of export.

Despite many setbacks caused by political conflicts or natural disasters, the economic achievements of the People's Republic of China are quite considerable, especially when compared to those of other developing countries. For example, the production of grain increased from 113 million tons in 1949 to 318.22 million in 1980 and production figures for cotton rose from 445,000 tons to 2.7 million.

Simultaneously in the industrial sector, the production of coal went up from 32 to 620 million tons, that of crude oil from 120,000 to 106 million tons, and that of steel rose from 158,000 to more than 37 million tons.

Due to the new policy of apportionment, incomes have risen dramatically in the last few years. Today, the annual income of a peasant is 310 Yuan. This may still not seem to be very much, but it must be remembered that the peasants can provide for many of their needs from their private allotments. The average annual income in the industrial sector is 826 Yuan per person. The incomes of the peasants rose by approximately 14.7% between 1982 and 1983; that of the labourers and industrial employees only by about 3.5%.

These figures for the growth in production are admirable, but they fall short of the expected rise in the general standard of living.

The major economic problem of the last three decades has been the explosive **growth in the population.** In 1949, the population was just slightly more than 500 million. In just 35 years it has nearly doubled to 1.008 billion inhabitants on the mainland. Maoist policy regarded the large population as being China's most valuable resource and thus ignored all early warnings by demographers. Since then politicians have become very much aware of the problem. Consequently, the **one-child family policy** is being propagated throughout the nation, except in those regions inhabited by minorities. Those who comply with it can expect material benefits, those who do not may lose bonuses or be required to pay kindergarten and school fees.

This family plan ordinance might be considered to be a massive intrusion into the private sphere and a curtailment of personal freedom. However, China has no other alternative left if it does not want to risk a Darwinian reduction of its population as a result of famine.

Regional Section

Regions and Towns

	Page
Beijing and the North	207
(Beijing, Tianjin, Heilongjiang, Liaoning, Jilin, Inner Mongolia, Hebei)	
Beijing	207
Tianjin	221
Harbin	222
Changchun	223
Shenyang	224
Hohhot	225
Baotou	227
Chengde	228
Beidaihe/Shanghaiguan	230
Shijiazhuang	231
Shanghai and the East	233
(Shanghai, Shandong, Anhui, Jiangsu, Hubei, Hunan, Jiangxi, Zhejiang, Fujian)	
Shanghai	233
Jinan	237
Taishan	238
Qufu	240
Qingdao	241
Nanjing	242
Wuxi	245
Suzhou	248
Wuhan	251
Changsha	254
Hangzhou	255
Fuzhou	258
Quanzhou	259

Xi'an, the Centre —————————————————————— 261
(Shaanxi, Shanxi, Henan, Gansu, Ningxia)
Xi'an ——————————————————————————————— 261
Taiyuan ————————————————————————————— 269
Datong —————————————————————————————— 270
Luoyang ———————————————————————————— 273
Kaifeng ——————————————————————————————— 278
Lanzhou ——————————————————————————————— 279
Dunhuang —————————————————————————————— 280

Guangzhou and the South East ————————————— 283
(Guangdong, Guangxi and Hainan Island)
Guangzhou ——————————————————————————— 283
Nanning ———————————————————————————————— 286
Guilin ——————————————————————————————————— 288
Hainan ———————————————————————————————— 291

The South West —————————————————————————— 292
(Sichuan, Yunnan, Guizhou)
Chengdu, Leshan and Emei Shan ——————————————— 292
Chongqing, Dazu ——————————————————————————— 295
The Yangzi Gorges ——————————————————————————— 297
Kunming ——————————————————————————————— 300
Xishuangbanna ————————————————————————————— 302

Xinjiang, the North West —————————————————— 303
(Xinjiang)
Urumqi ——————————————————————————————— 303
Turfan ———————————————————————————————— 304
Kashi (Kashgar) ———————————————————————————— 306

Tibet/Qinghai-Plateau ——————————————————— 307
(Tibet, Qinghai)
Lhasa ———————————————————————————————— 307
Xigaze ——————————————————————————————— 311
Gyantse ——————————————————————————————— 313
Xining ——————————————————————————————— 313

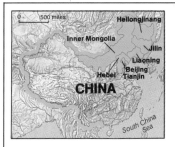

Beijing and the North

Beijing

Beijing, the largest city in China, extends over an area of 16,800 sq. km/6,486 sq. miles. Its present population is more than 9 million. Most important of all, it is the political centre of the People's Republic. The leading members of both state and party reside here. The National People's Congress convenes in Beijing and most of the central authorities, agencies, and ministries are located in the city.

Beijing is the youngest of all Chinese imperial cities. It became the centre of the nation at the time when the Mongols consolidated the north and the south into one huge empire. The city is first mentioned under the name of Ji; it was made a prefecture after the unification of the empire under Emperor Qin Shi Huangdi. During the Tang Dynasty it was named Youzhou. Around 1000 A.D. the city became the capital of the dynasties founded by the northern tribes and was given various names. Kublai Khan, the Mongol emperor, was the first to have a large palace city erected, which became renowned under the name of Dadu or Khanbalik. Its fame was partly due to the accounts of young Marco Polo, who had spent a number of years at the palace. Unfortunately, the palace was destroyed entirely as the Ming emperors drove out the Mongols. The imperial city as it stands today was built under the third Ming emperor.

The basic structures of the city built under Ming emperor Zhu Di are still recognizable today. The imperial city was patterned according to strict geometric rules. All of the important buildings are situated on a central north-south axis. Many of the streets (laid out in a chessboard pattern) have remained unchanged since the reign of Kublai Khan.

The first place a visitor in Beijing will go to is **Tiananmen Square;** from here one can reach all of the major sites in just a few minutes.

Tiananmen Square, or **Square of Heavenly Peace,** was built following the victorious revolution in 1949. Extending over 50 hectares, it is probably the largest square of this sort. Standing at the centre of the square is the **Monument to the People's Heroes,** an obelisk that bears inscriptions taken from Mao Zedong and Zhou Enlai. Its base is adorned with reliefs depicting various scenes from the revolution.

Facing towards the north from here, one will see the **Gate of Heavenly Peace,** Tiananmen. It lies directly behind Chang'an

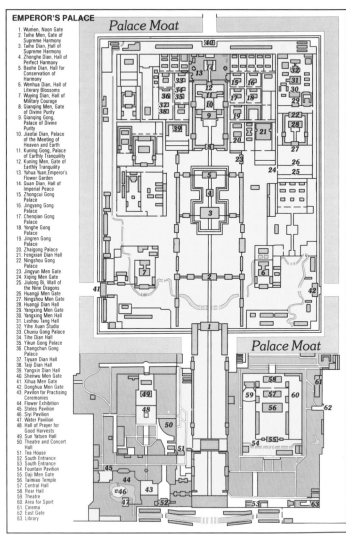

EMPEROR'S PALACE

1. Wumen, Noon Gate
2. Taihe Men, Gate of Supreme Harmony
3. Taihe Dian, Hall of Supreme Harmony
4. Zhonghe Dian, Hall of Perfect Harmony
5. Baohe Dian, Hall for Conservation of Harmony
6. Wenhua Dian, Hall of Literary Blossoms
7. Wuying Dian, Hall of Military Courage
8. Qianqing Men, Gate of Divine Purity
9. Qianqing Gong, Palace of Divine Purity
10. Jiaotai Dian, Palace of the Meeting of Heaven and Earth
11. Kuning Gong, Palace of Earthly Tranquility
12. Kuning Men, Gate of Earthly Tranquility
13. Yuhua Yuan, Emperor's Flower Garden
14. Quan Dian, Hall of Imperial Peace
15. Zhongcui Gong Palace
16. Jingyang Gong Palace
17. Chenqian Gong Palace
18. Yonghe Gong Palace
19. Jingren Gong Palace
20. Zhaigong Palace
21. Fengxian Dian Hall
22. Ningshou Gong Palace
23. Jingyun Men Gate
24. Xiqing Men Gate
25. Jiulong Bi, Wall of the Nine Dragons
26. Huangji Men Gate
27. Ningshou Men Gate
28. Huangji Dian Hall
29. Yangxing Men Gate
30. Yangxing Men Hall
31. Leshou Tang Hall
32. Yihe Xuan Studio
33. Chuxiu Gong Palace
34. Tihe Dian Hall
35. Yikun Gong Palace
36. Changchun Gong Palace
37. Tiyuan Dian Hall
38. Taiji Dian Hall
39. Yangxin Dian Hall
40. Shenwu Men Gate
41. Xihua Men Gate
42. Donghua Men Gate
43. Pavilon for Practising Ceremonies
44. Flower Exhibition
45. Steles Pavilion
46. Siyi Pavilion
47. Water Pavilion
48. Hall of Prayer for Good Harvests
49. Sun Yatsen Hall
50. Theatre and Concert Hall
51. Tea House
52. South Entrance
53. South Entrance
54. Fountain Pavilion
55. Daji Men Gate
56. Taimiao Temple
57. Central Hall
58. Rear Hall
59. Theatre
60. Area for Sport
61. Cinema
62. East Gate
63. Library

Palace Moat

Palace Moat

208

Avenue, which runs from west to east. It is the former entrance gate to the imperial city, once called "Forbidden City" because the common people were not allowed to enter it. **Wumen Gate,** located right behind it, is the entrance to the **Imperial Palace.** Farther to the north, one can also see the pavilion on the summit of **Coal Hill.**

The first thing one can see towards the south is the **Mao Mausoleum,** built in 1977, and, directly behind it, **Qianmen Gate.**

On the eastern side of the square stands a large building complex. Its northern wing houses the **Museum of the Chinese Revolution** and its southern one the **Museum of Chinese History.**

The National People's Congress convenes in the **Great Hall of the People,** which is situated on the west side. It has a meeting hall that can hold over 10,000 people. Important official receptions, festivities, or banquets also take place here. The southern wing of this building contains a number of smaller meeting rooms and the offices of the privy council. For several years now, this public hall has been open for visitors. Of special interest are the 30 reception rooms – one for each province – that have been decorated with provincial handicrafts.

Old Beijing was divided into four cities. The Outer City was where the common people could reside. Qianmen Gate, which is located to the south of the Mao Mausoleum, marked the border to the Inner City.

The entrance to the Imperial City was through Tianmen Gate. Wumen, or Midday Gate, was the passage to the Forbidden City, the Imperial Palace itself.

The **Imperial Palace** extends over an area of approximately 720 sq. m/861,11 sq. yards. It is surrounded by a 10 m (33 ft) wall, in front of which is a moat 50 m (164 ft) wide.

The palace is supposed to have 9,999 rooms, one less than the Palace of the Celestial Emperor. According to legend, the latter had 10,000 rooms. However, it should be mentioned that each space enclosed by four columns counts as a room in Chinese architecture of the antique period. The number 9,999 also seems to have its origins in legend as a count taken in 1958 only revealed 8,886 rooms. At any rate, the palace is so immense that the tourist can't possibly see it all in the brief time available to him. Therefore, the following description will just focus on the essential parts of the site.

One enters the palace through the u-shaped Wumen, or **Midday Gate.** At the centre, rising above the u-shaped vermillion wall, is a tower with a double roof covered by glazed yellow tiles. It is flanked by four pavilions from which it got its name: "Tower of the Five Phoenixes". During the Qing Dynasty it was common practice for the civil servants to gather here just before daybreak to await an audience with the emperor. Once past the gate, a way leads across **Gold Water Bridge,** which is made of white marble. Only the emperor could use the path along the middle of the bridge and the central gate of Wumen.

Then follows the **Gate of Supreme Harmony,** Taihemen. Behind this gate lies the largest courtyard of the palace. Close to 90,000 people can fit in this area extending over 30,000 sq. m (35,880 sq. yards). During the major ceremonies the honorary guard, military personel, and civil servants would form up here and pay homage to their emperor on bended knee.

Bordering the courtyard to the north is Taihedian, the **Hall of Supreme Harmony.** It is the largest hall of the palace and, at the same time, the largest wooden construction built in ancient China. Measuring 37 m (121 ft) in height, it was also the tallest building in imperial Beijing. No other building in the city was allowed to surpass this one in height; it would have been a sign of disregard for imperial authority. The building is supported by 72 huge vermillion columns. The six central columns surrounding the throne are decorated with gilded dragons, the symbol of imperial power. The throne stands on a platform 2 m (6.5 ft) high, which is also richly decorated. Dragon symbols cover the folding screen and the roof as well.

In order to reach this hall one has to climb a wide marble staircase with white marble balustrades. The ramp in the centre is reserved for the emperor. It is a huge slab of stone with dragons and symbolic clouds

carved on the surface. There are two narrow stairways on either side of it. The emperor was carried up the ramp in his sedan.

The Hall of Supreme Harmony was used for major ceremonial events, such as the festivities taking place after an ascension to the throne, larger audiences, or the ceremonies conducted on special festive days.

Next comes the **Hall of Complete Harmony,** Zhonghedian, a smaller building somewhat resembling a pavilion or a bower. The emperor used to rest here before the great ceremonies began and rehearsed his part or made final consultations with his masters of ceremonies. This hall also contains a throne and a number of tripods and incense vessels; two open imperial sedans are on display.

On the same terrace, lies the last of the three great halls, the **Hall of Preserving Harmony,** Baohedian. Here the emperors used to put on banquents for the representatives of the nobility on such occasions as the new year's festivities. It was also here that the imperial examinations were held under the Qing emperors. Anyone wanting a higher civil office was first required to pass this examination. At the centre of the hall stands yet another large throne. The five-piece backdrop is richly decorated. Symbolic figures made of bronze, incense vessels, cloisonné vases, and fans of peacock feathers surround the throne.

The halls located on the western and eastern side presently contain various exhibits from the palace treasury, including paintings, calligraphies, uniforms and costumes belonging to the emperor and the empress, jewellery, and implements.

A large marble staircase stands at the exit of the Hall of Preserving Harmony. Once again, the central path between the three marble terraces is covered by **stone reliefs.** Here lies the largest stone in the entire palace. It is a slab 16 m (52 ft) long and weighing close to 200 tons.

The purple wall that follows next, with its **Gate of Heavenly Purity,** Qianqingmen, is located on the central axis and marks the border between the Outer Court and the Inner Chambers. Four lions made of gilded bronze stand in front of the gate. Several large bronze water kettles stand along the wall that were also plated with gold at one time. The kettles still have visible scratch marks on them. On different occasions towards the close of the last century, plundering foreign soldiers peeled the gold off. The imperial family, court ladies, concubines, and eunuchs lived in the inner chambers. Behind the gate, in line with the north-south axis, lies the **Palace of Heavenly Purity,** Qianqinggong. The emperors usually chose to locate their sleeping quarters here. The last ceremony that ever took place in the palace was the wedding of Pu Yi, the last of the emperors. This happened in 1922, some 11 years after his abdication. Next is the **Palace of Union,** Jiaotaidian. This is the place where empresses were enthroned and

where they celebrated their birthdays or cultivated silkworms in the spring. Under Emperor Qianlong it was transformed into a hall of seals. Today, the hall contains an exhibit of 25 imperial seals made of jade.

The last hall in the Inner Chambers is the **Palace of Earthly Tranquility,** Kunninggong. It served as the empresses' sleeping and leisure quarters. Also contained within it is the completely red room where the imperial conjugal nights took place.

Having passed through the **Gate of Earthly Tranquility,** one arrives at the final section of the site, the **Imperial Garden** which dates back to the Ming era. Miniature stone landscapes, ancient pines and cypresses, ponds, bridges, pavilions, terraces, bamboo, and flowers; together they form a perfect example of Chinese horticulture.

The palaces to the rear are flanked on either side by the **Six Western Palaces** and the **Six**

Eastern Palaces. These were also used as sleeping quarters by the empresses, concubines, and eunuchs. Supposedly more than 1,000 concubines and even more eunuchs were living at the palace at certain periods during the Ming Dynasty.

Visitors usually go to the Six Eastern Palaces because the Museum of the Treasury is located there. It is found in the **Hall of Mental Cultivation,** Yangxingdian, formerly the private quarters of Emperor Qianlong and the dowager Ci Xi. The museum exhibits include a chime, two imperial costumes, weapons of the emperor, jewellery belonging to the empress, cloisonné and jade works, extremely valuable religious objects, and Buddha figures or stupas made of gold and encrusted with precious gems. A huge block of carved jade weighing 5 tons may also be seen here.

The exit to the Imperial Palace is the **Gate of Divine Wisdom,** Shenwumen, located behind the imperial flower garden.

Across from the northern gate of the Imperial Palace stands **Coal Hill,** Jingshan. The origin of its name remains a mystery. According to local tradition, the coal supplies for the palace were once kept on this spot. When weather conditions are good, it is worth climbing up the hill as the view of the Imperial Palace with its golden-yellow tiles reflecting in the light is beautiful. Towards the north one sees the Bell and Drum Tower. To the west lies Beihai Park with its large white pagoda. South of it is Zhongnanhai, where the Central Committee of the Communist party has its seat.

In the hot summer months the court would move to the cool gardens of the **Summer Palace.** The Summer Palace could be reached by ship directly from the Imperial Palace. This change of residence was an occasion for a splendid procession. Hundreds of smaller boats accompanied the emperor's large dragon ship.

The **Summer Palace** is situated to the northwest of the city. The emperors of the Jin Dynasty set up the first gardens there in the 12th century. This was continued by all of the succeeding dynasties, including the last one, the Qing. The basic structures of the contemporary site date back to the era of Emperor Qianlong (1736–1795). He had work done on it in a large scale. During the second half of the 19th century the site was destroyed several times, usually by foreign troops. They completely devastated it in 1860. The present site was restored in 1903. The deposed emperor Pu Yi was allowed to live there for a while. In 1924 the republic decreed that the site be opened to the public.

As far as the scenery is concerned, the 290 hectare site can be divided into two sectors. To the south lies the artificial **Kunming Lake.** A boat ride takes one past the 150 m (492 ft) long **Bridge of the Seventeen Arches** and the marble **Jade Belt Bridge.** These

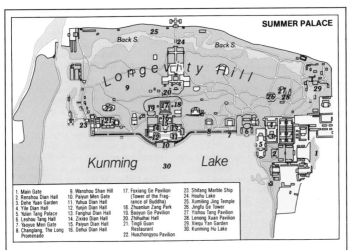

1. Main Gate
2. Renshou Dian Hall
3. Dehe Yuan Garden
4. Yile Dian Hall
5. Yulan Tang Palace
6. Leshou Tang Hall
7. Yaoyue Men Gate
8. Changlang, The Long Promenade
9. Wanshou Shan Hill
10. Paiyun Men Gate
11. Yuhua Dian Hall
12. Yunjin Dian Hall
13. Fanghui Dian Hall
14. Zixiao Dian Hall
15. Paiyun Dian Hall
16. Dehui Dian Hall
17. Foxiang Ge Pavilion (Tower of the Fragrance of Buddha)
18. Zhuanlun Zang Park
19. Baoyun Ge Pavilion
20. Zhihuihai Hall
21. Tingli Guan Restaurant
22. Huazhongyou Pavilion
23. Shifang Marble Ship
24. Houhu Lake
25. Xumiling Jing Temple
26. Jingfu Ge Tower
27. Yishou Tang Pavilion
28. Lenong Xuan Pavilion
29. Xiequ Yan Garden
30. Kunming Hu Lake

further subdivide the lake. The latter is located by the **West Dyke,** also a man-made construction which is an imitation of the scenery at West Lake near Hangzhou, where there is a similar dyke.

Wanshou Mountain and the numerous buildings found along its slopes make up the second sector.

One enters the palace at the **East Gate** and arrives at a section where the affairs of state were once conducted. The main building here is the seven-roomed **Hall of Benevolence and Longevity,** Renshoudian. Bronze dragons and phoenixes stand in front of the hall, together with a huge legendary creature. Dowager Ci Xi and Emperor gave audiences in this hall. The buildings to the north and south of it were used as offices for the ministries and administrative bodies.

In a westerly direction, behind the Renshoudian, is the residential sector. Here are the **Hall of Joy and Longevity,** Leshoutang, the summer residence of the empress dowager, and the **Hall of Jade Clear Ripples,** Yulantang, which was last occupied by Emperor Guangxu. To the north of Renshoudian lies **Deheyuan Garden** and the **Hall of Enjoyment,** Yiledian. The latter also has a three-storeyed stage, built in commemoration of the empress dowager's 60th birthday.

She used to watch the performances from a cubicle in **Yiledian Hall,** just accross from the stage. Nearly all of the halls in this part of the site have been preserved in their original form.

Situated along the northern shore of Kunming Lake is the recreation

213

and amusement area. A 728 m (2,388 ft) long **covered walkway** known as Long Corridor stretches along the shore of the lake in an east-west direction. Its ceiling and beams are decorated with paintings depicting ancient legendary landscapes and scenes.

A huge ornamental gate, **Gate of Dispersing Clouds,** or Paiyunmen, stands by the shore about halfway down the walkway. This is where the ascent to the summit of Wanshou Mountain begins, to the large **Tower of Buddhist Incense,** Foxiangge, and the Buddhist **Temple of the Sea of Wisdom,** Zhihuihai, located at the top. One will pass numerous halls and pavilions on the way up. A stone stairway towards the end of the trail may make the going a little more difficult. From the summit there is a beautiful view down each side of the mountain and of Kunming Lake. If the weather is fair, one may even be able to see the West Mountains. The **Temple of the Sea of Wisdom** is a rectangular building, the four sides of which have been covered with glazed green tiles. Small figures of Buddha rest in niches along the walls. On the northern slopes of Wanshou Mountain stand buildings and stupas with some elements of Tibetan style.

If one follows the walkway farther towards the east, one will get to **Tingliguan Restaurant** (its name means "listening to the song of the golden oriole"). Imperial recipes are excellently prepared here. Unfortunately, the restaurant is often very crowded at noon. At the end of the walkway is the famous **Marble Boat.** The empress had it built with funds that were meant to be used for refitting the navy.

Many Chinese like to visit this beautiful site in the summer. Consequently, it is often overcrowded, especially along the shores of Kunming Lake. Those who are looking for a quieter spot should retreat towards the northern slope of Wanshou Mountain and go to **Rear Lake.** At the eastern end of this lake is the **Garden of Harmonious Interests,** Xieguyuan, which is often referred to as the "garden within a garden". It is also easy to reach from the main entrance, the East Gate, if one walks due north. The garden was modelled on the southern Chinese style of garden landscaping. Four building complexes surround a lotus pond, which is lined with willows at its edges. A covered walkway connects thirteen pavilions to one another. The bridges spanning the pond break up the area into smaller perimeters. The appearance of the garden is different in each one of these.

It is also worth visiting this site in the winter. Since Lake Kunming is shallow, it is frozen over for at least two months and thus offers enough room for thousands of skaters. Many people, especially older men, take advantage of the cold northerly winds and let their beautifully made kites rise up into the clear blue sky.

One of the larger historical sites the city has to offer, the **Temple of Heaven,** is actually the largest temple complex in all of China. Extending over 270 hectares, this site is three times the size of the Imperial Palace, but there are just a few buildings on it.

It was erected under the Ming emperor Yongle in 1420. The Ming and Qing emperors used to make two annual pilgrimages to the Temple of Heaven in order to ask the Emperor of Heaven for a rich harvest or to make harvest sacrifices to him.

The temple is generally entered through the **Western Gate of Heaven.** It takes one directly to a large courtyard, at the centre of which stands the **Hall of Prayer for Good Harvests,** Qiniandian. The temple has a unique three-storeyed circular roof covered with blue tiles. It was built in 1420 and has been restored many times since then. It burned down in 1889, when it was struck by lightning. After that it was rebuilt in its original form. The temple measures 30 m (114 ft) in diameter and 38 m (125 ft) in height. A gilded globe crowns the roof. The entire hall was constructed without steel girders or nails. Columns, beams, and a complicated system of brackets support the roof.

The 28 vermillion columns have symbolic meaning. The four columns standing in the middle are the strongest. They are entwined by golden dragons, which stand for the four seasons. Another twelve columns are spaced around these in a circle, representing the twelve months of the year. The outermost ring of twelve columns are symbolic for the 12 hours of the day. In

contrast to present day practice, imperial days were divided into twelve units of two hours each. The ceiling is decorated with magnificent carvings and paintings. At the centre of the ceiling are images of a dragon and a phoenix, the symbols for the emperor and the empress.

Then one moves on in a southerly direction, through the **Altar of Prayer for Good Harvests,** Qinianmen. If one follows a somewhat longer and elevated path, one will arrive at the **Imperial Heavenly Vault,** Huangqiongyu. It is a round hall, also covered by a roof of glazed blue tiles, that was used as a storage place for ceremonial objects like the commemorative tablets of the God of Heaven. There is not a single cross-beam in this hall; the roof is entirely supported by a unique system of graded brackets.

An echo wall surrounds this hall. It was constructed in such a way that it is possible to carry on a conversation with a person standing at some distance away, just as long as one faces the wall whilst speaking. However, when there are too many tourists talking there will be enough distortion to make communication very difficult. There are three other echo spots marked by stones on the floor of the hall. If one calls out while standing on the first stone, one will hear a single echo. On the second stone one can hear a double echo and on the third stone a tripple echo.

The last building that follows is the **Circular Mound Altar**, Huanqui, a round white marble terrace constructed in three levels. The total height is 5 m (16 ft) and the topmost terrace has a circumference of 30 m (98 ft). The tiles covering the terrace are placed in symbolic order. The stone at the centre is surrounded by a ring of nine tiles. The successive rings have 18 tiles, then 27, and so on times nine. In ancient China odd numbers were considered to be lucky. The highest of the odd numbers was reserved for the emperor.

Two low walls surround the altar that are also covered by blue tiles. The first one is round and the second one square, in accordance with the ancient cosmological notion that the heavens were round and the earth a square slab.

The stone at the centre of the topmost terrace was designated as the centre of the earth by the Chinese. If you stand on this stone and say something, you will hear your own voice amplified.

The Chinese say that if one has not seen the **Great Wall,** one has never been to China. It would indeed be difficult to find a tourist who did not stand on top of the Great Wall at least once during his trip to China. It is undoubtedly one of the most impressive constructions ever to have been built by mankind.

Some 2,500 years ago, the Chinese principalities had to erect bulwarks in order to protect themselves from the warlike nomadic tribes of the north. Emperor Qin Shi Huang Di (221–210 B.C.) was the first to have the various sections of walls joined and enlarged to form one huge bulwark. Even at that

time, the wall ran in an easterly direction from the province of Gansu across Inner Mongolia, Shaanxi, Shanxi, Hebei, all the way to the eastern part of the province of Liaoning. The course of the wall has not changed much since then, with the exception of the few hundred miles added on to the west by the Han Dynasty.

The Ming emperor Taizu was the last person to have the wall rebuilt in fear of the return of the Mongols. The wall had previously been made entirely of earth but the emperor had it reinforced with tiles and stones.

The Chinese call their wall Wan Li Chang Cheng, "10,000-Li Long Wall". Ten thousand Li are equal to about 5,000 km (3,100 miles). In fact, the wall from the Ming era is somewhat longer. It measures 6,350 km (3,946 miles) in length; an incredibly huge construction, which cosmonauts in orbit are still able to discern with their bare eyes.

The tourist will usually take the bus or train from Beijing to **Badaling,** which is approximately 80 km (50 miles) from the centre of the city. The bus journey leads through **Juyongguan Pass.** In the middle of this ravine stands a stone archway that bears the **Terrace of Clouds,** Yuntai. Of special interest are the inscriptions on the inside of the archway. They include texts in Chinese, Sanskrit, Tibetan, Tungusic, Uighur, and Mongolian. Juyongguan Pass was once the most important gateway to the capital from the north.

The wall close to Badaling has been rebuilt numerous times right up to the modern period, so that it is very well preserved. If one walks on top of the wall – either in a westerly or an easterly direction – one soon arrives at the steep approaches to the watchtowers with their battlements and embrasures. Alarm towers were set up on top of the more prominent elevations in the distance, which could be seen from afar. Fires were lit on top of these towers if there was an alarm and so the information could be immediately conveyed to the next command post.

The Badaling section of wall is about 8 m (26 ft) high and nearly 7 m (23 ft) across at the base. Although it is somewhat narrower at the top, there is still enough room for six horses to move along side by side. Steps were cut into the steep embankments at certain intervals, which made it possible to get to the top of the wall from the outside.

Apart from the Great Wall, one can also see the remains of the older sections of walls scattered throughout several provinces. When all of these are taken together, they cover a distance of about 50,000 km (31,000 miles).

On the way back from the Great Wall one can stop off and visit the **Ming graves,** Shisanling, some 50 km (31 miles) north-west of Beijing. Thirteen of the 16 Ming emperors were buried here. Zhu Di, the third Ming emperor, chose this particular site because it is shielded by mountain ranges to the west, north, and east. The valley opens up into the Plain of Hebei to the south, where the Dragon and Tiger Mountains form a natural gateway to the burial site.

First one encounters the **Sacred Gate** which is made of white marble. Directly behind it is the **Great Red Gate,** Dagongmen. It has red walls, three entranceways, and a roof covered with glazed yellow tiles. Stone slabs standing on both sides bear the following inscription: "All military and civilian dignitaries must get off their horses at this point". The entire site was once surrounded by a 40 km (25 mile) long rampart. Only a few remains of it are still to be seen today.

Behind the main gate is a small pagoda with a large slab of stone resting on the back of a turtle figure. To the rear of this pavilion the **Avenue of Souls,** sometimes referred to as the Path of Stone Figures, begins. Twenty-four animal figures and twelve human ones, the latter representing military or civilian dignitaries and high officials, seem to indicate that they will continue to pay homage to and protect the emperor beyond death. The Path of Souls ends in front of the **Dragon and Phoenix Gate.**

Two of the graves are open to the public: Changling and Dingling. **Changling,** containing the remains of the third Ming emperor, Yongle, is both the oldest and the largest. However, the burial-mound itself has not been uncovered so far. Therefore, most visitors will choose to visit **Dingling grave,** containing the remains of Ming emperor Wan Li. It was uncovered in 1956. It is said that more than 30,000 people worked each day for a total of six years in order to complete this grave. The costs were equal to the sum taken in by land taxes levied throughout the entire nation for a period of two years.

The grave site is surrounded by a high wall; its gate opens up into the first courtyard. A path crossing over an elevated terrace leads to the second courtyard. All that has remained of the sacrificial hall located in the second courtyard are the stone floor and the stumps of the former columns.

Two small exhibition halls stand one on each side of the third courtyard, containing displays of objects found at the grave site. Among these are two precious crowns made of gold and set with gems and pearls.

At the end of the third courtyard is a stairway leading up to a towering stela. The entrance to the grave itself is located behind it. However, if there are too many visitors, one may have to climb down the rear side of the burial-mound and then come out again in front of the stela.

The **Underground Palace** has three main halls and two side ones. Huge marble gates 3.3 m (11 ft) high and 1.7 m (6 ft) wide divide the three main halls. Each one of the doors weighs 4 tons.

Three stone thrones stand in the central hall. The tombs of the emperor and both of his wives lie in the rear chamber. Twenty-six chests full of treasures were discovered during the excavations of the site. Both of the side halls are empty.

Other imperial burial sites still within the sector of Beijing are the graves of the Western and Eastern Qing.

The **Eastern Qing graves** are located 125 km (78 miles) outside of Beijing in the district of Zunhua, in the province of Hebei. This site is not much different from the Ming graves. Of the 15 graves, the one containing the remains of empress dowager Ci Xi is both the largest and the most important. It has been uncovered and is now open to the public. Fine reliefs and Buddhist inscriptions line the marble walls of the Underground Palace. Tourists seldom come here because they usually spend no more than a few days in Beijing. Furthermore, a special permit is needed to visit this site.

The **Western Qing graves** are in Lianggezhuang, Yixian District, about 100 km (62 miles) south-west of Beijing. Four Qing emperors, three empresses, three concubines, as well as a number of princes and princesses rest here. Not one of the graves at this site has been uncovered so far.

Beijing has a number of beautiful parks, a few of which deserve to be introduced at this point. To the west of the Imperial Palace, in the area where Kublai Khan's capital Dadu once stood, lies **Beihai Park** (North Sea Park). Both the **Great Jade Vessel** in the **Round City** (Tuancheng) and the **Iron Wall** (Tieyingbi), located on the north shore of the lake, date from this period. The **Round City** is situated by the south gate of the park and is surrounded by a round wall 5 m (16 ft) in height. Its main attraction is a 1.5 m (5 ft) high **Buddha figure made of white jade.** The robe of the figure is studded with rubis and emeralds. The **Great Jade Vessel,** a basin 60 cm (24″) in height and 1.5 m (5 ft) in diameter, stands in the Pavilion of the Jade Vessel. It is said that Kublai Khan once used it as a container for wine.

Walking towards the north from the Round City, one will arrive at a small bridge that leads to the **Jade Flower Isle.** On the summit of the elevated island stands the **White Dagoba** Baita, a Tibetan style stupa built in 1651 in honour of the visiting Dalai Lama. A covered walk winds along the north shore of the island. **Fangshan Restaurant** is also located here. It prepares imperial dishes, but at prices that are also almost imperial. It is also very difficult to obtain a reservation for a table. The **Iron Wall** and the **Nine Dragon Screen** are found to the north of the park. Worth seeing as well is the **Palace of the Ten Thousand Buddhas,** Wanfolou. Emperor Qianlong had it built in celebration of his mother's 80th birthday. There are ten thousand niches along the three-storeyed building; a gilded Buddha once stood in each one.

Behind the Gate of Heavenly Peace, just before one arrives at the entrance to the Imperial Palace, are two more large parks. The one to the west, **Zhongshan Park** (Sun Yatsen Park), is a favourite recreation spot for the inhabitants of Beijing because it is located right in the centre of the city. Behind the large flower garden stand seven tall cypresses that are thought to be more than 1,000 years old. To the rear of the park is the Sun Yatsen

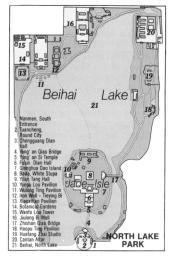

1. Nanmen, South Entrance
2. Tuancheng, Round City
3. Chengguang Dian Hall
4. Yong' an Qiao Bridge
5. Yong' an Si Temple
6. Falun Dian Hall
7. Qionghua Dao Island
8. Baita, White Stupa
9. Yilan Tang Hall
10. Yuequ Lou Pavilion
11. Wulong Ting Pavilion
12. Iron Wall – Tieying Bi
13. Xiaoxitian Pavilion
14. Botanical Gardens
15. Wanfo Lou Tower
16. Jiulong Bi Wall
17. Zhishan Qiao Bridge
18. Haopu Ting Pavilion
19. Huafang Zhai Studio
20. Cantan Altar
21. Beihai, North Lake

Hall. This is where the body of Dr. Sun Yatsen, first president of the 1911 Republic, was laid out in state.

To the east of Tiananmen lies the **Working People's Palace of Culture.** It presently contains a basketball court, an open-air stage, a cinema, and other recreational facilities. The Imperial Ancestry Temple of the Ming and the Qing emperors once stood here. The terrace of the **Altar of Earth and Harvest,** Shejitan, located to the rear of the site, is still very well preserved.

Many of those living in Beijing like to spend the weekend at the West Mountains, some 20 km (12 miles) outside the city. For people who enjoy taking long walks through beautiful scenery, **Fragrant Hill Park** (also known as Xiangshan Park) can be recommended. Several of the emperors had temples and pavilions built here some 700 years ago. In the northern section of the park stands the Lamaist **Bright Temple,** Zhaomiao, which was built in honour of the Tibetan Pantchen Lama in 1780. Standing to the west of it is a beautiful octagonal pagoda, Linlita. It is seven storeys high and covered with glazed tiles. copper bells hanging from the corners of each story tinkle even in the slightest breeze.

To the north of the park, on the eastern slopes of Fragrant Hill, stands the **Temple of Azure Clouds,** Biyunsi. It was built in 1366, towards the end of the Yuan Dynasty. Its major attractions are the Hall of the 500 lohans, with its gilded wooden statues approximately 1.5 m (5 ft) in size, and the Vajra Stupa, or **Diamond Pagoda.** Both of its floors are made of white marble. The upper one is decorated all the way around with reliefs. At the centre of the top platform stands a white dagoba, which is in turn surrounded by two other dagobas and a number of smaller pagodas.

The **Temple of the Sleeping Buddha,** Wofosi, is also located on the West Mountains. Although the temple generally goes by this name, it is officially called "Temple of the Universal Spiritual Awakening", Shifangpujue. It dates back to the 7th century A. D. The most interesting statue here is the **Sleeping Buddha** found in the fourth hall. This figure, which weighs 54 tons, was apparently cast in 1321, at the time of the Mongol rule. It represents a legend which describes Buddha's attainment of Nirvana.

The figure is over 5 m (16 ft) long, well proportioned, and sculptured in a naturalistic style. Buddha is lying on his side, one hand supporting his head and the other resting on his body. He is surrounded by twelve statues representing his disciples.

Beijing's best preserved and most important temple site is the **Lamaist Temple Yonghegong,** situated in the eastern part of the city. This site was once the residence of Emperor Yongzheng, before he ascended the throne. The palace was transformed into a monastery after his death. The Four Gods of Heaven and one Buddha Maitreya stand in the first hall. In the following hall one can see the Buddhas of the Three Worlds: Buddha Sakyamuni, Kasyapa, and Maitreya. They are flanked by 18 lohans standing on each side of the hall. Tsongkhapa, the great Buddhist reformer and founder of the Yellow Cap Sect, is honoured in the fourth hall. The almost 6 m (20 ft) bronze figure of Tsongkhapa is an imposing appearance. Behind it is the Mountain of 500 lohans, a carving made of sandalwood. The lohan figures themselves are made of gold, silver, copper, iron, and tin.

The most interesting of all the statues is found in the last hall, Dafolou, the **Hall of the Great Buddha.** At the centre of the three-storeyed building constructed of wood stands an 18 m (59 ft) statue of Buddha Maitreya, the Buddha of the future. It is carved out of a single sandalwood log.

The side halls contain numerous figures from the seemingly endless Lamaist Buddhist pantheon.

Beijing, as a cultural centre, has a number of theatres, stages, and halls to offer. Since – unlike other cities of the world – there is practically no night life in Beijing, one should take the opportunity of watching a performance at the Peking Opera or an acrobatics show. The ensembles at Beijing are ranked among the very best of the nation.

Shopping can be taken care of at the **Friendship Store** located near the embassies; it is the largest in all of China. Here one can obtain both Chinese export goods and imported foreign wares. Beijing's largest shopping street is **Wangfujing.** It runs from north to south, due east of the Beijing Hotel.

Also well known is **Liulichang,** Beijing's area of antique shops. It was restored to its original form in 1983 and 1984. Other than antiques, one can also obtain jewellery, porcelain, Paintings, sculptures, scrolls, lacquered works, and old books here. Internationally known is the **Rongbaozhai Studio** at Nr. 19 Liulichang. Valuable originals and reproductions are sold here and costly paintings restored.

Tianjin

Tianjin is not really one of China's tourist attractions, as it has few cultural or historical highlights to offer. In the past, many tourists have become acquainted with Tianjin simply because all the hotels in Beijing were booked up. This is highly unlikely to happen now, because many hotels have been built in Beijing since then. Nevertheless, someone spending several days at Beijing may still want to make a day's journey to Tianjin. It is the third largest city in China, with 7.8 million inhabitants. Along with Beijing and Shanghai, it is also one of the three administrative centres of the country. It can be reached quite comfortably by train in about two hours.

Tianjin is only 120 km (75 miles) from Beijing. It is located on the Bay of Bohai and it has the largest man-made harbour in China. This makes Tianjin one of the largest industrial and commercial areas of the country. Its opportune position by the ocean, at the confluence of five tributaries of the navigable Haihe, and its location on the Beijing-Shanghai railway also make it an important junction in northern China.

Ships up to 10,000 tons can dock at the modern **Xingang Harbour** and smaller craft can make it up the Haihe directly to Tianjin. The city has a lot of heavy industry, including iron and steel mills and chemical enterprises. Watches, cameras, and electric instruments are also produced here. Many Chinese hotels and skyscrapers have elevators that were made in Tianjin.

Excavations have shown that there was a larger settlement in this area in the early centuries prior to the birth of Christ. During the reign of the Mongols, Tianjin was a fortified city bearing the name of Zhigu, which roughly translated means "buy and sell". This indicates that it must have been an important commercial centre back then already.

The garrison was further fortified during the Ming era, when a wall was erected all around it. The harbour at Tianjin was coveted by the foreign powers at the middle of the last century, the latter being willing to gain access to the Chinese market with the use of violence if necessary. In 1858, the Qing regime had to sign the Treaty of Tianjin, thereby giving the British and French the first concession rights. In 1860, British and French troops marched from here to Beijing where, among other things, they destroyed the Summer Palace. Other European nations followed suit. By the end of the century, nine foreign powers had established themselves in this city.

Anyone who decides to remain in the city ought to visit the **Park on the Water,** Shuishang Gogyuan, which is located on the south-western outskirts of town. It is the largest park of the city. This particular site with its lakes and islands also has a zoo, a theatre, and numerous smaller pavilions to offer. **Jinshan Park** is also situated to the south of the city. **Xigu Park** and **Beining Park** are found to the north.

It is also worth taking a walk to the old quarter of the town to visit the **Renmin Bazaar** (People's Bazaar). A stroll along the narrow lanes with their innumerable small shops – and large department stores – provides one with a good insight into the daily life style of a large Chinese city.

Outside the city itself, in the **district of Jixian,** which is still a part of the city's administrative sector, one can visit the **Dule Temple.** Dule means solitary fortune. The temple houses a statue of Guanyin, the Goddess of Mercy.

Built during the Tang Dynasty and then restored in 984, the temple ranks as one of China's oldest wooden buildings.

Another place worth visiting in the district of Jixian are the **Panshan Mountains.** Temples, pagodas, waterfalls, bizarre rock formations, and pine forests all render a memorable impression of typical Chinese mountain scenery.

Harbin

Harbin, the capital of Heilongjiang, the northernmost province of China, is located by the Sunghua River, in the middle of the fertile northern Chinese plain. The name is derived from the Mongolian Arjin, which is what this relatively unimportant settlement was called up until the last century.

The Russians brought about rapid progress in this city when they began to build a railway in 1896. Harbin was then joined to the main Trans-Siberian Line. In the years that followed, Russian merchants and missionaries came to live in Harbin. They set up factories, stores, and churches. Many of the buildings at Harbin, especially the 30 orthodox churches, recall the extent of Russian immigration.

Other foreigners soon followed suit. The former sleepy fishing village of Harbin quickly developed into an important junction in northern China and ultimately emerged as a major industrial and commercial centre. Finally, more than 100,000 foreigners coming from 36 different countries were residing in Harbin. Banks, hotels, bars, gambling saloons, appartment buildings, and expensive villas began to spring up.

All this building and modernization work was carried out despite the inhospitable weather. The average temperature from December to February is −30°C (−4°F) and snowfall is very heavy. During this time the inhabitants of Harbin buy their milk in frozen bricks, which they thaw out again at home. Thawed pears are considered to be a delicacy and are consumed during the Spring Festival. On this particular festive occasion, as well as during the New Year's Festival (based on the Chinese moon calendar), one may witness another one of Harbin's peculiarities. During these festive days, the people all over China hang up lanterns. The same practice is also to be found in Harbin, but here the **lanterns are made of ice.** Water is frozen in a jar and then hollowed out and decorated with fine carvings on the outside. A candle can be lit inside of it, and the extreme temperature keeps the lantern from melting.

Just as in many Japanese cities, numerous **ice sculptors** practice their art here during the winter. Large blocks of ice are cut out of the Songhua River and then brought to one of the parks alongside the riverbanks. The sculptors quickly transform the blocks of ice into unique works of art – flower vases, carp, birds, skaters, pavilions, lanterns and, above all, the great heroes of Chinese mythology take shape. In the evenings these are lit up and innumerable people come to relax in this wonderland of ice after they have finished work.

Harbin proudly calls itself the city of parks. There are 13 of them in this city, most of them along the banks of the Songhua River.

The **Park on the Riverbank,** Jiangpan Gongyuan, extending over an area of 10 hectares, is one of the largest and most beautiful of these. It offers the inhabitants of Harbin numerous recreation facilities, from restaurants to a watersports centre.

Situated in the middle of the river is **Sun Isle,** Taiyang. Its lawns, flower-gardens, and pavilions make it an ideal place to go for walks. During the summer, one can go to **Sun Isle Park** for picnics or simply to enjoy the natural beach.

At the centre of the city, not far from the railway station. is the **Children's Park,** Ertong Gongyuan. The children have a great time riding on the 2 km (1.2 mile) long model railway. A small diesel locomotive can pull up to two hundred of them at one time. The part of the railway personnel is also played by the children.

Not far from the railway station is the **Provincial Museum** of **Heilongjiang.** Its displays focus on the history of the province, but a number of extinct animals are also shown.

The largest temple of the province is also located at Harbin. It is the Buddhist Temple **Jile Si,** which wasn't built until 1924. The major attraction here, other than the main hall with its statue of Buddha Amitabha, is the **Pagoda Qiji Futu Ta.**

The rare northern Chinese tiger can be seen at the zoo located in the southwestern part of the city.

Changchun

The city of Changchun is located on the Yitong River and has a population of 1.5 million. It has been the capital of Jilin Province since 1954. During the 30's it became the capital of the state of Manchuguo, which was established by the Japanese. They named the city Xinjing (New Capital). The last emperor of the Qing Dynasty, Pu Yi, was reinstated by the Japanese. He had previously assumed the throne and then been deposed while still an infant.

The **Imperial Palace** to the north-east of the city used to be Pu Yi's residence. It is a relatively small and recent construction, not to be compared with the old palaces in Beijing or any other former imperial city. The basic structure of the site is like that of most other palaces. The outer perimeters were designed for receptions or ceremonies; behind them is the interior palace with the private chambers of the imperial family. After the defeat of the Japanese, Pu Yi was taken prisoner by the Soviets and then later extradited to the Chinese. They sentenced him to a long term of prison for treason and collaboration with the Japanese aggressors. He died as a free man in Beijing. His memoirs were published under the title "I Was Emperor of China".

Otherwise, Changchun has no sites of historical interest to offer. It is known nationwide for its **car industry.** The first car factory in China was constructed in 1953; today it produces buses, trucks, and tractors for the greater part. The large black official limousines, "Red Flag" (hongqi), were also manufactured here until three years ago. It has been phased out since then because the high costs resulting from the limited production were considered to be excessive. Occasionally, tourists may get the chance to visit the **film studios** in Changchun, which enjoy a good reputation throughout the country. The favourite place for the inhabitants of the city to go for excursions or recreation is **Xinlicheng Reservoir,** situated 12.5 km (8 miles) miles outside the city on the upper course of the Yitong River.

Shenyang

Shenyang, the capital of Liaoning Province with 4 million inhabitants, ranks as one of the largest cities in China.

Shenyang first became historically important when the Manchu united under their feudal lord Nurhaci and established control over North East China at the beginning of the 17th century. They made Shenyang their capital and gave it the Manchu name of Mukden. The son of Nurhaci, Abukai, founded the Qing Dynasty in 1636. Eight years later, he was able to conquer Beijing and extend his rule over all of China. The Qing moved to the palaces in Beijing, but often returned to Shenyang to pay homage to their ancestors.

The Russians set up their administrative centre here during the construction of the East China Railway. Later it was used as a base by the Japnese, who transported the natural resources they had exploited in the area to their homeland. The Mukden Incident, when shots were exchanged between Japanese soldiers and Qing troops, was used by the Japanese as an excuse to declare war on China.

Today, Shenyang is the most important cultural and industrial centre of north-east China.

The **Imperial Palace,** a relic from the period of the conquest of China by the Manchu, was built in 1636. It is occasionally referred to as the **Little Imperial Palace,** Xiao Gugong, when compared to the Imperial Palace in Beijing. It was the residence of the first Qing emperors before they moved their capital to Beijing. As a sign of homage to his ancestors, the great Qing emperor Qianlong had the palace enlarged during the middle of the 18th century. The main gate of the palace faces south as usual. In the eastern section of the palace there is a large octagonal hall, Dazheng Dian, combining Manchurian, Chinese, and Mongolian styles. The roof is covered with glazed yellow tiles, the imperial colour. Mighty red pillars entwined by golden dragons support the roof. Ten smaller pavilions flank the hall, which today contain an exhibition of weapons, uniforms, and armour. The Qing emperor held important ceremonies in the central part of the palace. Behind this, are the private chambers. At the entrance to these there is a large three-storey pavilion, the **Tower of Phoenix,** where banquets took place. In the western section, which was added on later by Emperor Qianlong, there is an open-air stage and, behind it, the imperial library.

Nurhaci, unifier of the Manzhu tribes and conqueror of North China, lies buried in the **Imperial Grave of the East** (Dongling). One steps into the burial site through the large entrance gate and continues along the **Path of Souls,** lined by various stone statuettes. Having passed the first inscribed stela, one arrives at the Hall of Ancestry Worship. Behind yet another stela with the inscription "Grave of the Emperor Taizu", or Nurhaci, lies the unopened burial-mound.

The **North Grave,** Beiling, the burial-site of his son Abukai, is much larger. It measures over 400 hectares and is surrounded by a wall. Behind the entrance gate there is also an **avenue of stone statues** which include two figures of horses – reproductions of Abukai's favourite steeds. Then one arrives at the **"Square City",** the interior grave-site, which also encloses an ancestry hall and a second stela and is surrounded by high walls. The burial-mound of the first Qing emperor, also said to contain his first wife as well as various concubines, has not been opened so far.

Otherwise, all Shenyang has to offer is the **Lamaist temple Shisheng Si** and, if one is interested in the products and efficiency of Shenyang's industry, the **Liaoning Exhibition Hall.**

Hohhot

Hohhot, a Mongolian name meaning "blue city", is the capital of the autonomous province of Inner Mongolia, Neimenggu. Altan Khan, feudal lord and leader of the eastern Mongolian tribes, founded the settlement in the middle of the 16th century. Hohhot is situated on the south rim of the Gobi Desert, just 200 km (124 miles) from Datong. The dry and cold climate is brought about by the continental land masses in the north. The winters are extreme because of the cold northerly winds from Siberia. The average temperature in June and July is 77°F (25°C).

The greater part of the Mongolian steppe-plateau (1,000 m/3,280 ft above sea level on average) is desert region. The rest of the area is only suitable for raising stock. Sheep and goats are usually grazed here. Farming is only possible in the south-western part of the province, where the Yellow River (Huanghe) flows in a wide arch through Inner Mongolia. After the great Mongolian onslaught of the 13th century, in the course of which Dschingis Khan and Kublai Khan established an incomparable empire, the Mongolians never again rose to such heights. Mongolian freedom fighters – with the support of the Russians – took advantage of the fall of the Qing Dynasty in 1911 to sever Outer Mongolia and declare it an independent state. During the 30's, many Mongolians joined the communist freedom fighters in their struggle against the Japanese. Upon the foundation of the People's Republic, Inner Mongolia was declared an autonomous province. Of its approximately 20 million inhabitants, only 2.5 million are Mongolians. With the exception of a few Hui and Manchu, the remainder are all Han Chinese, who started coming there during the Ming Dynasty and then arrived in ever greater numbers after 1949.

Hohhot developed into a modern industrial city after 1949, especially in the sector of wool and leather processing as well as chemicals and mechanical engineering.

Today, tourists can still live in yurts, the traditional felt tents of the nomads. Of course, these have been comfortably furnished specifically for tourists. The programme of activities includes traditional **mounted games, wrestling matches,** and **folkloric presentations** that always take place during important festivities and are sometimes put on exclusively for the benefit of tourists. Besides this, Hohhot still has a number of interesting historical sites to offer.

The **Temple of the Five Pagodas** was built during the rule of Qing emperor Yongzheng (1723–1735). Only the **Diamond Pagoda,** the base of which is adorned with Mongolian, Tibetan, and Sanskrit inscriptions, is still in good condition. Five pagodas and one pavilion rise up from the terrace.

An 18th century **mosque** is located near the north gate of the old town.

Inside the old town itself stands the **Lamaist temple Xilitu Zhao,** built in Tibetan style with a 15 m (49 ft) high Dagoba, a pagoda also built in Tibetan style.

The **Dazhao Monastery,** a combinaton of Chinese and Tibetan architectural styles, was built under the direction of the Mongolian feudal lord Altan Khan, who converted his subjects to the Lamaist Buddhism practiced by the Gelugpa Sect (Yellow Cap Sect). The monastery contains a **silver Buddha** and is therefore known locally as the **Temple of the Silver Buddha.**

In the eastern part of the city an old pagoda still stands which was built around 1000 A. D. of wood and bricks. The base of this 43 m (141 ft) structure is of particular interest consisting of stylized lotus blossoms. It is known locally as the **White Pagoda.**

Approximately 10 km (33 miles) south of the city is the **grave of the concubine Wang Zhaojun.** This lady features in many Chinese legends, stories and operas. Zhaojun was an expectionally beautiful concubine at the court of Emperor Yuan (48–33 B. C.) of the Western Han Dynasty. In order to make peace with the warlike Huns of the north, the emperor offered to give their king a princess in marriage. Since no one was about to consider giving up one of the favourite princesses or concubines to the "barbarians" from the north, Zhaojun, whose beauty had not yet come to the notice of the emperor, was chosen to go. When he saw her for the first time as she was about to depart, he regretted his decision, but by then it was too late.

In the legends, Zhaojun's sacrifice is praised as a patriotic deed. One pagoda stands on top of her burial-mound and another in front. Wang Zhaojun's life is depicted in an exhibition hall.

From Hohhot, one may also journey to the **communes** in the area and gain an impression of the living and working conditions of the Mongolian cattle-breeders and farmers.

Baotou

The city of Baotou was once a small trading post. It became an important commercial centre in the 30's, when it was connected to Beijing by rail. In the 50's, connections to Northwest China, Central China, and Sichuan were established by the construction of a railroad to Lanzhou. Today, Baotou has a large iron and steel plant and ranks as the most important industrial city in Inner Mongolia after Hohhot. Its present population is 1.5 million.

The folkloric programme in Baotou is very similar to the one offered in Hohhot.

The only worthwhile attractions are situated at quite a distance from the city itself. Some 70 km (43 miles) to the north-west is the **Lamaist temple Wudang Zhao.** It was built at the end of the 17th century and once housed over 1,000 monks. As was the case in Tibet, they were driven out of their monasteries during the Cultural Revolution.

It is nearly 300 km (186 miles) to the **tomb of Dschingis Khan** in Yijin Horo, who died in 1227. There are three halls at the burial-site. The bodies of Dschingis Khan and his three wives lie in the middle hall and that of one of his sons and his wife in the eastern hall. The weapons and instruments of the great Khan are exhibited in the western hall.

Chengde

Chengde, also known under its former name of **Jehol,** is located in the province of Hebei, 260 km (162 miles) north-east of Beijing. The beautiful landscape of Chengde with its many mountains, valleys, forests, and rivers, incited Qing emperor Kangxi to have a summer palace erected there. Its construction was

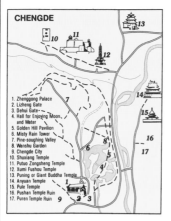

CHENGDE

1. Zhenggong Palace
2. Lizheng Gate
3. Dehui Gate
4. Hall for Enjoying Moon, and Water
5. Golden Hill Pavilion
6. Misty Rain Tower
7. Pine-soughing Valley
8. Wanshu Garden
9. Chengde City
10. Shuxiang Temple
11. Putuo Zongsheng Temple
12. Xumi Fushou Temple
13. Puning or Giant Buddha Temple
14. Anyuan Temple
15. Pule Temple
16. Pushan Temple Ruin
17. Puren Temple Ruin

begun in 1703 and did not terminate until 1790, during the rule of Emperor Qianlong. The buildings at this site reflect the political ambitions of the Qing, who sought to strengthen the ties within the empire and with Tibet especially. The summer residence thus incorporates replicas of

the Potala, the palace of the Dalai Lama in Lhasa, as well as several Tibetan temples and monasteries.

For hundreds of years, the imperial court moved regularly to Chengde during the summer and conducted the affairs of the empire from there, including the reception of foreign representatives. It was not until 1820, when Emperor Jiaqing (1796–1820) was struck by lightning here, that the emperors no longer dared to return to Chengde and the residence began to fall into a state of dilapidation.

The palace site is situated on the northern edge of the city, surrounded by a wall 10 km (6 miles) long that winds its way across mountains and valleys. The 560 hectare site not only includes palaces, temples, halls, and pavilions, but also beautiful landscapes and gardens, making it the residence with the largest imperial garden still in existence today. In the same way that the buildings reflect a variety of Chinese styles, including those of national minorities, the garden architecture combines the styles of North and South China.

The entrance to the palace site is through the **Lizheng Gate** in the south. It is adorned with inscriptions in Chinese, Manchurian, Uighur, and Tibetan. The palace itself is composed of four large building complexes. The **Hall of Modesty and Honesty** was used by the emperors for great ceremonies and receptions. It was constructed from nanmu wood, a highly precious wood especially imported to Chengde from south-west China, Sichuan and Guizhou.

The imperial bedroom is in the **Hall of Clouds and Water.**

If one looks towards the north from within the halls in the **Pine-soughing Tower** one will see a beautiful lake which is intended to remind one of the landscapes in southern China. By the shores and on the islands of the lake are several pavilions, towers, and halls once used for recreational purposes.

From the **Misty Rain Tower** on the northern shore, one could once view an expansive steppe-like landscape with grazing deer. It was here that Emperor Qianlong had picnics to receive Mongolian nobles, and the sixth Dalai Lama, and others.

Outside the palace walls are the **Eight Outer Temples,** originally eight groups of buildings with 11 temples in all. Only five of these, located to the north and east of the summer residence, still remain.

Directly to the north is the largest of the temples, **Pu Tuo Zong Sheng.** Since it was modelled on the Potala Palace in Lhasa, it goes by the name of **"Small Potala".** It was constructed in 1766 in honour of a number of nobles from the northwest, who had personally made the journey there to congratulate the emperor and his mother on their birthdays. In the front section there is a remarkable gate of honour made of glazed bricks, the reproduc-

tion of a gate located at Behai Park in Beijing. In the rear section is the Great Vermillion Terrace, 43 m (141 ft) high and built on two levels: a white terrace below and a red terrace above. Behind it is the main hall, covered with glazed green tiles and a gilded rooftop. The hall contains statues and groups of figures from Tantra Buddhism (Lamaism) found in Tibet.

East of here is **Xu Mi FuShou Temple,** a replica of the Tashi Lhunpo Monastery in Xigaze, the residence of the Pantschen Lama, spiritual leader of the Tibetans. It was erected in 1780 as a gesture of welcome when the 6th Pantschen Lama visited Chengde. The main hall is covered by a roof made of gilded copper tiles with eight golden dragons adorning the ridge. The site is complemented by a pagoda constructed out of glazed bricks.

At the most distant point in the north-eastern section of the site, stands the **Pu Ning Temple,** the **Temple of Universal Peace,** often referred to as the "Giant Buddha Temple". The entire structure is a mixture of Chinese and Tibetan styles. The 36 m (118 ft) high main hall at the back is flanked by several smaller Tibetan constructions. It encloses a huge statue of Bodhisattva Avalokiteshvara, the tutelary god of the Tibetans of whom the Dalai Lama is believed to be the incarnation.

The wooden figure is 22 m (73 ft) in height, has a circumference of 15 m (49 ft) and weighs 110 tons. It has twenty-two arms, each one holding an eye and a magical instrument. A Bhuddist statue measuring 1.4 m (4 ft) in height stands on the Bodhisattva crown.

The **Anyuan Temple** added on to the eastern section of the wall was also constructed by order of Emperor Qianlong in 1763. It is also called "Ili Temple" because it was modelled on a temple in Ili in Xinjiang Province. The roof of the temple is covered with black-glazed tiles and there is a large figure of Ksitigarbha Buddha inside.

Pule Si, the Temple of Universal Joy, also known as "Round Pavilion", was built in honour of Mongolian nobles. It has a very remarkable coffered ceiling made from wood, depicting two large dragons at the centre playing with a pearl.

Beidaihe/Shanhaiguan

The city of **Qinhuangdao** is 300 km (186 miles) due east of Beijing and it can be reached by plane in half-an-hour or just short of 5 hours by train from Beijing. This seaport has few attractions to offer, but it is only 30 km (19 miles) away from Beidaihe, the bathing resort to the south-west.

What is otherwise nearly unthinkable on an excursion through China – a day spent swimming – is part of the daily activities here. The climate even stays mild during the hot summer months, which is why the Han emperors had country houses

and villas constructed here. Many rich Chinese and foreigners owned summer houses in the area at the beginning of this century. In 1949, after the foundation of the People's Republic, it was turned into a recreation site for high cadres and merited workers or farmers, who would go there for health treatments at the expense of the government. Even Jiang Qing, Mao's widow, and Lin Biao, once thought to be Mao's successor, used to own villas here.

Recently, part of the site has also been opened up to tourists as well. They can bathe at the west beach, which has been reserved for the national travel agency of China, Lüxingshe.

In Beidaihe one is usually accommodated in attractive, small bungalows. The hotels were also built as bungalow-sites.

It is also worthwhile paying a visit to the **Lotus Rock Park** (Lianhuashi Gongyuan) in Beidaihe. The park got its name from the many bizarre rocks shaped like lotus blossoms. The former Minister of Defence Lin Biao, once designated as Mao's successor and later removed from office prior to his death in a plane crash over Mongolia, used to live here during the summer. In the vicinity of the park there is a row of temples called **Temples of the Guanyin Fairies,** which are almost three hundred years old.

Shanhaiguan is located about 30 km (19 miles) to the north-east on the border of Liaoning Province, where the Great Wall ends in the Bay of Bohai. It is known for the large fortress at the end of the Great Wall.

The fortifications of Yuguan were built as early as the 7th century. In the centuries that followed, the pass at Shanghaiguan was continuously at the focal point of the wars between the Chinese and the

A Ming vase with typical blue and white design.

nomadic tribes from the north. After the Ming emperors ousted the Mongolians, they had the Great Wall enlarged and the fortress in Shanhaiguan rebuilt. The site that can still be seen today dates back to 1681.

On their march of conquest to China, the Manchu armies also crossed over the Shanhaiguan Pass. They were able to convince the officer in command to join their side and he simply opened the gates for them.

The rectangular fortress spans about 4 km (2 miles). It has four gates, of which the eastern one is the most famous. It bears the name "Tianxia Diyiguan", **First Gate on Earth.** A few weapons and uniforms are on display in the tower structure over the gate. Another attraction is **Jiangnu Temple,** situated about 10 km (6 miles) east of the fortress, in the village of Wangfushi. It houses the statue of the legendary Meng Jiangnu.

It is told that Meng Jiangnu's husband was recruited for compulsory labour on the Great Wall under the rule of Emperor Qin Shi Huang Di. Meng Jiangnu set out to look for her loved one but was unable to find him. At this point she began to weep so bitterly that the Great Wall burst open and revealed the body of her husband. Like so many others, he had been a victim of the hard labour. Out of despair, she flung herself into the sea near Shanhaiguan.

The said temple and the huge cliff from which she flung herself into the sea both commemorate this popular legend.

The latter still bears her name today.

Shijiazhuang
Few tourists come to Shijiazhuang, the "Village of the Stone Family", as the name translates from the Chinese. Nevertheless, those people

who travel by train to south China, may just put in a brief stop at Shijiazhuang. Some 100 years ago, it is highly unlikely that anyone except the people living in neighbouring villages knew of the place, which only had 500 inhabitants at that time.

Progress came to the city with the construction of the railway from Beijing to Zhengzhou at the turn of the century. Today, Shijiazhuang has a population of nearly 900,000. It is a decidedly modern city: new homes, wide avenues and streets, all of which were built after 1949.

Shijiazhuang is the capital of Hebei Province and an important juncture for two major railroads, one from Beijing to Guangzhou and the other from Taiyuan to Dezhou, in the province of Shandong. Modern industry, especially textiles, has established itself in the city. To the west of the city there are coal, iron ore, marble, and limestone mines.

Attractions in Shijiazhuang are scarce. First of all, tourists are offered a tour to a hospital. It is the **International Peace Hospital,** which also bears the name of a Canadian physician: Dr. Norman Bethune.

This social-minded physician, who sympathized with the Communist Party, first applied himself to the provision of medical assistance for the industrial workers in Canada, before joining the Republicans in the Spanish Civil War to help establish medical services for the front lines.

He felt drawn to China even before the defeat in Spain. In 1937 he arrived there and began to practice at the International Peace Hospital a year later. He died on November 12th, 1939, from an infection contracted during an operation.

An **exhibition hall** has been added to the hospital which is dedicated to Dr. Norman Bethune and which documents his life and work.

His grave is in the **Martyrs' Cemetary** on the east side of the city.

The only other place worth visiting in the city itself is **Dongfeng-hong Exhibition Hall,** where local handcrafts are displayed and sold.

Anyone who spends more than one day in the city could make an excursion to the **Zhaoxian Circle,** where one can see one of the oldest bridges in North China, **Zhaozhou Bridge** – also called "Big Stone Bridge". Thirty-eight large boulders were placed side by side and fitted together in a complicated system to span a river 50 m (164 ft) wide. The bridge was constructed at the beginning of the 7th century. About 50 km (31 miles) north of Shijiazhuang is **Zhengding,** a city of temples, monasteries, and pagodas. One should certainly pay a visit to the **Long Xing Monastery,** built more than 1,400 years ago. Also worth visiting is the **Hua Ta,** the Flower Pagoda from the 12th century; next to it there is also a massive brick pagoda from the Tang Dynasty.

Shanghai and the East

Shanghai

Shanghai, the largest city in China with nearly 12 million inhabitants, has no exceptional historical attractions to offer. Nevertheless, it still draws millions of tourists. Foreigners associate the present city with its past reputation. A banking and commercial centre and largest seaport in China, it was also known as an El Dorado for adventurers and opportunists and for its bars and prostitution; Shanghai is said to have had the longest bar in the world. It is not without reason that the word "shanghai", meaning the press-ganging of seamen by getting them drunk and then carrying them off to the ships, is found in every dictionary directly following the word Shanghai.

No trace of all this is left in contemporary Shanghai. Even though the Seaman's Club is still in existance, drunken brawls seldom occur and, if they do, the authorities are quick to intervene.

Shanghai has a different kind of attraction for the Chinese as well. Anyone who has the chance to visit this city will scrape all his money together, borrow some if necessary, take along a list of wishes from relatives and friends, and then go shopping there. The stores along **Nanjing Road** in the downtown area have the most abundant, best, and most modern supply of goods in China.

The inhabitants of Shanghai are an urban people – more open-minded, more modern, more flexible, and more alert than the rural people. However, they are also more hectic and subject to more stress.

Because of all this, they are often regarded as being snooty and arrogant by the other Chinese. But everything has its price. The inhabitants of Shanghai pay for the abundance of material goods with an acute lack of housing space. The floor space per person is a mere 3 to 4 sq. m (32 to 43 sq. ft).

Shanghai is situated on the East China Sea coast, south of the estuary of the Yangzi. Two large rivers run through the city: the Huangpo and the Wusong.

Only a small fishing village was located here in the early days. Shanghai did not develop into a commercial centre until the start of the Ming Dynasty. The seaport rose in importance as the foreign powers began to get involved in China. The city had some 500,000 inhabitants in the middle of the 19th century. Due to the first compulsory agreement made after the Opium War, China was also forced to open Shanghai to foreigners. In the following decades, the town centre was divided up into concessions which were under the exclusive control of foreigners and even had their own legal systems. The Chinese were forbidden to enter these areas.

Traces from this past colonial era are still visible in the buildings along the **Bund,** the promenade by the Huangpo.

Because of its favourable position in terms of traffic facilities, Shanghai rapidly developed into the industrial and commercial centre of China after 1949. Nearly two million industrial workers in 8,300 enterprises produce one eighth of the gross national product and one third of all exports in China. With a turnover capacity of 90 million tons per year, 30% of the maritime trade is transacted through the seaport of Shanghai.

Shanghai has also emerged as the political and intellectual centre of the country over the decades. It was here that the Communist Party was founded, that great labour revolts were witnessed, where the Cultural Revolution reached its peak, and where the members of the now sentenced and imprisoned "Gang of Four" came from. And even today, politicians from Shanghai make up a higher proportion of the leading elite than politicians from any other Chinese city. There are 200 research institutions and 43 institutes for higher education in the city and 43 professional ensembles provide it with music, dance, singing, operas, acrobatics, and ballet. Additionally, there are four film studios and the city has its own television station.

The rapid rate of construction is a visible sign for the vitality and expansionist drive of this city. Since the centre of the city is overcrowded, one satellite town after another is being erected at the city limits.

The first place tourists usually make for is **Nanjing Road** – the largest business street in Shanghai, perhaps even in China (where, for example, there are cafes that serve gâteaux) – and then they go on to the **Bund.** It borders on the Huangpu River; the multi-storey buildings of the former colonial powers are located along the side of the city. Here one can see hundreds of shadow-boxers at 6 in the morning. Old masters instruct the young people in the art of Kung Fu Boxing.

A boat leaves the Bund twice a day for a **tour of the seaport** lasting about three hours. It sails down the Huangpu, past freighters, docks, and warehouses, all the way to where the Huangpu empties into the Yangzi River. The junks everyone would like to capture on film are becoming more and more scarce.

The city has a permanent display of Shanghai industrial productivity in the **Industrial Exhibition Hall** – a remarkable building constructed in the confectionary style of the Stalin Era. There is an exhibition of handicraft products in the right wing of the building, but the whole thing rather resembles a department store.

The **Museum of Art and History** is located on the Henannanlu. Besides neolithic ceramics, terracotta statuettes of the Qin and Han Era, and porcelain objects from

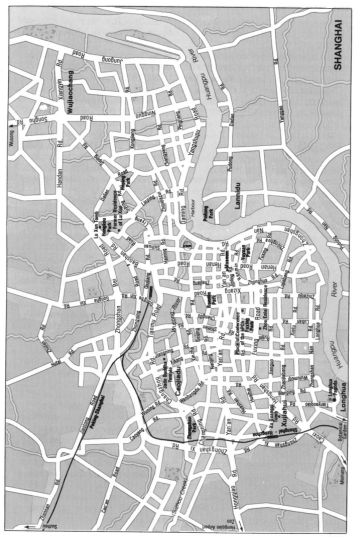

SHANGHAI

235

various periods, the most interesting attraction is the exhibition of paintings.

Because there are few historical attractions, Chinese tour guides will often suggest a visit to a **Palace for Children.** At least 11 of these are found in the city. These institutions provide exceptionally talented children with special assistance in their free time. The largest Palace for Children is on 64 Yanan Road.

This marble villa was once the residence of a colonial master. Currently, 2,000 children come here each day either to play or to attend the special advancement courses. The institution of Palaces for Children can be traced back to the work of the Chinese Welfare Association, which was founded by the widow of Dr. Sun Yatsen, Mrs. Song Qingling, and provided a great many children with assistance, especially during times of revolution and war.

There are few jade statuettes of Buddha in China. Two of these are found in the **Temple of the Jade Buddha,** Yufosi, situated on the west side of the city. There are three main halls in this Buddhist temple. The Treasure Hall of the Great Hero contains a Buddha triad: three large gilded figures that represent the Buddha rulers of the three eras of the world. The first jade statuette of Buddha, a 1.9 m (6 ft) seated Buddha Sakyamuni, is on the first floor of the next hall at the rear. The second jade statuette, a 96 cm (38″) Buddha in a lying position, can be seen in the western section. Both of them are originally from Burma; a monk brought them back to China from a pilgrimage as presents.

South of Renmin Road is the **old town** of Shanghai, often referred to as "Chinatown". It is easy to get lost in the crooked and narrow alleys, but somehow one always manages to find the way to one of the large streets that encircle the old town. Countless small stores make it a good place to go shopping in. Numerous small restaurants offer fast foods as well as special dishes. In front of **Yuyuan Garden,** there is a large square. An old tea house standing there on stilts in the middle of a pond offers cocoa with jasmin tea as its specialty.

The **Yuyuan Garden** is a site well worth seeing. This garden was built in the style of the gardens at Suzhou in the second half of the 16th century by a high official named Yu. The artful composition of water, artificial hills, boulders, pavilions, and gates make the 2 hectare site seem much larger. The inner garden is more compact and thus appears more romantic than the ample configuration of the outer garden. The Dragon Walls are remarkable. The coping was constructed in the form of waves that terminate in large dragon heads.

Tourists with a special interest in history or literature could, for example, go and see the **meeting place of the First Party Congress of the Communist Party** on 76 Xingye Road or the **residence of the first President of the Republic, Dr. Sun Yatsen,** in the vicinity of Fuxing Park. In **Hongkou Park** on the north side of the city there is the grave of China's most important modern writer, Lu

Xun, some of whose works have also been published in the English language. An exhibition hall on the same location documents his life and work.

On the western bank of the Huangpo, on the far south side of the city, is one of the few historical attractions of the city: the seven-storeyed octagonal **Longhua Pagoda,** 41 m (135 ft) high and built in the style of the Song Dynasty. It dates back to 977. Supposedly a temple and a pagoda stood here as early as 247 A.D., but they were destroyed during the wars of the Tang Dynasty. It is one of the largest pagodas in South China. The temple was restored in 1064 and is now located to the north of the pagoda.

Excursions to the rural districts under the administrative control of the city are also possible. There are a few attractions in the districts of Songjiang and Jiading – temples, pagodas, or gardens – that can be recommended to those who stay in Shanghai for a number of days. Such an excursion could well be combined with a visit to a peasant village. The peasants in the surrounding areas of Shanghai rank among the wealthiest of the country. They own private, often two-storeyed, houses with gardens. The average housing space here is 20 to 30 sq. m (215 to 323 sq. ft) for each person. These homes have televisions, radios, washing machines, sewing machines; the luxury items in contemporary China. Recent economic reforms permitting private enterprise and reopening the free market combined with great con-

sumer demand – Shanghai has a population of 12 million – caused the income of the peasants to soar.

Jinan

Jinan, the capital of the province of Shandong, presently has a population of 3 million. The capital of the province as early as 1368, it also became its commercial centre during this century, following the construction of the railway to Qingdao on the coast in 1904. The Yellow River, Huanghe, runs north of the city and to the south lies the sacred mountain Taishan.

Jinan is still known today as the **City of Springs.** Three large springs at the centre of the city deserve special mention. The **Spouting Spring,** Baotuquan, is located south-west of the old town. The water bursts out of the earth in three fountains up to 3 m (10 ft) high. There is also a **memorial hall** here for a Chinese **poetess and artist, Li Qingzhao,** born in Jinan in 1084. **The Spring of the Black Tiger,** Heihuquan, is located south-east of the old town. The spring water pours out of the mouth of stone tigers into a pond which explains how the name came about. At the centre itself is the **Pearl Spring,** Zhenzhuquan.

The waters from numerous springs run into the **Five Dragon Pond** Wulongtan. It is located about half a mile south of the **Spouting Spring.**

Daming Lake to the north of the city is also fed by spring water. There is a large park around it with trees, covered walks, and pavilions.

Within the park there are also garden plots. It is said that the poets and artists used to meet for a glass of wine in **Tingyuan Garden.**

Also situated to the south is the **Provincial Museum of Shandong,** in which natural and historical objects are on show, such as the objects from the Neolithic Longshan Culture discovered in Shandong.

The 285 m (935 ft) **Thousand Buddhas Mountain,** Qianfoshan, rises up 3 km (2 miles) south of the city. The numerous reliefs and sculptures there date back to the Sui Dynasty (589–618), but most of them were destroyed during the Cultural Revolution. From here one has a good view of the Huanghe Valley.

There are a few interesting attractions in the **district of Licheng,** situated north of the city. These include a 7 m (23 ft) Buddha head on Mt. Fohui dating from the year 1035 and the **Dragon Cave Mountain** containing numerous cliff sculptures. It is said that the people used to pray here to the Dragon King for rain. One of the oldest stone pagodas in China is the **Four Gates Pagoda,** Simen Ta, which was built in 611. It has four arched gates at the base, approximately 2 m (7 ft) high.

From Jinan one can go to the village of Longshan in the district of Changqing. Here one can visi the excavation-site of the Longshan Culture, which was discovered in 1928. This culture, known for its black ceramics, must have established a centre here around 4000 to 3000 B. C.

Taishan

Mt. Taishan in the province of Shandong is one of China's five sacred mountains. The foot of the mountain can be reached from the district town of Tai'an, approximately 50 km (31 miles) south of the capital Jinan.

The 1,540 m (5,069 ft) mountain has many majestic peaks and ridges, pines and cypresses hundreds of years old, waterfalls, and countless temples. The emperors used to make pilgrimages to Mt. Taishan from the 3rd century onwards in order to pay homage to the Celestial King. Innumerable inscriptions have been left there by scholars and artists.

The best time to climb the mountain is in May and October. A cable car takes one up part of the way. However, most visitors choose to tackle the mountain on foot. The ascent is not very difficult, but it is recommended that you take along a pair of sturdy shoes.

First of all, people pay a visit to **Taishan Temple** which is located at the foot of the mountain. It was built during the Han Dynasty and then enlarged under the Tang and the Song. The emperors used to make sacrifices to the mountain here. **Tiankuang Hall** is the main building. Measuring 48 m (157 ft) in length 19 m (62 ft) in width, and 22 m (72 ft) in height it is one of the most impressive buildings in ancient Chinese architecture. It stands on a terrace that is enclosed by a white stone railing. Red columns and a complicated system of brackets support the roof, which has been covered with glazed yellow tiles. Inside is a remarkable mural 62 m

(203 ft) in length and 3 m (10 ft) high that dates back to the Song Dynasty (960–1279). It depicts the God of Mt. Taishan making a tour of inspection around the mountain.

Impressive as well are the **157 stelae** at the temple site. Among them is one of the oldest slabs of stone ever to have been found in China, dating back to 209 B.C. It bears an inscription by Li Si, the chancellor of Qin Shi Huang Di, the first emperor of China.

The visitor has a choice between a western or an eastern route of ascent. The latter is preferred by most because it has more atractions to offer. After following the trail for some 500 m (1,600 ft) one arrives at the Daizong Gate. From here it is still another 9 km (6 miles) to the summit, up no less than 7,000 steps. After going over a short and winding stone stairway, one will soon arrive at the **Palace of the Red Gate,** a site containing several buildings that were erected in 1626 in honour of the Goddess of the Coloured Clouds. Then come the **Sacrificial Hall for the Celestial Queen,** formerly a **Taoist convent,** and the **Valley of the Stone Sutras.** Here an ancient calligrapher perpetuated the Diamond Sutra (Vaijrasutra) on the face of a cliff in 50 cm (20″) high characters.

Half way up to the summit one arrives at the **Doumu Palace,** a former Buddhist monastery. Behind it is a path lined with several hundred-year old cypresses leading to the **Gate Halfway to Heaven,** or Zhongtiang Gate. Here are restaurants as well as hotels in which to spend the night. Not far from Zhong-

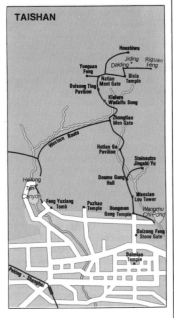

tiang Gate stand the three towering **Wudafu Pines.** Wudafu was a high official title during the Qing Dynasty. It is said that Emperor Qin Shi Huang Di once took rest under these pines and then gave them this honorary title. The pines that presently stand there, however, are only 250 years old. From here 1,200 stone steps lead up to the **Southern Celestial Gate,** Nantianmen. This is the most difficult part of the ascent and is therefore called **Ladder to Heaven.** Continuing along **Paradise Road,** past houses, stores, restaurants, and hotels, one arrives

239

at the **Temple of the Coloured Clouds,** Bixia Ci. Its roof is covered with tiles made of bronze and iron. Small bronze bells hanging from all four corners of the main hall ring constantly in the breeze.

At the summit stands the **Temple of the Celestial King.** An octagonal balustrade winds its way around the summit of Mt. Taishan. Numerous visitors spend the night on top of Mt. Taishan in order to see the unique Taishan sunrise. During the summer, the day breaks around three thirty in the morning. Then the clouds begin to glow red as the sun makes its appearance like a ball of fire emerging from the sea.

Qufu

Qufu's most famous son is **Confucius,** the greatest of the Chinese philosophers, at least as far as the enduring influence of his teachings is concerned. He was born in 551 B. C. here in Qufu, the capital of the state of Lu.

The bus journey from the railway station Yanzhou to Qufu takes half an hour, and the first thing one sees on arrival there is the **Confucius Temple** which completely dominates its surroundings. The construction of the temple was begun just one year after the death of the philosopher in the year 478 B. C.

On the orders of the rulers of the various dynasties the temple complex was repeatedly restored and extended. In time it became the Mecca of the Confucian religion. The complex covers an area of 22 hectares, and the buildings are symmetrically arranged along a north-south axis which is one kilo-

metre (about half a mile) in length. It contains 53 large archways and numerous halls, pavilions and shrines.

Approaching from the south, one passes through several archways before reaching one of the first main halls, the **Kui Wen Hall,** an imposing wooden skeleton construction with a three-tiered roof covered in glazed tiles. It dates from the year 1191 and was formerly used to house documents, books and offerings.

Then one passes through the **Dacheng Gate,** the seventh gate, to arrive at the **Xing Pavilion,** (Xing Tan). According to legend, it is here that Confucius sat under the shadow of tall Gingko trees, teaching his pupils. The next hall is the **Da Cheng Hall,** the central building of the temple. It stands on a terrace and covers an area of 1,800 sq. metres (19,375 sq. ft). The front roof is supported by ten massive marble columns decorated with magnificent bas-reliefs portraying dragons coiling and twisting around them. This hall was formerly used for the celebration of the great ceremonies in which offerings to Confucius were made. It is possible to view the ceremonial objects in the hall which also include some musical instruments.

On both sides of the hall stelas are displayed. There are about 2,100 of these stone slabs in Qufu, and all of them are of great historical importance, as their inscriptions represent a most important source of information about the past. Among them are 100 stone reliefs which were discovered in the graves of the Han Dynasty (206 B. C.–220 A. D.). Then comes another large hall, the **Qindian,** constructed in 1018 and which has undergone several restorations since then. It is here that offerings were made to the wife of Confucius.

To the east of the temple lies the **Residence of the Kong Family** (Kong is Confucius' family name), where his descendants lived. During the period of the Han Dynasty, Confucius' descendants were made members of the aristocracy in recognition of the achievements of their famous ancestor. The buildings in this complex which covers an area of 16 hectares are grouped around nine courtyards. The **Great Hall,** (Datang), still contains its original furnishings. Inside, there is a chair upholstered in tiger skins, where, according to tradition, Confucius used to sit when teaching his disciples. A red lacquered writing desk contains the official seals, writing instruments and other requisites. The other buildings served to accommodate guests and to entertain them. They were also used to house the guards and servants. In the family's own appartments we find gold and silver objects, jade and ivory, copper vessels and priceless silk garments.

Passing through the **North Gate** of the town, and after a walk of approximately 1 km (half a mile), one reaches the **Confucius Wood,** (Konglin), where Confucius and his descendants are buried. The wood, which has a circumference of 7 km (about 4 miles), is planted mainly with pine and cypress trees, dotted among which are nearly 1,000 stelas, as well as pavilions and halls.

Further sights of interest in Qufu are the **Temple of Duke Zhou,** whose brother Wu Wang is considered to be the founder of the Zhou dynasty (1100 B. C.), the **ruins of the Halo Palace,** official residence of the State of Lu, and the **grave of Shao Hao, one of the legendary Five Emperors.** The latter is also China's only pyramid-type grave. On account of the enormous number of stone blocks used in its construction, it was commonly known as the "Hill of Ten Thousand Stones".

Qingdao

Qingdao is perhaps better known under the old spelling of the name, Tsingtau, which means "blue island". At first this referred only to the small offshore island, but later it was applied to the little fishing village on the coast.

Qingdao's transformation into an important trading and industrial centre is a very recent development in which the Germans played a not inconsiderable role. In 1898 they succeeded in forcing the Chinese emperor to relinquish Qingdao and the Jiaozhou (Kiaotshou) Bay. After World War I Qingdao was occupied by the Japanese and was not returned to China until 1922. The presence of the German colonists has left its mark on the appearance of the town, and is still visible today in its architecture.

Today, Qingdao has almost two million inhabitants. It is surrounded on three sides by the sea; to the west by the Jiaozhou Bay, to the south and to the east by the Yellow Sea (Huanghai). The climate is mild and refreshing, particularly in summer and this has helped to make Qingdao a very popular holiday resort. To the west, in the Jiaozhou Bay, lie the **Great Harbour,** (Dagang), and the **Small Harbour,** (Xiaogang). The **Qianhai Pier** was formerly used as a landing stage. Today, this 440 m (just over ¼ mile) long jetty is directly linked to the Zhongshan Road and is ideal for a brisk walk.

At the end of the pier is a small octagonal pavilion. It is a favourite spot for popular sports. Older people gather here early in the morning for shadow boxing while the younger generation prefers jogging.

To the east of the pier is the **Maritime Museum** which houses China's oldest **aquarium** where rare sea-creatures may be observed.

The wide **sandy beaches** to the south are ideal for bathing. The seven beaches are equipped with changing cabins and showers.

The **Zhongshan Park** with an area of 800,000 sq. metres (8,611,120 sq. ft) is the largest in Qingdao. Over 300,000 trees of 300 different species are to be found there, including peach and cherry trees, tea bushes and a collection of medicinal herbs. In the autumn one can enjoy the sweet intoxicating scent of the cinnamon blossoms.

The Lu Xun Park, named after china's most famous modern writer, is to be found further south along the coast. Narrow paths lead through the rocky park covered in pine trees. Here in the south one can still see the **old villas,** built in the European style, which once belonged to wealthy colonists.

Today, they have been transformed into a sanatorium and health spa for workers.

To the east of the city rises the 1,333 m (4,373 ft) high **Laoshan** mountain which is famous throughout China for the purity of its spring water. On the summit of this mountain some small **Taoist Temples** are to be found.

Nanjing

Nanjing, capital of Jiangsu Province, is situated on the south bank of the Yangzi river, and today boasts a population of 3.7 million. Nanking developed into a modern metropolis after 1949. The city can look back on more than 2,000 years of history. From the third century A. D. until the tenth century, it had been the capital of several of the southern dynasties who had been forced to retreat from the northern tribes.

After his victory over the Mongols, the first Ming Emperor chose Nanjing as his capital because he preferred the security offered by the south.

Between 1853 and 1864, the peasant rebels of the Taiping Revolt made Nanjing the capital of their heavenly kingdom. From 1927 to 1949 the Guomindang government of Tschiang Kaischek had its headquarters in Nanjing before the National Army was driven back over the Yangzi river at Nanjing by the Red Army, and soon afterwards, it retreated to Taiwan.

A fair number of Chinese would prefer to have Nanjing as capital city once again. Its atmosphere is modern and sophisticated, and the city itself is particularly beautiful. The wide avenues can be identified by their trees, e. g., one avenue is planted exclusively with plane trees, another with Himalaya cedars, etc.

In the East Zhongshan Road stand the **ruins of the Palace of the First Ming Emperor.** According to historical records, it must have been comparable, both in size and in the furnishings it contained, with the Imperial Palace in Beijing.
One can view the remains of the **Midday Gate** (Wumen), as well as the **Dragon Bridge** and the remains of **Fengtian Hall.**

Across the road, on the northern side of the Zhongshan Road, is the **Nanjing Museum.** It has archaeological finds from Jiangsu Province on display dating from the Neolithic Age to the present. There is also an exhibition of paintings, and an antique shop has been installed in the West Wing.

If one continues in an easterly direction, one passes through the **Zhongshan Gate** set in the well preserved ancient city wall which was constructed under the Ming dynasty, and soon one reaches the

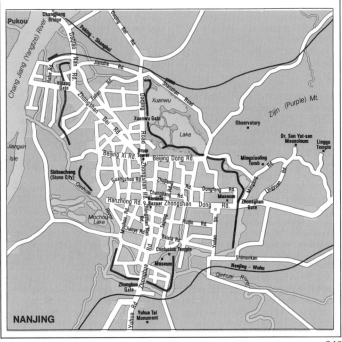

Purple Mountain (Zijin Shan). The centre of attraction here is the **Mausoleum** built in 1929 to honour **Dr. Sun Yatsen.** He was born in 1866 in the province of Guangdong, studied medicine and practised in Honolulu and Hongkong. Later he went to Tokyo and devoted himself to politics. After the fall of the Qing dynasty he became first president of the Republic of China. He died in 1929 in Beijing.

In the forecourt stands a bronze statue of Dr. Sun. The pathway to the tomb itself is 480 m (roughly ¼ mile) long, and is reached by a series of 392 steps. The summit offers a magnificent view. In the funeral hall there is a statue, 5 m (16 ft) high and in a sitting position, and behind this, the sepulchre is to be found.

The first Ming emperor lies buried to the west of the Sun Yatsen mausoleum. His tomb was constructed in 1383, and the first person to occupy it was the empress who died much earlier than her husband. It was not until 16 years later (1398) that the emperor followed her to the grave. Access to this grave is similar to that of the Ming graves in Beijing, first one passes through an entrance gate, then along a pathway lined by stone figures. Animals, fabulous creatures, ministers and generals, all hewn out of stone, stand guard at the tomb of the emperor. The road then curves to the north and leads directly to the grave of the emperor which, however, has not yet been opened. Experts are of the opinion that it is most probably larger than the only other grave among the

Ming graves at Beijing, which has been opened so far.

To the east of the Sun Yatsen Mausoleum lies the **Soul Valley** (Ling Gu). **Soul Valley Temple** which was constructed in 1381, has unfortunately not survived in its original state. In the main hall there is a statue of the Buddha Sakyamuni with two of his disciples and 18 lohans. To the east of the temple is a **Memorial Hall for the Monk Xuanzang** from the Tang period. This monk became famous on account of his journey to the West, to India, the home of the Buddha, and also for his translation of the Buddha's works. Relics of this monk are kept in the hall, and parts of his skull are preserved in a small thirteen-storey pagoda, carved out of wood.

The most interesting building is the **Beamless Hall** (Wuliang Dian), which was formerly used for the worship of Buddha Amitabha. It is constructed solely of stone slates and contains neither wood nor nails. Today, stone tablets have been hung in it, which bear the names of thousands of those who fell in the revolutionary wars.

Behind this hall stands the nine-storey **Ling Gu Pagoda,** erected in 1929. Each floor has an accessible stone gallery. The ascent of 252 steps up the 60 m (197 ft) high pagoda is rewarded with a magnificent view, as is the case with almost all pagodas.

The **Taiping Museum** is located in the southern part of the city in the former palace which was once the residence of the king of the Taiping rebels. The Taiping peasant rebels succeeded in conquering almost the entire southern part of China, and for a period of eleven years they ruled their Kingdom of Heavenly Peace from Nanjing. The first hall contains an exhibition of the life of Hong Xiuquan, leader of the Taiping revolution. In the second hall historical objects are exhibited.

The south Zhongshan Road leads to Nanjing's largest city gate, the **Zhongshua Gate.** It is more than a mere gate, however. It is 128 m (420 ft) long, 8 m (26 ft) wide, it contains four archways, three inner courtyards and 27 casemates which are located on the side of the outer gate facing the city, thus making the whole complex a secure fortress. From the terrace of the outer gate one can look down on the south suburbs of the city.

The **Rainflower Pagoda** (Yuhua-tai), is situated there and used to be a place of pilgrimage for many Buddhists. According to an ancient legend, the God of the Heavens was so moved by the intensity of the fervent prayers of a monk at this spot that he changed the rain into flowers. Everywhere in Nanking, small brightly coloured stones are on sale, and they are put into water to intensify their colours. They are called Yuhua, that is, **Rainflower Stones.** From 1927 onwards, the Guomindang army used the pagoda as a place of execution, especially for their Communist opponents. After 1949 a heroe's cemetery and a memorial to the martyrs were erected at this spot.

To the north-west of Nanjing there is a great construction which is the pride of both the city and the Chinese people, it is the **Yangzi Bridge.** In 1960 the Soviet Union and China were engaged in an ideological conflict which resulted in a withdrawal of all economic and technical aid on the part of the Russians. It became a matter of national prestige to construct this bridge alone, and within a space of eight years they had succeeded. The bridge is of vital importance for the infrastructure of the country, as there are only three major bridges over the Yangzi river which acts as a natural boundary, separating the south of China from the north.

The railway runs along the lower storey of the bridge and is double tracked. The overall length of the bridge, including the ramps, is 6,772 m (22,217 ft). The upper storey is for cars, cyclists and pedestrians. The actual bridge between the towers on both sides of the river measures 1,577 m (5,174 ft).

The **Xuanwu Park** is a nature paradise on the north-west side of the city. A boat trip on **Lake Xuanwu** is to be highly recommended. In the lake are five large islands on which a wide variety of plants and trees grow. There is also a large swimming pool, an open-air theatre, a zoo and other entertainments.

Wuxi

Wuxi belongs to that group of towns worth visiting because of their magnificent scenery. The town is situated on the northern bank of Lake Taihu in a region which belongs to the fertile Yangzi estuary. It is within easy reach of Nanjing, Shanghai

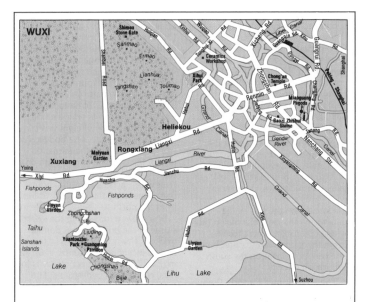

and Hanzhou, and is therefore a popular place with the Chinese for excursions. The name Wuxi means literally "no tin". Over 2,000 years ago the name of the town was Youxi, which means "has tin". During the Han dynasty the tin reserves became exhausted, and the town was soon renamed Wuxi – "no tin".

Up until this century, Wuxi remained a small, sleepy market town. Then in the thirties, foreign and Chinese industrialists from Shanghai began to invest in the textile industry, particularly in the manufacture of silk. As a result, the population increased rapidly, and today it stands at 800,000. Silk production is still one of the most important industries in Wuxi.

The process of **silk manufacture** begins in the summer months. Everywhere in the countryside surrounding the town, particularly on the north bank of Lake Taihu, the extensive mulberry tree plantations are to be seen. The leaves of these trees are used to feed the silkworms, which are often reared by the peasants as a means of providing a secondary source of income. When the silkworms have spun themselves into their cocoons, they are collected by the peasant farmers and delivered to the spinning mills.

The favourable climate in this region enables the farmers to harvest up to three times a year, usually one wheat and two rice harvests.

On the north bank of Lake Taihu fish-farming is carried on. Lotus flowers and water chestnuts are cultivated in separate ponds along the side of the lake.

The main attraction the town has to offer is **Lake Taihu.** It covers an area of almost 2,500 sq. km (965 sq. miles) and is thus China's fourth largest inland lake. Over 90 islands are dotted about the lake which has a maximum depth of only 3 m (about 10 ft).

It is possible to take a half-day excursion to some of the islands by boat.

In the northern part of Lake Taihu lies the **Tortoise Head Peninsula** (Yuantou Zhu), which is so called because its shape resembles that of a tortoise's head. The island can be reached by ship or via the bridge connecting it with the Li Garden. The shores of the island are planted with cherry trees which are a magnificent sight in spring when in full bloom. A landscape of natural and artificial hills, pavilions and a rocky coast to the south, as well as a number of tea houses make the island a popular choice for an excursion.

To the north, you can follow a road across a bridge to a workers' sanatorium which was constructed as a place of recuperation for older and deserving workers.

Tourists are mainly accommodated in hotels on the north bank of Lake Taihu. In front of the Hubin hotel lies the magnificent **Li Garden.** It was laid out in 1929 according to the plan of an older park. Particularly worthy of attention are the beautiful stones which have been used to create imaginative miniature landscapes. The Taihu stones are famous throughout China, and were formerly placed in the gardens of the emperors. Centuries ago, these stones were thrown into the lake, and they took on these bizarre shapes after a number of years.

The **Mei Garden** is situated on the north shore of the lake behind the Taihu hotel. It was formerly the private garden of a high official. This garden is characterized by its numerous plum trees, and a visit here when they are in full bloom is an experience never to be forgotten. The **Nianqu Ta Pagoda** is only fifty years old, and from the top there is a wonderful view over the lake.

Xihui Park is situated in the western part of the town. Its name is a composite of the names given to the two hills which border it on each side, Xihand and Huishan. The park contains several smaller gardens, tea houses and the **Wuxi Museum.** A **pagoda,** which is also the town's emblem, is perched on top of Xishan.

The most beautiful garden in the Xihui park is the **Jichang Garden,** which is to be found immediately to the right of the park entrance. The garden was originally laid out in the 16th century, but had to be restored several times since then. The Emperor Qianlong was so enchanted by this garden that he ordered an exact copy to be constructed in his summer palace.

In this park the **Second Spring under the Heavens** is to be found, which is supposed to have been discovered by a Tang scholar. Being a tea expert, he reached the conclusion that the water from this spring was the second best in the whole of China for the preparation of tea.

On the Huishan hill there is a very malleable type of clay which was discovered some centuries ago, and which on being dried became very hard and suitable for firing. The famous Huishan Pottery Industry grew up and flourished in the surrounding region. After 1949 this industry, which had fallen into decay, was revitalized, and today, production is directed at the tourist market and the export trade. This is the reason why one sometimes comes across an image of the Virgin Mary or a model of Santa Claus among the traditional statues representing Chinese legendary figures.

The **Imperial Canal,** also known as the **Grand Canal,** flows through the town of Wuxi from the northwest in a southerly direction. A network of several smaller canals crisscrosses the various districts of the town. With its total length of 1,794 km (1.087 miles) from Beijing to Hangzhou, this is one of the world's longest artificial waterways. The second emperor of the Sui dynasty, Yang Di, ordered the construction of this canal in the year 605 in order to connect the imperial city of Xi'an and also Luoyang with the fertile regions of the Yangzi delta. It was from this point that the grain was then transported northwards. The Mongol emperors were responsible for the construction of the link with Beijing, which is still in use today.

A boat journey through the town of Wuxi on the imperial canal is an

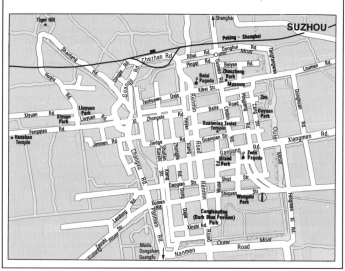

ideal way of enjoying the busy scenes of life on the waterway. It takes one past old junks and magnificent arched bridges. Old houses with steps leading down to he water's edge line the route of the canal. Here, women are to be seen washing clothes, and sometimes even vegetables.

Suzhou

Suzhou is situated south of Wuxi and on the banks of the imperial canal. Today, the town has a population of 600,000.

Suzhou has been given many names in the past. The Europeans called it "Venice of the East" because its numerous small canals, narrow streets and pleasant climate all served to remind them of the Italian town. The Chinese are not less reticent in their praise of this town. They like to refer to Suzhou as a paradise on earth and quote the old saying: "Heaven has paradise, but the earth has Suzhou and Hangzhou".

The first European traveller to discover Suzhou was Marco Polo, and he was enthralled by the town. He gave an account of the silk industry here and praised the quality of the silk that was manufactured, remarking that the inhabitants of the town earned their livelihood with the silk they produced and with trading. He also counted a grand total of 6,000 stone bridges in the town. Today, there are a mere 300. Fortunately, some of the atmosphere and excitement of the town that fascinated Marco Polo has survived to the present day.

The narrow streets, the white-washed houses with black tiled roofs, tiny front gardens and small narrow pavements all contribute to the special atmosphere that characterizes this town.

Suzhou's claim to fame rests on its magnificent gardens. In the preceeding centuries rich merchants, high government officials and landlords chose to construct their small but very beautiful gardens here, usually with the help of famous artists. Suzhou thus developed into

Delicately painted Chinese silk fan.

a cultural and intellectual centre. It offered all the advantages of town life, yet at the same time the gardens and surrounding region provided the opportunity to enjoy country life. The art of gardening consisted of grouping together in perfect harmony the greatest possible number of landscapes in a confined space, all of which offered opportunity for relaxation and rest, but which also created the illusion of size and spaciousness.

The **Liu Garden** (Liuyuan) is Suzhou's largest garden. It belonged originally to a government official named Xu, but it was subsequently sold to the Liu family. One walks through this garden clockwise, passing through the western and northern sections where artificial rock landscapes predominate. There is also a very beautiful peach tree garden in the northern part. To the east, there are halls, pavilions and foyers. Also in this section of the garden is the largest Taihu stone, a rock of bizarre shape, six feet high and weighing five tons. Also worthy of mention are the magnificently carved windows in the foyers and halls. Their purposes is to direct the visitor's attention to particular views. They are called huo chuang in Chinese, which means living windows.

The **Fishermen's Garden** (Wangshiyuan is one of the smallest in Suzhou, but it is also one of the most romantic. The entrance gate offers no hint of the beauty that lies hidden behind it. This small area presented an enormous challenge to the artistry of the landscape gardener who planned it. The aim was to present a pattern of ever-changing landscapes, and this has been achieved to perfection. The winding path constantly alters direction, and so at every corner a new view is presented to surprise and

delight the visitor. The garden was originally laid out in the 12th century, but later fell into decay. It was restored in 1770 by the government official Song Zongyuan.

Also worth visiting is the **Garden of the Modest Official** which is much more extensive. The entrance to the garden lies at the eastern end. Its large-scale lay-out bears more resemblance to a park than to a garden. The inner garden is hidden behind a wall, and here, water dominates the scene. Little zig-zag bridges artfully placed between water and shore decorate the artificial lake in a manner which charms and fascinates the eye of the beholder. The path along the shore leads through halls and pavilions, miniature landscapes, and hills and valleys. The **Little Flying Rainbow Bridge** spans the lake, and its reflection in the water looks like a rainbow. It is absolutely unique in Suzhou.

The **Garden of Waves** (Canglangting), is the oldest garden in Suzhou. It was originally constructed in 1044, but experienced repeated destruction and restoration. The last time this happened was in 1873 during the Taiping rebellion.

Three kilometres (1.8 miles) to the north-west of the town lies **Tiger Hill** (Huqiu) which is 30 m (98 ft) high. It was here in the year 473 B. C. that the King of Wu, Fu Cha, had his father, King Helue, buried. According to legend, a white tiger then appeared to guard the burial place, and so the hill was named after it.

Somewhat higher, the **Pool of the Sword** is to be found, and it is here that King Helue together with

3,000 swords is supposed to have been buried. On top of the hill is the 46 m (151 ft) high **Pagoda of the Cloudy Rock** (Yunyansai Ta). The first six storeys date from the tenth century, the seventh storey was rebuilt in the seventeenth century.

There are two pagodas in Suzhou which visitors should see. The **North Temple Pagoda** (Beisi Ta) is 76 m (249 ft) high. The present building dates from 1582. It is possible to ascend by the gallery pagoda, and the upper storey offers a splendid view of the town.

The **Twin Pagoda** (Shung Ta) dates from the tenth century and is situated in the eastern part of the town. The two pagodas stand only 30 m (98 ft) apart. Each of them contains yet another pagoda, and on top of the roof they have an umbrella-like fixture which resembles the Tibetan or Indian stupas.

Suzhou is famous for the craft of **silk embroidery.** Animal figures such as cats, dogs, birds and fish are the favourite motifs. Some of these pieces are double embroidered, so that the back of the silk looks as perfect as the front, and the best masters of the craft are even able to embroider a different picture on each side of the silk.

Wuhan

The city of Wuhan with almost four million inhabitants is situated on the Yangzi. It is the capital of the province of Hubei, and due to its central geographical location it has become an important modern industrial centre. The Yangzi flows from Shanghai in a westerly direction through Wuhan into the province of Sichuan. Two main railway lines meet here: the north-south line from Beijing to Guangzhou, and the east-west line from Shanghai via Nanchang to Chongqing and Chengdu.

Wuhan is an amalgamation of three formerly separate towns, Wuchang, Hankou and Hanyang.

Wuchang is the oldest of the three towns and it had a major role in the Republican Revolution. It was here that the republican troops were victorious over the imperial army, and as a result, the rebellion spread over the whole of South China.

Hankou was originally just a small fishing village. In 1858 the English were the first to gain concession rights in Hankou. Their intention was to capture the huge market in the Yangzi region as far as Sichuan. The traces of the former presence of the colonial powers are still very much in evidence in the townscape of Hankou.

Hanyang, which lies to the west of the Yangzi and to the south of the Hanshui river, is the smallest of the three towns. It was there that China's first steelworks were constructed at the end of the last century.

The great **Yangzi Bridge,** spanning China's longest river, connects Wuchong with Hanyang. Until its construction in 1957, the river could only be crossed by ferry. The total length of the bridge is 1,670 m (5,479 ft). The railway tracks take up the lower storey with the upper storey reserved for vehicles. The bridge is of vital importance for both the general infrastructure and the economic integration of the country because the Yangzi river is the geo-

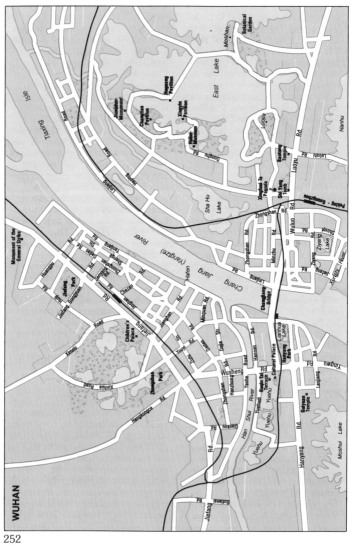

WUHAN

Tixing Isle

Road

Hepu

Lijiang Road

Monument of the General Strike

Huangpu Rd

Jiefang Park

Jianghan Rd

Jiefang Rd

Ximalu

Xinhua Road

Zhongshan Park

Hangkongcao Rd

Xiaoxu Rd

Children's Palace

Jiefang Rd

Zizhi Rd

Jianghan Rd

Jianghan Rd

Dingdao Rd

Shengli Rd

Zhongshan Rd

Chezhan Rd

River (Yangtze) Jiang

Hefen Rd

Minquan Rd

Daja St.

Taiye Rd

Yanhe Rd

Jianghan Rd

Han Shui River

Zhongshan Rd

Hanzhong Rd

Hanlan Rd

Yanhe

Wusheng

Yuehu

Yuehu Rd

Yuehu

Guiyuan Temple

Hanyang Rd

Moshui Lake

Jietang Rd

Buddino Rd

Sha Hu Lake

East Lake

Moshan

Botanical Garden

Houyuan Pavilion

Juishan Monument

Changtian Pavilion

Xingyin Pavilion

Haihuo Monument

Lianghu Rd

Xinphui Ta Pagoda

Shi Yang Tomb

Dianchi Rd

Beishou Temple

Luoqia

Luoyu Rd

Luoshi Rd

Nanhu

Zhongshan Rd

Zhongshan Rd

Minzhu Rd

Wuluo Rd

Peking - Guangzhou

Changjiang Bridge

Lianhua Lake

Hanyang Palace

Cultural Palace

Yuehu-Sport Rd Terrace

Shouyi Rd

Ziyang Rd

Ziyang Rd

Xiao-Zhi-Kou Rd

Yingwu Rd

Yinghu Lake

Xiaonan Lake

graphic feature which forms a natural border between North and South China.

The recent decades have seen the development of some very important industries: agricultural and other machinery, car manufacture, shipbuilding and china's largest iron and steelworks.

Nonetheless, this modern industrial town can still offer the tourist a number of sights of historical and geographical interest. The **East Lake** (Donghu), 33 sq. km in size, with hills, parks and walks along the shore, is a lovely recreation centre in the eastern section of Wuchang. There are over 70 pavilions, towers and arcades along the shore and in the parks, all of which create the atmosphere of a typical Chinese landscape.

On the north-east shore of the lake stands the **Xing Yin Pavilion** (Pavilion for the Recitation of Poetry) which is dedicated to the memory of the patriotic poet **Qu Yuan,** who lived over 2,300 years ago and is still greatly revered. The **University of Wuhan** is situated on the southern shore, and to the east of it lies the **Botanic Gardens.**

Snake Hill coils its way through Wuchang. **The Tower of the Yellow Crane** (Huanghe Lou) once stood here, but it was unfortunately destroyed by fire in 1884. The 1,600-year-old tower is now in the process of reconstruction with the help of drawings and paintings from the Yuan and Ming dynasties. One old legend tells how the tower got its name. The landlord of a small tavern there was frequently visited by a mysterious immortal being,

who, as payment, painted a yellow crane on the wall which used to descend and dance for the guests. The landlord became a very rich man as a result. One day, the immortal returned, played a tune on his jade flute and lured the yellow crane down from the wall, mounted it and flew away, never to return. In gratitude for the riches the yellow crane had brought him, the landlord constructed the tower in its honour. To the east of the mountain stands the 10 m (33 ft) high **Shenxiang Pagoda,** a three-tiered stupa built in 1343.

There are two more pagodas on the **Hongshan Mountain** which were constructed at a more recent date.

Tortoise Hill (Guishan) rises up on the west bank of the Yangzi, directly opposite Snake Hill. The main object of interest here is the **Lute Pavilion** (Guqin Tai) which is also called the Boya Pavilion after a famous musician of the Era of the Warring Kingdoms (476–221 B. C.). He is supposed to have destroyed his zither out of grief at the death of a friend and never to have played again.

Not to be missed is the **Hubei Province Museum,** situated on the west bank of the Donghu lake, as the objects discovered in the tomb of Prince Yi of Zeng in 1978 at Suixian are on display. This tomb dates from the year 433 B. C. Almost 7,000 objects were excavated, and the most spectacular of these is a set of bronze chimes. It consists of 65 bronze bells which are attached to a three-tiered wooden frame. They are rung with wooden hammers and the largest of them with long wooden sticks. The biggest bell weighs 200 kg (440 lbs). The total weight of the chimes is 2.5 tons. It was found undamaged in the tomb and can be considered to be one of the best and most exciting finds from this period.

The Buddhist **Temple Guiyuan** is 400 years old. Among the treasures of the temple is an almost complete collection of Buddhist writings which numbers 54,000 volumes. Also worth visiting are the Hall of 500 lohans and a Buddha Sakyamuni statue made of white jade and weighing three tons. Like the other two jade Buddhas in Shanghai, this statue also comes from Burma.

Changsha

Changsha, the capital of the province of Hunan, the fish and rice province as it is commonly called, has 2.5 million inhabitants. Ten years ago, the city took on a new significance for Chinese tourism because nearby in the **village of Shaoshan** Mao Zedong was born, he went to school in Changsha and later was a teacher there. In the meantime, since the politically motivated aspects of tourism have receded into the background, considerably fewer tourists find their way to Changsha. However, an excursion to **Shaoshan,** which lies 100 km (62 miles) west of Changsha, and where Mao Zedong was born in 1893, the son of a prosperous farmer, is still worth the effort. The bus journey takes one through a wonderful terraced landscape covered in green rice fields. Individual farms stand on little hills surrounded by trees which circle

them in welcome shadow. The working animal found here is the water buffalo, which loves to wallow in the little ponds during his work-breaks. Even today, Shaoshan is a picturesque village, surrounded by hills covered in woods.

The **house** in which **Mao** was born is today a museum and is open daily. Adjacent buildings exhibit photos and documents of Mao's revolutionary life.

In 1911, the 18-year-old Mao went to the city of Changsha and attended the **Teachers Training College** Nr. 1 there where he later taught and founded the first Marxist teaching and research group.

In the north of the city at the foot of a hill stands the **Pool of the Clear Water,** Qingshui Tang. Mao lived in the house at the pool for a short time and there for the first time instigated the founding meeting of the Hunan Party Committee.

In the middle of the river Xiangjiang lies the **Island of Oranges,** Juzizhou. The island, which is 5 km (3.1 miles) long and only 50 to 150 m (492 ft) wide, is a popular tourist destination because of its beautiful parks which are full of orange trees and pavilions. Nearby, Mao's poem "Changsha", is carved on a huge stela.

Today, the **University of Hunan** is situated on the **Yuelu Shan Mountain** west of Xiangjiang river. The 300 m (984 ft) high hill is scenically very attractive and a climb to the top to appreciate the magnificent view is well worth the effort. Half-way to the top one comes upon one of the oldest temples in the province, the **Lushan Temple.**

A few miles west of Changsha is the site of an unusual discovery which was made in 1972. During the opening of a grave dating from the Han dynasty, near the village of **Mawangdui**, a virtually undisturbed grave containing several interlocking coffins was discovered. In one of these coffins lay the extremely well-preserved body of a woman aged about 50 years and born between 190 and 140 years B.C.

The grave lay about 20 m (66 ft) underground and due to a naturally ocurring clay stratum was luckily perfectly isolated so that neither air nor water could enter. The corpse was so well-preserved that investigations were even able to show what her last meal was and which illnesses she had suffered from.

The grave, the body, the numerous objects including red lacquered articles, pots, bamboo articles, musical instruments and beautifully preserved silk material, as well as the coffins are now on show in the **Hunan State Museum** in the northeast of the city.

Hangzhou

The city of Hanzhou with 1 million inhabitants, is an important junction for traffic in the hinterland of Shanghai. The Imperial Canal ends here, and roads and railway lines leading to the large Eastern provinces of Jinagsu, Anhui and Zhejiang cross here. Hangzhou is the capital of Zhejiang Province.

In the meantime the city has become an extremely popular tourist centre. For centuries it has been renowned for its **West Lake.** In spite of the fact that there are 36 lakes with this name in China, when one speaks of the "West Lake" it is the West Lake, Xihu, near Hangzhou which is meant.

The lake is, in fact, relatively small, only 5 sq. km (almost 2 sq. miles); it is divided by the **Su-Causeway** and the **Bai-Causeway.** These dykes are man-made and bear the names of two of the most famous poets of the Tang and Song epochs, and who spent part of their lives here, Li Bai and Su Dongpo. Artists have always been drawn to this area and have painted or sung of the beautiful landscape. **Three Pools Reflecting the Moon** San Tan Yin Yue, is the largest of three islands in the outermost lake. On this island in turn is found another tiny lake in which innumerable goldfish swim. One can cross this lake by a small bridge, pass by a pavilion, stones and lotus flowers, thereby reaching a pavilion on the water's edge where three small stone pagodas stand in the water. During the festival of the moon, candles are lit in the pagodas, and the round window openings of the pagodas are covered with paper cutouts. In the evening light it appears as if many moons are reflected in the water thus giving the island its name.

In the North lies **Solitary Island** on which the 38 m (125 ft) high **Solitary Hill** is located. The island is connected to the mainland by the Bai-Causeway on the west side and on the north side by a bridge. As early as the 13th century the Imperial palaces were situated on this hill because this is the point with the most beautiful view of the lake. On the northern slope stands a pavilion with an inscription of the Qing-Emperor Kangxi.

On the western shore in a traditional Chinese building is the centre of the **Xiling Stone Engraving Company.** They are known throughout the world on account of their studies on Chinese stone inscriptions. **Zhongshan Park** is in the south and the **Provincial Library** is situated next to it.

On the western side of the island where the Bai-Causeway is situated stands the **Broken Bridge,** Duanqiao. The bridge was, in fact, never broken and does not look as if it ever intends to break. One of China's best known sagas originates

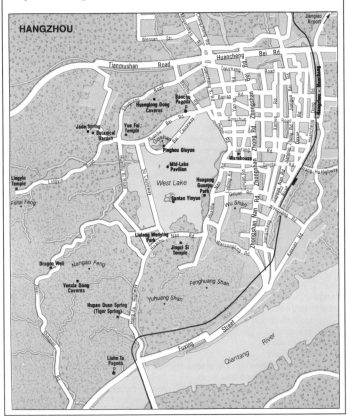

HANGZHOU

Jiangiao Airport

Wensan Str

Moganshan Rd

Zhongshang Rd

Tianmushan Road

Huancheng   Bei Rd

Liyuchang   Rd

Baochu Rd

Hangzhou-Nanchang

Rapian   Rd

Huanglong Dong Caverns

Baochu Pagoda

Qingchun

Jade Spring

Botanical Garden

Yue Fei Temple

Yan   Rd

Zhongshan

Xinhua

Road

Qinghua

Huanhu Bei Rd

Bai-Causeway

Pinghou Qiuyue

Jiefang   Zhong   Rd

Warehouse

Qingtai

Mid-Lake Pavilion

West Lake

Huagang Guanyu Park

Hang-Hu Highway

Lingyin Temple

Lingyin

Qinjian Rd

Santan Yinyue

Wu Shan

Zhongshan Nan Rd

Wanghiang Rd

Feilai Feng

Liulang Wenying Park

Nan   Rd

Wansongling   Rd

Zhongshan

Kaixuan Rd

Dragon Well

Nangao Feng

Jingci Si Temple

Yanxia Dong Caverns

Fenghuang Shan

Hupao Quan Spring (Tiger Spring)

Yuhuang Shan

Liuhe Ta Pagoda

Fuxing   Street

Qiantang   River

256

from this area. The story goes that the White Snake came down to the earth in the guise of a woman and while on this bridge fell in love with a mortal youth.

The legend has a tragic ending, however. The White Snake was buried under a pagoda by a jealous and wicked monk. This **Lei-Feng Pagoda** has, in the meantime, disappeared; it used to stand on the southern shore of the West Lake.

Another pagoda, the **Baochu-Pagoda** which stands on the summit of the 200 m (656 ft) high **Mountain of the Precious Stone,** Baoshishan, is part of the distinctive panorama of the West Lake. The mountain probably got its name in earlier times when jade was found there. The needle-shaped 45 m (148 ft) high pagoda was built in 1933 but dates back, however, to an earlier building from the year 968.

Hangzhou's most famous pagoda is the **Pagoda of the Six Harmonies,** Linhu Ta, named after a Buddhist temple which used to stand nearby. The octagonal pagoda is built from brick and wood and is 60 m (197 ft) high. The outer building of the galleried pagoda has 13 floors but only every second gallery can be reached from the inside. The present building is 800 years old. It was thoroughly restored in 1900 and 1949.

On the northern shore of the lake is the grave of a general of the Southern Song dynasty who even today is admired as a great patriot: **General Yue Fei.** He steadfastly fought against the Northern Jin Dynasty. In the end, however, he was betrayed by his own followers

and executed. Nevertheless, he was highly regarded by the people and twenty years later he was rehabilitated posthumously by imperial decree. **The Temple of Honour** with its monument was built as early as 1220.

One enters the temple through a large red entrance gate. Going straight through, one reaches the main hall where a large statue of the general stands. The back and side walls show paintings of scenes from his life. The grave lies to the left of the entrance. It is reached through a small door and faces some **stone figures** similar to those we know from the Ming graves. Here there are two horses, two tigers, two sheep and six important dignitaries guarding the way to his grave. Beside Yue Fei lies the burial place of his son.

On both sides of the entrance one sees two kneeling iron figures behind bars. These are the people who were involved in the conspiracy against Yue Fei; now they are condemned to kneel forever in this humiliating position before his grave.

To the west of the West Lake lies one of the biggest and most beautiful temples in South China, the **Lingyin Temple.** It was founded in 326 by an Indian monk who believed that the region was inhabited by "hidden deities" (i. e. Lingyin), and he claimed to recognize in a mountain here one of India's holy mountains. The Hall of the Four Kings of the Sky comes first, followed by the Hall of the Laughing Buddha, the Maitreya Buddha. Behind this stands the 700-year-old statue of Wei Tuo, a tutelary deity, which is carved from one single piece of camphor wood.

The Hall of the Great Buddha is 33 m (3,573 ft) high and contains a 19.6 m (64 ft) high figure of the sitting Buddha Sakyamuni, which is also made from camphor wood. In front of this hall on both sides stand two nine-tiered pagodas dating from the 10th century.

Across from the entrance rises the 209 m (685 ft) high **Peak which flew over from India** Feilai Teng, where over 300 reliefs and sculptures depicting Buddhist deities and dating from the 10th to the 14th century are to be seen.

The main attraction is the Laughing Buddha with his wide smile and fat stomach. He is depicted playing with a string of worry beads and is surrounded by numerous smaller figures.

Longjing tea, one of the finest of Chinese teas, comes from the region of Hangzhou. The **village of Longjing** which means dragon fountain is well worth a visit. Between April and September the tea pickers can be seen working in the large plantations. The best tea is that from the first spring harvest and is produced in April; this type is hand dried in pans. The village, however, also has a mechanically operated drying system.

Fuzhou

Fuhou, which is the capital of the Fujian Province, has about 1 million inhabitants. Although the region became part of the empire in 221 B. C. under the Emperor Qin Shi Huang Di, due to its great distance from the capital it managed to maintain a certain independence. As late as the 10th century it succeeded in establishing, for a short time, an independent kingdom.

The importance of the city is due to its foreign trade. Fuzhou is one of the harbours which in the last century was opened to foreign powers. Almost half of all Chinese living abroad originate from the Fujian Province. This is also true for a large percentage of the population of Taiwan. Since 1949, Fuzhou has lost most of its importance in the southeast as a harbour because directly across from it lies Taiwan and the area between mainland and island is a military area of conflict.

In the middle of Fuzhou on the western slope of a barley 60 m (197 ft) high hill stands the characteristic landmark of the city, the **White Pagoda,** Baita. The brick building dates from the year 904 and had to be restored in the 16th century after a fire had destroyed it. The 41 m (134 ft) high pagoda is entirely covered in whitewash, which circumstance explains its name. The accompanying temple hall, Baita Si, is used today as a **library.** On a hill across from it stands its counterpart, namely the 35 m (115 ft) high **Black Pagoda,** which dates from about the same period.

Fuzhou, like the city Hangzhou and several other cities, has a West Lake, Xihu. It is situated in the northwest of the city and possesses a whole series of sights worth seeing, including the **Provincial Museum** and the **Zoo.** The shores are planted with banyan trees and willows, whilst attractive pagodas and pavilions provide opportunities for relaxation and pleasure.

In the east of the city rises the **Drum Mountain,** Gushan. At the summit lies a flat drum-shaped stone which is supposed to give rise to drum-like sounds during heavy rain. Half-way up the mountain stands the biggest temple in the city, the **Temple of the Hot Springs,** Yongquansi. A white jade statue of Buddha is found within. There are two rare ceramic pagodas worthy of mention to be found in this 900-year-old temple area, the **Thousand Buddhas Ceramic Pagodas** which stand in front of the hall of the four kings of heaven. The temple houses a tooth of Buddha which is honoured as a relic.

In the northern suburbs is the grave of the well-known **General Lin Zexu.** In the 19th century he resolutely fought against the opium trade; in Guangzhou (Canton) he openly burnt 20,000 cases of opium. Later on he was held responsible for the military defeat by the English.

Quanzhou

The old harbour city of Quanzhou lies 150 km (93 miles) south of Fuzhou on the coast. An old ship-wreck dating from the 12th or 13th century was recovered in 1974 from the bottom of Quanzhou Bay. Remains of her cargo, perfumes and spices in particular, were found. This discovery confirmed that, Quanzhou was, already at that time an important overseas harbour. From here trade extended to the whole of

southeast Asia. In addition, historical records confirm that Quanzhou, as regards size and importance, was at least as significant as the Egyptian port of Alexandria. The **Quanzhou Ship** is nowadays exhibited in a **museum.**

During the Tang Dynasty, in the 8th and 9th centuries, the importance of sea trading grew and eventually superceded even the silk road which was one of the oldest overland trading routes to Europe.

The most important sight worth seeing is the **Kai-Yuan Temple** dating from the year 686. Originally it was called the Lotus Flower Temple. According to legend, Buddha permitted lotus flowers to grow on a mulberry tree as a sign to a monk that he should built a temple on that spot. Later, on the orders of the Tang Emperor, Xuanzong, he was named Kaiyuan, which was also the motto of his period of rule.

The main hall is an exceptional example of Chinese temple building; it is supported by one hundred stone columns which are decorated with bas-reliefs of flying musicians. The upper halves of the figures depict the female body and the lower halves the body of a bird. Some columns are reminiscent of Greek columns. On either side of the main hall stands an octagonal, five-storeyed **Stone Pagoda.** There are inscriptions and carvings of Buddha on each of the eight sides of the building. The **East Pagoda,** Zhenguo Ta, is 48 m (157 ft) high, the **West Pagoda,** Renshou Ta, only 44 m (144 ft) high. Together they represent the emblem of the city and are used as a trademark for many of the commodities produced by the city.

An ancient bridge, built in the middle of the 11th century, crosses the Luoyang River. The **Luoyang Bridge** is a wonderful example of ancient Chinese bridge architecture. The 800 m (2,625 ft) long bridge is supported by 47 pylons and used to have seven pavilions, nine stone pagodas, and stone balustrades on either side.

Outside the **East Gate** of the city on top of the **Lingshan Mountain** there is an old graveyard. It is written in the records of the Tang Dynasty that Mohammed, the founder of Islam, sent four missionaries to Quanzhou. Two died in the city and were buried on Lingshan Mountain. Half-way up, under a small pavilion are five stone plaques depicting scenes of the lives of the two missionaries and marking their graves.

The people called them the **Holy Graves of Islam.** Later, missionaries and traders from overseas who died in Quanzhou found their last resting place here. Islam was introduced into China as long ago as 651. In Quanzhou alone lived quite a number of Arabian missionaries who adhered to Islam. In 1010 they built their first mosque. This **mosque** which is also known as the Unicorn Temple, is modelled on the type found in Damascus. Numerous inscriptions in Arabic record the building and restoration of the mosque commanded by Ahmed of Jerusalem in the year 1310.

Other religions also flourished in the tolerant atmosphere of this old trading city. Even today, there are many reminders of the simultaneous co-existence of several religions, e. g. Buddhism, Taoism, Islam, and Manichaeism.

Three kilometers (1¾ miles) west of the town on top of the **Wushan Mountain** stands a huge **stone statue** of **Lao Zi, the founder of Taoism.** Across on the other side in the caves of the mountain are several large Buddhas.

A small **Manichaean monastery** is situated under a huge banyan tree on the top of **Wanshan Mountain.** Manichaeism is a religion which is based on the duality of light and dark and contains elements of both Buddhism and Christianity. It first found its way to China in the 7th century. A stone tablet near the monastery commemorates the work of the Manichaean mission.

The journey from the town to the coast takes about half an hour. An old octagonal tower built in 1162 and which used to serve as a navigational guide can still be found there. From this **Tower of the Two Sisters-in-Law** one can enjoy a wonderful view across the Taiwan Straits and the East Chinese Sea. According to legend, the wife of a sailor and her sister-in-law used to come here every day to wait for her husband to return from the sea. Every day they carried up a stone. Because the husband took so long to return they managed to build up a 21 m (69 ft) high tower.

Xi'an, the Centre

Xi'an

It is not without reason that Xi'an is today one of China's most important and popular tourist centres. Xi'an is, after all, the birthplace of Chinese culture, and was also the capital city of many dynasties for a period of 2,000 years.

Primitive tribes from prehistoric times found fertile, easily worked loess soil in the Wei river valley. Many neolithic villages of the Yangshao culture were discovered here and provide powerful evidence for the existence of a highly developed culture. The first big basic communities originated here. West of modern Xi'an, on the Feng River, was the capital of the Western Zhou Dynasty (1110–770 B. C.). Later on the capital was transferred to Hao on the opposite river bank. Qin Shi Huang Di, who unified the empire, built his capital in Xianyang in 221 B. C., 15 km (9 miles) northwest of Xi'an on the Wei River. When this palace grew too small for him, he built the A-fang Palace on the south bank of the river, which, however, was never completed.

The capital of the Han dynasty which followed, was situated a few miles north of Xi'an and was called Chang'an (Eternal Peace). The Eastern Han moved their capital to Luoyang, and after their downfall the kingdom disintegrated. Xi'an thus lost its significance as the centre.

The Sui Dynasty was the first to reunite the kingdom once more. They founded their capital in what is today Xi'an and called it Daxing (Great Prosperity).

The Tang Dynasty which followed, and whose reign brought China to new economic and cultural heights, enlarged the city and gave it back its old name from the Han epoch: Chang'an. During the Tang Dynasty (618–906) Xi'an developed into the centre of the Asiatic world, and with 1 million inhabitants was probably the largest city in the world then. Chang'an was the most eastern point of the silk road, via which countless traders and missionaries reached China. The excavation of the market place brought to light Persian, Egyptian and Byzantine coins. Thousands of merchants from the four corners of the earth lived in Chang'an in those days, and numerous foreign religions came to China. Buddhist, Taoist, Islamic, and Nestorian churches and communities lived side-by-side. The contact with foreign cultures and scientists enriched the Chinese way of life. Central and Near Eastern dances and songs were performed at court. The young Italian explorer Marco

261

Polo also reached Xi'an by the silk road.

The rectangular shaped Chang'an which was bigger than the inner city of Xi'an today was surrounded by a 37 km (23 mile) long city wall. The Imperial Palace was situated in front of the northern city gate, and the government buildings stood in front of the palace. The whole city was constructed like a chess board: the streets running from north to south and from east to west. With the fall of the Tang dynasty Xi'an's role as capital and Imperial city ended. The city was only rebuilt when the Ming emperors came to power. The city wall, which can still be seen today, surrounded Xi'an in the Ming epoch but it covered only a seventh of the area of the illustrious city of Chang'an. The **Small Wild Goose Pagoda** which in the Tang epoch was situated in the middle of the city, is today outside the city walls towards the south.

It was only in the 1930's that Xi'an regained some of its political

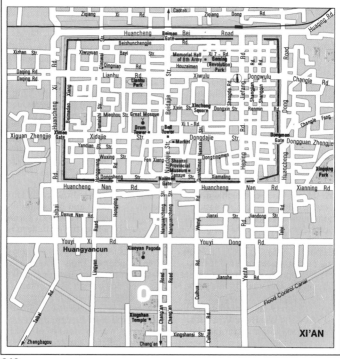

importance. In 1935, after the end of the Long March in which the Red Army marched more than 10,000 km (6,200 miles) right across China, the Communists established a base in Yan'an, which lies 80 km (50 miles) north of Xi'an. Here the leaders of the Communist Party, including Mao Zedong, set up their headquarters and from this point they carried out their operations against the Japanese and later against the Guomindang Army.

Today, Xi'an (Western Peace), including the incorporated administrative districts, covers 2,295 sq. km (886 sq. miles) and has 2.8 million inhabitants of which 1.5 million live in the inner city. In summer it is hot and dusty, especially in the months of March and April when the loess winds sweep over the plateau. August-September constitute the rainy season. The principal crops are wheat and above all cotton, which is processed in the local mills. The area produces large quantities of coal.

The principal sights of interest here are of cultural and historical importance. First and foremost the two wild geese pagodas are to be recommended.

The **Great Wild Goose Pagoda,** Da Yan Ta, lies at the very southern end of the city, in the middle of the **Temple of Great Benevolence,** Da Ci'en Si, which the Tang emperor Gaozong erected to the memory of his mother.

The famous Buddha monk Xuanzong, returning from India where he had studied for many years, came to Xi'an and commenced his monumental translation of sacred texts.

The pagoda was built in 652 A.D. in the centre of the temple in order to preserve his works and was originally called the Sutra Pagoda, Jing Ta. There are several explanations for its present name which it received at a later date. One legend tells of a certain monk who was forbidden to eat meat and was tested by Buddha. He sent him a wild goose which he allowed to fall dead from the skies in order to tempt him. The monk, however, recognized Buddha's sign and decided to erect a pagoda in memory of the incident. This is supposed to have occurred in India and Xuanzong brought the story home with him. The present building dates from the year 701–704 A.D. and is a magnificent example of the earlier period of Tang architectural design. The pagoda is built entirely from bricks which are arranged in such a way that their design creates the impression of a wooden building with beams, pillars and roofs.

The seven-storeyed pagoda is 64 m (210 ft) high and is accessible to the highest floor. On the lowest level there is a stone tablet commemorating the journey of the monk Xuanzong.

The **Small Wild Goose Pagoda,** Xiao Yan Ta, lies 1.5 km (roughly 1 mile) south of the southern city gate. The square pagoda was built in the years 707–709 A.D. and is also made of bricks. It used to have 15 storeys but two collapsed in an earthquake. The remaining 13 reach a height of 43 m (141 ft). Its storeys are not as high as those of its larger twin and its overall appearance with its tapering contours is one of elegance and grace. It stands in the **Temple of Blissful Happiness,** Jianfu Si, which was built in 684 A.D. to commemorate the death a year earlier of the Emperor Gaozong. The 36 m (118 ft) high **Bell Tower,** Zhong Lou, situated in the town centre, is the city emblem. The present building dates from the year 1582; although an older version was constructed during the Ming Dynasty in 1384. In earlier times the time was sounded out from the tower. The 2.5 ton heavy bell, dating from the 15th century, stands today on a stone pedestal in the northwest corner. The building which is constructed entirely from wood with no other materials of any kind is in the Ming style. From the tower there is an excellent view over all four city gates. Not very far to the west from here stands another smaller tower, the **Drum Tower,** Gu Lou, which has been restored several times since it was first constructed in the year 1370. A wooden building which today houses an antique shop also stands on the square stone pedestal at this spot. In the early days the closing of the city gates was proclaimed by the banging of drums.

The present **city walls** were constructed between 1376 and 1378 by command of the Ming Emperor Hongwu. He had handed the city over to his son who adopted the title "King of Qin". The city was replanned and the present-day wall was erected on the old foundation-wall of the former Forbidden City of the Tang emperors. It is one of the best preserved defensive systems of any Chinese city. The wall is 12 m

(39 ft) high, 15–18 m (49–59 ft) wide at the base and 12–14 m (39–46 ft) wide at the top. The West Gate is the largest. A few years ago the city began a thorough restoration of the walls and gates. The old moat system around the walls is undergoing reconstruction and will be used as a park. Setting out from the Drum Tower and following several narrow alleys one reaches the Huajue Alley and the **Great Mosque,** Qing Zhen Si. Islam reached China and Xi'an in the 7th century, by way of the Silk Road. This quarter of the city is inhabited mainly by Hui Moslems who are recognized as having independent nationality and, therefore, enjoy special privileges. The mosque is built in the Chinese style. Right at the entrance stands a memorial gate such as is found in Confucian temples and the minaret looks more like a pavilion than the traditional Islamic building. Only the prayer hall which dates from the 14th century contains elements of the Near Eastern and Arabian style. The inscriptions on the eastern-facing prayer wall are in Arabic. The library also contains many works in Arabic. Five times a day there is a call to prayer. The mosque was established in 742 A.D. with the support of the Emperor Xuanzong. During the last few years the some-what neglected structure has been restored – a further indication that religious freedom is once more guaranteed.

Not very far from the South Gate the **Shaanxi Provincial Museum** in an old Confucian temple is located. Plenty of time should be reserved for this museum which exhibits unique examples of 3,000 years of Chinese historic art. There are three main divisions: the first section shows historic finds from several dynasties; the second consists of sensational life-size stone sculptures and bas-reliefs; the third most famous section is that of the Forest of Tablets, an ancient record of Chinese history engraved on over 2,000 stelas.

The **Exhibition of Historical Finds** is chronologically ordered. Among these fascinating exhibits there are bronzes dating from the Zhou epoch (1100–221 B.C.); decorated bricks from Qin and Han dynasty palaces and graves, old coins and a model of the oldest seismograph in the world. The second section features objects from the Sui and Tang Dynasties including ceramics in the three coloured glaze of the Tang epoch, Tang horses, wall paintings recovered from tombs, and many discoveries documenting trading links with the West.

The **Exhibition of Stone Sculptures** – unique in China – presents seventy life-size stone animals and many Buddhist sculptures and bas-reliefs. The largest stone figures are almost 2,000 years old, such as the life-size rhinoceros and an ostrich which date from the Han dynasty. Particularly interesting exhibits are the four bas-reliefs with horse figures which come from the Emperor Taizong's tomb (626–649 A.D.). Two of these were removed to the United States in the 1930's. Some of the remaining reliefs are damaged because they were broken into smaller pieces for easier transport.

The **Forest of Tablets** which covers 6 halls, consists of a collection of over 2,000 stone tablets. One hundred and fourteen of these tablets are of particular interest since they depict the twelve classical works of Confucius with 560,000 characters. The Nestorian tablet which commemorates the foundation of the Nestorian community in 781 A.D. and the building of a chapel is also exhibited. It is easy to recognize, having a cross on top and some Syrian writing. **The Xingqing Park** which was formerly one of the Tang emperor's palace lies outside the city walls. Today it is situated outside the southern city gate and offers a wide variety of recreational facilities. Several of the former palace buildings have been rebuilt in the classical Chinese style. One-third of the area is covered by a lake whose shores are filled with pavilions, tea-houses, and bridges. The Neolithic Yangshao culture can be studied in the **Banpo Museum** which lies about 10 km (6 miles) east of Xi'an. The Neolithic village was discovered in 1953. The excavations brought to light the remains of the village and its huts, as well as a pottery workshop and a graveyard. An exhibition hall occupies 3,000

A bowl from the Neolithic period.

sq. metres (32,290 sq. ft) of the 5,000 sq. metre (53,820 sq. ft) village. The plans of round houses and rectangular community buildings, as well as harvest silos, pottery remnants and skeletons, can be seen.

Two smaller exhibition halls which are situated in front of the main hall have selective findings of stone work tools, bones and pottery on show. On the basis of certain evidence, the archaeologists believe that the society which was based here was a matriarchal one.

Some clay pottery shards even show traces of readable characters: examples of very early forms of Chinese writing.

The aforementioned Monk Xuanzang, famous through his great Indian journey and his translation works, is buried in the **Xiangjiao Temple,** 30 km (19 miles) south of Xi'an. Xiangjiao means: may religion prosper. The temple was built in 669 A.D. The main hall, which contains a jade Buddha, a bronze statue of Buddha and a laughing Buddha made of porcelain, has red pillars and a green roof. East of the main hall stands the library which owns six palm leaf pages dating from the Song dynasty. There are three pagoda covered tombs in the western corner. The largest five-storied pagoda is built on top of Xuanzang's earthly remains; the two three-storeyed pagodas on either side are dedicated to his two disciples. The Xiangji Temple with its 33 m (108 ft) high pagoda stands south of the city. At that time, the temple was assigned to the Buddhist Sect of the Pure Land. The Great

Hall, the Jingang Hall and the monks' living quarters are all preserved.

Xi'an's main tourist attraction and probably the most important archaeological find of the century is the **Mausoleum** of the **Emperor Qin Shi Huang Di,** which lies 35 km (22 miles) east of Xi'an in the Lintong district. The 47 m (154 ft) high burial mound has not yet been excavated. It is planned, however, that digging should begin in the near future. Tomb no. 1, situated 1.5 km (almost 1 mile) to the east of the burial mound, contains over 6,000 terracotta warriors as well as weapons and chariots. The tomb was discovered only in 1974. In 1979, a huge hall was built right over the excavations which cover 14,260 sq. metres (153,493 sq. ft) of ground. Several hundred of the figures have been completely restored and put into position again. The figures stand in battle formation in eleven long dug out rows; they include archers, crossbowmen, charioteers and officers, all between 1.8 m and 1.86 m (approx. 6 ft) in height. Every head is individually and uniquely modelled, no two faces are alike.

Qin Shi Huang Di came to the Qin throne when he was only thirteen years of age. With his attacking forces and mobile army he later succeeded in subduing six other separate kingdoms.

Very shortly after his ascent to the throne he gave the order to begin work on his monumental tomb. It took many thousands of workers 36 years to complete. The tomb was totally subterranean: pillars, walls

and a wooden ceiling protected it from the earth covering. In 206 B.C. the grave was plundered and later on the ceiling collapsed.

Only a few metres to the north of the grave site (no. 1) there are two other graves. Grave no. 2 contains about 1,400 cavalry soldiers and their horses. It has not yet been completely excavated. Grave no. 3 which contains a group of officers still has to be completely examined.

Two smaller exhibition halls on both sides of the entrance contain various finds and terracotta figures, as well as drawings and models which document the whole site.

Recently, a special exhibition was opened. A bronze model of a recently discovered Qin war chariot which is one of the most important finds at this site, is on display.

At the foot of Lishan near the Qin mausoleum are the **Huaqing Hot Springs** which were known as long as 2,800 years ago. The ruler of the Zhou dynasty built a palace here in the 8th century B.C. and the emperors of suceeding dynasties knew the value of this lovely spot. Emperor Taizong of the Tang dynasty enlarged the palace complex and renamed it **"Palace of the Hot Springs",** Tangquangong. His follower Xuanzong gave it its present name: Palace of Purity, Huaqinggong. Together with his concubine Yang Guifei he used to come here to spend the winter months.

Each face of the 7,000 terracotta figures is individually modelled, no two are the same.

When visiting the palace complex one enters a room which contains a sunken bath which the beautiful concubine is supposed to have used. In front of this is the **Pool of the Nine Dragons.** Later the building was taken over by Taoist monks who built a number of Taoist temples on the slope. Half-way up stands a small temple built in the classical style, commemorating the Xi'an incident of 1936 which resulted in the alliance between the Guomindang and the Communists against the Japanese. Chiang Kaishek who was recuperating here was betrayed by his own officers, arrested and was forced to negotiate. An attempt to escape failed and he was recaptured on the spot where the pavilion stands today.

Four springs supply pure water at 43°C (109°F) which is particularly effective against rheumatism and skin diseases.

One part of the complex is a sanatorium which is reserved for the sick and those taking the waters.

The **Xianyang Museum** which is 20 km (12 miles) west of Xi'an in the old capital of the Qin dynasty exhibits historical finds dating from the Qin and Han epochs. These include a cavalry army of small sized terracotta figures found in the tomb of a Han general.

A visit to the Xianyang Museum can be combined with an excursion to the **Tombs** of the **Han** and **Tang Dynasties.** In **Maoling** there are a total of ten graves which date from the Han epoch, and resemble small pyramids. They are grass-covered, and none of them has as yet been opened.

The grave of the Han general, Huo Qubing lies about 1 km (almost 1 mile) east of Maoling. On the orders of the emperor he was honoured with an exceptionally large mausoleum because of the great service he did in suppressing the Xiongan (Huns). In front of the grave stand enormous stone figures and statues. Further stone sculptures are on show at the Maoling Museum.

The **Graves** of the **Tang Emperor** are found about 80 km (50 miles) east of Xi'an. The grave of the Taizong emperor **Zhaoling** is the largest and was built on a naturally occurring hill in 636 A.D. Over 167 other graves belonging to the emperor's family and high government officials are found in the surrounding area. The **Zhaoling Museum** has several grave-stones from these, as well as relics from the smaller graves, on show.

The third Emperor Gao Zong and his Empress Wu Zetian, who was previously a concubine, are buried in the third grave. After his death she became the only woman to become empress in her own right and she reigned for fourteen years. The grave complex consists of three hummocks which include the grave hill itself and two smaller ones which form a natural entrance gate to the whole complex. Here at this point begins the long row of stone figures including horses, generals, and dignitaries, as well as two 6 m (20 ft) high stelas.

On the right side of the tomb stands a group of 61 stone figures representing envoys from the various Chinese national groups, as well as foreign lords and nobles who took part in the funerary rites. Unfortunately, the heads are missing from all of these figures. Some of the neighbouring graves have been opened, including those of **Princess Yong Tai, Prince Zhang Huai** and the **Prince Yi De.** Although these are significantly smaller they contain some fine murals and smaller clay figures with the typical Tang three-coloured glaze, which are well worth seeing.

A journey by land always offers the opportunity to stop and visit a **farmhouse.** Most of the peasants live in loess huts or caves. The **loess caves** are usually built in an excavated square with one open side which is used as the entrance. The other three sides are connected up to cave living rooms. The firm loess can be worked smoothly and straightened easily. The living space can actually be very comfortable. Loess is, in fact, the only available building material in the area.

Taiyuan

Taiyuan, the capital of the province of Shanxi, lies about 500 km (310 miles) south-west of Beijing, on the northern edge of the fertile Taiyuan plain which stretches along the banks of the river Fenhe, and is surrounded by mountains. This modern and industrially important city has about 2.2 million inhabitants.

Archaeological finds verify the earlier existence of neolithic settlements at a time when the Taiyuan plain was still covered by a huge inland sea. In the Era of the Warring Kingdoms (475–221 B. C.) the city

was known as Jinyang. The nomadic peoples from the north used to cross the strategically important Taiyuan plain on their war campaigns; here the entrance to the fertile valleys at Huange and the Wei River opened up and this is also where the heart of Chinese culture was to be found.

During the Ming Dynasty, the viceroy for Shanxi Province lived in Taiyuan. The influential secret society, the "White Lotus", was centered in Taiyuan. It played an important role in the Boxer rebellion at the beginning of the century.

The most important sight to be seen in Taiyuan is the **Temple of the Two Pagodas,** Shuangta Si, situated in the south-east of the city. The two 400-year-old, 54 m (177 ft) high pagodas are the city emblem.

The **Chongshan Temple** is situated in the city itself, its foundation dates back to the Tang epoch. The temple was restored and renovated by the Ming emperors but was unfortunately damaged by fire about a century ago. Apart from the entrance and a bell tower, the main hall is still standing, and is open to visitors. There is a statue of the **Goddess of Mercy** on show.

The **Shanxi Province Museum** in Taiyuan is also well worth a visit. The museum is housed in an old Taoist temple and has a good selection of Neolithic pieces, a bronze work from the Shang Dynasty, weapons, coins, and grave objects on show. A collection of Buddhist sutras is exhibited here, besides examples of calligraphy and paintings by a well-known 4th century painter.

There is a large selection of temples and temple complexes in the area around the city. We shall mention just a few of these, e. g. the **Temple of the Minister of Jin** which lies north-west of Taiyuan in the township of Lancun. It is dedicated to a minister of the Jin Fief who lived during the Zhou epoch, and who was also mentioned and admired by Confucius.

In the district town Lingfen **Iron Buddha Temple** is located (Dayun Si) which was founded during the Tang Dynasty.

Above a 6 m (20 ft) head of Buddha stands a tile-decorated pagoda which rises to a height of 30 m (98 ft).

The most remarkable temple park in the area, however, is the **Jin Temple of Ancestors,** Jinci, which is situated at the foot of the Xuanweng Mountain and about 25 km (15 miles) from Taiyuan. The park consists of about 100 temples, pavilions and halls. The temple was constructed in the fifth century B. C. in honour of a prince of the Northern Wei Dynasty, Prince Shuyu who was lord of a fief here in the earlier Zhou epoch. Later rulers continued to pay homage to this prince and further enlarged the whole complex.

When one enters by the main door and continues straight on, one comes to a large terrace which in earlier times was also used as a stage; after crossing over a small bridge, one comes to another smaller terrace. Behind this terrace stand the Bell and Drum Towers which flank the Hall of Offering. Behind the Hall of Offering one crosses the "Flying Bridge", which is built in the form of a cross, and enters the main hall of the complex, the **Hall of the Venerable Mother,** Shengmu Dian. The hall was erected in 1030 to honour the mother of Prince Shuyu. Well worth seeing is the exceptional collection of 44 terracotta figures in the inner hall. One represents the mother herself, others her ladies-in-waiting and her eunuchs. Each statue has unique individual features and differently carved clothes.

East of the main axis stands the **Prince Shuyu Temple** and the **Temple of Honour of the God of War, Guanyu.**

South-west of Taiyuan in the surrounding mountains, there are several smaller grotto complexes which cannot, however, be compared to those in Longmen or Yungang. The **Tianlong Mountain** has 20 grottos which date from the Tang epoch but which are unfortunately badly damaged. On the Longshan (the Long Mountain) there are Taoist cave temples which date from the first century of the Mongol dynasty (Yuan).

Datong

Datong, which means "Great Unitiy", is situated on a high plain in the north of the Shanxi province near the inner Mongolian border. An eight-hour train journey from Beijing, which partly follows the Great Wall, is needed to reach Datong.

The land here is not particularly fertile and since the city lies in the dry dusty north Chinese plain, the continual dust and cold winds from the north do not enhance the quality of life here. The average yearly temperature is 6°C (43°F); in summer it reaches 38°C (109°F), whereas in winter it can drop as low as −30°C (−22°F). Only five months of the year are frost-free.

Datong is one of the northern industrial cities. Coal mining and the construction of agricultural machinery are the main industries. Nowadays the city has about 900,000 inhabitants.

During the Era of the Warring Kingdoms (475–221 B.C.), Datong existed as a settlement in the Zhao state. During the Han Dynasty it was the chief town of the Pengcheng district. Two hundred years later, it served as capital of the Toba people who founded the northern Wei Dynasty. The Yungang Cave Temples date from this period, i.e. around the 5th century A.D. During the Tang epoch it was the capital of the Yunzhou district and in the year 1048 it finally got its present name of Datong which was given to it by another foreign dynasty, the Liao.

The two large monasteries, the **Huayan Monastery** and the **Shanhua Monastery,** date from the Liao Dynasty (916–1125). Around the year 1400, the thirteenth son of the first Ming emperor lived in Datong as military governor. He was responsible for erecting the still intact **Nine Dragon Wall.** The city walls of Datong also date from the Ming epoch.

If you are interested in arts and crafts you have the choice of visiting either one of the two **carpet factories** – one is in the city centre, the other in the southern suburbs – or

the **porcelain factory** which is in the east of the town.

The **Huayan Monastery** (Huayan is the name of an early Buddhist sect) is in the centre of the city. It was built in 1062 during the Liao Dynasty by the Khitan people. During subsequent dynasties, in particular during the time of the Mongols, it was destroyed several times and rebuilt. The present complex is not quite as big as the original building. During the Ming Dynasty, the monastery was divided into the Upper and Lower Monasteries.

The central building of the Upper Monastery is the Da Xiong Bao Dian Hall (The Treasury Hall of the Great Hero) which was built in the year 1140 and has stood undamaged for over 800 years. One reaches the Hall by a flight of stairs and a terrace constructed in the style of the Liao Dynasty. The Great Hall itself contains five enormous Buddha figures which date from the first half of the 15th century. The walls of the hall are decorated with 5 m (16 ft) high painted murals which are, however, only a hundred years old.

The Bojiajiao Hall in the lower Huayan monastery serves as a library. Previously there were 579 volumes of Buddhist writings stored on unique, beautifully built shelves. Unfortunately, the books have been lost and it is in fact astounding that the hall has been so well preserved, since it was used at the beginning of the Ming Dynasty, as the official state granary. The wonderful wooden ceiling and the murals have probably been restored but the style of the Liao period was maintained. The clay figures, Buddhas, Bodhisattvas and hosts of other holy figures and gods, are with a few exceptions the originals.

In the south of the city the **Shanhua Monastery** is situated which is also known as Kaiyuansi because it was built during the reign of the Tang Emperor Kaiyuan (714–741). This monastery is one of the few 12th century buildings which has survived relatively intact. It was rebuilt in this period after having suffered serious damage. The Great Hall, together with the Huayan monastery halls, are exceptional examples of Liao architecture. Five large statues of Buddha stand in the hall, and the walls are adorned with murals.

The **Yungang Cave Temples** lie about 16 km (10 miles) west of the city. Together with the caves in Dunhuang and those at Longmen near Luoyang, these are some of the most important examples of Buddhist cave art in China. Both large and small caves honeycomb over half a mile of cliffs. Work on this cave complex began during the time of the northern Wei Dynasty over 1,500 years ago. At the suggestion of the monk Tan Yao, who had found a protector of Buddhism in his emperor Wen Cheng, the first five great Buddhas were hewn from the sandstone in the year 460. During the following 40 years, 1,000 caves with over 100,000 richly decorated figures were completed. The capital was moved to Luoyang in the year 494 and over the years the cave complex passed into oblivion.

Fifty-one thousand figures have survived until the present day, the biggest of these being a 17 m (56 ft) high sitting Buddha, whereas the smallest figures are barely 2 cm (3/4″) high. As well as the larger statues there are numerous small niches in the caves, filled with scenes portraying flying celestial beings, scenes that recount Buddhist legends, flowers, buildings and many other designs.

Of the remaining 53 caves, the 21 most important are divided into three groups: the central, eastern and western groups, of which the most important is the middle group (caves 5–13). In cave No. 5, carved out of a single stone, sits a 17 m (56 ft) high Buddha. His ear alone measures 3.1 m (10 ft), the foot 4.6 m (15 ft) and his middle finger 2.3 m (7 ft). The figure was completely plastered with clay and later during the Tang Dynasty painted all over. On both sides of the entrance there are two Buddha figures under a Bodhi tree, the tree of knowledge, where Buddha the philosopher sat and reached the highest state of enlightenment. Walls and ceiling are full of little niches which are decorated with heavenly beings flying like a halo around the great Buddha.

Cave No. 6 is also well worth seeing. In the centre of the square cave stands a 15 m (49 ft) high, two-storeyed, four-cornered pillar which reaches right up to the roof. On each of the upper four corners stand smaller nine-storeyed pagodas supported on the backs of elephants. This cave contains a series of Jataka tales which relate the story of the

Buddha Sakyamuni, beginning with his birth and ending with his entry into nirvana. These stories are depicted on the three walls of the cave, as well as on the four sides of the pillar.

Cave No. 7 is divided into two chambers; the lower one contains a Bodhisattva seated on a lion. The other three walls are decorated completely with niches and figures, including six worshipping Bodhisattvas. The ceiling is decorated with flying celestial beings and lotus flowers which are the symbol of purity.

Cave No. 8 is noted for its two unusual exhibits, which show strong Indian influence. One is a statue of Vishnu (Kumarakadeva) with five heads and six arms, sitting on a peacock; and the other is a Siva (Mahesvara) possessing three heads and eight arms, and sitting on a bull. Cave No. 12 is also divided into two chambers. The front chamber has niches which are hewn in the form of a wooden house with alcoves. The capitals supporting the eaves are reminiscent of Persian pillars. The upper half of the main wall is decorated with numerous heavenly musicians. Cave No. 13 is particularly beautiful and contains a 13 m (43 ft) high Buddha Maitreya (the Buddha of the Future).

The Eastern Group of Caves (1–4) has withstood the effects of wind and weather over the centuries less well. Apart from Buddha statues, the caves contain mainly pillars hewn to resemble pagodas. Cave No. 3 is the largest of the whole complex. Across the cave, far up on the 25 m (82 ft) high cliff right-angled holes are visible and the most probable explanation is that a projecting structure, possibly a temple, once stood there. Today, however, the only objects in the cave are two Bodhisattva figures and a statue of Buddha which date from the Tang and Sui Dynasties.

In the western complex, cave number 15 is well worth seeing. It contains 10,000 small sitting Buddhas. One of the oldest caves, No. 16, was laid out by the monk Tan Yao. In the centre of the cave stands a large Buddha and the walls are covered in thousands of smaller Buddhas. Cave No. 19 also contains one of the larger Buddha figures to be found here in Yungang, i. e. the 16.7 m (55 ft) high seated Buddha Sakyamuni. The almost 14 m (46 ft) high seated Buddha from cave 20 stands outside today because the front part of the cave has collapsed. The remaining caves 22–53 are less remarkable.

Not only the wind and rain are responsible for the damage in the area, nearly 1,400 statues have been stolen and sold abroad. Many figures are missing limbs or heads, some were wantonly mutilated but others were carefully and deliberately removed by antique hunters.

Loyang

Today, there are 900,000 inhabitants in the city which lies in the western half of Henan province, only a few miles south of the Hunanghe (Yellow River). Luoyang has as much historical significance for China as Xi'an. For centuries it was the great rival of Xi'an which lies only 400 km (248 miles) to the west. Early Neolithic settlements have also been discovered in the region around Luoyang. In the time of the Eastern Zhou Dynasty, around 770 B.C., it was the capital. Until 1000 A.D. it served as the capital for nine different dynasties. The **Temple of the White Horse,** Baima Si, was the first Buddhist temple to be built in China. During the Han Dynasty the first Chinese university was also founded here. When the Mongols elevated Beijing to the status of imperial city, Luoyang and Xi'an lost most of their importance. The former imperial city and cultural centre of the country, had only 90,000 inhabitants in 1949, the year the People's Republic of China was founded. During the last decade, however, it has regained some of its old importance in having become an important industrial city which, for example, can boast of one of China's largest tractor factories employing 27,000 people.

The **Longmen Caves,** situated 12 km (7 miles) south of the city on the Yellow River can be considered the most important historical and cultural structure in Luoyang. The river flows in a northerly direction between two mountains, behind which, according to legend, a dragon lived. This explains how the area came to be known as Longmen which means "Dragon Gate". The Longmen Buddhist caves date from about 494 A.D. when the Emperor Xiao Wen of the Northern Wei Dynasty moved his capital to Luoyang. Construction work on the complex was carried out over a period of 400 years. The cave complex extends to both sides of the river; the caves are hewn out of the steep cliffs and therefore provide natural protection for the many sculptures and reliefs found there. The complex on the western bank is well preserved, whereas those on the east side are unfortunately almost completely destroyed. Altogether there are 2,100 caves and niches, 40 stone pagodas and over

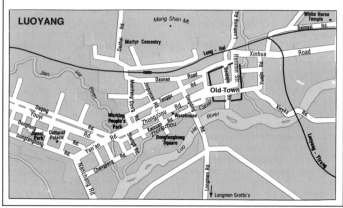

100,000 figures, including the biggest Buddha statue which is over 17 m (56 ft), and the smallest which is only 2 cm (¾″).

The **Qian Xi Temple Cave** is the first large cave and dates from the middle of the 7th century. Its centre is occupied by the Buddha Amitabha on his throne, flanked by two Bodhisattvas and his two disciples. On either side of the entrance stand two guardian deities.

Then there are three further caves. The **middle Bin Yang Cave** was started in the year 500. The main figure is an 8.5 m (28 ft) high sitting Buddha Sakyamuni, situated between his two disciples and two Bodhisattvas. Musicians and dancers circle a lotus flower on the ceiling above. In the **southern Bin Yang Cave** it is possible to follow the development of both design and style because the caves were begun during the time of the northern Wei and only finished when the Tang epoch had begun. The **northern Bin Yang Cave** contains a 7.6 m (25 ft) high Amitaba Buddha. At the entrance are two wonderful bas-reliefs depicting Dharmapalas (guardian deities).

Fifteeen thousand smaller Buddha figures fill the **Cave of the Ten Thousand Buddhas,** Wan Fu Dong, which dates from the Tang epoch, 680. The wall behind the central Buddha consists of 54 lotus flowers upon which smaller figures are seated.

The **Lotus Flower Cave,** Lian Hua Dong, gets its name from the enormous lotus flower which decorates the ceiling. Here also the smallest of all the figures is found which is ony 2 cm (¾″) high.

The **Feng Xi'an Temple** is the most imposing part of the whole complex and also the largest. The main figure is a Vairocana Buddha which even though it is in the seated position is still over 17.14 m (56 ft) high. Although the facial features are very simply modelled, the figure somehow radiates a moving sense of peace and contemplativeness. The Buddha is not only flanked by the disciples Kasyapa and Anada but also by two Bodhisattva figures. Impressive, too, are the two fierce guardian deities with their demonic faces. The Gu Yang Cave is also of great interest. It contains many small niches, as well as important inscriptions dating from the Northern Wei Dynasty, and is the oldest cave in the complex. The **Yao Fang Cave** houses ancient medical texts on stone tablets.

The above mentioned **White Horse Temple,** Baima Si, dates back to the year 68 A. D. The Eastern Han Emperor Yong Ping is reputed to have had a vision of Buddha, where-upon envoys were sent to India in order to study Buddha's teachings. They only reached present-day Afghanistan but returned with two Indian monks who according to legend were riding on two white horses.

Later on they were buried in the temple. The present buildings date from the 16th century; the halls and figures are in good condition, a bell from the same period is also well preserved. Well worth seeing are the artistically made 18 lohan figures.

South-east of the temple stands the 13-storeyed, 24 m (79 ft) high **Cloud Embracing Pagoda,** Qi Yun Ta, which dates from the 12th century. The name Qi Yun means "that which greets the clouds"; it is possible that this pagoda used to stand in the middle of the temple complex.

The **Luoyang Museum** is on the Zhongzhou Road right in the middle of the city centre. Five different halls are filled with over 2,000 objects dating from Neolithic times up to the Tang Dynasty. Particularly interesting and highly significant historically are the bronzes which date from the Zhou era. This verifies the theory

Figure of a camel carrying five musicians on its back. The three colour glaze is characteristic of the Tang period   (c. 723).

that the Bronze Age did in fact initially begin in the Luoyang region. Some stelas and inscriptions from the first imperial Han university can still be seen. The famous Tang tricolour glazed ceramics, including horses, camels, and interesting human figurines which came over the Silk Road from Central Asia, are well worth seeing.

In the **Imperial City Park,** Wangcheng Gongyuan, there are two **smaller tombs** of **nobles** who lived in the Han era. The tomb from the Western Han Dynasty (205–225 B.C.) was discovered in 1956 during the construction of the railway station and was later moved to its present position in the park. It is so far the oldest tomb where the walls are decorated with murals that has been discovered. The second tomb, dating from the Eastern Han Dynasty (25–200 A.D.), came to light when a road was being built and was also transferred to the park.

In April, when the peonies are blooming, the park looks like a huge flower exhibition and is a popular attraction. At the entrance stands a huge station of Chairman Mao Zedong.

At the foot of the Mangshan Mountains north-west of the city is the area where in earlier times during the Sui Dynasty (605) the huge imperial granaries were built and used for nearly 500 years. So far 287 silos, which were built 5–7 m (16–23 ft) below the ground, have been discovered. Eleven of these have been excavated and can be visited.

General Guan of the Shu state, who lived in the time of the Three

Kingdoms (220–280), is honoured and prayed to as a war god even today by the Chinese. His picture can even be found in the homes of Chinese farmers because he is the most powerful god in the popular belief of the people. His head is believed to be buried in the **Guan Lin Temple** 8 km (5 miles) south of the city.

Behind the third temple hall surrounded by an octagonal red wall stands the 20 m (66 ft) high grave barrow.

Anyone who visits the city in April when the peony flowers are in bloom can also participate in the **Lantern Festival** which occurs at the fun-filled annual market fair. The most extraordinary sight, however, is the exhibition of palatial lanterns. These large imaginative works of art are usually assembled from paper and thin wood only. When dusk falls, their full effect can be admired. The tradition of lantern building goes back as far as 2,000 years.

One of the Buddhist five holy mountains, the Songshan, lies only roughly the same distance from Zhenzhou which is the capital of Henan Province. The Songshan Mountain Range has 72 peaks stretching over an area of 60 km (37 miles). The Junji peak which is 1,494 m (4,900 ft) is the highest. For centuries the Songshan has been known as a holy mountain and has innumerable monasteries and temples.

The chief town of the district is **Dengfeng** and from here it is easy to visit all the most important sights.

Only 4 km (about 2 miles) to the south lies the **Zhongyue Temple** which stands on an earlier foundation dating back to the Qin Dynasty (221–206 B. C.). The Han emperor, Wu Di, restored and enlarged the temple. Today's complex is more recent-from the Qin Dynasty. After going through the **Zhonghua Gate,** one passes along a 650 m (2,132 ft) long path flanked by 10 buildings. The four **Iron Guards,** dating from 1064, are very rare. They stand guard in a boxing stance and with grotesque faces protect the small pavilion to which the emperors brought their offerings. There are over 30 cypresses which are over 1,000 years old still standing in the courtyards.

The most famous monastery in the Songshan Mountains is the **Shaolin Monastery** which lies at the foot of the Shaoshi Mountain about 13 km (8 miles) north-west of Dengfeng. It was built during the Northern Wei Dynasty (495 A. D.). In 527, the Indian monk Bodhidharma (in Chinese Da Mo) went to Shaolin and founded the Chan sect. Today it is known, especially in Japan, as Zen Buddhism. Bodhidharma is thought to be the founder of Shaolin boxing which is a particular form of Chinese martial boxing. Some monks still practice this art form today and in recent years have succeeded, even in China, in making kung fu and shaolin films popular once more. At the beginning of the 7th century some of the shaolin boxers earned a place as guardians of the first Tang emperor. This in turn meant that the monastery enjoyed generous imperial patronage. The renovation work begun some time ago should be completed soon. One enters the monastery by the **Mountain Gate,** Shanmen; well worth seeing are the Halls of **Bodhidharma** and the **Ten Thousand Buddhas.** They contain valuable wall paintings depicting 500 lohans.

In another hall there is a wall painting showing a scene where thirteen shaolin monks are practising their art before the Tang Emperor Li Shimin.

Left of the entrance about 300 m (984 ft) away one reaches the **Pagoda Forest,** Ta Lin. This is the graveyard where for over 1,000 years the abbots and their famous monks were buried. Over 200 grave pagodas dating from various epochs permit one to study the architectual development in pagoda construction over the years. Of particular interest are the pagodas of the Yuan era, the age of Mongolian rule, which resemble Tibetan stupas. They have cupola-shaped pedestals and long thin shafts at the top of which one or several umbrellas are placed.

Some 5 km (3 miles) north-west of Dengfeng stands **China's oldest pagoda,** the **Songyue Ta.** The twelve-storeyed brick pagoda over 40 m (131 ft) high and dates from the year 520. It is in remarkably good condition.

Apart from a few other temples, a visit to the **Guard Towers** which date from the Han era, and the **Gaocheng Observatory** is highly recommended. The latter is named after a well known modern astronomer and mathematician and dates back to the time of the Mongols (1368–1644).

Kaifeng

Kaifeng lies in the east of Henan Province only about 75 km (47 miles) from the capital town Zhengzhou and near the Yellow River, Huanghe. Kaifeng is one of the former imperial cities. Even before the reunification of the empire it was the capital of the Wei state. In the year 600 the Sui emperor built the Great Canal, or **Imperial Canal** as it is also known. Thus, Kaifeng had access to Luoyang and the rich cities of the east coast. This in turn encouraged its development as an important trading city. From 900 until 1127 it was the capital of several dynasties which did not, however, rule over the whole of the Chinese territories. During the reign of the Northern Song Dynasty (960–1127) the city had over 1 million inhabitants. In 1644 when the Manchus were driving the imperial Ming Dynasty troops south, the city officials are supposed to have breached the Yellow River dykes in order to defeat the conquerors from the north. The city was completely flooded and more than 300,000 people are said to have perished.

The **Xiangguo Temple** in the city centre used to be one of China's most famous temples. It was destroyed in 1644 during the above-mentioned flooding. The present buildings date from the 18th century. A gold-plated wooden statue of the Goddess of Mercy, Guanyin, and a 5 ton heavy bell from the Qing Dynasty are particularly worth seeing.

The **Dragon Pavilion,** Longting, stands on what used to be the Song imperial palace. Emperor Kangxi built it in 1692 and gave it its name. Between the steps leading up to the pavilion, which stands on a slope, winds the figure of a black stone dragon.

In the north-east of the old town stands the **Iron Pagoda,** Tieta, whose fame reaches far beyond the walls of Kaifeng. It gets its name from the brownish red glazed bricks which cover the outer walls. It was built in 1048, is 55 m (180 ft) high and has thirteen floors.

During the Ming Dynasty, a high official of the town Kaifeng ordered a 2 m (about 6 ft) high **Iron Rhinoceros** statue to be made, which was supposed to protect the city from flooding. Later on it became a victim to further flooding. In 1691 it was luckily found again and dug up. Today it stands in the **Huilong Temple** 2 km (roughly 1 mile) north of the northern gate. One of the largest earlier brick pagodas

was the **Fan Ta** pagoda which dates from the year 977, and was situated in the Yuwangtai Park in the south-west of the city. It has unfortunately fallen down and today only three floors remain; the pagoda now measures 31 m (102 ft) in height.

Lanzhou
The largest city in north-west China, and the capital of the Gansu province, is Lanzhou which has two million inhabitants. The city lies on the upper reaches of the Huanghe (Yellow River) and is an important junction for traffic between the centre and the north-west. Railways connect the city with Xi'an, with Xining in Qinghai Province, with Urumqi in Xinjiang Province and with Baotou which lies in Inner Mongolia. Because of this, the importance of the bigger industries has grown during the last thirty years, e. g. locomotive and wagon

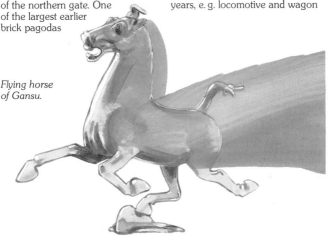

Flying horse of Gansu.

factories, the petrochemical industry and metalworking factories. Lanzhou is also the centre of China's nuclear research industry.

Some 2,000 years ago, Lanzhou was a strategically important trading centre having access via the Silk Road to Central and Near East Asia. The Han General Huo Qubing, who had opened up the western areas for trade, stationed his troops in Lanzhou and from there controlled all the trading routes.

The climate in Gansu is strongly influenced by the great Siberian continent. The summers are warm and dry, whereas in the winter months the temperatures can easily fall to $-20\,°C$ $(-4\,°F)$. In the fertile Huanghe valley wheat, millet, tobacco and melons are grown. The overall view of the city is undisturbed by the big industrial complexes because these are situated on the outskirts of the city.

The city occupies narrow stretches running along the shores of the Huanghe. In the centre, across from the Friendship Hotel, the Gansu Provincial Museum is situated. Exhibits include interesting Neolithic pottery pieces and sacrificial urns in bronze dating from the Zhou Dynasty. The most famous exhibit, however, is the bronze statue of the "Flying Horse of Gansu" which is supported by a single hoof on a swallow-like foot. The figure was discovered in a tomb dating from the Eastern Han era (25–220).

In the south of the city, near the railway station, lies the **Park** of the **Five Wells,** Wuquanshan Gongyuan, which is a popular excursion centre for local people on holidays and feast days. The **Chongqing Si Temple** dates from the year 1392 and stands within the park boundaries. Worth seeing is the 5 ton iron bell and 5 m (16 ft) bronze Buddha dating from 1370. The zoo is located nearby. North of the Huanghe the 1700 m (5,577) high **Mountain of the White Pagoda** rises up. The **White Pagoda** is octagonal has seven floors and is 17 m (56 ft) high. All around the hill pavilions and temples are grouped.

From July until November when the water level of the Huanghe and the Liujiascia Lake is high enough, it is possible to take a three-hour boat journey to visit the **Temple Cave** of the **Thousand Buddhas,** Bingling Si. In a 60 m (197 ft) high cliff, rising up from the shores of the lake, there are over 183 grottoes and niches, as well as a 27 m (88 ft) high figure of Buddha. It is possible to walk through the cave complex along steps and wooden galleries. The buildings date from the time of the Northern Wei Dynasty. They were started in the year 513 and were not finished until well into the 19th century. Most of the sculptures and reliefs date from the Tang era. The cave complex is often compared to those found at Longmen and Yungang; it dates from the same period, although it is much smaller. The cave temple was, in fact, forgotten with time and was only rediscovered in 1952.

It takes 5 hours to reach **Labrang Monastery** (Labuleng Si) near Xiahe. It is one of the six largest holy places of the Tibetan Lamas. The monastery was built in 1708 and used to shelter up to 4,000 monks. It was a popular pilgrimage centre for followers of Lamaism from Tibet, Qinghai, Gansu and Inner Mongolia. Particularly worth seeing are the gold-plated bronze statues of Buddha which are found in a temple built in the Tibetan style. The walls of the building are plastered white, the ceiling friezes are reddish brown and the roofs are gold-plated – i. e. it has the typical appearance of a Tibetan monastery.

Dunhuang

The city, which has 80,000 inhabitants, lies on the very western edge of Gansu Province, not far from the borders to Qinghai and Xinjiang. This remotely situated oasis city can be reached by travelling to Liuyuan by train and continuing from there by bus or by taking a plane from Langzhou. It must be said, however, that planes to Dunhuang do not operate very frequently.

In earlier times Dunhuang was among the important stopovers on the Silk Road. Here it divides itself into the northern route which leads via Hami, Turfan, Kuqa and Aksu to Kashgar. The southern route follows the northern edge of the Kunlun range which surrounds the Taklimakan Desert, then passes through Khotan and Yarkand and finally reaches Kashgar. Dunhuang is famous throughout the world and China itself because of the famous **Mogao Caves** which were formerly a Buddhist holy city and are full of unique well-preserved cave paintings. The **Mogao Caves** are situated about 27 km (88 miles) southwest of Dunhuang in a small oasis which bears the nam Qian Fo dong or "Cave of the Thousand Buddhas". The 1,600 m (5,249 ft) high cliff rises up at the shore of the river Danghe, and here over thousands of years Buddhist artists carved out caves, grottos and niches in three overlying levels. Buddhism reached China from India by means of the Silk Road. Until well into the 7th century the Silk Road was travelled by the famous Chinese monks on their pilgrimages to Buddha's homeland.

Thus, the earliest Buddhist communities developed as early as the first century A. D. The building of the Mogao Caves began in 366. As late as the 11th century this was one of the most important Buddhist places of worship. As the importance of the sea trading routes grew and the Silk Road declined in importance, Dunhuang also faded into the past and was forgotten. The complex was only rediscovered in 1900. The finder, a man called Wang Yuanlu, notified the authorities as to his spectacular find but because they showed no particular interest he began to sell the priceless documents, scrolls and treasures to foreign archaeologists. 492 caves have been preserved; they contain 2,450 sculptures and wall paintings covering an area of 450,000 sq. m (4,843,755 sq. ft). The caves vary in size from 1 m (roughly 3 ft) to 40 m (131 ft). Many of the cave paintings are remarkably well preserved thanks to the extremely dry climate. Archaeologists, artists and visitors are particularly impressed by the Apsaras, the heavenly flying deities. Today the latter's influence can be seen in the arts and crafts produced in China's workshops.

Artists from several dynasties left their influence on the various styles. Dates of completion and dynasties are indicated by inscriptions in each cave. In the oldest cave, No. 275, the cave paintings largely depict scenes from the life and works of the Buddha Sakyamuni. Scenes from normal everyday life such as hunting, working, fishing can, however, also be seen. Cave No. 249, which also dates back to the Wei Dynasty shows hunters on horseback with their bows and arrows chasing after gazelles and tigers. Cave No. 296 has scenes of caravans loaded with cargo traversing the Silk Road. There are also scenes from the life of Prince Sudan who sacrificed his life to save that of a hungry tiger.

Ninety-five grottoes have survived from the time of the Sui Dynasty (589–618). The influence of Indian art and culture which can easily be seen in the earlier caves, dominates less and less. This can be seen for example in the statues which show bodies of quite different proportions with enormous upper torsos and richly ornamented clothing.

The largest group is made up of 213 caves dating rom the Tang Dynasty (618–907). The latter can often be identified by the figures and themes they feature. During the Tang Dynasty, the sect of the Pure Land exerted its influence. It preached a philosophy which tried to bring Buddhism and the simple people closer together. Accordingly it was no longer necessary to fulfill complicated meditative exercises in order to reach a state of perfection. According to the rules of this sect, all that was now required was to call

continuously on Buddha Amitabha in order to be allowed to enter into nirvana. Buddha Amitabha, the Buddha of Eternal light, together with scenes of the paradise of the pure land also decorate these caves.

In cave No. 96 stands a 33 m (108 ft) high statue of Buddha; another large Buddha statue 26 m (85 ft) high is in No. 130; cave 220 is famous for its finely depicted scenes of musicians and dancers. Cave 158 contains the sculpture of a sleeping Buddha. The Tang grottos usually consist of several rooms: entry, main hall and back room.

The following dynasties produced fewer new caves since during the Tang era almost all the available space was used up by the Tang artists. The later work, therefore, consisted mainly of renovation.

The sand dunes of Taklimakan desert reach almost to the city limits. Near the city and lying between the enormous sand dunes is the **Crescent Moon Lake** which owes its name to its unmistakable form.

The **Ringing Sand Mountain** lies on the southern outskirts of the city. When one slides down the huge sandy slopes a peculiar ringing sound arises due to the rubbing of the sand.

In Dunhuang the Silk Road divides into the northern and southern branches. After about a 60 km (37 miles) drive in a south-westerly direction one reaches the **Yangguan Mountain Pass.** There are still some 2,000 year old watchtowers standing there from the Han dynasty. From the Yangguan Pass there is a wide uninterrupted view across the Taklimakan Desert.

Guangzhou and the South East

Guangzhou

Guangzhou, which is better known to most Europeans as Canton is the largest city in South China, with a population of over three million people. The city has as its emblem five goats and for that reason it is sometimes called "city of the goats". An old legend tells how in ancient times five celestial beings riding on goats visited the city. Each of the goats was carrying a rice plant bearing ears of grain which the gods presented to the town in the hope that Guangzhou would never again experience famine.

To the north of the city in **Yuexiu Park** stands the **Goat Monument** which is the city emblem carved out of stone. Beside it is the **Tower which overlooks the Sea** (Zheu Hai Lou), constructed in 1380 and destroyed by fire in 1686, and then rebuilt. During the Opium War it was occupied by the French and English. Two canons on top of the tower, supplied by the German firm of Krupp, are a present-day remind-

er of that time. **The History Museum of Guangzhou** is located in this five-storey tower. It has objects from the Qin and Han Dynasties on display, but in particular documents of the period of the Taiping Rebellion and the Opium Wars. The museum also contains valuable clocks and vintage car models which were presented to the Lords of Guangzhou during the colonial era by foreign businessmen. Not far from the tower stands the **Monument to the Republician Revolutionary Dr. Sun Yatsen.**

In the lower part of the park is the **Sun Yatsen Memorial Hall** erected in the style of the Imperial Palace buildings and with a blue roof. It was built in 1931 and financed by money donated by Chinese people living abroad. The hall which is large enough to hold 5,000 persons is used as a theatre and congress centre. In the park in front of the hall is a large statue of Sun Yatsen.

In the 19th and 20th centuries this city was a centre of revolutionary activity, and there are several monuments to the hereos and martyrs of recent Chinese history. There is the **Mausoleum of the 72 Martyrs** who died in 1911 in the first unsuccessful rebellion against the Qing government. The **National Institute of the Peasant Movement** is in a former Confucian temple building where Mao Zedong once taught and also directed the peasant revolts. The **Memorial Park for the Martyrs of the 1927 Revolt** honours 6,000 Communist supporters and workers who fell in

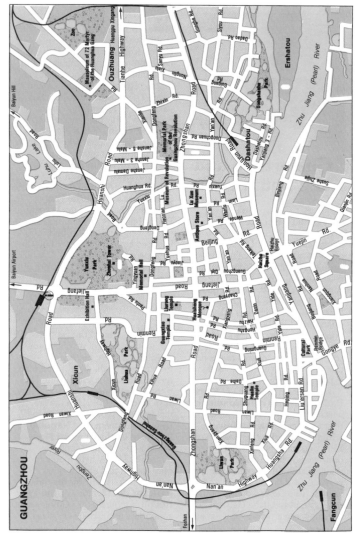

GUANGZHOU

Zengbu River

Liwan River

Baiyun Airport

Baiyun Hill

Likee Road

Liuhua Road

Huanshi Road

Zoo

Mausoleum of 72 Martyrs of the Huanghua Gang

Huangpu Xingang

Ouzhuang

Tianhe Highway

Guangta Rd.

Sanyu Rd.

Xiang

Nongjian

Road

Zhirxin Rd.

Dongfeng Rd.

Xianie

Memorial Park of the Guangzhou Revolution

Yan'an Rd.

Zhongshan

Road

Dongpu

Dengfeng Rd.

Rd.

Dadao

Sanyu Rd.

Suzu Rd.

Sanxia Rd.

Ershatou

Zhu Jiang (Pearl) River

Dashatou

Houjinin Road

Dongchuan Road

Dashatou Park

Dongjiaohua Park

Yanjing 3 - Rd.

Yanjing 3 - Rd.

Dabao Rd.

Jianshe 6 - Malu

Jianshe 3 - Malu

Jianshe Dalu

Huanghus Rd.

Huaxiang

Museum of Revolution Rd.

Xiaobei Rd.

Yuexiu

Rd.

Lu Xun Museum

Yuexiu Rd.

Lilu Rd.

Wenming Rd.

Wende Rd.

Yuexiu Park

Zhenhai Tower

Tingzuan Road

Jiaoquan Rd.

Yuehua Rd.

Dongfeng

Antique Store

Beijing

Road

Jiaoji Rd.

Yan'an Rd.

Dongfeng Rd.

Guangxou Rd.

Wuxian Rd.

Yan'an Rd.

Haizhu Square

Haizhu Bridge

Yuejin Road

Yuejin Road

Binjiang

Road

Sushe Zhije

Jiefang

Memorial Hall

Exhibition Hall

Jiefang

Rd.

Jiefang

Road

Chaoyang

Rd.

Jieyang Rd.

Dazin Rd.

Yide Rd.

Yide Rd.

Qixian Rd.

Xicun

Rd.

Zhongshan

Xiwan Road

Liuhua River

Liwan Park

Rd.

Liuhua

Road

Guangxiao Temple

Liurong Temple

Youshiking Mosque

Renmin

Rd.

Panfu Rd.

Liwan

Road

Ruya Road

Zhifu Road

Dongfeng

Nanan.

Zhongshan

Road

Kuangcang Rd.

Hongshu Rd.

Renmin

Rd.

Daihe Rd.

Shipuang

Huaiin

Temple

Liwan

Road

Heping

Cultural Park

Renmin Bridge

Bujang Rd.

Gongye Rd.

Lu Ersan Rd.

Gongye Rd.

Feihan

Nan'an

Road

Zhongshan Highway

Highway

Liwan Park

Xian Rd.

Bodhixy

Xinfeng

Nan'an

Highway

Huangsha Rd.

Zhu Jiang (Pearl) River

Fangcun

the revolt against Tschiang Kai Shek.

The **Guangxiao Temple** is the oldest temple building in the city and is presumed to date back to the 4th century. In the course of time it has been frequently altered and restored. A famous Indian monk is reputed to have lived here in the 7th century. The two **Iron Pagodas** which are among the oldest in China and date from the 10th century are worth viewing. The western pagoda, however, has fallen into disrepare with only three tiers remaining.

The **Temple of the Six Banyan Trees** (Liurong Si) is today the seat of the Buddhist Society of Guangzhou.

In the centre of the small park stands the **Flower Pagoda** (Hua Ta) which was constructed in 1097. It is possible to climb to the upper floor, from which vantage point one can view the city.

Behind it there are three unprotected statues of Buddha which had been dragged away during the Cultural Revolution, but at present, a new hall to house them is under construction.

To the south of the monastery stands what is probably China's oldest **mosque** (Huaisheng Si) built around 627. All the buildings are in the Chinese style of architecture with the exception of the 25 m (82 ft) high minaret.

The **Temple of the Ancestors of the Chen Family** (Chenjia Ci) in the West Zhongshan Road is in a poor state of repair, not least due to the fact that it was used as a warehouse during the Cultural Revolution.

In the **Pearl River** is the **Island of Shamian,** which is separated from the rest of the city by a narrow canal. It was once a concession area in the hands of the English and French and is easily recognizable as such by its Victorian architecture. Close to the island of Shamian is one of the largest **open-air markets in Guangzhou.** The selection of goods and wares on offer is varied and exciting, but may not always appeal to European tastes.

It is said that the "Cantonese eat anything that has four legs" and this and much more besides is to be had here: snakes, frogs, tortoises, cats. owls, etc. The fact that some of these creatures have only two legs, or even none at all, is of no account.

The **Mountain of the White Cloud** (Baiyun Shan) in the northeast is a popular recreation area for the inhabitants of Guangzhou. One passes temples, pavilions and tea houses to reach the top of the 382 m (1,253 ft) high peak where one is rewarded with a magnificent panorama of the city.

A four hour bus journey southwards takes one to **Cuiheng** in the district of Zhangshan, the birthplace of Sun Yatsen. The reddish brown house of the Sun family was designed by Sun Yatsen himself. In the courtyard stands a tropical tree which he brought back from Honolulu. There is an exhibition room with documents and personal possessions of Sun Yatsen himself on display.

Thermal Springs are located in the vicinity of the administrative centre Conghua and 80 km

(50 miles) north-east of Guangzhou. The water has a temperature of between 50 and 60 °C (122 and 140 °F).

For tourists interested in arts and crafts the town of **Foshan** 20 km (12 miles) south-west of Guangzhou is well worth a visit. It is particularly famed for its **paper cuts** and **paper lanterns.** It is possible to visit most of the craft factories and to observe the artists and craftsmen at work. The production of ceramics can look back on a one thousand year old tradition. Also in Foshan is a particularly beautiful **Temple of the Ancestors** (Zumiao) decorated with a myriad of fine sculptures, ornamented roofs and scenic reliefs.

The **Seven Star Cliffs** (Qixing Yan) lie 118 km (73 miles) to the west of Guangzhou near the administrative centre of Zhaoqing. This group of cliffs is so spaced that it strongly resembles the seven stars in the constellation of the Great Bear. There is a legend that the stars fell from heaven and formed cliffs where they landed.

The highest of these hills is the Shishi which contains a cave with over 300 calligraphic signs engraved on the stone. An underground river makes it possible to traverse the cave by boat. The region is presently undergoing development as a tourist centre.

Nanning

Today Nanning has about half a million inhabitants. Since 1959 it has been the capital of Guangxi, the autonomous region of the Zhuang people.

For centuries Guangxi has been a disputed territory. The Han Chinese fought with non-Chinese peoples over it. The Emperor Yin Shi Huang Di managed to annex Guangxi to his kingdom, but he was unable to prevent it breaking away again. In the last phase of the Tang Dynasty a separate state developed. The Ming Emperors were forced to conquer the troops of the Yao, and in the last century there was a ferocious outbreak of the Taiping Rebellion in this region. Following this, the English, who were already established in Guangzhou, and the French in Vietnam tried to gain influence in the province. In 1907 Nanning was declared a free trading town.

In recent years, peace in Guangxi has been threatened once again due to the worsening relations between China and Vietnam. The border between these two countries is in the south-western part of the province.

Nanning enjoys a subtropical climate. The best time of the year to travel there is April-May and September-October. The scenery in this region is particularly beautiful. The main agricultural products are rice and sugar cane. Tropical fruits such as mangos, lychees, pineapple and watermelon are also cultivated.

Many of the non-Chinese minorities live in this province. The twelve million Zhuang are the largest ethnic group in Guangxi Province which they share with other smaller groups such as the Yao, Dong, and Miao.

In Nanning there is an **Institute for Minority Ethnic Groups** where members of these nationalites

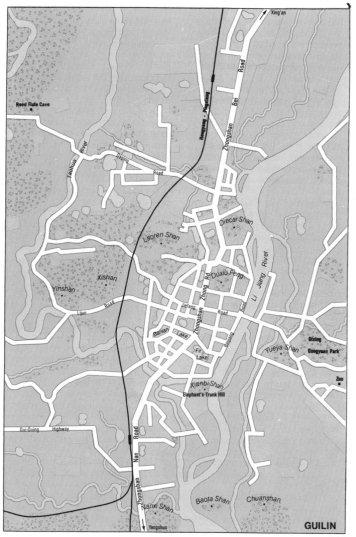

Xing'an

Reed Flute Cave

Taohua River

Daqing Road

Hengmen – Pingshang

Zhongshan Bei Road

Laoren Shan

Diecai Shan

Xishan

Yinshan

Duxiu Peng

Li Jiang River

Zhong Rd

Lijun Road

Jiefang Road

Zhongshan Road

Banian Lake

Fir Lake

Bailong Road

Qixing

Yueya Shan

Gongyuan Park

Zoo

Xianbi Shan

Elephant's Trunk Hill

Gui-Quing Highway

Nan Road

Zhongshan

Baota Shan

Chuanshan

Nanxi Shan

Yangshuo

GUILIN

are trained as teachers and where the culture and language of these peoples is studied. A visit to this institute provides one with an opportunity to learn more about these minorities in China.

One of the biggest folklore festivals is the **Dragon Boat Festival** at the beginning of June which, according to the Chinese Moon calendar, is always celebrated on the fifth day of the fifth month. Each year several hundred thousand visitors celebrate this festival, the highlight of which is the dragon boat race.

In **South Lake Park** (Nanhu Gongyuan one can admire tha plant life of the subtropical world: the orchid garden, medicinal herb garden and Bonsai exhibition should not be missed.

The **Guangxi Provincial Museum** is situated just north of South Lake Park and is devoted to the history of the various nationalities of the region.

Some 20 km (12 miles) to the north-west of Nanning in the karst mountain region there is a remarkable stalactite cavern, the **Yiling Yan Cave,** where coloured light effects emphasize and highlight the fantastic stalactite forms.

Guilin

No other scenery in China is so unique, so indescribably beautiful yet mysterious, nor calls forth such breathless admiration on the part of visitors as the karst region around Guilin.

The hills taper upwards like cones, they rise like slender columns and form an incredible panorama when viewed from a distance. From certain vantage points the hills appear to resemble all sorts of objects and creatures: animals, pagodas, needles, plants and it is not surprising, therefore, that the native population has bestowed the most imaginative names on them.

Over 300 million years ago this region was submerged under an extensive sea. Certain geological phenomena contributed to the formation of the landscape during the course of millions of years: folds occured in the earth's crust, the water level subsided and erosion took its toll.

Guilin has become one of the most popular centres for Chinese and foreign tourists alike. The town is situated in the north of Guangxi Province and has a population of 380,000. During the reign of the Emperor Yin Shi Huang Di this region was connected to central China by the construction of a canal which joined the Xiangjiang River, a tributary of the Yangzi, to the Lijiang which flows through Guilin. During the Japanese invasion (1937–1945) thousands of Chinese fled to Guilin which had to accommodate over a million people at that time.

The name Guilin means "Cassia Tree Wood" (cinnamon trees). These trees line the wide avenues and in autumn, when they are in bloom, their sweet intoxicating scent fills the air.

Unique Beauty Peak (Duxiu Shan) stands on the former site of the **Princely Mansion.** On account of its shape, it tapers upwards to reach a considerable height, it is also called "The Pillar Under the Southern

Heaven". The rising and setting sun covers it with shimmering golden and purple light. On the west flank 306 steps lead up to the summit and to the **Gate of the Southern Heaven** (Nantianmen). **Dushu Cavern** on the eastern side resembles a giant stone chamber with windows and furniture made of stone. **Crescent Pool** is visible on the north flanks. The palace was built in 1393 for the Prince of Jingjiang, a grandson of the first Ming emperor. Today the polytechnic school occupies the buildings.

For an even better view of the town, its surroundings, and the river Li one should go to the top of the **Mountain of Many Colours** (Diecai Shan). Sometimes it is also referred to as the "Piled Brocades Hill" because the narrow layers of rock strata glistening in rainbow colours in the light of the evening sun resemble heaped bales of silk. The mountain has four peaks, of which **Bright Moon Peak** 223 m (723 ft) is the highest elevation in Guilin. From this point one can make out the river Lijiang flowing along the base of the mountain. To the south, **Unique Beauty Peak** Mount Fubo and Elephant Trunk Hill are to be seen.

Located half-way up there is a small cave, open on both sides and therefore full of draughts, which explains how it came to be named **Draught-Producing Cave.** There are also many carvings and sculptures on the mountainside.

To the south of the Mountain of Many Colours, on the western bank of the Lijiang, Mount Fubo rises up. The mountain is sometimes called

Whirlpool Hill because a lot of turbulence arises along its banks when the river waters reach their highest point. The entrance to the **Returned-Pearl Cave** (Huanzhu Dong) is at the base of the mountain. Legend tells of an ancient dragon who guarded a shining pearl in the cave. One day, a curious fisherman crept into the cave and stole the precious pearl. Full of repentance, however, he returned it to the dragon shortly afterwards. Having passed through the cave one emerges on the banks of the Lijiang. Here, one can admire a stone column almost 3 m (about 10 ft) in length which hangs down from the ceiling and ends just a few inches from the floor. There is an old story that a general of the Han period was trying out his sword at this spot and cleaved through the stone while doing so. A flight of steps leads upwards through the mountain where there are some very fine Buddhist stone sculptures and inscriptions to be seen.

Elephant Trunk Hill is located a stone's throw away from Lijiang Hotel on the banks of the river Li. A round cave on the shore separates the mountain from a stone column projecting into the water. It does not require much imagination to discern the shape of an elephant in it. On the summit there is a small three-tiered brick pagoda from the period of the Ming Dynasty.

The karst mountains contain a multitude of **stalactite caverns** some of which are open to tourists. The entrance to the **Reed Flute Cave** (Ludi Yan) lies at the foot of Guangming Hill, some 7 km (about

4 miles) from the town centre. It is around 600,000 years old and received its name from the reeds that hid the entrance to it until its discovery in 1956, and which were used for making flutes. From various archaeological finds, however, we know that it was once used as a place of refuge by local inhabitants. The passage through this cave is 500 m (1,640 ft) long and leads along easily accessible paths and steps past a multitude of grotesquely formed stalagmites and stalactites. The guides point out the fantastic shapes of lions, plants and herbs, fruits, stone drapes and stages, which all adorn the walls and are cleverly spotlighted. The centre of the cavern is known as the **Crystal Palace** and can accommodate up to a thousand people. A row of stones in this hall is linked with a well-known legend, the combat between the king of the apes Sun Wukong and the Dragon King which took place in the Crystal Palace.

One of the most important sights of Guilin is the **Seven-Star Park** (Qixing Gargyuan). The position of the seven hills resembles that of the star constellation, the Great Bear, thus giving the park its name. Just beyond the entrance one crosses the **Bridge of Flowers,** a stone bridge, dating from the Song Dynasty and restored during the Ming Dynasty, which is surrounded by massed banks of flowers. The entrance to the **Seven-Star Cave** (Qixing Yan) is on the north-west slope of the Putuo Shan, the four eastern hills of the park. The cave consists of three storeys of which only the middle one

is accessible. The subterranean river occupies the lower storey which lies 10 to 15 m (33 to 49 ft) below. The upper level is theoretically accessible but is not open to the public. Sightseers traverse a passage 800 m (875 yds) in length which, like that of the Reed Flute Cave is illuminated by coloured lights. Also on the **Putuo Shan** is the **Putuo Temple** from which there is a magnificent view of the town, as well as the **Cavern of the Goddess of Mercy** (Guanyin Yan) behind the temple. The **Cave of the White Crane** (Baihe Yan) has stalacmite formations on the ceiling which resemble flying cranes.

The **Nanxi Mountain** to the south and also the **Xishan** and **Yinshan Mountains** to the west also contain stalacmite caves.

The climax of any journey in this region is a **boat trip on the River Lijiang.** The trip begins in the town itself at the back of the Lijiang Hotel if the water level is sufficiently high and it takes approximately six hours to reach Yangshuo. At low water level the trip begins with a two-hour journey by bus to Yangdi in the south in order to join the boat and the remainder of the trip to Yang-shuo takes almost three hours.

Starting at Guilin, the boat first passes **Elephant Trunk Hill** and **Pierced Hill** where the hole in the hill glistens like a moon in the reflection of the evening sun. Then comes **Pagoda Hill** and **Fighting Cocks Hill**. Suddenly, **Beauty of Crown Hill** which is very similar in appearance to an imperial crown appears; there is a spring of pure water to be found in the grotto within it. Just before Xingpeng stands **Screen Hill**. Its rock face rises sheer above the water and the structure and colour of the stone combine to create the illusion of nine dancing horses, giving the imaginative observer the impression of a giant natural painting before him.

After **Xingping** the hilly landscape becomes more dense and the peaks are reflected in the clear water of the river whose banks are lined with green bamboo groves. The fishermen, some of whom use tame cormorants to help them fish, can be observed in their long and narrow bamboo boats. The boat journey finally ends in **Yangshuo,** a small town which the hoards of tourists and visitors have turned into a giant bazaar. On the return bus journey a stop is usually made at a giant banyan tree reputed to be 1,300 years old.

Gourmets should visit the small **restaurants in Guilin** along the Zhangshan Road. The dishes made with the meat of frogs, badgers, snakes and armadillos are considered great delicacies and usually these animals are to be found in small cages in front of the restaurants.

Hainan

Hainan is the biggest of almost 5,000 Chinese islands in the South China Sea. It is the second largest Chinese island after Taiwan and has a population of about six million people, including members of the Li, Miao and Hui ethnic minorities. The island has been opened to tourists only in the last two years, but it is planned to develop it further as a tourist and recreation centre as its excellent climate and wonderful scenery make it an eminently attractive place for visitors.

The capital of the island, **Haikou,** is situated in the north and is surrounded by groves of giant coconut palms.

Just five km (about 3 miles) outside Haikou stands the **Temple of the Five Government Officials** in memory of five important officials who were sent into exile here during the Tang and Song Dynasties. A stone fountain in the temple courtyard is reputed to have been erected on the instructions of Su Dongpo, a poet of the Song era.

At the southern tip of the island there are magnificent sandy beaches for bathers as well as exotic scenery to delight the visitor, who usually takes up residence in the little harbour town of **Sanya.** Not far from here is the **End of the World** (Tianyahaijiao). This spot is surrounded by the old town of Yazhou in the west, Mount Maling in the north and the sea to the south. In between, on the beach are several hundred large smooth stones with rounded contours, many of which bear inscriptions, such as "end of the world", "corner of the world", and "pillar in the south heaven". Nearby is the **South Gate of the ancient city of Yazhou.** The prefect of Yazhou in the 11th century, Cheng Zhe, is reputed to have been responsible for the inscription "end of the world".

Also worth a visit is the hill known as **"The Stag Turns its Head".** A legend of the Li people tells how a brave hunter pursued a certain stag, which, when it saw that there was no escape, turned round and was transformed into a beautiful fairy. The hunter fell in love with her and they were married and lived happily ever after.

To the north of the Sanya hotel is a palisade village belonging to the Li ethnic group, known as **Coconut Village.**

One of the best places for bathing is the **Great East Sea,** a narrow bay well protected from the elements, so that even in winter the temperature does not drop below 20 °C (68 °F).

The South West

Chengdu

Chengdu which has 3.9 million inhabitants is the capital of the most highly populated province in China namely Sichuan which has 100 million inhabitants. The name Sichuan means "the Land of the Four Rivers", and here is the centre of one of China's main granaries. The **Red Basin** is surrounded on all sides by mountains which protect it from the cold air masses which come down from the north thus providing it with an attractive climate. Only 100 km (62 miles) west of Chengdu begin the high mountain ranges. The Gongga Shan is, at 7,556 m (24,789 ft), Sichuan's highest mountain and it extends in a westerly direction as far as the Himalayas.

Chengdu was famous as far back as the time of the Han Dynasty in particular for its artistic **Brocade Weaving.** Even today it is known as the "Brocade City" and the river Jinjiang which flows through the city is known as the "Brocade River". It is also known as the "Hibiscus City" because the King of Shu planted the city walls with hibiscus in the 10th century.

Because of its isolated and remote situation Sichuan has always been difficult of access. Hence, separate or virtually independent kingdoms were often established here and it has often proved a haven for religiously or politically persecuted people.

Even today it is not the most popular or most visited tourist area but perhaps because of this it is to be particularly recommended. Here it is still possible to see many of the old sights and traditions which have died out elsewhere. There are the traditional tea houses, for example, where amateur musicians present Sichuan operas, where the tea tastes particularly good, and where the atmosphere and customs have both remained unchanged.

The **Temple** of the **Duke Wu** in the southern outskirts of the city commemorates a famous statesman who was chancellor of the Shu state, Zhuge Liang (181–234). As early as the 3rd century a temple was erected in his honour. The present buildings, however, date from the year 1672. Behind the entrance door stand six stone tablets under the shade of some ancient cypress trees; the oldest of these is from the year 809. In the Liu Bei Hall stand statues of King Liu Bei and his grandson. On the right hand wall there stands another statue to Zhuge Liang; the latter is gold-plated and is flanked on either side by statues of his son and grandson. Before them are three copper drums which are supposed to have been used by Zhuge Liang's troops as cooking pots by day and alarm drums at night. West of the temple King Liu Bei's tomb is found.

Of interest in the western suburbs is **Du Fu Thatched Cottage,** Du Fu Caotang. Du Fu (712–770) one of the most famous poets of the Tang epoch, retired to Chengdu in 759 and lived there for four years in a thatched cottage. During this period he composed 240 poems. His works are more often than not very critical of the times and reflect the condition of the disintegrating Tang kingdom. His work has survived until the present and it is part of today's basic school education to be able to recite some of the Du Fu stories. During the course of the years the buildings have developed into a commemorative temple. There are statues of the poet on show in several halls and other halls are filled with his works and translations. One hall contains paintings based on the poet's verses by well-known artists.

The **Wang Jian Tomb,** Wang Jing Mu, also lies west of the city.

Wang Jian was a general of the Tang army. After the fall of the Tang Dynasty in 907 he proclaimed himself Emperor of Shu. He died in 918 and was buried here. His grave is somewhat on the small side – 14 stone bows support the vaults of the 23 m (75 ft) long grave – but the stone pedestal on which the casket rests is exceptionally valuable. This pedestal is decorated on three sides with reliefs depicting groups of musicians of the Tang era. These include 24 musicians and two dancers. A stone statue of Wang Jian stands in the back chamber. The contents of the tomb are displayed in two special halls on either side of the tomb.

The **Monastery** of the **Precious Light,** Bao Guang Si, which lies 18 km (11 miles) east of Chengdu in Xindu Province is one of the most beautiful and famous of this province's monasteries. It is believed to date from as early as the time of the Eastern Han Dynasty (25–200). However, the present halls date mainly from the 17th century. Behind the entrance gate and the Hall of the Kings of Heaven stands a thirteen-floored pagoda which is 30 m (98 ft) high and dates from the Tang era.

Well worth seeing are the Thousand Buddha Tablet and the Hall of the Five Hundred Lohans. The lohan figures are up to 2 m (about 6 ft) high and completely covered in gold. Tourists are usually allowed to take a break in what was formerly the abbot's chamber. A relic of Buddha is exhibited here and there are valuable paintings on show in the Garden Hall.

The **Riverview Pavilion Park,** Wangjiang Lou Gongyuan, stretches all along the river Jinjiang in the south-west of the city. This attractive pavilion, which is right on the river bank, has four floors and is artistically and elegantly built. Some of the halls in the park are dedicated to the poetess Xue Tao (768–831) who is supposed to have lived here. Over 100 different varieties of bamboos grow here.

To the west of the Guanxian district, about half-way up the Minjiang, 57 km (35 miles) from Chengdu, it is possible to see the oldest functioning **Irrigation System** in China: **Dujiangyan.** In 256 B. C. Li Bing, Lord of Shu, devised an irrigation system for controlling the floodwaters. Using the natural conditions of the river and its surroundings he constructed a system which not only permitted the irrigation of the surrounding contryside but also permitted the control of the spring floods. Although the present system has been modernised and changed the principle remains the same as in Li Bing's time.

From the **Pavilion** of the **Dragon Being Subdued,** Fulong Guan, there is a magnificent view. Here also stands a four-ton stone statue of Li Bing which is almost 2.9 m (about 9 ft) high and 1,900 years old. It was only found in 1973 and put on exhibition. Nearby one can see a three-legged iron vessel decorated with flying dragons. The **Temple** of the **Two Kings,** Erwang Miao, lies on the eastern shore of the Minjing River and is actually built on the slope. It is dedicated to Li Bing and his son. It is reached by a hanging bridge which stretches from the manmade island located in the middle of the Minjiang.

Leshan and **Emei Shan** are easily reached from Chengdu although it is better to include an overnight stay for these excursions. **Leshan** lies about 167 km (104 miles) south of Chengdu and is renowned for its **Great Buddha** which stands on the bank of the river Minjiang. At 71 m (232 ft) high it is the world's largest statue of the sitting Buddha. Its ears alone are 7 m long and the feet which are just above water level can accommodate over 100 people at a time. Its construction was begun in 713 and it took 90 years to complete. One can see the Buddha from on board ship or climb down from his head. Right behind his head, on Lingyun Hill there is a little monastery, and a series of steep steps which one can descend. West of Leshan lies one of the four holy mountains of Buddhism, **Emei Shan.** The first temple was built here in the 2nd century. Some time later the mountain was consecrated to the Bodhisattva Samantabhadra who was one of the forerunners of Buddhism in China and is supposed to have lived here on the Emei Shan. Legend has it that he climbed up to the top of the mountain on the back of a white elephant. The Elephant Bathing Pool and the Samantabhadra Hall commemorate this legend. In the hall stands a bronze elephant on whose back Samantabhadra sits in a lotus flower. The whole statue is 7.3 m (24 ft) high and weighs 62 tons. From the bottom of the mountain there is a path 63 km

(39 miles) long winding its way to the top of the 3,099 m (10,167 ft) high **Golden Peak,** Jinding. From the summit it is possible to experience a rare natural phenomenon; the **Shining Glory of Buddha.** It is a particularly frequent occurence in the autumn months when it can be observed almost daily. When the sun shines through the clouds in the late afternoon it appears in the form of a rainbow cross. Many highly devoted Buddhists took this as a sign from Buddha and hurled themselves off the mountain to their death below. Previously there were over 200 temple buildings on Emei Shan, today there are 20. The beauty of the mountain alone merits a journey; there are rare plants and flowers everywhere.

This is also the **home** of the **Giant Panda.** This protected rare endangered species lives only in Sichuan and the border regions to Tibet, Qinghai and Shaanxi. A good place to visit while in the region is of course **Chengdu Zoo** which has thirteen pandas as well as several baby bears which were born in the zoo. This is a great achievement because the animals are extremely sensitive and rarely breed in captivity.

Chongqing

The most popular way to visit Chongqing is to take a boat trip on the Yangzi River. The city is situated at the confluence of the Yangzi and Jialing Rivers, has six million inhabitants and is China's fourth biggest city. During the past few years in the course of an administration reform several other administrative districts were added to the greater city area. The Chongqing administrative area now comprises over 13 million people.

The harbour is wonderful; high up on the steep banks where the two large rivers meet the old town is situated. Innumerable narrow alleys and flights of steps run through the incalculable maze of old, black tiled houses, sometimes they even stand on pillars; here and there, sprouting up in the middle is a modern new building. A cable car railway situated on the banks of the river takes you high up into the city centre just like in Hong Kong. There is another cable car running across the Jialing River.

During the Tang epoch, Chongqing was known as Yuzhou and even today the city is known by the nickname Yu for Chongqing. The Emperor Zhao Dun of the Southern Song Dynasty (1127–1279) then changed the name to Chongqing in order to celebrate the occurence of two happy events in his family. The name means "double good luck". First of all he was prince of the prefecture and later he became emperor.

Between 1939–1945, i. e. for the duration of the second world war Chongqing served as the capital. The Guomindang government took refuge here from the Japanese. The Communist Party also had local headquarters in Chongqing.

Today, the city government has its headquarters in what was once the residence of the Guomindang government. The building is right across from the **People's Hotel,** Renmin Binguan. Hotels do not usually pertain to the most exciting tourist attractions in a city but in this case the exception is the rule. The hotel is entered by a traditional gate of honour. After having crossed the courtyard, one mounts a wide staircase to reach the imposing building which is constructed in the traditional Imperial Palace style. The central building is round with a three-tiered roof which is covered in blue-glazed tiles and is a copy of the Temple of Heaven in Beijing. On both sides there are connected wings. White marble, red pillars, and blue tiles emphasize the outside of the building which was erected in the 50's. From the top of **Pipa Hill** (Pipa Shan) there is a magnificent view over the whole town. The park which is laid out on the surrounding hill is particularly worth visiting, especially later in the evening when the sparkling lights of the city are spread out at one's feet. On the way up to the peak one comes across the **City Museum.** The **Natural History Museum** is situated in Beipei; but the only thing really worth seeing there are the dinosaur skeletons.

During the war against Japan, the former southern branch of the Chinese Communist Party was based on the banks of the Jialing River where the director was Zhou Enlai who later on became Prime Minister. The house where he lived on **Zhongshan Street** is a museum today. Chongqing has two thermal spas. The **Northern Thermal Spa** in Beipei which is north-west of Chongqing produces water with an average temperature of 35 °C (95 °F). The park complex has

swimming pools with changing rooms, nearby there are some Buddhist buildings. The **Southern Thermal Spa** is in more beautiful surroundings. It is situated 25 km (15 miles) south of the city and here too it is possible to go swimming.

One of the three biggest bridges across the Yangzi River is in Chongqing. The 1.5 km (almost 1 mile) long **Yangzi Bridge** was finished in 1980.

On the southern shore of the Jialing River near the Jialing Bridge the **Cassia Gardens,** Gui Yuan are situated. The cinnamon tree (cassia tree) blooms in the autumn and its sweetish smell wafts through the air.

The **Gate which Greets the Heavens,** Chao Tian Men, stands at the confluence of the Yangzi and Jialing Rivers. From here one can look down the slope towards the river banks, and here in the old town near the harbour it is possible to begin a leisurely stroll through the attractive narrow lanes and up and down the steep steps. The colourful hustle and bustle on all sides where the free markets offer vegetables, herbs and the famous "rotten eggs" is something not to be missed.

On the edge of the city of Chongqing, one can visit wonderful parklands where the **Academy of Fine Arts** is situated. Here, students from the south-west provinces can study various subjects. There are exhibition rooms where excellent examples of their work are on show, e. g. modern oil paintings, traditional water colours, sculptures, ceramics, lacquer art and graphic works.

The **Institute of Painting** trains the outstanding artists of the south-west provinces. They are among the very best that the country produces. Some examples of their work are on show in some of the rooms. The artists themselves do not appear very often but one person is always there to demonstrate the traditional water-colour techniques to visitors. There are introductory lectures on the history of Chinese art, as well as the different styles in Chinese art. For those who are interested in further discussions there are plenty of people willing to converse.

Dazu, which lies 160 km (525 miles) west of Chongqing, is well worth a visit. A five-hour bus journey is necessary to reach it and two days or so should be allowed for this trip. In the Dazu district there are approximately forty hills with altogether 50,000 Buddhist sculptures and reliefs. The latter were made 500–700 years earlier than their more famous precursors at Dunhuang, Yungang or Longmen. In the middle of the 9th century many Buddhists fled from persecution to Sichuan. Here in Dazu they found enough rich patrons and sponsers to enable them to construct a huge cave temple complex. Two hills can be visited at the moment, several other sites are being renovated.

The **Northern Mountain,** Beishan, lies only 2 km (1.2 miles) north of the city. A 20 minute walk brings one to the top. Work began here in 892 and was continued for over 250 years. Well worth seeing is a huge scene bearing the title "Amitayus Dhyana Sutra" which is a representation of the teachings of the Buddha Amitabha who is

honoured as Lord of the Western Paradise. Niches and grottos contain over 600 figures representing the horrific as well as the heavenly sides of life.

Some 15 km (9 miles) north of Dazu stands the **Treasure Chamber Hill,** Baoding Shan. The sculptures here are bigger and more colourful. Almost all of them depict scenes clarifying the teachings of Buddha. One particularly fine figure is the statue of the Goddess of Mercy, Guanyin, who is a representation of the Bodhisattva Avalokiteshvara and who can possess up to 1,000 arms and 11 heads. The Guanyin figure at Baodingshan has exactly 1,007 arms and covers an area of 88 sq. m (947 sq. ft). Not very far from this point lies the **Sleeping Buddha.** The prostrate figure is 31 m (102 ft) long, not counting the lower part of his legs which are not complete. Heavenly as well as wordly rulers lament the passing of Buddha who is just about to enter nirvana.

The Yangzi Gorges

The Yangzi River which is 6,300 km (3,915 miles) long is China's largest river and the world's third largest. It rises in the Qinghai Plateau and first flows in a southerly direction. Then it turns in an easterly direction and winds its way to the East China Sea. One of the most interesting scenic areas is the **Yangzi Gorges** which lie between Yichang and Congqing (see "Trying to Reach Heaven", p. 51). The regular boats are called "The East is Red" and are numbered in sequence.

Each boat has 22 two-bed cabins at the bow under the bridge which are reserved for tourists. Recently, however, luxury cruise ships have began operating. They are better equipped and are solely for the use of tourists. A major advantage of such ships is that they will stop at any particular points of interest whereas the regular scheduled ships do not.

About 50 km (31 miles) west of the district town Wanxian, which lies high above the river, one reaches the first tourist attraction, the **Stone Seal Mountain,** Shibaozhai. The scheduled ships stop here for several hours. This 30 m (98 ft) high rectangular stone block looks, from a distance, like a huge stone seal, hence the name. Legend has it that on this spot there was a small spring from which rice steadily flowed with which the monks fed themselves. When one of the monks tried to enlarge the spring it stopped flowing. The Ying Emperor Jiaqing (1797–1821) ordered a pagoda to be built up the

side of the cliff. The lower floors nestle close to the cliff, only the upper floors stand on the mountain itself.

The Zhang Fei Temple stands on the southern bank of the river in the Yunyang district. It was built during the time of the Warring Kingdoms (3rd century B. C.) in honour of a general of Shu. The Yangzi Gorges begin immediately behind the town of Fengjie. On the northern shore, directly before **Kui Men,** on a hill at the entrance gate to the Qutang Gorge, stands the **City of the White Emperor,** Baidicheng. A king of Shu is supposed to have proclaimed himself emperor and built his imperial city on this spot. Right at the peak stands the **Temple of the White Emperor,** Baidi Si.

Up until this century, any crossing of the Yangzi Gorges was a dangerous and exciting experience. Underground reefs, rapids and whirlpools were hazards that caused many victims because the small junks were

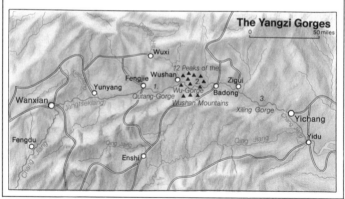

often hard to manoeuvre. Within the gorge itself, the river varies in width between 200 and 300 m (656 and 984 ft) although at its narrowest point it is only 80 m (262 ft) wide. At low water only 3,000 m^3 of water per second flows through the gorge but at high water this can rise to between 40,000–80,000 m^3. Then, the rate of flow rises from 4 km (2.4 miles) per hour to 11.5 km (7.1 miles) per hour and at the rapids it can reach a speed of 25 km (15.5 miles) per hour. The gorges from Fengjie to Yihang stretch for over 200 km (124 miles). The natural **Kui Men** gate at Baidicheng is formed where two precipitous cliffs face each other. The **Qutang Gorge** which is only 8 km (5 miles) long is also the narrowest of the three gorges. Shortly after the Kui Men one passes a cliff covered in lots of small rectangular holes. The legend tells how the bodyguard Meng Liang wanted to find a safe burial place for his general and tried to build a ladder or steps up the cliff face. Today, therefore, the spot is referred to as **Meng Liang's Steps.**

On the northern bank, high up on the cliff face it is possible to recognise small, very long narrow crevices which in fact look like old bellows; the place is known as **Bellows Gorge,** Feng-Xiang Xia. Archaeologists have since discovered that they contained skeletons. It is assumed that the crevices once served as graves.

The second gorge is the 40 km (25 miles) long **Sorcerer's Gorge,** Wu Xia. Twelve imposing mountain tops dominate the sides of the river. The best known of these is the **Peak of the Beautiful Goddess,** which is a lofty needle-like peak lying directly beside the actual peak and which from a distance has the appearance of a woman. According to the legend, it is the goddess Yao Ji, who is the goddess of protection for all ships. At **Beishi** one crosses over the border between Sichuan and Hubei.

About 14 km (9 miles) before the town of Zugui, the **Perfumed River** flows into the Yangzi. It flows down from the karst mountains and because of this its water is crystal clear. A famous concubine from the Han Dynasty, Wang Zhaojun, is supposed to have been born in this region. According to legend she washed her hair in the river. A pearl from the jewels in her hair once fell into the water and since then it has been perfumed so sweetly.

Xiling Gorge which is 75 km (47 miles) long, is the last and longest of the gorges. It used to be the most dangerous gorge and contained many hidden rapids, whirlpools and sandbanks. There are many smaller gorges within this gorge, and all of them have unusual names. **Sword Gorge** and the **Military Manual** are just two examples. **Cow Gorge, Oxen Liver Gorge** and the **Horse's Lung** are other unusual appellations. The names are based on legends or on the particular appearance of the cliffs. The name **Empty Boat Gorge** has a story attached to it.

It is said that whoever tries to pass Xiling Gorge must at this point throw all his cargo overboard, otherwise the boat itself would go under.

Hence the origin of the name "Empty Boat Gorge", Kongling Xia.

The exit of Xiling Gorge is **Nanjing Pass.** The city of **Yichang** lies 6 km (3.7 miles) away. In 1979 a huge hydroelectric dam, Gezhouba, was completed here.

Kunming

The capital of the province of Yunnan is the city of Kunming which has two million inhabitants. On the south it borders Vietnam, Laos and Burma and in earlier times it was the trading centre for traffic to Southeast Asia. The Emperor Qin Shi Huang Di (221–211 B.C.) was the first to construct overland routes to Yunnan. For centuries the ties which bound the area and its peoples to Imperial China were so loose that sometimes independent kingdoms of non-Chinese peoples arose. Then the Mongols overran the area and incorporated it into the empire. The "City of Eternal Spring" is another name for Kunming. It is situated on a 1,900 m (6,233 ft.) high plateau surrounded by mountains on every side so that the climate all year round is mild and pleasant. The average yearly temperature is 18 °C (64 °F). Yunnan is the home of many minority nationalities which is evident in the streets of Kunming. The women of these minorities can be seen in their colourful national costumes and there are plenty of shops selling the special materials needed to make them, as well as the distinctive jewellery and musical instruments which characterize the individual groups.

North of the city is the **Yuantong Park** and at the beginning of February when the cherry and peach trees are in bloom the magnificence of the scene is a sight to behold. The eight-cornered pavillion, the **Yuantong Temple,** which dates from the Tang Dynasty, is also situated in the park. The **Zoo** is situated in the north of the park.

The **Green Lake,** Cuihu, is situated west of the park. This is a popular recreation area for the people of Kunming who can relax on the lawns, riverbank walks, temples and pavillions.

The **Provincial Museum** is in the city centre and among its exhibits are a variety of cultural objects from the minority nationalities of Yunnan.

For those people who are particularly interested in the history and culture of Yunnan's minorities, a visit to the **Institute for National Minorities** is highly recommended.

In the south-west of the city there are two brick pagodas: the **West Temple Pagoda,** Xisi Ta, and the **East Temple Pagoda,** Dongsi Ta. Both are square thirteen-storey high buildings. Each floor is filled on all sides with small Buddha niches. On the uppermost floor stand huge stone peacocks on each corner. If one drives in a southwesterly direction, one comes to the **Park with the Magnificent View,** Daguanlou Gongyuan. The **Hall of the Magnificent View,** Daguanlou, which was built in 1696, gave the park its name. From here one can look far across over **Dianchi Lake** and the **Western Mountains** with their cliff temples. On each side of the entrance to the hall stand two large stone tablets praising the beauty of

Kunming and recounting the history of Yunnan.

The 330 sq. km (127 sq. mile) large **Dianchi Lake** is the sixth largest freshwater lake in China. It is possible to take a lake cruise along beside the Western Mountains and watch, at close range, the fleets of sailing junks.

The **Western Mountains** consist of four high peaks. On the shore side of the Luohan Mountain high up on the cliff face one can see a Daoist cliff temple. The climb to the top is breathtaking; in places one must pass through narrow tunnels hewn out of the cliff rocks by the monks, and finally one reaches **Dragon's Gate,** the Longmen, from where there is a wonderful view across the lake.

At the foot of Taihua Mountain lie two monasteries: Taihua Monastery and **Huating Monastery.** The latter was restored in recent years and is renowned for its hall containing 500 lohans. In the main hall stands a golden Buddha trinity.

The **Black Dragon Pool** is situated in a beautifully landscaped park 15 km (9 miles) north of the city. In earlier times it was believed that a dragon lived in this pool. In Chinese mythology the dragon is regarded as the lord of the water, the rivers, and the seas.

The **Qiongzhu Temple** which lies 11 km (7 miles) west of Kunming is well worth seeing, in particular for its 500 lohan figures. Although the group dates only from the end of the last century it is famous because of its folkloric influence. The life-like, cheeky, sometimes funny depiction of these Buddhist holy men is in sharp contrast to the more usual presentation. The lohan figures in Huating Monastery are similar in appearance.

The **Golden Hall,** Jindian, which was built in 1671 and is found in the northeastern suburbs of the city, is almost totally constructed of bronze: beams, pillars, arches, roof tiles, window frames and even the people and animal figures are all made of bronze. The entire hall weighs over 200 tons.

The highlight of any tourist's visit to the area is a trip to the **Stone Forest,** Shilin, which lies 120 km (74 miles) south of Kunming. This spectacular landscape is often compared to that of Guilin and indeed both areas underwent similar geological formation. The type of stone involved is the same, ie. karst, which forms towering limestone pillars between 5 m (16 ft.) and 30 m (98 ft.) high formed by the subsidence of a lake and erosion. A 1,200 m (3,937 ft.) long marked pathway leads through the stone labyrinth which consists of fantastically shaped rocks which resemble people, animals, swords and pagodas. The pathway leads to the **Lotus Peak** on which a small pavillion stands. From here there is a wonderful view over the whole Stone Forest which covers an area of 80 hectares. The **Ashma Cliffs** which resemble a beautiful woman of stone, remind one of the legend of the Yi people and which tells of the unhappy ending to a passionate love story. The heroic Ashma is said to have been turned to stone and there she stands to the present day waiting for her lover.

It is possible to spend the night in a small hotel where folklore demonstrations are sometimes held.

The small **Sani Village** which is at the entrance to the Stone Forest belongs to the Sani people who are Yi nationals. The inhabitants are in fact better off than their appearance suggests. In recent years they have been able to make a good living from national costumes and jewellery which they make to sell to tourists.

Xishuangbanna

The autonomous region of the Dai nation, Xishuangbanna, lies in the very south of Yunnan Province and borders onto Laos and Burma.

The 6000,000 inhabitants of the region are made up of thirteen different nationalities. One third of these are Dai (Thai). The climate in the region is subtropical, warm and humid. The average yearly temperature is around 21°C (70°F). Jungle still covers over 100,000 hectares of land. Rare types of wood are found here, including mahogany, teak, camphor, and sandalwood. Kiwis, mangos, bananas, coconuts and papayas can be bought at the market. The area produces up to three rice crops per year.

Travellers to the area must fly in small two-propeller planes from Kunming to Simao; the flight lasts one hour and it is followed by a six-hour bus journey overland. It is possible to stay in the capital Yunjinghong. Accommodation is available on the banks of the river Lancang or nearby.

First on the list of things to see and do is a visit to a Dai village. The Dai people are extremely hospitable and sometimes one is even invited to eat in someone's house – that is of course if the group is not too large. They live in bamboo houses which stand up on 2 m (6 ft.) high poles. The poles afford protection against flooding, mud, or even wild animals.

April is a particularly good month in which to visit the area because this is the time of the **Dai Water Festival.** According to the Dai calendar, this occurs on the 24th day of the sixth month; in early April, according to our calendar. This is the end of the dry season and the beginning of the half-yearly monsoon rain season. The festivities last three days and begin with the **Dragon Boat Race** which is particularly popular with the young people. The boats are 40 to 50 m (131 to 164 ft.) long and can hold up to 60 rowers. The second day is a wet one because from morning until night people splash each other with water and there is much fun and laughter. On the third day one visits the market and calls on friends and relatives.

It is possible, however, to see folk dances and folk singing at other times of the year.

A boat trip on the Lancang River (called the Mekong in Indochina) makes it possible to experience the tropical plant world. One also can see the **summer residence** of the former Dai Kings. The jungles are full of elephants, tigers, leopards, huge snakes, wild boars, bears, gold-haired apes, gibbons and mungos.

Of the many varieties of birds to be seen the rhinoceros bird is particularly interesting.

Sunday is **market day** in Yunjinghong and an opportunity to browse there should not be missed. Farmers of many different nationalities and their wives come there from the surrounding villages and offer their produce for sale. Even the shops in the city are open on Sunday.

Buddhism was widely spread among the Dai people in early days and almost every village had its own temple. Unfortunately, very few now remain. Particularly in the 1970's during the Cultural Revolution, their religion was suppressed and the temples destroyed or turned into storehouses or granaries. One temple which survived is the **White Pagoda** or **Damenglong.** Damenglong is about 50 km (31 miles) south of Yunjinghong near the Burmese border. This pagoda has more in common with the architectural styles of southern Asia than the typical Chinese style. From the middle of the base rises a three-floored 16 m (52 ft.) high pagoda, which resembles a Tibetan stupa. It is surrounded by eight smaller pagodas. At the entrance stand two stone peacocks. The peacock is a good luck symbol for the Dai.

Some 15 km (9 miles) west of the town Menghai, west of Yunjinghong, stands the **Buddha Pagoda.** It is rectangular and 15 m (49 ft.) high. The roof which resembles a pavillion, is supposed to symbolise the headdress of the Buddha Sakyamuni.

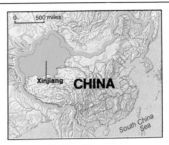

Xinjiang, the North West

Urumqi

Urumqi, once a caravan station on the northern route of the Silk Road, is today the capital of the autonomous region of Xinjiang. It is at the northern foot of the Tianshan mountain range, about 900 m (2,953 ft.) above sea level. The name means "rich pastures" and the town is situated in an oasis east of which the 5,445 m (17,864 ft.) high Bogdo Shan rises with its snow-capped peaks.

The majority of the inhabitants are Uighurians, but other peoples such as the Hui, Han Chinese, Kirgis, Ubeks, Kazaks and Mongols live here as well. Most are Moslems and this fact is reflected in the town's architecture with its thirty mosques and various buildings in the Islamic traditional style.

The **Red Mountains** on the east bank of the Urumqi River provide a wonderful view over the town. In the light of the rising and setting sun the rock walls give off a red-coloured glow. The town has adopted them as its emblem. Pagodas have been built on two hills in order to prevent the return of two evil dragons. An old legend tells how these dragons often laid waste the land until they were driven out by the Heavenly Mother of the Western Heaven.

In the 7th century one of the Tang emperors undertook the transformation of the mountain into a centre of Buddhist worship. Numerous temples and monasteries were built at the foot of the mountain and on its slopes. These were completely destroyed at the beginning of this century when the region was under military control. An essential part of any visit to Urumqi is a day trip to the **Heavenly Lake,** about 50 km (31 miles) to the south-east of Urumqi. It lies 1,900 m (6,233 ft.) above sea level at the foot of Bodga Shan. The waters of the lake, which has a maximum depth of 90 m (295 ft.), glisten jade-green, and its banks are lined with willow and cypress trees. The lake sparkles against a background of azure-blue sky and silver glaciers; here nature's colours can be enjoyed in all their glory.

The tourists are ferried by boat to the opposite shore in order to visit the dwellings of the nomad Kazaks.

On a hillside stands the **Temple of Happiness and Longevity** which the Qing emperor, Qianlang had built in the 18th century to commemorate the successful resistance to foreign invasion and the quelling of internal revolts. It is also known as the **Iron Slate Temple** on account of its unusual roof which is covered in iron slates. **The Temple of the Heavenly Mother of the Western Heaven** is built into the rock face.

The **Xinjiang Provincial Museum** was founded in 1953. The Hall of Cultural Relics has approximately 1,000 objects representing over 5,000 years of Chinese history on view. They extend from the primitive societies of the Early Stone Age to the feudal era which lasted into the 19th century. There are stone tools and pottery from the Neolithic period, as well as bronze and jade objects, silks, paintings and coins from later civilizations. The great trading era with the West via the famous Silk Road is documented by silver coins from Persia and gold coins from the Eastern Roman Empire. The Hall of Murals contains 124 copies of Buddhist murals, the originals of which are located in various caves including the famous murals of the Beizeklik Caves. The Hall of Mummies contains China's oldest and best preserved mummy, the body of a woman who lived 3,200 years ago. There are also mummies from the Han period as well as the mummy of Zhang Xiang, a famous general of the Goachang kingdom in the 7th century.

It is possible to undertake excursions to the **nomad communities** and villages in the surrounding countryside. On such occasions the Kazaks usually provide refreshment in the form of buttermilk bread and mare's milk. Folklore displays and the famous **exhibitions of horsemanship** by the Kazaks are not to be missed.

Turpan

Turpan once belonged to the chain of important stations along the ancient Silk Road. The valley of Turpan offers a panorama of unforgettable scenery: desert, dunes, gorges and mountains as well as wooded oases. Right in the centre of the valley lies the Moonlight Lake (Aydingkol Lake) which covers an area of 152 sq. km (59 sq. ft.).

Turpan has the distinction of being both China's hottest and lowest region. The valley of Turpan lies 154 m (505 ft.) below sea level and is thus the second lowest point on the earth after the Dead Sea. The chain of mountains around the valley prevent the penetration of cool winds, and as a result, summer temperatures can rise as high as 47,5°C (117°F). Rainfall is minimal, but the valley is still a fertile region thanks to melted snow and ice from the glaciers in the Tianshan mountain range which is used for irrigation purposes. In order to prevent rapid evaporation, the glacial waters are channelled down to the valley by means of a series of underground canals.

The hottest place in the valley is the **Mountain of Flames.** Its surface can reach temperatures of up to 75°C (135°F). From the distance it appears to glow like fire in the intense sunlight, hence its name. Turpan is famous throughout China for its excellent grapes and melons. One of the best grapes grown there is a variety which has no pips and has a sugar content of around 20%. The Hami melons taste sweet and refreshing and can weigh up to 15 kg (44 lbs) each.

Some 40 km (25 miles) east of Turpan lie the ruins of a once prosperous town, **Gaochang.** The ruins are surrounded by the old city wall which is 5 km (3 miles) long and between 2 and 8 m (6 and 26 ft.) high. The foundations of the buildings can still be clearly distinguished. The walls were built of pressed clay and contained gates strategically placed to the north, south and west. The town was divided into three sections, the inner city, the outer city area and the palace centre. The remains of the old pottery workshops have shown that elaborate vessels for the purpose of storing wine were once manufactured here.

On the way to Gaochang, down in the Kiziltagh Valley lie the ancient Buddhist grottos known as the **Caves of Beizeklik.** At the turn of the century, European archeologists became interested in this site, but regrettably they took many of the interesting and valuable finds back to Europe.

Not far from Gaochang lie the **Graves of Astona.** "Astona" means capital in the Uighurian language. This burial place for high government officials and common citizens alike spans the period from the Western Jin to the Tang Dynasty. The graves have yielded important finds to archeologists and historians. The hot, dry climate has kept the mummies in an excellent state of preservation. More than 2,000 books and documents were discovered in the graves. The wealth and prosperity of this region during the period of trade with the Western world along the Silk Road is documented by finds of ceramics, coins and silks.

The **Imin Minaret** stands 2 km (almost 1 mile) east of Turpan. This brick building, decorated with geometrical patterns in the typical Uighuric style, is 44 m (144 ft.) high and two hundred years old. The Imam Imin Gola was responsible for the construction of the minaret, and after his death in 1770, his son, Sulaiman, ordered work on the building to continue, which accounts for its other name, the **Sulaiman mosque.**

Kashgar

The town of Kashgar (200,000 inhabitants) in the west of Xingjiang Province at the foot of the Pamir Mountains has been open to tourists since 1983.

It is not an easy place to reach. It lies about 1,000 km (624 miles) away from the provincial capital, Urumqi, and lacks good road and rail connections. Air traffic to the town is irregular, depending on prevailing weather conditions.

And yet 2,000 years ago Kashgar, then known as Shule, was one of the most important stations on the Silk Road. From this point the trade routes branched: to the south, towards India and Pakistan, and then to the west over the Pamir Mountains to embrace the Scythian and Persian kingdoms and finally reaching the Roman Empire.

Kashgar came under Chinese rule for the first time in 200 B.C. when the Han general, Zhang Qian, led a military expedition to the lands of the western peoples and also established trading routes.

From the 2nd to the 7th century the Kashgar region belonged to various Turkestan kingdoms. It was not until the Tang Dynasty that the Chinese emperors succeeded in bringing it under military control once more. From the 10th century onwards, Kashgar began to lose its importance as a trading station as the newly discovered sea routes began to supersede the centuries-old Silk Road.

For centuries, the Kashgar region as well as the whole of Xinjiang was disputed by different rulers, and the Qing emperors ruthlessly suppressed several bloody revolts.

At the turn of the century it was of more than passing interest to diplomats, secret service agents and adventurers, as the English, Russians and Chinese all sought to bring Turkestan within their sphere of influence, with the Chinese basing their claim in historical rights.

One of the most famous adventurers in Kashgar at this period was the great explorer, Sven Hedin, and it was from here that he started his many expeditions to the dessert regions and to Tibet.

The present-day hotel in Kashgar was formerly the residence of the Russian diplomat Petrowky (1882–1903). Nearby are the busy streets of the **bazaar** and the mosque.

The weekly market takes place at the square in front of the **Id Kah Mosque.** This mosque is the largest in China and can hold up to 8,000 people. It is rightly considered one of the most beautiful buildings in the whole province. To the north-east of the mosque lies the **Tomb of Apak Hodscha,** the burial place of Islamic saints. The 72 persons interred here are descendants of Muhatum

Adscham, an Islamic missionary famous throughout Central Asia. Five generations lie buried here, among them Apak and Yusuf Hodscha. The tomb complex which was built in 1620 was once a rich foundation possessing lands, mills and farms. Within the tomb there are 58 coffins. An empty grave nearby is presumed to have been the last resting place of Yakub Beg, who, in 1862, led a revolt against the Qing regime. The circumstances of Yakub Beg's subsequent demise are still the subject of controversy; Chinese historians claim he committed suicide whereas the Uighurians are convinced he was murdered. In any case, after the suppression of the rebellion his grave was desecrated and his head sent tot Beijing as a sign of victory.

To the north of Kashgar, there are 3 Buddhist caves known as the Caves of the Three Immortals, set into a steep cliff face on the south bank of the Qiakmakh River. In one of them there are well-preserved murals to be seen.

Roughly 30 km (18 miles) to the east of Kashgar lie the ruins of the once flourishing town of **Hanoi** which fell into decay in the course of the 11th century. The remains of a temple and the old water supply system can still be seen.

When weather conditions are good, it is possible to distinguish two glaciers lying to the south-west, Kongur which is 7,719 m (25,324 ft.) high, and Muztagata, 7,546 m (24,757 ft.) in height. These are two of the highest peaks in the Pamir range of mountains.

Tibet/Qinghai Plateau

Lhasa

Lhasa is the capital of the sparsely populated autonomous region of Tibet which has only 1.9 million inhabitants. The city is situated on the river Lhasa which is a tributary of the Yarlung Zangbo which transverses Tibet from west to east before swinging south and flowing into the Gulf of Bengal as the Brahmaputra.

The Yarlung Zangbo valley which lies at an altitude of 3,700 m (12,139 ft.) is enclosed by the Himalayas in the south and the Transhimalayas in the north, it is the most densely populated area of Tibet. Lhasa, Xigaza and Gyantse – all of which are open to tourists are also situated here.

The Tibetan King Srongtsan Gampo who was responsible for unifying the kingdom ordered a palace to be built on Marpori, the Red Mountain, in the 7th century. He called it the "Palace of Immortality".

Today, the **Potala Palace** stands on top of Marpori. The Fortress of the Gods, the seat of the Dalai

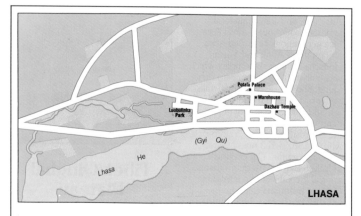

Lamas since the time of the great fifth Dalai Lama looks as if it has grown up out of the mountain. Its golden roofs greet the visitors and pilgrims approaching from far away; long after the sun has set its roofs glisten in the darkening valley.

The great fifth Dalai Lama, Lobsang Gyatso, started building in the year 1661. First the **White Palace** was erected; it is so-called because its gigantic walls have always been whitewashed. Half a century later work was completed on the **Red Palace** which rises from the white walls in the middle like an enormous tower. The Dalai Lamas' private apartments are found there. The palace is nearly 400 m (1,312 ft.) long in an east-west direction and from north to south it is 350 m (1,148 ft.) long. The thirteen-storeyed palace covers an area of 130,000 sq. m (1,399,307 sq. ft.) and stands 117 m (384 ft.) above the valley. The building is constructed from wood and stone only; the walls are on average about 3 m (10 ft.) thick but in places they are 5 m (16 ft.) wide. More than 15,000 pillars support the rooms which number nearly 1,000. The architectural style is Tibetan but the pillars and roofs in particular show the influence of Chinese artists and craftsmen. Craftsmen from India and Nepal are also believed to have participated in the construction.

A climb up the steep stone steps brings one to a big courtyard which lies half-way up and is entered by the east gate. Here, in earlier times, the religious feasts and festivities were held in front of the Dalai Lama and other important lamas. It was here they watched the ceremonies, the dances and the singing.

The seminary for the older monks and the dormitories used by the 154 lamas who once lived here are both located east of the terrace. From the terrace one reaches the main eastern hall, the most spacious in the White Palace which is supported by 64 pillars.

Having walked along the twisting paths and passed by innumerable little chapels one reaches the Red Palace. Here in the Red Palace are the largest ceremonial halls, 35 small chapels, four meditation halls, and in the western main hall the eight burial shrines of the 5th and 7th–13th Dalai Lamas. In the tschortens (stupas) which stand over three storeys high rest the embalmed bodies of the Tibetan Dalai Lamas. The tschorten of the 5th Dalai Lama is 14.85 m (48 ft.) high and covered with 3,700 kg (8,140 lbs.) of gold. Diamonds, pearls, turquoise, agates, coral stones and many other precious gems are used to adorn the tschortens.

The burial shrine of the 13th Dalai Lama is similarly decorated with gold and precious stones and stands 14 m (46 ft.) high. The wall paintings in the Western Hall are of great historical and artistic value; they depict the life of the 5th Dalai Lama including his audience with the Qing Emperor Shunzhi in Beijing.

In the north-eastern section of the Red Palace one can see the Avalokiteshvara Chapel which although it is believed to be the oldest part of the palace is still standing and was built when construction work first started by Srongtsan Gambo.

The private apartments of the Dalai Lama are found on the upper floors. Up until last year it was possible to visit them but this has become more difficult because the lamas once again have judicial rights to the palace and they don't particularly like the thought of tourists visiting their Sacred halls. It is still possible, however, to climb up onto the roof. Standing practically in the midst of the golden roofs which rise over the tombs of the Dalai Lamas one has a magnificent view over the city and the whole Lhasa valley.

From this vantage point one can also look across to the centre. Here, in the old quarter of the town stands the holiest of holy Tibetan temples – the Jokhang. The latter forms the central building of the **Tsuk-Lug-Khang** in which, in earlier times, all the most important Tibetan government departments were located: ministeries, municipal authorities, the offices of the regents, law courts and prison. The Tsuk-Lag-Khang is encircled by the 800 m (2,625 ft.) long **Barkhor,** or Sacred Way – a ritual path which praying Tibetans follow in a clockwise direction. The most devout measure the way by prostrating themselves on the ground. They throw their bodies to the ground, stand up, walk a few paces and then throw themselves lengthwise in the dust again. Today, among the jostling crowds found on the Barkhor are many pilgrims and traders. Ceaselessly they spin their prayer wheels and let their beads slip through their fingers. An even bigger Sacred Way used to encircle the whole old town, the 7 km (4.3 miles) long Lingkhor. Unfortunately it is now interrupted in several places by new buildings and streets. In the olden days – and there are some who do it even today – the pilgrims who arrived here after weeks or months of travelling over the mountains would first visit the Lingkhor, which was then connected to the Potala, before continuing to the centre and the Barkhor.

At the entrance to the Tsuk-Lag-Khang stands an old dried-up tree stump which is all that remains of a willow that the Chinese Princess Wen Cheng is supposed to have planted here on the occasion of her marriage to Srongtsan Gambo. Before the entrance the pilgrims throw themselves innumerable times to the ground in prayer. The "Cathedral of Tibetan Buddhism", the Jokhang, is reached through the main prayer hall which is supported by red pillars and contains a throne used by the Dalai Lama. The four sides of the hall are filled with many smaller chapels containing statues of Buddha or Bodhisattva. Right across from the entrance stands a statue of the twelve-year-old Buddha Sakyamuni, Jobo. The statue, richly decorated with gold and precious stones, was the wedding present of the Princess Wen Cheng to her future husband. On the second floor there are more chapels and government rooms. From the roof of the Jokhang on top of which there are smaller golden roofs there is a view right across to the Potala Palace.

An interesting statue of King Srongtsan Gambo stands in a side chapel in the main hall. The small Buddha figure in his headdress signifies that he is honoured as a reincarnation of the Bodhisattva Avalokiteshvara. The latter is the patron saint of all Tibet. Even the Dalai Lamas consider themselves as a reincarnation of the Bodhisattva. He is flanked on both sides by two female figures representing a Nepalese woman and the Chinese Princess Wen Cheng, both of whom he took as wives.

About 7 km (4 miles) from the city centre there is an enormous park in which the **Norbulingkha** (Precious Stone Garden) is situated. The park was built in the second half of the 18th century on the orders of the 7th Dalai Lama. From then on it was used by the Dalai Lamas as their summer residence which is why the Potala is known as the winter residence. In 1954 it was restored and rebuilt under the auspices of the present Dalai Lama, the 14th. There is a huge reception room inside, whose walls are decorated with paintings of more recent historical events and containing a throne for the Dalai Lama. It is possible to visit not only the chapels, meditation rooms, the huge library, but also the private apartments of the Dalai Lama and his family.

There are three important monasteries in Lhasa which were regarded as the pillars of the Tibetan state: Galdan, Dripung and Sera. In these three monasteries all the most important monks and state officials are trained.

Galdan Monastery was razed to the ground during the Cultural Revolution. Nothing has remained of it. Today, the faithful are trying, with the support of the government, to raise funds for the monastery to be rebuilt.

Drepung Monastery ("Rice Heap") which dates from the year 1416, was founded by a pupil of the reformer Tsongkhapa, who is regarded as the founder of the Yellow Hat Sect which is predominantly found in Tibet. It is situated about 6 km (3.7 miles) west of the city at the foot of a 5,600 m (18,372 ft.)

high mountain and was previously the largest monastery in Tibet, housing over 10,000 monks. Before the Potala was built, the official residence of the Dalai Lama was in Drepung.

It is not particularly easy to walk through the monastery because it is first necessary to climb up the slope in the thin high mountain air. The living quarters and the storeroom are the first rooms to be encountered below. Then, further up come the larger prayer rooms, dukhangs, which contain priceless statues including one of the Tsongkhapa.

The pantheon of Tibetan Buddhism is sheer confusion. Everywhere there are countless statues including earthly as well as heavenly Buddhas, Bodhisattvas, which occur again and again in various representations, Dakinis, which are heavenly celestial beings, Dharmapalas, protectors of learning, others with weapons and terrifying faces, guardian deities, local gods which are usually gods from the ancient Tibetan natural religion, holy men, saints, higher Lamas and teachers such as the founder of the Yellow Hat Sect Tsongkhapa.

Sera Monastery is situated about 5 km (3 miles) north of Lhasa. It was also founded by followers of Tsongkhapa – in the year 1419. Nearly 5,000 monks used to live here and the monastery was famous throughout all of Tibet for the quality of its academic teaching. It is similar to but smaller than Drepung Monastery.

On the way to Drepung Monastery one passes by the small Netschung Monastery which houses the **State Oracle.** Up until recently the oracle was always consulted before any important official decision was made. The oracle priests could be either monks or laiety. First they would be put into a trance and then the god Pehar would speak through them. The lamas of the Netschung Monastery would then translate the usually unintelligable speech. The last of the oracle priests, who were also involved with the resistance of the Tibetan people and the flight of the Dalai Lama, are today also living in exile in India.

Xigaze

The arduous journey to Xigaze involves taking the Gyantse Road which lies at an average height of 4,000 m (13,123 ft.) and is one of the most impressive experiences in life that a person can have. The snake-like road with its hairpin bends winds its way at dizzying heights along the side of the mountain, passing glacier filled mountain peaks. On the way one passes little villages, fertile valleys, herds of cattle, and of course, the inevitable yaks, that unassuming beast of burden so beloved by the Tibetans both for work and for food.

Xigaze is the seat of the Pantschen Lama, second highest spiritual leader after the Dalai Lama. The fifth Dalai Lama bestowed the title of Pantschen Lama on his old teacher as a sign of his respect for him and out of feelings of gratitude. The latter is a reincarnation of the Buddha Amithaba and in the Buddhist hierarchy stands higher than a Bodhisattva. The Dalai Lama himself is known as the incarnation of the Bodhisattva Avalokiteshvara. At the beginning of this century when the English, Russians and Chinese were disputing the sovereignty of Tibet, it was not an uncommon tactic to try and play the Pantschen Lama and the Dalai Lama off against each other. The present Pantschen Lama, the 10th, is today the vice-representative of the National People's Congress in Beijing. At the time that the Dalai Lama was making his escape to India, the Pantschen Lama was negotiating with the Chinese. However, he still had to spend the duration of the Cultural Revolution in prison. After 18 years in prison, he was allowed for the first time, in 1983, to visit his residence, the Tashi Lhunpo Monastery, which was built by a pupil of the reformer Tsongkhapa in 1447. Following generations continued to enlarge and improve the buildings.

The Maitreya Hall is one of the outstanding features of the monastery. The 9th Pantschen Lama had it built in 1914. It is hard to overlook the 30 m (98 ft.) high red coloured rectangular building. A 26.2 m (86 ft.) high completely gold-covered statue of the Buddha Maitreya (the Buddha of the Future) stands in the middle. More than 229 kg (504 lbs.) of gold and 115 tons of copper were used to make the statue.

About 85 kg (187 lbs.) of gold 15 tons of silver and countless precious stones decorate the 11 m (36 ft.) high burial tomb of the 4th Pantschen Lama which dates from the year 1662. He was the 16th abbot of the Taschi Lhunpo Monastery and is held in particularly high esteem, even today.

The golden roofs of the burial chapels of the Pantschen Lamas dominate the whole monastery complex. A huge stone wall has been erected on the side of one of the mountains which stand right behind the monastery. On feast days, thangkas religious picture scrolls made from material – often even silk is used – are hung there and can be seen from miles around.

Since his Tibetan visit this monastery has once again become the summer residence of the Pantschen Lama. Although it used to be possible to view these rooms this is no longer the case.

Today, the tents of nomads on pilgrimage can once again be seen in front of the monastery. Behind the monastery is the traditional place where the corpses are dismembered and the pieces left for the vultures. This ceremony takes place in the presence of the closest family members only and is out of the question for other Tibetans or tourists to attend.

The main street in Xigaze runs in front of the spartan guest house. It is here in the evening that the young people gather. It is also possible to see a brigade. Beside the living quarters of the Tibetans are workshops where the holy objects needed for the monasteries are made.

Visitors to a Tibetan family will be offered tchang which is beer made from fermented barley or else Yak butter tea by the host.

On the return journey to Lhasa it is possible to take the northern road which runs along the northern side of the Yarlung Zangbo back to Lhasa. The road leads across a pass surrounded by glacier filled peaks.

Gyantse (Gyangzi)

Tourists to Tibet usually stay for about six days. As well as visiting Lhasa it is possible to see the city of Xigaze which is about 300 km (186 miles) west of Lhasa. The journey which lasts 8–10 hours takes one first into the Lhasa River valley; after crossing this valley one reaches the Yarlung Zangbo River. From here the surrounding mountains rise up. This route involves crossing two passes which lie at heights of 4,700 (15,420 ft.) and 4,900 m (16,076 ft.) respectively.

One should also make a short stop in the city of Gyantse. Up until this century it was an important trading city because it was here that the caravans met on their way to India, Sikkim, Burma and Nepal. From here it was only a short journey to Tibet's two most important cities, Lhasa the principal seat of the Dalai Lama and Xigaze home of the Pantschen Lama. Apart from the home-produced traditional luxury articles which were once available here such as silk, brocades and jade, it was possible to buy Scottish whisky and Swiss watches. According to one British diplomat in 1910 the market in Gyantse was comparable to Oxford Street in London.

The **fortress** of the old town which stands high up on the hill and which dominates the entire valley can be seen from a long distance.

The second most striking building is the monumental **Gyantse tschorten.** It stands in the middle of a high monastery complex, surrounded by a big red wall. Unfortunately, most of the buildings now stand in ruins.

The ground plan of the 14-storeyed tschorten resembles a Tibetan mandala which is a rather peculiar diagram used by the monks as a meditation object. On top of a rectangular base stands the circular tschorten. There is a covered passage leading to small chapels and niches on each floor. On the very tip of the tschorten is a big chapel which contains a larger-than-life golden Buddha. The building dates from the beginning of the 15th century and is still one of the most interesting examples of Tibetan architecture.

Next to the Tschoerten stands a big prayer hall which is luckily still undamaged. Inside there are countless smaller chapels and statues including a bronze statue of the Buddha Maitreya which stands over two storeys high.

Xining

Xining with its 400,000 inhabitants is the capital of Qinghai Province. It is situated over 2,000 m (6,562 ft.) above sea level in a fertile plateau region in the north-east of the province. The town can be reached by train from Lanzhou, which is 200 km (656 ft.) away.

About 70 km (43 miles) to the east of Xining is China's largest lake, **Qinghai Hu,** more commonly known as **Koko Na.** Trips to this lake are available to tourists and start at Xining.

The town is of interest to tourists because of the **Monastery of Kumbum** (Ta'er Si) which is considered a holy place by the Tibetan Buddhists because it is the birthplace of Tsangkhapa (1357–1419), the great lama and Buddhist reformer who founded the Gelugpa Sect (Yellow Caps). Work on the monastery began in 1560, and in its heyday over 4,000 monks lived there.

The architectural style is pure Tibetan, easily recognizable by its whitewashed walls, its redbrown roof friezes and the gilded roofs.

At the entrance stands a 14 m (46 ft.) high stupa with eight smaller ones behind it.

The central building is the Hall of the Golden Roof which is reputed to stand at Tsongkhapa's place of birth. In the hall itself, a 12 m (39 ft.) high stupa marks the exact spot where Tsongkhapa is presumed to have been born. There is a golden statue of the founder of the sect, about 1.3 m (4 ft.) in height, affixed to a niche in the stupa. The library with its collection of Buddhist writings and sacred texts is also to be found in this hall.

Attached to the hall is the Jokhang, i.e., Buddha Hall, a building which dates from the year 1557. It contains a gilded statue of the Buddha Maitreya; next to him are Tsongkhapa and two of his disciples. All three figures are worked in gold and silver. The most impressive of all the Tsongkhapa statues stands in the Dipankara Temple to the northeast of the main hall. To the east of it one can see a group of trees known as the Holy Trees. There is a legend which tells how a sandalwood tree sprang up at Tsongkhapa's place of birth. This present group of trees is revered because it is believed to be descended from the original holy tree.

The great Congregation Hall, a Meditation Hall in which the monks assemble for prayers and devout meditation is supported by 108 pillars which symbolize the 108 volumes of the Kandshur, the sacred text of Buddhism. After the death of the thirteenth Dalai Lama, a group of high Lamas set out to find the reincarnated Lama. Pursuing a vision that they had experienced, they came to the monastery of Kumhum. In a small village nearby they discovered a small boy whom they pronounced to be the reincarnated Dalai Lama after a series of tests and examinations. This child became the fourteenth and present Dalai Lama.

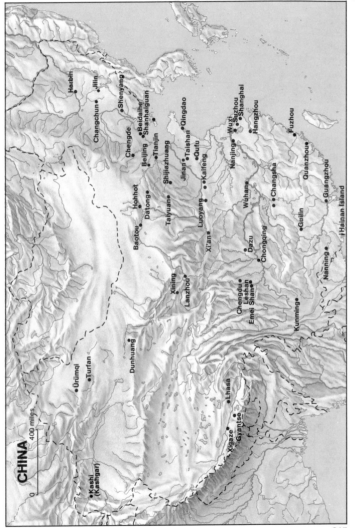

CHINA

0 _____ 400 miles

Kashi (Kashgar)
Ürümqi
Turfan
Dunhuang
Xining
Lanzhou
Xi'an
Chengdu
Leshan
Emei Shan
Lhasa
Gyantse
Xigaze
Kunming
Nanning
Chongqing
Dazu
Guilin
Guangzhou
Quanzhou
Hainan Island
Changsha
Wuhan
Fuzhou
Hangzhou
Nanjing
Wuxi
Suzhou
Shanghai
Kaifeng
Luoyang
Qufu
Taishan
Jinan
Qingdao
Taiyuan
Shijiazhuang
Tianjin
Beijing
Datong
Hohhot
Baotou
Chengde
Beidaihe
Shanhaiguan
Shenyang
Changchun
Jilin
Harbin

315

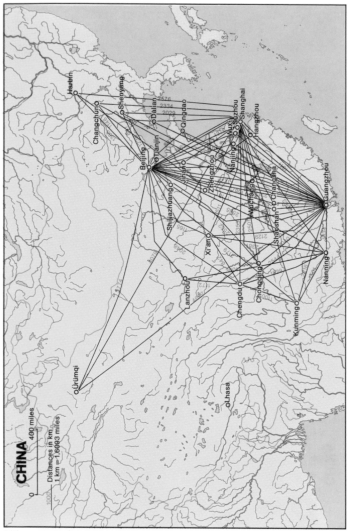

CHINA

Distances in km.
1 km = 1.6093 miles

0 _____ 1000

0 _____ 400 miles

Useful Information

Currency

The Chinese currency is called **renminbi** (people's money; renmin = people, bi = money). The basic unit is the yuan. One yuan is divided into 10 jiao or 100 fen. One jiao is 10 fen. All denominations are issued as bank notes; 1, 2, 5, 10, 50 and 100 yuan notes; 1, 2 and 5 jiao notes, and finally 1, 2, and 5 fen notes. The three fen units are also issued as coins.

The importation and exportation of renminbi is strictly forbidden. When exchanging currency, tourists receive **currency certificates** instead of renminbi. These certificates have the same value as renminbi but are only valid in certain shops, in hotels and tourist agencies. The currency certificates are issued in the following denominations: 100, 50, 10, 5 and 1 yuan; in 5 jiao (= 50 Fen) and in 1 jiao (= 10 Fen),

The currency certificates may be exported but have no value whatsoever outside China.

It is possible to **exchange certificates** in all hotels, as well as in Friendship Stores and other tourist shops. Sometimes it is possible to use the certificates in factories which are visited by large numbers of tourists. The exchange rate is fixed daily. **Travellers cheques** are also accepted and in some shops and hotels it is possible to use credit cards. At present the ten big credit

cards are accepted. Unused Chinese currency certificates can only be exchanged at the border and customs posts. Since only certificates and not cash can be re-exchanged people are advised to use up their coins and notes. For current rates of exchange ask at your bank or travel agency.

Foreign Exchange Certificates

The Foreign Exchange Certificates have the same value as the Chinese currency renminbi. Tourists are only ever given Foreign Exchange Certificates. In tourist agencies, hotels and friendship shops only these are accepted.

Units: yuan and fen. One yuan = 100 fen. Notes: yuan 50, 10, 5 and 1; fen 50 and 10; no coins are issued.

Entry Regulations

Tourists visiting the People's Republic of China need a valid **visa** issued by the Chinese authorities. Normally the travel agent will apply for the necessary papers. In addition, special permission from Luxingshe, the official Chinese travel authorities in Beijing, is needed for tours. Normally the travel agent automatically receives this when booking an organised tour. For individual travellers it is important to know that in the meantime 452 cities have been exempted from this requirement. The **passport** must be valid for a period of at least two months after the proposed date of leaving the country. The group visa is held by the courier. When entering the country an additional declaration of health must be filled out, giving details of any past or present serious illnesses. These forms are available at the point of entry.

Spirits totalling 1.5 litres and up to 400 cigarettes can be imported duty free. It is important to declare watches, tape recorders, cameras, movie equipment, jewellery and other valuables as well as any currency.

The **copy** of this **customs declaration** must on no account be mislaid since it has to be produced when leaving the country. All declared goods must be re-exported as well as any remaining currency.

The authorities are particularly strict in controlling the export of antiques or other art objects. Only antiques bearing a red wax seal are allowed to leave the country. It is advisable to keep all currency exchange receipts as well as receipts for purchases in case they are demanded by customs officials. Antiques and valuable art objects for which there is no proof of purchase may be confiscated without compensation at the border.

In general, controls are not over strict but spot checks must be expected. Travellers from Tibet, however, can reckon with particularly stringent controls.

Booking and Travel Preparations

For the last two years China has been open to individual travellers but this is more an exception and will remain so for some time to come.

Travel agents in most countries now offer a choice of organised tours of China. It is worth studying the brochures carefully in order to find the most suitable route. Very few agents offer standardized routes for which they need special permission from the China International Travel Service of Luxingshe, the official Chinese travel authorities.

Deviations from the prescribed travel route are generally not allowed. The advertised tour programme is subject to change because Luxingshe reserves the right to alter any tour at short notice. The China International Travel Service has the right to select means of transport, hotels and restaurants. The foreign travel agents have only limited control over the preparation and organization of the travel route and programme.

Basically, the conditions offered to all travel agents are the same. So it is simpler for the tourist to make his choice based on a comparison of prices. One exception are the luxury tours because the small number of luxury hotels can be booked direct by the travel agent. When deciding the best time to travel it is wise to take into account the extremes of climate in the different parts of China. The best time to travel for those not able to stand severe heat is in the months April/May and September/October.

Several books are available on China and its culture which enable the tourist to build up a picture of the country and its people beforehand. Information on China can also be obtained from the Tourist Office of the People's Republic of China.

Visas are generally applied for by the travel agent. The Chinese Embassy issues a visa for organised tours; this requires leaving one's passport at the travel agent's for a number of weeks.

Health and Medical Care

Medical attention is in any event guaranteed. The bigger hotels have their own emergency clinics, in others a doctor will be sent for immediately on request.

Not only Chinese natural healing methods (with herbs, acupuncture) will be used; western medical methods and treatments are also available. Medical costs are extremely low.

What can be expensive, however, is the cost of an emergency journey home.

In any event, it is strongly recommended to take out full **health insurance coverage** which covers both illness and accidents. This is usually available as an exclusive insurance package from the tour operator together with luggage, personal liability insurance and cancellation insurance.

Inoculation

Inoculation for travellers from Europe and the U.S.A. is no longer obligatory. Travellers from other areas, however, especially those intending to stay for prolonged periods may be required to provide evidence of certain vaccinations. In any event it is better to make enquiries at your travel agent's or the Chinese tourist authorities prior to leaving for China.

Malaria prophylaxis is not usually required or necessary. One exception, however, is a journey to the extreme south which is tropical. The health authorities and the tropical medicine experts often give conflicting advice. There have been no reported cases of malaria in China in recent years.

Medicines

It is advisable to pack sufficient supplies of any medicines which are taken regularly.

It is also a good idea to take remedies along for the **common cold** and **stomach upsets.** Many tourists complain of catching cold because of the great climatic differences from region to region. Buildings and buses are also often equipped with air-conditioning which makes one prone to colds.

Unfortunately, diarrhea is also an unpleasant occurrence. Toilets are hard to find once away from the hotel, or even worse, they are in an indescribable condition.

Sun tan lotion is also necessary during the summer and it is not always possible to find it in China.

Women are advised to take sanitary towels or tampons with them since neither are readily available in China.

Language
Most groups have two **interpreters** at their disposal – a permanent Chinese guide and a local guide. Don't be surprised if even the interpreters have difficulty understanding each other. The Chinese language has a large number of dialects which vary tremendously. Rutonghua – the North Chinese dialect is the standard language.

English is rarely spoken and if at all then in the cities.

If you are out and about on your own therefore, it is a good idea to take a map along with you.

In recent years several competent **phrase books** have appeared on the market. An important consideration when buying such a book is that the Chinese characters are given alongside the latin letters. Even with the aid of the latin transcription Chinese is difficult to pronounce, but should all else fail you can always show your interlocutor the Chinese characters.

Crime
Incredible tales are told of incidents involving foreigners from the early days of tourism in China. It is claimed, for example that socks and shirts which people had thrown away were returned to them, or that people were given their change of 1 fen a day after they had made their purchase. Such stories should no longer be accepted as the norm. Gestures like those mentioned above would be impossible today due to the sheer numbers of tourists visiting China.

Moreover, crime is on the increase of late especially in large cities and in particular among young people. Nevertheless, China can still rank as one of the safest countries in the world. Very few crimes are commited against foreigners because the punishment is so severe.

Tourists should still keep an eye on their valuables however, especially when in a crowd. What is more, one cannot assume that having lost something, the person who finds it will have the honesty to return it.

In several towns in southern China, street traders can be remarkably persistent. Foreign exchange certificates are also a much desired item since the Chinese can use them to purchase imported goods. It is however, illegal to exchange foreign exchange certificates for renminbi and you also have the problem of spending or otherwise getting rid of the currency before you leave the country.

Clothing

Since tours involve a large amount of overland travel and even cultural activities in the evening in China do not require very formal clothing, it is advisable to pack light casual and sportswear. Most hotels offer their guests a laundry service but they are not always reliable and therefore it is better not to entrust your hotel with garments requiring special care or made of delicate fabrics.

It should also be remembered that since China is such a large country it is made up of many different climatic zones. Particularly in the spring and autumn, the northern part of the country can experience very cold spells. In the extreme north as well as in the steppe and desert regions, temperature extremes are quite normal.

Comfortable shoes are a must and a light raincoat is also indispensable.

Some old travel guides recommend limiting oneself to conservative. clothing. For remote country regions as well as where ethnic groups have settled it is certainly better to avoid clothing which might be considered outrageous or revealing. In the bigger cities, however, the Chinese are becoming increasingly fashion conscious.

Food and Drink

Chinese cooking is famous throughout the world and even if foods which are unknown or unrecognisable are served one should not miss the opportunity to try out everything offered. Very unusual dishes such as snakes, cats or armadillos are not usually served any more.

It is, however, possible to order a **speciality menu** for between 15 and 20 yuan in most cities. Individual dishes can also be ordered.

It is sometimes better to eat in restaurants rather than in a hotel where the food is not of such a high standard.

Drinks are served with meals and are included in the price. The most common drinks are a good spicy beer and lemonade, though the lemonade is usually very sweet. Mineral water is also available.

In the meantime it is possible to order imported drinks but these must be paid for with currency certificates (tourist currency). The bars of larger hotels offer imported spirits as well as Chinese drinks. Do be careful, however! Chinese schnapps is more than 50% proof.

Hotels

Apart from the few luxury hotels which have recently opened in Beijing, Shanghai, Nanjing and Guangzhou, foreign tourist agents have no say as to the choice of hotel. The Chinese tourist agency allots hotels according to availability, to the various groups shortly before they arrive.

For a surcharge of about 20 yuan it is possible to book a room in a luxury hotel, provided of course that one is available.

The quality of hotels is not standardized. In remote, off-the-beaten-track areas one can expect simple accommodation. Rooms offered to tourists, however, all have a bathroom and toilet and in many cases a writing table and television. Hot water and tea leaves are always available in hotel rooms.

Nearly all hotels have currency exchange offices, post office facilities and laundry services. Washing which is given in the morning is returned that same evening. The bigger hotels have shops, hairdressers, ironing services, recreation rooms, bars and often a medical service.

Shopping
Tourists are only too willingly taken to the **Friendship Stores –** Yougi Shangdian – which are found in all the cities. These shops usually offer an extensive selection of Chinese merchandise destined for export, as well as some imported goods. In these shops – just as in the hotels – payment can only be made with currency certificates (often referred to as tourist currency).

It is of course possible to shop in other **department stores** and shops. The usual special offers are to be found and can be paid for in renminbi. It is not possible to bargain about prices in the shops; in any event all articles have price tags. On the **free market** and with individual traders the case is somewhat different; the stands are usually found in the places where the tourists are likely to be sightseeing. Here the customer is more or less expected to **bargain** and because of this high prices are usually asked.

Sometimes small statues or old coins are offered for sale. It is better to be careful where such objects are concerned since the customs authorities can declare them cultural objects or antiques and, since there are no exit permits for them, can confiscate them when you leave the country.

All antiques which may be officially exported can be bought in special shops and have a red wax seal.
When buying handicraft articles or handmade objects one should remember that these are often made

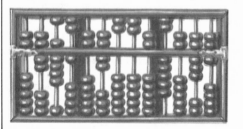

The abacus which is the traditional Chinese adding machine is still used in shops everywhere.

locally and are found only in a particular region. Very often they can be bought only in a particular city and nowhere else.

In some cases it is possible to buy direct from the factory during a visit. The goods, such as woven silk and ceramics are usually offered at much lower prices than elsewhere.

There is no limit to the quantity of any particular purchase that one can export. It is advisable, however, to check the **import regulations** for your particular home country. It is perhaps better to check these regulations before leaving for China. **Please note:** In accordance with the "Convention on International Trade in Endangered Species" (**CITES**), you should make a point of not buying any souvenirs, the production of which involves the use of wild animals or wild flowers. In China's case this applies in particular to objects made of ivory (from elephants). The importation of such articles is banned by many countries anyway.

Customs Regulations
A detailed customs declaration must be filled out on entering the country. The following must be specifically mentioned: currency, technical and electrical apparatus as well as any personal valuables. These may not be disposed of within China and must be shown on leaving the country if required to do so.

The **copy** of this **customs declaration form** must be shown on leaving the country so care should be taken not to mislay it. It should be kept together with one's passport in a safe place.

The importation of radios, weapons, amunition, drugs, any literature politically not acceptable to the Chinese government, as well as pornographic material (here the Chinese authorities are much stricter than in the West) is strictly forbidden. Antiques and objets d'art must have the official red seal before leaving the country.

It is also illegal to import or export anything belonging to another person. The importing or exporting of renminbi is forbidden too.

Picture Taking and Filming
Video and other small cameras are permitted without any special permission. For 16 mm and above, special permission is required. There are, in fact, only a few restrictions to normal photography. Just as in western countries the photography of military installations is strictly forbidden.

Restrictions are however placed on the photography of certain tourist attractions, especially in Tibet. Be sure to follow any regulations and restrictions since they are usually strictly applied.

It is now possible to buy Kodak and Fuji film in the Friendship Stores. It is better, however, to take a supply of flash bulbs, batteries and other extras with you.

Post Office Facilities

Post office facilities are found in almost all hotels. Postcards can be bought in hotels and other tourist areas.

From Beijing a letter to Europe takes 4 to 7 days. A letter to America takes on average slightly longer – from one week to 10 days. The farther one travels into the country, the longer the post takes; from remote areas it can take 2 weeks.

The Chinese post also accepts parcels. However, only unsealed parcels are accepted.

It is somewhat more complicated to receive post or news from home, in particular because in most cases one does not know in advance in which hotel one will be staying. The best course of action is to leave word with one's tourist agency at home that any urgent news can be telexed or telegraphed to the China International Service in Beijing. They will know which group is staying in which hotel and can pass on the message.

Phone Calls

In China, any telephone call within an area code is free. Nearly all hotels have telephones in the rooms. It is also possible to make free calls within the city with these phones.

To telephone outside the local area one has to go through the operator. It is also possible to telephone outside of China. First it is necessary to fill out the form which one gets at the post office or from the switchboard in the hotel. Using this completed form one registers the call. It is then possible to make the call even from one's room.

It is also possible to send **telegrams** from the post office or from the hotel lobby desk. The bigger hotels also offer a **telex service.**

Tipping

In China, attitudes towards tipping are gradually changing. Officially it is still frowned upon, but quite often tips are accepted and, in some cases, even expected. A small tip may well improve services rendered.

Travel

In China, attitudes towards tipping are gradually changing. Officially it is still frowned upon, but quite often tips are accepted and, in some cases, even expected. A small tip may well improve services rendered.

Individual travel can be somewhat more problematic. **Regular scheduled buses** are often overcrowded and are few and far between in the evenings.

Most hotels have **taxi services** and it is necessary only to ask at the front desk. The charge depends on the distance travelled as well as the make of the car. One often has to search for a taxi stand, however, in order to make the return journey. These are usually located near the hotels or the Friendship Stores. It is impossible to find a taxi any other way; it is not possible to order one by telephone or to stop one in the street. However, anyone who wants to leave the group for a few hours or a day can, in principle, engage a taxi for that time.

Recently it has become possible to hire **bicycles** from certain hotels. Be careful, however! The bicycles are heavier than Western models so you might experience initial difficulties.

Bicycle accidents are not an uncommon sight on Chinese streets. Do, therefore keep an especially close eye on traffic; as a cyclist you will have to give way to motorists.

Rickshaws pulled by bicycles which had disappeared off the streets for many years have once more made their appearance. During the Cultural Revolution they were declared degrading and banished. Today, rickshaw drivers have to have a state licence but are independent operators.

Travel within China is by bus or plane. Quite often it is necessary to travel longer distances by train. **Long Distance** travel by train is usually in special first class sleeping cars called "the soft class" by the Chinese.

Only four-bed compartments are available. The 2nd class is also known as the "hard class" by the Chinese. Train journeys are comfortable and friendly, although the trains travel at an extremely slow pace,

between 50 and 60 km (30 and 38 miles) per hour. For shorter trips one travels in the normal sitting carriages (soft class) which are reserved for tourists or higher officials.

The Chinese airline is known as the **Civil Aviation Administration of China** (CAAC). They use Boeing 747's, Boeing 707's, Boeing 737's, Iljuschin 62's, Trident and Super VC planes. Smaller propeller machines such as Antonow are used on short haul flights. The CAAC serves over 115 airports and 166 inland flights. It is not known for its punctuality and many flights are dependent on good weather. Delays are to be expected at any time.

Food is not served on shorthaul internal flights. Drinks, sweets and small souvenirs are, however, available.

Luggage
On inland flights as well as long distance flights 20 kg of luggage is permitted. The controls within China are somewhat more relaxed than in other countries.

It is advisable, however, to bring strong, well-made, sturdy luggage because organised tours involve situations where damage can easily occur. It is prudent to take out a **travel insurance policy** which covers luggage.

Luggage transport is taken care of by Luxingshe (China International Travel Service) so it is not necessary to carry one's baggage.

Newspapers and Magazines

A journey to China involves a complete rest from "news" of any kind, good or bad. This can be regarded as a good or a bad thing. **Foreign newspapers** and **magazines** are available in only a few cities such as Beijing, Shanghai or Guangzhou, and even there only in a limited number of hotels.

For the past couple of years, however, an English language newspaper – "**China Daily**" has been on sale. It is available free of charge in many hotels. Otherwise it costs between 10 and 15 Fen.

Naturally enough it reports mainly news from China and Asia. Looking at the world as it were from China, Europe is indeed very far away.

In Beijing itself other English newspapers are available.

Weights and Measures
Lengths
1 cun = 3.33 cm
1 chi = 33.33 cm
1 chang = 3.33 m
1 li = 500 m
1 gonli = 1 km

Weights
1 liang = 50 g
1 jin = 500 g
1 gongin = 1 kg

Area
1 mu = 0.066 hectare

Volume
1 sheng = 1 l

Electricity Supply

All hotels have 220 V. The problem is the **sockets.** It is very difficult to even recommend an adaptor because the sockets can even vary from province to province.

In the few luxury hotels there are normalized sockets. In some other hotels it is possible to ask at the reception for a suitable **adaptor.** In areas which are less frequented by tourists the problem can be more pronounced. If bringing an adaptor be sure and bring a three pin one with flat movable prongs. Even better, bring battery operated equipment or an accumulator.

Diplomatic Representation

Any tourist office or your travel agent should be able to give you the address of your embassy or consulate in the country you are visiting. We would advise you to keep the address and telephone number handy in case of loss or damage to personal effects, or should you have any other problems.

Information

Your travel agent as well as the various embassies and the offices of the China Tourist Board can provide the most up-to-date information. Your tourist office will also usually be able to provide a list of China tour operators.

The state run Chinese tourist office has its headquarters in Beijing and branches in the towns and cities which are open to tourists.

China Tourist Office
Glentworth Street
London NW1
Tel.: 01 – 93 59 427

China Tourist Office
Lincoln Building 60 E
42 ND Street, Suite 464

New York NY 10165
Tel.: 212 – 867 0271

Luxingshe
China International Travel Service
6, Dong Chang 'an Lu
Beijing
People's Republic of China

Further Reading

Travel Guides
Fodor's Guide to the Peoples
Republic of China; David McKay
Company, New York 1984
Kaplan, Frederic/de Keijzer, Arne J.
– The China Guidebook; Eurasia
Press, New York 1984
Nagel's Encyclopedia Guide to China;
Nagel Publishers, Switzerland 1979
Schwartz, Brian – China off the
Beaten Track; St. Martin's Press,
New York 1983

General
Bonavia, David – The Chinese;
Lippincott, New York 1980
Gernet, Jaques – Ancient China:
From the Beginnings to the Empire;
University of California Press,
Berkeley 1968
Hinton, Harold C., ed. – The People's
Republic of China, a Handbook;
Boulder Co., Westview Press, 1980
Kaplan, Frederic/Sobin, Julian –
Encyclopedia of China Today;
Harper & Row/Eurasia Press,
New York 1981

Chiona's Cultural Heritage
Chang Kwang-Chih – The Archaeology of Ancient China; Yale University 1977

Cotterell, Arthur – The First Emper-
or of China; Macmillan London Ltd.
1981
Sickmann, L./Soper, A. – The Art
and Architecture of China; Balti-
more 1956
Stalberg, Roberta H./Nesi, Ruth –
China's Crafts, The Story of How
They're Made and What They Mean;
University of California Press,
Berkeley 1977
Sullivan, Michael – The Arts of
China; University of California Press,
Berkeley 1977

Personal Accounts
Fairbank, John K./Chinabound: A
Fifty Year Memoir; Harper & Row,
New York 1981
Fraser, John – The Chinese: Portrait
of a People; Summit Books, New
York 1980
Kahn-Ackermann, Michael – China:
Within the Outer Gate; Parco Polo
Press, London 1982
Myrdal, Jan – The Silk Road;
Pantheon Books, New York 1979
Snow, Edgar – Red Star Over China;
Grove Press, New York 1971
Terrill, Ross, ed. – The China Differ-
ence: A Portrait of Life Today in the
Country of One Billion; Harper &
Row, New York 1979

Currency: Renminbi
Units: Yuan, Jiao and Fen
1 Yuan = 10 Jiao = 100 Fen
1 Jiao = 10 Fen

Banknotes: Yuan 10, 5, 2, 1
            Jiao 5, 2, 1
            Fen 5, 2, 1
Coins: Fen 5, 2, 1

Foreign Exchange Certificates
Units: Yuan and Fen

1 Yuan = 100 Fen
Banknotes: Yuan 50, 10, 5, 1
Coins: none

Places of Interest

Baotou —————————————— 227
Beidaihe —————————————— 230
Beijing —————————————— 207
Changchun —————————————— 224
Changsha —————————————— 254
Chengde —————————————— 228
Chengdu —————————————— 292
Datong —————————————— 270
Dazu —————————————— 297
Dunhuang —————————————— 281
Emei Shan —————————————— 294
Fuzhou —————————————— 258
Guangzhou —————————————— 283
Guilin —————————————— 288
Gyantse —————————————— 313
Hainan —————————————— 291
Hangzhou —————————————— 255
Harbin —————————————— 222
Hohhot —————————————— 225
Jinan —————————————— 237
Kaifeng —————————————— 278
Kashi (Kashgar) —————————————— 306
Kunming —————————————— 300
Lhasa —————————————— 307
Lanzhou —————————————— 279
Leshan —————————————— 292
Luoyang —————————————— 273
Nanjing —————————————— 242
Nanning —————————————— 286
Qingdao —————————————— 241
Quanzhou —————————————— 259
Qufu —————————————— 240
Shanghai —————————————— 233
Shanghaiguan —————————————— 230
Shijiazhuang —————————————— 231
Shenyang —————————————— 224
Suzhou —————————————— 249
Taishan —————————————— 238
Taiyuan —————————————— 269
Tianjin —————————————— 221
Turpan —————————————— 304
Urumqi —————————————— 303
Wuhan —————————————— 251
Wuxi —————————————— 245
Xigaze —————————————— 311
Xining —————————————— 313
Xishuangbanna —————————————— 302
Yangzi Gorges —————————————— 302

Contents

Photographs

Impressions in Pictures 6
Captions 48

Impressions

Trying to reach Heaven 51
A typical Tea House 57
"Hallo there. How are you?" 59
Beijing –
the City of the Dragon 65
King of the Road 69
Guilin – a Landscape Painting 71
Tibet – the Lands of Gods
and Demons 74
Morning Light 81
Zhongguo – the Middle
Kingdom 86
An Audience with China's
First Emperor 88

Information

China's History 95
Map Silk Road 114
☐ The Emperors of the
Ming Dynasty 130
☐ The Emperors of the
Qing Dynasty 131
☐ The Chinese Dynasties 132
The People's Republic of China 133
Geography 137
Climate 142
☐ Table Average
Temperatures 144
☐ Table Average Rainfall 145
☐ Table Seasons 146
Soil, Resources and Agriculture 148
Flora and Fauna 149
Map Vegetation Zones 150
☐ The Panda 153
Population 156
National Minorities 159

☐ National Minorities in China 161
Writing and Language 162
Philosophies and Religions 167
Art and Culture 178
Chinese Medicine 190
Chinese Martial Arts 192
Chinese Cooking 195
☐ Peking Duck 198
☐ Pidan 200
China's Economy 201
Regional Section 205
Beijing and the North 207
Plan Imperial Palace 208
Plan Summer Palace 213
Plan Beihai Park 219
Plan Chengde 228
Shanghai and the East 233
Town Plan Shanghai 235
Town Plan Taishan 239
Town Plan Nanjing 243
Town Plan Suzhou 248
Town Plan Wuhan 252
Town Plan Hangzhou 256
Xi'an, the Centre 261
Town Plan Xi'an 262
Town Plan Luoyang 274
Guangzhou and the
South East 283
Town Plan Guangzhou 284
Town Plan Guilin 287
The South West 292
Map Yangzi Gorges 298
Xinjiang, the North West 303
Tibet / Qinghai Plateau 307
Map Lhasa 308
Map China 315
Map Distances in China 316
Useful Information 317
Further Reading 327
Money 328
Places of Interest 330
Contents 331
Personal Notes 333

Map

Please note:
Every effort was made to ensure that the information given was correct at the time of publication.

However, as it is not possible for any travel guide to keep abreast of all changes regarding passport formalities, rates of exchange, prices, etc., you are advised to contact the appropriate authorities (embassy, bank, tourist office ...) when planning your holiday.

The publishers would be pleased to hear about any omissions or errors.

Personal Notes

Hildebrand's Travel Guides

Vol. 1 Sri Lanka (Ceylon)
Professor Manfred Domrös and
Rosemarie Noack

Vol. 3 India, Nepal
Klaus Wolff

Vol. 4 Thailand, Burma
Dr. Dieter Rumpf

Vol. 5 Malaysia, Singapore*
Kurt Goetz Huehn

Vol. 6 Indonesia
Kurt Goetz Huehn

Vol. 7 Philippines*
Dr. Dieter Rumpf
Contributions by Dr. Gerhard Beese
and Wolfgang Freihen

Vol. 9 Taiwan
Professor Peter Thiele

Vol. 10 Australia
Michael Schweizer and
Heinrich von Bristow

Vol. 11 Kenya
Reinhard Künkel and
Nana Claudia Nenzel
Contributions by
Dr. Arnd Wünschmann,
Dr. Angelika Tunis and
Wolfgang Freihen

Vol. 13 Jamaica
Tino Greif and Dieter Jakobs

**Vol. 14 Hispaniola (Haiti,
Dominican Republic)**
Tino Greif and Dr. Gerhard Beese
Contribution by Wolfgang Freihen

Vol. 15 Seychelles
Christine Hedegaard and
Clausjürgen Eicke
Contributions by Wolfgang Debelius

Vol. 16 South Africa
Peter Gerisch and Clausjürgen Eicke
Contributions by Hella Tarara

Vol. 17 Mauritius
Clausjürgen Eicke
Contributions by Peter Gerisch,
Joachim Laux and Frank Siegfried

Vol. 18 China
Manfred Morgenstern

Vol. 19 Japan
Dr. Norbert Hormuth

Vol. 21 Mexico
Matthias von Debschitz and
Dr. Wolfgang Thieme
Contributions by Werner Schmidt,
Rudolf Wicker, Dr. Gerhard Beese,
Hans-Horst Skupy, Ortrun Egelkraut,
Dr. Elizabeth Siefer, Robert Valerio

Vol. 24 Korea
Dr. Dieter Rumpf and
Professor Peter Thiele

Vol. 25 New Zealand
Robert Sowman and
Johannes Schultz-Tesmar

Vol. 26 France*
Uwe Anhäuser
Contribution by Wolfgang Freihen

* in print

Hildebrand's Travel Maps

1. Balearic Islands Majorca
   1:185,000, Minorca,
   Ibiza, Formentera
   1:125,000

2. Tenerife 1:100,000,
   La Palma, Gomera,
   Hierro 1:190,000

3. Canary Islands
   Gran Canaria 1:100,000,
   Fuerteventura, Lanzarote
   1:190,000

4. Spanish Coast I
   Costa Brava, Costa
   Blanca 1:900,000,
   General Map 1:2,500,000

5. Spanish Coast II
   Costa del Sol, Costa
   de la Luz 1:900,000,
   General Map 1:2,500,000

6. Algarve 1:100,000,
   Costa do Estoril
   1:400,000

7. Gulf of Naples
   1:200,000,
   Ischia 1:35,000,
   Capri 1:28,000

8. Sardinia 1:200,000

*9. Sicily 1:200,000
   Lipari (Aeolian) Islands
   1:30,000

11. Yugoslavian Coast I
    Istria – Dalmatia
    1:400,000
    General Map 1:2,000,000

12. Yugoslavian Coast II
    Southern Dalmatia –
    Montenegro 1:400,000
    General Map 1:2,000,000

13. Crete 1:200,000

15. Corsica 1:200,000

16. Cyprus 1:350,000

17. Israel 1:360,000

18. Egypt 1:1,500,000

19. Tunisia 1:900,000

20. Morocco 1:900,000

21. New Zealand
    1:2,000,000

22. Sri Lanka (Ceylon),
    Maldive Islands
    1:750,000

23. Jamaica 1:345,000
    Caribbean 1:4,840,000

24. United States,
    Southern Canada
    1:6,400,000

25. India 1:4,255,000

26. Thailand, Burma,
    Malaysia 1:2,800,000,
    Singapore 1:139,000

27. Western Indonesia
    1:12,700,000,
    Sumatra 1:3,570,000,
    Java 1:1,887,000,
    Bali 1:597,000,
    Celebes 1:3,226,000

28. Hong Kong 1:116,000,
    Macao 1:36,000

29. Taiwan 1:700,000

30. Philippines 1:2,860,000

31. Australia 1:5,315,000

32. South Africa
    1:3,360,000

33. Seychelles General Map
    1:6,000,000,
    Mahé 1:96,000,
    Praslin 1:65,000,
    La Digue 1:52,000,
    Silhouette 1:84,000,
    Frégate 1:25,000

34. Hispaniola (Haiti,
    Dominican Republic)
    1:816,000

35. Soviet Union General
    Map 1:15,700,000,
    Western Soviet Union
    1:9,750,000,
    Black Sea Coast
    1:3,500,000

*37. Madeira

38. Mauritius 1:125,000

39. Malta 1:38,000

40. Majorca 1:125,000,
    Cabrera 1:75,000

41. Turkey 1:1,655,000

42. Cuba 1:1,100,000

43. Mexico 1:3,000,000

44. Korea 1:800,000

45. Japan 1:1,600,000

46. China 1:5,400,000

47. United States
    The West 1:3,500,000

48. United States
    The East 1:3,500,000

49. East Africa 1:2,700,000

50. Greece: Peloponnese,
    Southern Mainland,
    1:400,000

51. Europe 1:2,000,000
    Central Europe
    1:2,000,000
    Southern Europe
    1:2,000,000

52. Portugal 1:500,000

53. Puerto Rico,
    Virgin Islands, St. Croix
    1:294,000

54. The Caribbean
    Guadeloupe 1:165,000
    Martinique 1:125,000
    St. Lucia 1:180,000
    St. Martin 1:105,000
    Barthélemy 1:60,000
    Dominica 1:175,000
    General Map 1:5,000,000

55. Réunion 1:127,000

56. Czechoslovakia
    1:700,000

57. Hungary 1:600,000

59. United States, Southern
    Canada 1:3,500,000

*in print